Continuing Issues in Early Childhood Education

Carol Seefeldt

University of Maryland—College Park

MERRILL PUBLISHING COMPANY

A Bell & Howell Information Company

Columbus   Toronto   London   Melbourne

Published by Merrill Publishing Company
A Bell & Howell Information Company
Columbus, Ohio 43216

This book was set in Garamond.

Administrative Editor: David K. Faherty
Developmental Editor: Linda James Scharp
Production Coordinator: Linda Kauffman Peterson, Peg Connelly Gluntz
Art Coordinator: Ruth A. Kimpel
Cover Designer: Russ Maselli
Photo Editor: Terry L. Tietz

Photos in this text were taken by Carol Seefeldt and Richard Farkas.

Library of Congress Catalog Card Number: 89–62652
International Standard Book Number: 0–675–20935–8
Printed in the United States of America
1   2   3   4   5   6   7   8   9—92   91   90

About the Authors

Nita Barbour is chair of the Department of Education at the University of Maryland—Baltimore County where she was director of the Early Childhood Program. She has taught in child care, kindergarten, and at the elementary and secondary levels. Dr. Barbour was director of the Child Development Associate programs for Head Start at the University of Maryland—Baltimore County. She writes for professional journals and is co-author with Carol Seefeldt of *Early Childhood Education: An Introduction*.

Sue Bredekamp is director of professional development for the National Association for the Education of Young Children. She is the editor of *Developmentally Appropriate Practice in Early Childhood Programs Serving Children From Birth Through Age 8: Expanded Edition* and is the director of the National Academy of Early Childhood Programs. Dr. Bredekamp has taught in child care programs, preschools, and at the university level.

John E. Dopyera has taught in the teacher education programs at Syracuse University, Pennsylvania State University, and Pacific Oaks College, where he also served as dean of faculty. He has more than 30 years experience in conducting needs assessments and in designing, conducting, and evaluating training programs for education, human services, and business and industry.

Doris Pronin Fromberg is professor of Elementary and Early Childhood Education and director of Early Childhood Teacher Education at Hofstra University. She has been a curriculum and administration consultant to school districts and director of a Teacher Corps Project that developed field-based inservice consultation for teachers, administrators, and the community. With Leslie Williams, she is co-editor of the *Encyclopedia of Early Childhood Education* and author of *The Full-Day Kindergarten*.

Nancy George is a research associate at the University of Oregon with extensive background in the education of disadvantaged students and students with learning difficulties.

Russell Gersten is a professor in the College of Education at the University of Oregon. He has conducted numerous studies on the education of the economically disadvantaged with particular emphasis on early childhood education, reading comprehension, and aspects of effective teaching. He has served on the Association for Curriculum and Supervision Task Force on Early Childhood Education.

Stacie Goffin is an associate professor at the University of Missouri—Kansas City where she teaches undergraduate and graduate courses in early childhood education. She is co-author with Joan Lombardi of *Advocacy in Action: A Guide to Advocacy for Early Childhood Education*. Dr. Goffin has taught young children in a variety of programs and settings.

Alice Honig is professor of child development in the College for Human Development, Syracuse University where she has served as program director of the Children's Center and Family Development Research Program for more than 13 years. She is author of *Parent Involvement in Early Childhood Education* and co-author with Ronald Lally of *Infant Caregiving: A Design for Training*.

Melissa Kaden is an intern supervisor at the University of Massachusetts—Amherst. She is a doctoral candidate in early childhood education at the University of Massachusetts and has been an instructor at Greenfield Community College and the University of Massachusetts. Ms. Kaden has taught young children in a variety of settings, including child care, preschools, and public schools.

Margaret Lay-Dopyera has taught young children in public schools and university laboratory schools. A faculty member of Syracuse University since 1967, she has had major responsibility for designing and implementing model teacher training programs, and served as associate dean for academic programs in the School of Education. With her husband, John Dopyera, she is co-author of the textbook, *Becoming a Teacher of Young Children*.

ABOUT THE AUTHORS

Gayle Mindes is associate professor at Roosevelt University and chair of early childhood programs. She taught in the original Head Start Program, and has teaching experience at every level from preschool through college with both disabled and normal students. Dr. Mindes is chairperson of the Elementary Schooling Commission for the Chicago Association for the Education of Young Children and is author of *Kindergarten: What Should Be?* and the Association for Supervision and Curriculum Development's monograph, *Early Childhood Screening.*

Dennis R. Moore is a doctoral student at Arizona State University where he serves as chair of the graduate student council.

Raymond S. Moore is a developmental psychologist; former teacher, principal, and city school superintendent; university professor; college dean and president; and United States Office of Education officer. Known for his pioneer research, experimentation, and writings on work-study, school-entry age, and home education, Dr. Moore is currently chair and chief executive office of the Moore Foundation.

Gail Perry teaches child development science and early childhood education at the University of Massachusetts. She worked on conceptualizing and implementing Head Start supplementary training as the Child Development Associate program. As associate director of the National Child Research Center, she instituted the teacher education center. Also at that Center, she directed the 1976 Bicentennial National Symposium on Early Childhood Education. She also started a parent cooperative and has taught young children in a variety of preschool settings.

Mary Salkever is deputy director of the Maryland Committee for Children, Inc., a private, non-profit organization in Baltimore, Maryland. She has taught Head Start, elementary school, and college for the past 20 years. For the past 15 years she has coordinated training for child care providers, including work site training in parenting education at businesses. She has written about children with special needs and consulted with groups and associations across the nation on the issues of child care for children with special needs.

Susannah Sheffer is the editor of Growing Without Schooling and *Life Worth Living: Selected Letters of John Holt* published by Ohio State University. She writes extensively about home education for Holt Associates, Inc., and has been involved in the home school movement for more than six years.

Janet Singerman is deputy director of the Maryland Committee for Children, Inc., a private non-profit organization in Baltimore, Maryland. For the past six years she has been working with employers who are investigating the development of responsive family policies, programs, and practices within the workplace.

ABOUT THE AUTHORS

Carol Seefeldt is professor of human development at the Institute for Child Study, University of Maryland where she received the Distinguished Scholar/Teacher Award. She has worked in the field for more than 30 years, teaching child care through the third grade. In Florida, Dr. Seefeldt served as regional training officer for Project Head Start. Her research emphasizes early childhood curriculum, intergenerational attitudes, and the effects of competition on child growth and development. With Nita Barbour, she is co-author of *Early Childhood Education: An Introduction,* second edition.

Preface

Issue—a matter for discussion, a point for debate and disagreement, or a matter of dispute—is what this text, *Continuing Issues in Early Childhood Education,* is all about. Designed for the graduate student in early childhood education, the text is designed to foster discussions, debates, disagreements, and disputes that can lead to the generation of questions. Those questions, in turn, will lead to more research and study, and to the development of an ever-clearer understanding of the past and the present that will enable us to adapt to, and make progress in, the future.

Today's early childhood educators must know the theory and research supporting differing viewpoints in order to make decisions that are not based on personal bias and predilection, nor on simplistic, naive opinions. Rather, decisions should be based on an understanding of the complexities involved in each new, potentially controversial, polarizing issue. *Continuing Issues in Early Childhood Education* can assist the student of early childhood in developing the expertise necessary to be a reflective decision maker.

Five issues that confront the field of early childhood education in our nation are presented in this text. Within each of the five issues, selected topics are examined. The five issues, which have persisted in the field are the following:

- *Who is responsible for early education? Who is responsible for funding, operating, and monitoring?*

The issue of who will be responsible for education came to a head when President Nixon vetoed the child care bill of 1971. In doing so, Nixon carefully selected his words, saying that as a nation, we were not ready to "communize" our children through group care. Whether the family, churches, private associations, or local, state, or federal governments are responsible for the funding, implementation, and monitoring of early education is clearly a persistent issue in the field.

Stacie G. Goffin describes the role of government in the early care and education of young children. Her chapter, "Government's Responsibility in Early Childhood Care and Education: Renewing the Debate," takes the position that our government should assume a strong role in early childhood education.

Susannah Sheffer, on the other hand, in the chapter "The Child Is Not the Mere Creature of the State: The Family as Primary Educator," advocates that the family is solely responsible for the education and care of children—not just young children, but all children.

Mary Salkever and Janet Singerman, in the chapter "The Origins and Significance of Employer-Supported Child Care in America," describe the role of business in providing care for young children.

- *When should early education begin? In infancy? At age two, age four, or age five? Or should education be delayed until the child is seven or eight years of age?*

Most psychologists and educators agree that infants are efficient learners, and many have advocated beginning education during infancy. Using critical- or sensitive-period theory and research, some have suggested beginning education at age three or four. Today, using, at least in part, the concept of sensitive periods, school systems offer kindergarten for three and four year olds.

Others, however, using the same idea of sensitive periods, deplore the idea of early education. The fragility of the young child, and the susceptibility of the entire period of early childhood, are used as rationales to delay education until later in life, when growth and development is not as sensitive.

Alice Sterling Honig, in the chapter "Infant/Toddler Education Issues: Practices, Problems, and Promises," reviews the literature on infant care and education. Frankly concerned about the issue of quality, Honig cites research to point out the harm that can occur when infants and young children are not in programs of high quality. On the other hand, the fact that many families need child care is present. Referring to high-quality programs, Honig offers suggestions for the practice and promise of early education.

Often children's first exposure to education comes in the kindergarten. As the awareness of the importance of the early years has increased in our nation, the kindergarten has come under pressures. These pressures and issues are described by Gayle Mindes in the chapter "Kindergarten in Our Nation."

Raymond S. Moore, with Dennis R. Moore, in the chapter "When Delay Isn't Procrastination," takes the position that education should not begin during early childhood. They think that children are far better off learning and growing without schooling until much later in life, at least until after the sensitive period of early childhood has passed.

- *Who will teach young children? What qualifications are necessary to be an expert on early childhood education, and how will teachers acquire the necessary skills?*

Can anyone be an effective teacher of children under the age of eight? Should they have children of their own before being considered competent to teach others' children? Is a background of work with young children preparation enough to become an early childhood educator? Is a high school diploma, a child development certificate, or a bachelor's degree in early childhood necessary? Should a teacher experience 5 years of education and begin a career with a master's degree in education?

Piaget suggested that the younger the child to be taught, the more highly qualified the teacher should be. Former Commissioner of Education Harold Howe also called for the most sophisticated training and the development of a wide variety of skills for teachers of the very young.

But how will teachers acquire this knowledge and these specialized skills? Nita Barbour, in the chapter "Issues in the Preparation of Early Childhood Teachers," describes a variety of teacher-preparation programs, discussing the strengths and weaknesses of each. The issue of 5-year programs and the theory and rationale of the Holmes Group are also discussed.

Not all teachers of young children have degrees, however. The majority of people who work with young children, either in child care or in programs not associated with the public schools, are generally without any formal qualifications. The Child Development Associate program is one alternative to 4- or 5-year teacher preparation programs. Gail Perry, in the chapter "Alternate Modes of Teacher Preparation," describes the Child Development Associate program. She reviews the history and philosophy of early childhood teacher-preparation and illustrates how the CDA program was developed. The current status of the CDA program is discussed.

- *What should the curriculum contain? Is there a best curriculum? Does this curriculum consist of nurturing? Is it child centered or adult centered, or does it revolve around the computer?*

Curriculum is a word that provokes many images. For some, the word is associated with a picture of the whole child. For these, curriculum emerges from the teacher's understanding of the intellectual, physical, social, and emotional development of the child. This view is usually implemented through a program of free play or child-initiated activities. The curriculum is what happens as children and teachers interact with one another in the context of an enriched, planned educational environment. In the chapter "The Child-Centered Curriculum," Margaret Lay-Dopyera and John E.

Dopyera describe this curriculum and discuss how it differs from other curriculum models.

Doris Pronin Fromberg, in the chapter "Play Issues in Early Childhood Education," discusses play as the curriculum. In her chapter, she reviews the values and power of play in children's lives, and defines the issues revolving around play as the curriculum.

At the opposite end of the continuum are those who see curriculum as a set of goals and objectives, with specific and detailed instructions of how children will achieve each. Russell Gersten and Nancy George, in the chapter "Teaching Reading and Mathematics to At-Risk Students in Kindergarten: What We Have Learned from Field Research," suggest that direct instruction, based on carefully detailed goals and objectives, can only be of benefit for young children. Contrary to popular beliefs, Gersten and George point out that direct instruction is not associated with harsh discipline, punishment, or unhappy, dissatisfied children.

With increasing technology, other approaches to the curriculum are becoming popular. For some educators, the computer is seen as the curriculum. Melissa Kaden, in the chapter "Issues on Computers and Early Childhood Education," discusses the role of the computer in the curriculum. She employs the National Association for the Education of Young Children's Developmentally Appropriate Guidelines to assess the use of computers in early childhood education.

- *How will early childhood education be evaluated? How are programs, individual children, and groups of children evaluated? Should evaluation be formative, summative, or both?*

Given the many methodological problems that impede assessment of early education, evaluation has always been an issue. Should evaluation focus on children? the teacher? outcomes, such as children's achievement of specific goals and objectives? cost-effectiveness? or a combination of many variables?

As with any other educational experience, the effectiveness of early childhood programs must be evaluated. John E. Dopyera and Margaret Lay-Dopyera in the chapter "Evaluation and Science in Early Education: Some Critical Issues," review the process of evaluation in early education and give suggestions for future evaluation studies.

Sue Bredekamp, in the chapter "Achieving Model Early Childhood Programs Through Accreditation," suggests an alternative to the traditional models of evaluating programs. Through the accreditation process, program quality is enhanced, and evaluation is viewed as a continuation of the process of program growth and development.

Testing young children is not without controversy either. Some suggest that unobtrusive observations of children are the most efficient form of evaluation. Others, however, believe that standardized instruments, designed to asses factors from intelligence to self-esteem, can be valid assessment tools. In the chapter "Assessing Young Children," I present the issues involved in testing children.

I would like to thank the following reviewers for their insightful comments: Sandra DeCosta, West Virginia University; Doris Ditmar, Wright State University; and Elizabeth Stimson, Bowling Green State University. I am grateful to the Center for Young Children, College of Education, University of Maryland, under the direction of Marilyn Church, Elisa Klein, and June Wright; the Goddard Child-Development Center, NASA-Goddard Space Flight Center, under the direction of Barbara Karth; and the faculty, staff, and children of the centers used in the photographs throughout the text. Finally, the help of my editors at Merrill Publishing, Dave Faherty, Linda Scharp, Linda Peterson, and Peg Gluntz, is appreciated.

To conclude, this monograph will be successful if it stirs active debate and fosters thoughtful decisions based on an informed sense of the issues surrounding the definition of "best practice" in early childhood education. It is our hope that the text provides the impetus for your personal, continuing quest to improve the education of young children.

Carol Seefeldt

Contents

2

The Child Is Not the Mere Creature of the State: The Family as Primary Educator 27

Susannah Sheffer

3

The Origins and Significance of Employer-supported Child Care in America 43

Mary Salkever
Janet Singerman

PART TWO

When Should Early Education Begin? 55

4

Infant/Toddler Education Issues: Practices, Problems, and Promises 61

Alice Sterling Honig

5
Kindergarten in Our Nation   107

Gayle Mindes

6
When Delay Isn't Procrastination   121

Raymond S. Moore
with Dennis R. Moore

PART THREE
Who Will Teach
Young Children?   145

7
Issues in the Preparation of
Early Childhood Teachers   153

Nita Barbour

8
Alternate Modes of Teacher Preparation   173

Gail Perry

PART FOUR
What Should the
Curriculum Contain?   201

9
The Child-centered Curriculum   207

Margaret Lay-Dopyera
John E. Dopyera

10
Play Issues in Early Childhood Education   223

Doris Pronin Fromberg

11
Teaching Reading and Mathematics to At-Risk Students in Kindergarten: What We Have Learned from Field Research   245

Russell Gersten
Nancy George

12
Issues on Computers and Early Childhood Education   261

Melissa Kaden

PART FIVE

How Will Early Childhood
Education Be Evaluated?   277

13
Evaluation and Science in Early
Education: Some Critical Issues   285

John E. Dopyera
Margaret Lay-Dopyera

14
Achieving Model Early Childhood
Programs Through Accreditation   301

Sue Bredekamp

15
Assessing Young Children 311

Carol Seefeldt

Index   331

PART ONE

Who Is Responsible for Early Education?

Who will be responsible for the education of the very young is an issue as old as our nation. The early colonists ran into it when they passed the Old Deluder Satan Act of 1647 (Zais, 1976). Reflecting the Puritans' concern with religion and the ability to read the Bible, the Old Deluder Satan Act was passed by the General Court of Massachusetts making public education compulsory for every child. Although education was mandated by the state, parents had to provide the funding for children's education, and were even given the responsibility for teaching this mandated education.

Today, conflict and fundamental disagreement over who is responsible for the education of young children continues to be a major issue in early childhood education. Whether the government, family, private associations, or businesses have the primary responsibility for the funding, provision, and monitoring of education for very young children remains a provoking issue.

As a society, we are fairly clear that government is responsible for the education of children once they reach elementary school age. A well-defined legal structure, within a framework of constitutional provisions and statutory enactments, defines the authority and responsibility of federal, state, and local governments in the education of children above the age of five.

Given this framework, public education over the age of five is generally agreed to be the responsibility of the states. But the federal government has profound and far-reaching influences on state education systems, for all state and local educational activities are exercised consistently with federal constitutional requirements. Under the Constitution, Congress has the power to provide for the common defense and the general welfare of the United States. Thus the federal government, under the provision of providing for the general welfare, has historically acted to improve education, and to fund and provide for educational opportunity and equality for all children.

Nevertheless, very young children, those under the age of five, have not always been included in these provisions and acts. Whether at the federal, state, or local level, government's role in the education of the very young has wavered and vacillated throughout our history.

THE ROLE OF THE GOVERNMENT

Stacie G. Goffin, in the chapter "Government's Responsibility in Early Childhood Care and Education: Renewing the Debate," describes government's weak role in the education and care of children under the age of five. In response to specific crises and situations over the years, the federal government has fulfilled its role of caring for the general welfare of the population by funding specific early childhood programs. But these programs, with the exception of Head Start, were not extensive or long-lived.

During the depression of the 1930s, the Works Progress Administration established federally funded nursery schools. With the primary purpose of providing employment for unemployed teachers, the WPA nursery schools were for three, four, and five year olds and were administered through state departments of education and local school boards. The WPA nursery schools were viewed as successful. Hymes (1978) wrote, "The WPA nursery schools were generally good. Children were well served from 9 a.m. to 3 p.m. Food was good. Parents were highly pleased. And for the first time many children, in all parts of the country, from all backgrounds, had a chance to go to nursery school" (p. 5). Regardless, when the depression ended, the WPA ended, and the federal government's support for early education was discontinued.

A second time the federal government assumed responsibility for the education of the very young was during the Second World War. Now the problem was finding workers for jobs, not jobs for workers. So great was the need for workers that the federal government funded the Lanham Child Care Program, providing funds to factories employing working mothers for the establishment of day-care centers. Nearly 300,000 children were enrolled in these programs. When the war ended, however, men reentered the job market, the federal funds for child care went back to the government, and the women, without a whisper, went back to the home (Steiner, 1976).

A far different type of concern for the general welfare of our society prompted the support of the federal government for early education during the 1960s. Spurred by civil rights leaders, who demanded equality of educational opportunity for all children in our nation, and the research of Hunt (1961) and Bloom (1964), who documented the effects of early educational deprivation on children's intelligence and later educational achievement, the federal government funded Project Head Start. Head Start had its foundation in the idea that by intervening early in a child's life, or by compensating for a deprived background with enriching, educational experiences, all children could achieve. Thus the cycle of poverty would be broken, and equality of educational opportunity would be a reality.

Head Start is a documented success. *Lasting Effects After Preschool* (Lazar & Darlington, 1978) and *The Persistence of Preschool Effects* (Lazar, 1977) suggest that graduates of planned early childhood programs are more likely to complete high school and go on to vocational or academic training. Even though Head Start continues to be popular, the program reaches fewer than one-fourth of all eligible children today (Children's Defense Fund, 1989).

In her chapter in this book, Goffin documents government's neglect in the education and care of the very young. She points out that today, as in the past, not all families are self-sufficient. She makes it clear that the government has a responsibility in providing for the welfare of children and their families who are at risk and cannot provide for themselves.

As the federal government continues its neglect, local and state governments are assuming more control. Since 1979, at least eleven states have enacted some form of early education, and a few others are using existing school-aid mechanisms to fund programs (Grubb, 1987). Other states have formed commissions to study options and to provide care and educational experiences for children under the age of five. Day (1988) reports that local districts in at least fourteen states are providing for a significant portion of kindergarten funding for three and four year olds.

PRIVATE SPONSORSHIP OF EARLY EDUCATION

Responding to a variety of needs, other associations, organizations, and employers have offered provisions for child care or early education. Mary Salkever and Janet Singerman, in the chapter "The Origins and Significance of Employer-Supported Child Care in America," trace the role of business in caring for children under the age of five.

Hinting that others, not just the family or government, might share the responsibility for the care and education of young children, the authors describe a variety of employer-based child care programs and other suports for the care and education of children of workers. They describe how work styles and the needs of industry are interwoven with the care and education of the young.

Over the years, others, as well, have also sponsored programs for the very young. Private individuals, charities, and church groups, at various times in our history, have sponsored programs for the care and education of very young children. These programs had the same goal as the current Head Start program. Infant schools, popular during the 1830s and the 1840s, were funded by private individuals, industry, or charitable organizations in order to give very young children the education necessary to build citizens who were responsible, self-reliant, hardworking, and able to understand the importance of collective goals over individual needs (Kaestle, 1983).

Day nurseries, also funded by charitable groups or individuals during the later 1800s and early 1900s, were developed with the same goal. For low-income children in need of care and education, the day nurseries were supported in order to provide "a shelter for children of mothers who depended on their own exertions for their daily bread; but also to rear useful citizens among the class represented by the children we reach" (Grubb & Lazerson, 1977, p. 12).

THE FAMILY IS RESPONSIBLE

The day nurseries and infant schools were short lived. Lively discussion about the role of mothers in the education of very young children negated widespread growth of either the infant schools or day nurseries (Grubb & Lazerson, 1982). After all, mothers were supposed to care for their own children rather than work outside the home.

The attitude that parents, and specifically mothers, are responsible not only for the care of young children, but for their education as well, has prevailed throughout our history. The belief that only weak, inadequate, or selfish mothers would leave the care and education of children to others continues to limit and even negate the role of government or others in the education of the young.

Taking the argument that mothers are responsible for the education of young children a step further and in a different direction, Susannah Sheffer, in the chapter "The Child Is Not the Mere Creature of the State: The Family as Primary Educator," advocates the rights of families to educate and care for their children, not the state.

Describing the history and philosophy of the homeschooling movement, Sheffer presents the case for the family as responsible not only for the care of the young, but for the continuing education as well. She describes the role of the government in protecting parents' rights to educate their own children. The reasons courts have consistently upheld the right of parents to educate their own children are presented.

The fact that parents are the first teachers of children is not disputed, nor is the fact that parents remain as the most influential teachers of children. What is disputed is the fact that few families have the luxury to educate their own children. Families, even those who want to play an active part in their children's education, who want to be with their children daily, and who have the capability of teaching, must be able to afford this choice.

Sheffer points out that homeschooling is involved with more than a particular family in question at any given moment. Nevertheless, the fact that common education in a common public school is viewed as necessary for the free interchange of ideas with others, something essential for the survival of democracy, must be considered.

Perhaps if the variables of care and education of the young were not confounded, we as a society would better be able to accept the idea that government does have a role in, and responsibility for, early childhood education. Our clarity about government's role in the education of children, once of elementary school age, may be because older children care for themselves, and the role of the school—to educate—is not confused with the need for care. Thus the family's primary role and responsibility for care of children are protected.

To some, the government's assuming even partial responsibility for the toileting, dressing, and feeding of the very young may be upsetting or even frightening. In our society, the family, specifically the mother, is believed the primary giver of nurture and care to young children.

Regardless, the fact that democracy and education are so closely interwoven serves to guide decisions about responsibility for the care and education of the young. Just as governments assume roles in the education of older children, they can assume roles in programs for young children. Under the idea of providing for the general welfare of the nation, the federal government could, at the very least, take the initiative in setting and maintaining standards for programs for young children.

WHO WILL BE RESPONSIBLE?

As you read the following chapters, ask yourself

- What is the role of the local, state, and federal governments in the care and education of the young?
- How do the confounding variables of care and education negate or foster the government's support in programs for young children?
- Are all families in our nation capable, or do they have the luxury, of assuming total responsibility for the education of young children?
- How can the federal government fulfill the constitutional requirements to provide for the common defense and general welfare of very young children?
- As a society, have we come to grips with the role of women in caring for and educating children?
- Shouldn't industry, those who need workers, be responsible for the care of the very young?

After reading the following chapters, read John Dewey's *Democracy and Education*. React to Dewey's premise that common experiences in the public school are prerequisite for the preservation and improvement of a democratic society.

REFERENCES

Bloom, B. (1964). *Stability and change in human characteristics*. New York: John Wiley & Sons.

Children's Defense Fund. (1989). *A children's defense budget*. Washington, DC: Author.

Day, B. (1988). What's happening in early childhood programs across the United States. In C. Warger (Ed.), *A resource guide to public school early childhood programs* (pp. 3–32). Washington, DC: Association for Supervision and Curriculum Development.

Grubb, W. N. (1987). *Young children face the states: Issues and options for early childhood programs*. Madison, WI: Rand Corporation.

Grubb, W. N., & Lazerson, M. (1977). Child care, government and financing, and the public schools: Lessons from the California children's center. *School Review, 86+(2)*, 5–36.

Grubb, W. N., & Lazerson, M. (1982). *Broken promises: How Americans fail their children*. New York: Basic Books.

Hunt, J. M. (1961). *Intelligence and experience*. New York: Ronald Press.

Hymes, J. (1978). *Living history interviews: Book 2. Care of children of working mothers*. Carmel, CA: Hacienda Press.

Kaestle, C. (1983). *Pillars of the republic: Common schools and American society*. New York: Hall and Wang.

Lazar, I. (1977). *The persistence of preschool effects: A long term follow up of fourteen infant and preschool experiments*. Washington, DC: Administration of Children, Youth and Families.

Lazar, I., & Darlington, R. B. (1978). *Lasting effects after preschool*. Washington, DC: U.S. Department of Health, Education, & Welfare.

Steiner, G. Y. (1976). *The children's cause*. Washington, DC: The Brookings Institute.

Zais, R. S. (1976). *Curriculum: Principles and foundations*. New York: Thomas Y. Crowell.

1

Government's Responsibility in Early Childhood Care and Education: Renewing the Debate

STACIE G. GOFFIN
University of Missouri–Kansas City

Discussion of early childhood care and education is often organized within the trilemma of affordability, availability, and quality. Can parents locate care and education that promote the growth of their children at prices they can afford? For such discussions to fully address the issue, however, they must be expanded and framed as a "quadrilemma"; the question of responsibility must be added as a fourth variable. *Who* should assume responsibility for assuring children are cared for and educated in safe, healthy, and growth-promoting environments?

Dilemmas are situations requiring choices be made between equally disagreeable alternatives. Improving the quality of early childhood programs, for example, can make them so expensive they are unaffordable, and therefore inaccessible, to many parents and children—unless someone else helps with the responsibility to ensure that they are affordable, as well as accessible, and of high quality. Obviously, then, all four components of the "quadrilemma" are intricately intertwined, each significantly impacting upon, and being impacted by, the others. This chapter, however, focuses its attention on the component of responsibility, in particular, the responsibility of government to serve as a catalyst and enabler for accessible, affordable, and quality child care and education.

HOW GOVERNMENT BECOMES INVOLVED

Government involvement occurs at three levels—local, state, and national/federal—and in all three branches of government—legislative, executive, and judicial. General-

9

ly, the legislative branch makes laws, the executive branch administers laws, and the judicial branch interprets laws. The relationship between states and the federal government is described in the United States Constitution. State and local governments have primary responsibility for the education and the physical and mental health of children who reside within their state. In addition to planning and funding state programs, state and local governments also implement federal initiatives. The Constitution grants distinct powers to the national government to protect and promote the nation as a whole. Most children's programs, therefore, are a complex mixture of local, state, and federal interaction and finances.

Governments become involved in an issue when convinced it presents a problem they need to help solve. Their proposed solutions, if implemented, are called public policies. The policy-making process involves a series of steps, during which a problem's existence is identified and potential solutions are selected, implemented, and evaluated (Anderson, Brady, Bullock, & Stewart, 1984; Hayes, 1982; Kelman, 1987). Public policy, therefore, is a purposive, goal-oriented course of action constructed to deal with a problem or a matter of concern (Anderson et al., 1984); policies are proposed solutions by our local, state, and federal governments to try and solve societal problems.

Public policies include goals and objectives identifying what needs to be accomplished, a detailed description of how desired changes will be facilitated, and an analysis of what resources are available and needed for the plan to be successful. Public policies represent agreements that our governments will behave in certain expected ways (Morgan, 1983b). They represent a broad-based consensus about governments' responsibility in helping to solve a recognized problem and the kinds of solutions that will help resolve the problem (Kelman, 1987).

Although policies made by decision makers in Washington, in state capitals, and in city halls may seem far removed from our daily lives, the problems decision makers confront are the problems we are living, and the solutions they devise become the programs and practices early educators attempt to implement on behalf of children and families. Public policies for children and families, therefore, are solutions/plans of action that influence the circumstances of children's lives; they are part of the environment influencing children's development (Bronfenbrenner, 1974a; Bronfenbrenner & Weiss, 1983).

Public policies help define the social and economic context that describes the range of choices parents, early educators, and others can make for children. This critical understanding helps explain the significance of governments' role in early childhood care and education. Early childhood programs are part of children's child-rearing environments. Policies made by our governments about early childhood care and education can make it easier or harder to parent and for children to grow into competent, caring individuals. Public policies help make children's environments more or less supportive for their growth. When we analyze policies for early childhood care and education, we are trying to determine the validity of governments' solutions—to what extent do they help solve a problem and improve the circumstances of children's lives?

Public policies, however, are more than just decisions in favor of particular programs or services for children. They are also reflections of the kinds of relationships policymakers believe should exist among families, various levels of government, and the needs of children (Goffin, 1988). This conceptual context contributes to the value framework within which policy possibilities are contemplated.

Traditional responses to children's needs maintain that families have sole responsibility for rearing their children. Families are perceived as self-sufficient, capable of independently caring for their own needs and those of their children, and in control of their personal futures. As a result, the family that seeks help is frequently viewed as incompetent, rather than in need of support. When it does become necessary to respond to the needs of families, the local community and private enterprise are thought to be capable of meeting them. Under these circumstances, "accepting" government support is perceived as a sign of personal failure (Goffin, 1983, 1988).

This framework for public policy (often called a deficit approach) minimizes the role of government in creating a supportive environment for children's development. Government involvement, especially at the federal level, is viewed as intrusive into family affairs. Government assumption of responsibility, consequently, has historically tended to be crisis-oriented and available only for specific, narrowly defined problems (Goffin, 1983). The consequences for children and families of policies formed in this way appear to be loss of self-esteem, diminished family capacity to function (Bronfenbrenner & Weiss, 1983), and increasing numbers of impoverished and at-risk children (Children's Defense Fund [CDF], 1988; Grubb & Lazerson, 1988; Halpern, 1988).

Newer conceptualizations of children's issues argue for a different kind of relationship between government and its constituents and offer a different vision of government responsibility. In contrast to more traditional beliefs, these newer conceptualizations argue that society, as well as families, shares the responsibility for children's well-being. Because children's maximum development depends upon their opportunities to be supported by a nurturing family, services to children are increasingly understood as part of family—versus child—policies (Bronfenbrenner & Weiss, 1983; Goffin, 1983).

But families are not self-sufficient; they do not independently fulfill their own needs (Keniston, 1977; Edelman, 1981). Many of the problems facing families and their children are beyond individual control. Although children's needs can best be met within and by their families, society's support is needed to enable parents to fulfill their child-rearing responsibilities (Bronfenbrenner & Weiss, 1983; Goffin, 1983).

Within this framework, government involvement is seen as having the potential to be supportive, rather than intrusive, and children's well-being provides legitimate objectives for government actions. There are circumstances associated with children's growth that government involvement can help improve. Governments assume responsibility within this framework to help families succeed; programs and services are viewed as enabling, rather than indicators of family failure.

Currently, both these perspectives regarding the "appropriate" relationship between government and its youngest citizens coexist. Proponents of both these approaches truly believe they are advocating for children's—and society's—best interests. As a result, the United States lacks coherent policies describing its relationship with children and families.

In contrast, almost all European countries have recognized the importance and value of preschool programs for young children and increasingly provide universal, free, and voluntary early childhood programs (Kamerman, 1988). European countries have a long history of acknowledging children as a major societal resource and believe, consequently, that the whole society should share in the cost of child rearing (Kamerman, 1984).

Many advocates see the absence of explicit and coherent family policies in the United States as a failure to acknowledge the importance of society's support for children and families (CDF, 1988; Grubb & Lazerson, 1988; Kahn & Kamerman, 1987; Zigler, Kagan, & Klugman, 1983). The presence of such support would be a reflection of our understanding that families do not and cannot rear their children independently of an environment that supports their child-rearing efforts; supportive government involvement would be an acknowledgment of our collective responsibility for children.

Government Responsibility: The Debate Intensifies

Differing beliefs about the appropriate relationship among government, children, and families strongly influence the political context of policy-making, i.e., what policymakers will consider as a problem for government to solve and what solutions they will investigate. However, dramatic demographic changes are driving early childhood care and education and forcing policymakers to reexamine the existing relationship between families and governments and the need for early childhood programs. Consider the following statistics:

- Twenty-five percent of all children—47% of black children, 40% of Hispanic children, and 10% of white children—are born into, and spend their young years in, poverty (Halpern, 1988).
- In 1985, 49% of children under six and 62% of children 6–17 years old had mothers in the work force. By 1995, two-thirds of children under the age of six and three-fourths of schoolagers are expected to have employed mothers (Hofferth & Phillips, 1987).
- One million girls get pregnant each year, and half of them keep their babies (CDF, 1988).

- As the population of the United States ages, the percentage of young adults and children is diminishing, resulting in a smaller proportion of people who will be entering the labor force. Of today's three to five year olds, who will be entering the work force in the year 2005, one in four is poor, and one in seven is at risk of dropping out of school (CDF, 1988).

This long sequence of statistics vividly describes the changing demographics impacting upon children, families, and society. It reveals the increasing number of employed mothers, single-parent families, and impoverished children, and concern that the near future will have fewer workers with fewer skills. Changes in our economic system from an industry- to a service-oriented economy also mean that being poor is not necessarily restricted to families with unemployed parents. In 1985, 2.5 million children, or more than one-fifth of all poor children, were poor even though they had mothers who worked full-time (CDF, 1988).

The growing number of impoverished children who are at risk for school failure, the increasing number of employed mothers requiring child care for their children, and concern for the quality of our country's future labor force are causing local, state, and federal governments to reexamine their responsibility in supporting early childhood programs. Reaction to changing external circumstances as a rationale for government policy on behalf of children and families is consistent with the United States' crisis—versus prevention—orientation to family problems and continues a historical tradition. Furthermore, children are frequently used as vehicles for social reform (Grubb & Lazerson, 1988; Lazerson, 1971); i.e., they are used by society to help achieve purposes other than their well-being. Because of the statistics just cited, public policy intiatives currently focus on using early childhood programs to reduce teenage pregnancy and welfare rolls, facilitate women's productivity in the work force, reduce high-school dropouts, and ensure a competent future labor force.

Missing from this list as an important policy objective is the safety, health, and well-being of children. Perceived objectives structure what policies try to achieve and how they try to achieve it. The existing policy framework, consequently, tends to view children's programs either as a means for solving current social problems or as an assurance of future citizen productivity.

Furthermore, when these purposes for children's policies are placed alongside assumptions that argue for individualism, stay-at-home mothers, and family self-sufficiency, government involvement remains linked to short-term commitments and the resolution of crisis situations. This policy framework has important consequences for the way in which government supports early childhood programs. Government policy-making primarily occurs in three areas of early education: early intervention programs, child care, and parent education. None of these policy areas, however, represents new arenas for government involvement. Rather, current programs represent renewed government interest in becoming involved in helping solve current social problems through early childhood programs.

Early Intervention Programs

Early intervention programs, which are also called compensatory education, became the focus of intense interest in the 1960s when United States policymakers rediscovered poverty and President Johnson initiated "The Great Society," a series of federal policies designed to help eradicate poverty and social inequality. A key component of this effort was Project Head Start, which began in 1965 as a 2-week summer program focused on educational intervention for three and four year olds. It has since expanded to a 9-month preschool program focused not only on children's educational needs, but also on their nutritional and health needs, with an emphasis on family involvement and support as an enhancement to child development. Although funded at the federal level, Head Start programs are locally administered, sometimes through public schools, and thus involve several levels of government.

The basic program is a center-based, half-day preschool program serving predominately poor children between 3 and 5 years of age. Every program is mandated to provide education, health screening and referral, mental health services, social services, nutrition, and parent education. Project Head Start, therefore, is a comprehensive program, providing both services and educational programming to economically disadvantaged children and their families. Its comprehensiveness extends to its focus on children's social, as well as intellectual, competence (Zigler & Seitz, 1982). Consistent with its focus on helping children become more competent, Head Start is governed by federal regulations that help establish a minimum level of quality for all Head Start programs (Phillips & Zigler, 1987).

The focus on program quality reflects the purpose of compensatory education. Programs are designed to intervene in the lives of poor children to help compensate for their disadvantaged environments. The federal government has supported early-intervention programs because of their potential to help resolve the problem of poverty—by helping poor children escape the poverty of their parents by enhancing their potential for success in school.

Head Start has been in existence now for more than 24 years, and evaluations of its results, plus those of other early-intervention programs, have both reinforced and tempered the expectations of supporters. Early-intervention programs are based upon the concept of critical periods and the belief that changes in children's environments can result in increases in measured intelligence (Ramey, Bryant, & Suarez, 1985; Zigler & Seitz, 1982). The concept of critical periods argues that the first 5 years of life (others argue narrower age ranges) are the years most critical for intellectual development, most amenable to environmental enrichment, and, significantly, predictable of later achievement. Proponents of early-intervention programs argued, therefore, that the intellectual deficiency of poor children was because of their poor environments and that enriching their disadvantaged environments during the critical preschool years would remove their educational disadvantages when they formally began school.

Despite their conceptual comprehensiveness, however, most early intervention programs have targeted their efforts (and, consequently, evaluation focus) toward preparing economically disadvantaged children for success in public schools. This anticipated outcome has primarily been evaluated through measured gains on intelligence tests.

The initial optimism of proponents was dashed when early evaluation results found that, although children in Head Start programs showed gains on intelligence test scores (IQ) in comparison to children who had not attended such programs, these gains faded after the program's completion (Cicirelli, 1969), a finding that has been consistently supported (Barnett & Escobar, 1987; Consortium for Longitudinal Studies, 1979). The apparent fading of preschool participants' cognitive gains was a disappointment to those who believed that relatively short-term preschool intervention experiences would have substantial and lasting effects on intellectual competence, and provided an incentive to federal policymakers to remove their support and funding for Head Start (Zigler & Seitz, 1982).

In 1975, when this threat began to materialize, an investigation of the long-term effects of early-intervention programs was conducted by the Consortium for Longitudinal Studies. The Consortium analyzed the collective results of fourteen early-intervention programs. In addition, in a collaborative effort, the original participants in those fourteen early childhood programs were located and their success in school (rather than IQ scores) investigated (Lazar, 1980). The findings revealed that low-income children who had participated in these early-intervention programs were less likely than nonparticipating children to be placed in special education classes or to be retained in grade; participants were also more likely to meet school requirements and to graduate from high school, to have higher self-esteem, and to value achievement (Consortium for Longitudinal Studies, 1979). As a result of these findings on the long-term impact of early-intervention programs, Head Start received increased funding in 1980 and was placed in a "safety net" during President Reagan's two terms. Research on the positive impact of high-quality comprehensive early-intervention programs continues to amass, including evidence of reduced incidences of juvenile delinquency and teenage pregnancy (Berrulta-Clement, Schweinhart, Barnett, Epstein, & Weikart, 1984; Lally, Mangione, Honig, & Wittner, 1988; Seitz, Rosenbaum, & Apfel, 1985).

The results of the Perry Preschool Project (now known as the Cognitively Oriented Curriculum) received additional attention when program results were reinterpreted in terms of cost-benefit analysis (Berrulta-Clement et al., 1984). Cost-benefit analyses compare the costs and benefits of various alternatives in monetary terms, i.e., "Are early intervention programs good financial investments compared to other ways in which society could use its resources?" (Levin, 1988; Barnett & Escobar, 1987). The Perry Preschool Project found total cost benefits to taxpayers to average $28,000 per participant (Weikart, 1987); according to Weikart, taxpayers saved $5,000 for special education programs, $3,000 in crime costs, and $16,000 for welfare assistance, plus they gained $5,000 per participant in additional taxes. These kinds of verified benefits have provided popular support for early intervention programs—though it is important to note that the benefits that are arousing support for governments' continued involvement primarily target taxpayers and future employers, not children.

In addition to growing support for early intervention programs, there is also a growing need. In 1980, the United States had the highest proportion of its children living in poverty of any advanced Western nation, and the numbers have significantly increased since 1980 (Duncan, 1988). Children have replaced the aged as the poorest group in the nation (Halpern, 1988). Almost five million children younger than age six live in families below the poverty level (CDF, 1988), yet only 16% of eligible children are currently served by Head Start. In inflation-adjusted dollars, the federal government appropriated less money for Head Start in 1986 than in 1981; important components of the program have been weakened as a result (CDF, 1988).

In response to the results of the Perry Preschool Project and the growing number of children in poverty, concern for the productivity of the future labor force, and the demands for educational excellence, states have begun to fund early-intervention programs in the public schools. As of September 1986, fifteen states were offering prekindergarten programs for four year olds identified as at risk (Morado, 1986). Yet no state has committed the funds necessary to create the intensity and quality of services provided by effective early intervention programs (CDF, 1988; Phillips, 1988). "It makes no sense to cite evidence about the educational benefits of exemplary, high quality programs and then to enact programs with low expenditures, low ratios, low salaries, and inadequate teacher preparation" (Grubb, 1987, p. 42).

Furthermore, the positive impact of early-intervention programs has been achieved with high-quality, comprehensive programs with services provided to families as well as target children. In fact, analysis of the results of evaluation studies, especially the decline in IQ gains and the significance of family involvement in effective programs, has weakened the argument that preschool education *alone* can inoculate children against poor school performance (Barnett & Escobar, 1987; Ramey, Bryant, & Suarez, 1985; Ramey & Suarez, 1984). In addition, there is increasing awareness and concern about the economic segregation being perpetuated by early-intervention programs such as Head Start because, in essence, they segregate preschoolers from economically disadvantaged families into publicly funded programs for poor children (Grubb, 1987; Kagan, 1987, 1988; Zigler & Seitz, 1982).

The responsibility of state and federal governments would seem evident. Low-income children should have the opportunity to participate in Head Start or comparable programs in ways that address the issues of integration and family support. Funding needs to be provided not only to expand the program's size, but to assure program quality. Many low-income parents, however, need more than quality preschool programs; many are employed parents and parents in welfare-to-work training programs who also need full-day, full-year services.

Child Care

In 1985, 49% of children under six and 62% of children 6–17 years old had mothers in the work force, increases of 69% and 44% respectively since 1970. The largest increase in the last 10 years is in the proportion of children under age one with mothers in the work force, which rose 57% between 1976 and 1985. If current trends continue, by 1995, over three-quarters of school-age children and two-thirds of preschool children will have mothers in the work force (Hofferth & Phillips, 1987). As a result of these demographic realities, safe, healthy, and appropriate child care has become a necessity for families from all socioeconomic levels.

Unfortunately, a majority of children cannot be assured of such care (Zigler, 1987a). The issue of child care, more than any other early childhood education program, raises the specter of government invasion into family privacy and images of governmental child rearing. This kind of reasoning guided President Nixon's veto of the Comprehensive Child Development Act in 1971, which would have provided national direction and a comprehensive approach to child care programs.

> This legislation would be truly a long leap into the dark for the United States government and the American people.... This legislation would leap toward altering the family relationship ... [and] would commit the vast moral authority of the National Government to the side of communal approaches to child rearing over and against the family centered approach. (as cited in Ross, 1983, p. 175)

Currently, similar arguments are framed as warnings against "life style engineering" by the federal government (Christensen, 1988) and as pleas for government policies that would enable mothers to stay at home—versus provision of good care for children whose parents work outside the home (Christensen, 1988; Reiger, 1988; Schafly, 1988).

In the meantime, parents need child care to enable them to work; employers need employees who can work reliably and productively because they feel secure about their child care arrangements, *and* children need programs that facilitate their growth. Yet as Morgan (1983a) succinctly states it, child care policy is in chaos. The American child care system is primarily made up of separate and competing programs, each vying for scarce resources and arguing different purposes; missing is an overall policy for child care (Kahn & Kamerman, 1987; Morgan, 1983a).

Traditionally, child care has been a response to mothers who needed to work in order to be self-sufficient; child care, therefore, was provided to enable mothers to work—not to promote child development. Within this "welfare" context, child care has provided custodial rather than developmental care to children because mothers, not children, were designated as the program's target. This is reflected in state and federal government policies, which frame child care versus early-intervention programs. Policies linked to compensatory education have focused on the "educational" needs of poor children and, therefore, addressed the need for high-quality programming. In contrast, policies directed toward reducing welfare expenditures by placing mothers in the work force have viewed child care primarily as a service to enable mothers to work outside the home. The focus on cost reductions has been extended to the provision of child care, minimizing government support for quality as a policy issue (Phillips, 1988; Phillips & Zigler, 1987).

The debate over government responsibility for quality is most clearly represented in discussions about federal child care regulations; child care regulations are policy statements that guarantee child care environments do not fall below a prescribed baseline necessary for children's well-being (Morgan, 1980). The fact that no child care regulations exist at the federal level provides evidence of the federal government's lack of commitment to quality child care and its role in assuring it. Currently, standards are set by individual states and vary widely. As a result, the United States, in effect, has become a country with at least fifty different sets of child care policies, with few states having a coherent, statewide child care policy (Kahn & Kamerman, 1987). "One cannot identify any arena in national life with such large ramifications and so little, responsible, helpful federal presence" (Kahn & Kamerman, 1987, p. 261).

This debate is complicated by the fact that good child care is labor-intensive and expensive, up to $600 a month for preschoolers in major urban areas (Zigler, 1987b). As a result, a two-tiered system of child care is developing. Whereas wealthy parents can afford good child care (if available), a majority of families are being forced to purchase inappropriate and unsafe care (Kahn & Kamerman, 1987; Morgan, 1983a; Zigler, 1987b). According to Phillips (1987), "Good quality is seen by many as the luxury issue in child care" (p. ix).

This is exacerbated by the absence of sufficient federal and state support. The federal government has no program with the sole purpose of providing direct assistance to help lower-income families pay for child care. Only the Title XX Social Services Block Grant—which provides federal funds to states to cover a wide range of social service needs—is partially available for this purpose. But states' overall spending for child care in real dollars is still roughly at 1981 levels. In 1987, twenty-eight states spent less in real dollars for child care funded through the Title XX Social Services Block Grant than they did in 1981 (CDF, 1988).

In contrast, the largest federal effort to help families pay for child care is the Dependent Care Tax Credit. It allows a family to deduct between 20% to 30% of their annual child care expenses (up to a maximum expense of $2,400 for one child or $4,800 for two or more children) from their income tax bill. Because families must earn sufficient income to take advantage of such a deductible and be able to await receipt of the refund, this policy primarily supports more affluent families. Although tax credits help address the issue of affordability for some families, they fail to address the issues of availability or quality.

Desperately needed is a way to bring all these pieces together in a way that supports both parents' *and* children's needs. A consistent recommendation is the elimination of the programmatic and policy dichotomy between care and education

(Grubb, 1987; Kagan, 1988; Kahn & Kamerman, 1987; Phillips, 1988; Scarr & Weinberg, 1986). Children's care and education should be two prongs of a single, coherent policy that recognizes that (1) working parents need and want good care and education for their children, and (2) the care and education of young children are inseparable provisions.

One goal of state policy, which has become increasingly involved in early childhood programs since the early 1980s when program sponsorship and responsibility shifted from the federal to state and local levels, might be to integrate the different strands of early childhood education (Grubb, 1987). Because of their relative lack of previous involvement with early childhood policy, states have a fresh opportunity to control licensing, set standards, establish monitoring procedures, and encourage cooperative planning among diverse programs (Grubb, 1987; Kagan, 1988).

Another recommendation proposes that the public schools offer the solution to America's child care problem (Zigler, 1987a). Zigler suggests that schools become the prime sponsor of child care and a sponsor of three outreach programs: a family support system for first-time parents, support for neighborhood family child-care providers, and information and referral services. Zigler's proposal is currently under congressional consideration; the proposed legislation would fund a network of demonstration projects that would implement what Zigler calls the "School of the Twenty-first Century." Whether schools are the best sponsors for child care, however, is an issue of considerable debate (see, for example, Kagan & Zigler, 1987).

Still another proposal, the Act for Better Child Care (ABC) bill, sponsored by Senator Dodd and Representative Kilde, reasserts a federal role in child care. ABC attempts to create an infrastructure for child care by weaving together the current fragmentation through federal leadership and a more coherent state-based system. Morgan (1987) calls this approach one of "following the dots," connecting existing programs worth preserving (including school-based ones) and adding the necessary missing dots; she argues such an approach would preserve the quality of existing programs and strengthen families through an emphasis on informed parent choices.

Regardless of the solution one chooses, the reality is that child care has become a collaborative effort between families and caregivers, and children have become pawns in the debate over family life-styles and the question of responsibility. Grubb (1987) points out that the funding of public schools 150 years ago recognized parents could no longer educate their children as they did earlier on the family farm and in apprenticeship systems; he suggests that perhaps the time has come to extend this sharing of responsibility to earlier ages.

It is important that such a collaborative effort recognize child care as a significant component of children's child-rearing experiences and as part of a family's support system that enables parents to more effectively fulfill their child-rearing responsibilities (Goffin, 1988; Peters & Benn, 1980). "Time has come for the society—and thus federal and state government—to acknowledge child care as normative. Child care services should evolve and become as much a part of the social infrastructure as schools, libraries, parks, highways, and transportation" (Kahn & Kamerman, 1987, p. 246).

Parent Education Programs

Parent education programs provide information to parents to improve parenting skills. They are usually based on the premise that parents are a child's first and most important teacher and on the concept of critical periods (Powell, 1982). Similar to early-intervention and child care programs, parent education programs have focused on poor parents. In this instance, their need for "better education" in order to be effective parents is emphasized. Parent education has been seen as a way to improve "disadvantaged" home environments and, as a result, to improve children's cognitive functioning (Clarke-Stewart, 1981; Grubb & Lazerson, 1988; Powell, 1982).

These assumptions were reinforced when evaluations of early-childhood intervention programs found that program effectiveness was greater for those programs that also stressed parent education (Bronfenbrenner, 1974b; Consortium for Longitudinal Studies, 1979). As a result, public support for parent education programs grew rapidly during the 1970s and continues to expand, despite the fact that we still do not fully understand how parent education programs work (Clarke-Stewart, 1981, 1988; Powell, 1986). Currently, at least two states, Missouri and Minnesota, fund early childhood parent education programs that provide home visits and group meetings to participating parents. Significantly, both programs, delivered through the public school system, are available to all parents.

From a policy perspective, parent education programs emphasize parental care and assume public programs should focus on the "quality" of home child-rearing environments. Parent education programs have been promoted as an alternative to child care because they are cheaper and touted as more effective in teaching young children, while being more respectful of the parent-child bond—with the added potential bonus of their impact on the target child and siblings extending beyond the life of the program (Clark-Stewart, 1988; Grubb & Lazerson, 1988). By arguing that properly trained parents, regardless of economic and social circumstances, can by themselves shape their children's future, parent education programs reflect the assumptions of those who argue for family individualism and self-sufficiency.

The premises of parent education programs also make them difficult to deliver in ways that are sensitive to differing styles of parenting. Most parent education programs assume that parents—especially poor parents—need training. This basic premise tends to represent parents as "deficient" and parent educators as "experts"; it places parents in the role of knowledge recipients and parent educators in the role of knowledge givers (Grubb & Lazerson, 1988; Powell, 1984).

These premises, however, are being increasingly challenged by recognition and acceptance of the validity of a variety of parenting styles and the significance of the contexts in which families are embedded. These contexts, which include neighborhoods, community, work, social relationships, and government policies, influence parenting practices and are increasingly being incorporated into discussions of parenting and parent education (Goffin & Caccimo, 1986).

Traditional parent education programs are further challenged by the realization that parent behaviors do not affect children in a unilateral fashion. Children are not passive recipients of experiences and information; they actively contribute to their own growth and development and to family functioning (Clarke-Stewart, 1988; Goffin & Caccimo, 1986). Consequently, parenting is becoming respected as a challenging as well as highly personalized enterprise. Parent programs based upon these premises are being called family support programs (Weissbourd, 1983); parent support programs strive to strengthen parenting by being responsive to parents' individuality and respecting the responsibilities they have assumed as parents. Support programs share information with parents to assist—rather than change—parents' child-rearing efforts. Within this supportive framework, parent education and support programs have the opportunity to represent what Grubb and Lazerson (1988) call the "frontier of public responsibility"; they present the opportunity to move beyond a deficit approach to families (Cochran & Woolever, 1983) and to see the need for support by all families.

THE ROLE OF GOVERNMENT: SHARING THE RESPONSIBILITY

Every period of major social change has seen an expansion of public responsibility for children and families (Grubb & Lazerson, 1988). The question of whether or not government should become involved in family life avoids the current realities of society; government is already involved in family life through its policies for programs such as compensatory education, child care, and parent education. The more pertinent question asks, "How should government conceptualize its involvement?"

Historically, child and family policies have focused on children in need—in need because their families have been "inadequate" to the task of child rearing. This policy framework denies the complexity of poverty, underestimates the impact current demographic changes are having on all families, and ignores children's well-being—regardless of their socioeconomic status—as a legitimate responsibility of government.

Child rearing must be understood as a collective responsibility; *all* parents need support, e.g., parenting information and quality early childhood programs, in fulfilling their child-rearing responsibilities. Government needs to reconceptualize its relationship with children and families to assume responsibility for the ways in which it helps structure children's child-rearing environments. Such a request does *not* argue for government intrusion into family life or "government-run" programs; the request is for governments to assume their fair share of responsibility—not to attempt a "takeover." It is also important to place the value of early childhood programs in perspective. Early childhood programs are only part of a child's environment and cannot solely determine children's development or their future (Grubb & Lazerson, 1988).

Since President Reagan's election in 1980 and the advent of the new federalism, local and state governments have become the focus of child and family policies. However, a decentralized and diversified system of early childhood care and education still requires the federal government's support and backing. The federal government is needed not as the sole determiner of early childhood policies, but as provider of initiative, leadership, and needed financial support (Grubb & Lazerson, 1988; Kagan, 1988; Kahn & Kamerman, 1987; Zigler et al., 1983).

Because of its national perspective, the federal government has the opportunity to provide a broader context for public policies at state and local levels. It has the financial resources to assure that children, regardless of where they live, receive needed services. Lack of direction by federal government has resulted in unnecessary fluctuations in services, waste of human and financial resources, and lack of equity in service distribution (Kagan, 1987). Ultimately, it represents society's lack of commitment to assume public responsibility for the well-being of its children.

Policies of early childhood education and care have been a response to social, economic, and political issues. Debates on child care and parent and compensatory education have been—and continue to be—embroiled in other public policy issues such as women's rights, welfare, employment, teenage pregnancy, high-school dropouts, etc. In these instances, early childhood programs have been used to facilitate the achievement of other policy initiatives, but without concurrently considering the needs of children and families. Policies, however, can serve multiple purposes. Early educators need to advocate for the quality of early childhood programs and the needs of families as added policy objectives.

In conjunction with a historical preoccupation with children as low-cost vehicles of social reform and representatives of future productivity, public programs have had to be justified as economically efficient. "Our views of children as profitable vehicles of investment encourage a cost-benefit analysis of parenting and pedagogy . . . . Together with the cold-hearted calculation of long-term profits to be gleaned from early education, a public consciousness has been created of children as integers, as a category of investment, into which parents, educators, and the federal bureaucrats solicitously lay down their deposits, to be risked or reaped at future markets" (Polakow, 1986, p. 8).

Proponents of increased government responsibility often need to use these economic linkages for political purposes, but they must use them very carefully. Reliance on cost benefits perpetuates the instrumental use of children. Children must have advocates who value them in their own right—not just for what they will become. Nor can all decisions be made simply on the basis of costs and benefits; outcomes for children sometimes outweigh the costs incurred. If policies for children and families are made solely on the basis of "return on investment," children will suffer when "investors" seek a higher return or decide to sell short.

Public programs to feed children exist not because of a moral commitment to children, but because in the long run, it is more expensive *not* to feed them. Childhood poverty has a special horror not because the plight of poor children moves us, but because the developmental consequences of poverty are economically inefficient. In the public realm, we do not value children very highly; we care only for adults who have grown up "right", and we focus all programs on that future. (Grubb & Lazerson, 1988, p. 58)

Moving beyond a utilitarian approach to children's policies also creates an opportunity to expand beyond policies with a restricted emphasis on children at risk. The historic focus on children in need has resulted in a fragmented, categorical, and crisis orientation (Goffin, 1983; Grubb & Lazerson, 1988; Takanishi, 1977) and an evolving two-tier system of care and education for young children (Kagan, 1987, 1988; Kahn & Kamerman, 1987; Zigler, 1987b). Focusing only on the needs of impoverished children or children at risk also perpetuates governments' categorical approach toward child and family policy.

SUMMARY

As more and more children of all socioeconomic groups participate in inadequate and/or inappropriate early educational experiences, the needs of all children loom large. *All* children are placed at risk when their needs for safe and appropriate environments and responsive care and education—whether inside or outside their homes—are ignored. We *are* our governments, and it is *our* responsibility to assure that children are the beneficiaries of our collective caring.

REFERENCES

Anderson, J. E., Brady, D. W., Bullock, C. F., & Stewart, J. P. (1984). *Public policy in America* (2nd ed.). Monterey, CA: Brooks-Cole.

Barnett, W. S., & Escobar, C. M. (1987). The economics of early educational intervention: A review. *Review of Educational Research, 57,* 387–414.

Berrulta-Clement, J. R., Schweinhart, L. J., Barnett, W. S., Epstein, A. S., & Weikart, D. P. (1984). *Changed lives*. Ypsilanti, MI: High/Scope Press.

Bronfenbrenner, U. (1974a). Developmental research, public policy and the ecology of childhood. *Child Development, 45*(1), 1–5.

Bronfenbrenner, U. (1974b). *Is early intervention effective? A report on longitudinal evaluations of preschool programs*. Washington, DC: Office of Child Development, Department of Health, Education, and Welfare.

Bronfenbrenner, U., & Weiss, H. B. (1983). Beyond policies without people: An ecological perspective on child and family policy. In E. F. Zigler, S. L. Kagan, & E. Klugman (Eds.), *Children, families and government: Perspectives on American social policy* (pp. 393–414). Cambridge, England: Cambridge University Press.

Children's Defense Fund. (1988). A children's defense budget. *FY89: An analysis of our nation's investment in children*. Washington, DC: Author.

Christensen, B. J. (1988, May). Testimony before the Platform Committee of the National Republican Committee, Kansas City, MO.

Cicirelli, V. (1969). *The impact of Head Start: An evaluation of the effects of Head Start on children's cognitive and affective development.* Athens, OH: Westinghouse Learning Corporation.

Clarke-Stewart, K. A. (1981). Parent education in the 1970's. *Educational Evaluation and Policy Analysis, 3*(6), 47–58.

Clarke-Stewart, K. A. (1988). Evolving issues in early childhood education: A personal perspective. *Early Childhood Research Quarterly, 3*(2), 139–149.

Cochran, M., & Woolever, F. (1983). Beyond the deficit model: The improvement of parents with information and informal supports. In I. E. Sigel & L. M. Laosa (Eds.), *Changing families* (pp. 215–245). New York: Plenum Press.

Consortium for Longitudinal Studies. (1979). *Lasting effects after preschool* (Final report for HEW Grant 90C-1311). Ithaca, NY: Cornell University, Community Services Laboratory.

Duncan, G. J. (1988, June). *The economic environment of childhood.* Paper presented at a working converence on Poverty and Children, Lawrence, KS.

Edelman, M. (1981). Who is for children? *American Psychologist, 36,* 109–116.

Goffin, S. G. (1983). A framework for conceptualizing children's services. *American Journal of Orthopsychiatry, 53,* 282–290.

Goffin, S. G. (1988). Putting our advocacy efforts into a new context. *Young Children, 43*(3), 52–56.

Goffin, S. G., with Caccimo, J. (1986). *In partnership with parents.* Jefferson City, MO: State Department of Education, Division of Special Education.

Grubb, W. N. (1987). *Young children face the states: Issues and options for early childhood programs.* Paper prepared for the Center for Policy Research in Education, Rutgers University, New Brunswick, NJ.

Grubb, W. N., & Lazerson, M. (1988). *Broken promises: How Americans fail their children.* Chicago: University of Chicago Press.

Halpern, R. (1988). Major social and demographic trends affecting young families: Implications for early childhood care and education. *Young Children, 42*(6), 34–40.

Hayes, C. D. (1982). *Making policies for children: A study of the federal process.* Washington, DC: National Academy Press.

Hofferth, S. L., & Phillips, D. A. (1987). Child care in the United States, 1970 to 1995. *Journal of Marriage and the Family, 49,* 559–571.

Kagan, S. L. (1987). Early Schooling: On what grounds? In S. L. Kagan & E. F. Zigler (Eds.), *Early Schooling: The national debate* (pp. 3–23). New Haven: Yale University Press.

Kagan, S. L. (1988). Current reforms in early childhood education: Are we addressing the issues? *Young Children, 43*(2), 27–32.

Kagan, S. L., & Zigler, E. F. (Eds.). (1987). *Early schooling: The national debate.* New Haven: Yale University Press.

Kahn, A. J., & Kamerman, S. B. (1987). *Child care: Facing the hard choices.* Dover, MA: Auburn House.

Kamerman, S. B. (1984). Child care and family benefits: Policies of six industrialized countries. In R. G. Genovese (Ed.), *Family and change: Social needs and public policies* (pp. 60–67). South Hadley, MA: Bergin & Garvey.

Kamerman, S. G. (1988). An international perspective on child care. *Child Care Action News, 5*(3), 1, 7.

Kelman, S. (1987). *Making public policy: A hopeful view of American government.* New York: Basic Books.

Keniston, K. (1977). *All our children: The American family under pressure.* New York: Harcourt Brace Jovanovich.

Lally, J. R., Mangione, P. L., Honig, A. S., & Wittner, D. S. (1988). More pride less delinquency. Findings from the ten-year follow-up study of the Syracuse University Family Development Research Program. *Zero to Three, 8*(4), 13–18.

Lazar, I. (1980). Social research and social policy—Reflections on relationships. In R. Haskins & J. J. Gallagher (Eds.), *Care and education of young children in America: Policy, politics, and social science* (pp. 59–71). Norwood, NJ: Ablex.

Lazerson, M. (1971). Social reform and early childhood education: Some historical perspectives. In R. H. Anderson & H. G. Shane (Eds.), *As the twig is bent: Readings in early childhood education* (pp. 22–33). Boston: Houghton Mifflin.

Levin, H. M. (1988, June). *Cost-benefit and cost-effectiveness analyses of interventions for children in poverty.* Paper presented at a working conference on Poverty and Children, Lawrence, KS.

Morado, C. (1986). Prekindergarten programs for 4 year olds: State involvement in preschool education. *Young Children, 41*(6), 69–71.

Morgan, G. G. (1980). Regulating early childhood programs in the eighties. In B. Spodek (Ed.), *Handbook of research in early childhood education* (pp. 375–398). New York: The Free Press.

Morgan, G. G. (1983a). Child daycare policy in chaos. In E. F. Zigler, S. L. Kagan, & E. Klugman (Eds.), *Children, families, and government* (pp. 249–265). Cambridge, England: Cambridge University Press.

Morgan, G. G. (1983b). Practical techniques for change. *Journal of Children in Contemporary Society, 15*(4), 91–103.

Morgan, G. G. (1987). Two visions: The future of day care and early childhood programs. *Child Care Action News, 4*(6), 1, 6–7.

Peters, D., & Benn, J. (1980). Day care: Support for the family. *Dimensions, 9,* 78–82.

Phillips, D. A. (Ed.). (1987). Preface. *Quality in child care: What does research tell us?* Washington, DC: National Association for the Education of Young Children.

Phillips, D. A. (1988, June). *With a little help: Children in poverty and child care.* Paper presented at a working conference on Poverty and Children, Lawrence, KS.

Phillips, D. A., & Zigler, E. (1987). The checkered history of federal child care regulation. In E. Z. Rothkopf (Ed.), *Review of research in education* (Vol. 14, pp. 3–41). Washington, DC: American Educational Research Association.

Polakow, V. (1986). Some reflections on the landscape of childhood and the politics of care. *Journal of Education, 168*(3), 7–12.

Powell, D. R. (1982). From child to parent: Changing conceptions of early childhood intervention. *The Annals of the American Academy of Political and Social Science, 461,* 135–144.

Powell, D. R. (1984). Enhancing the effectiveness of parent education: An analysis of program assumptions. In L. G. Katz, P. J. Wagemaker, & K. Steiner (Eds.), *Current topics in early childhood education* (Vol. 5, pp. 121–139). Norwood, NJ: Ablex.

Powell, D. R. (1986). Research in review: Parent education and support programs. *Young Children, 41*(3), 47–53.

Ramey, C. T., Bryant, D. M., & Suarez, T. A. (1985). Preschool compensatory education and the modifiability of intelligence: A critical review. In D. K. Ditterman (Ed.), *Current topics in human intelligence* (Vol. 1, pp. 247–296). Norwood, NJ: Ablex.

Ramey, C. T., & Suarez, T. M. (1984). Early intervention and the early experience paradigm: Toward a better framework for social policy. *Journal of Children in Contemporary Society, 17*(1), 3–13.

Reiger, J. (1988, May). Testimony before the Platform Committee of the National Republican Committee, Kansas City, MO.

Ross, C. J. (1983). Advocacy movements in the century of the child. In E. F. Zigler, S. L. Kagan, & E. Klugman (Eds.), *Children, families, and government* (pp. 165–176). Cambridge, England: Cambridge University Press.

Scarr, S., & Weinberg, R. A. (1986). The early childhood enterprise: Care and education of the young. *American Psychologist, 41,* 1140–1146.

Schafly, P. (1988, May). Testimony before the Platform Committee of the National Republican Committee, Kansas City, MO.

Seitz, V., Rosenbaum, L. K., & Apfel, N. H. (1985). Effects of family support intervention: A ten year follow-up. *Child Development, 56,* 376–391.

Takanishi, R. (1977). Federal involvement in early education (1933–1973): The need for historical perspective. In L. G. Katz (Ed.), *Current topics in early childhood education* (Vol. 1, pp. 139–164). Norwood, NJ: Ablex.

Weikart, D. P. (1987). Curriculum quality in early childhood. In S. L. Kagan & E. F. Zigler (Eds.), *Early schooling: The national debate* (pp. 168–189). New Haven: Yale University Press.

Weissbourd, B. (1983). The family support movement: Greater than the sum of its parts. *Zero to Three, 4*(91), 8–10.

Zigler, E. F. (1987a). *A solution to the nation's child care crises: The school of the twenty-first century.* Unpublished manuscript.

Zigler, E. F. (1987b). Policy recommendations on child care. Testimony presented to the United States Senate Subcommittee on Children, Families, Drugs, and Alcoholism, June 11, 1987.

Zigler, E. F., Kagan, S. L., & Klugman, E. (1983). *Children, families, and government: Progress, perspectives, on American social policy.* Cambridge, MA: Cambridge University Press.

Zigler, E. F., & Seitz, V. (1982). Head Start as a national laboratory. *The Annals of the American Academy of Political and Social Science, 461,* 81–90.

2

The Child Is Not the Mere Creature of the State: The Family as Primary Educator

SUSANNAH SHEFFER
Editor, Growing Without Schooling

Somewhere, as you read this, a child is walking out of school knowing that he does not have to come back until (probably in consultation with his family) he decides to. Somewhere else, another child, who has just been asked where she goes to school, is answering, "I learn at home," or "My parents teach me," or perhaps, "I teach myself."

These children and their parents are among the small but growing minority of families (estimates ranged from 50,000 to half a million in the United States in 1988[1]) currently taking advantage of the fact that compulsory education in this country does not legally mean compulsory *schooling*. Though few Americans are aware of it and some, whether out of ignorance or a deliberate desire to discourage potential homeschooling parents, may act as if it is not the case, parents and children have the right to choose something else for themselves if government schooling—or schooling in general—does not seem to them the best option.

Those who choose homeschooling do so for many reasons, and practice it in many ways. Homeschooling families live in urban centers, in suburbs, in rural communities, on farms, in mobile homes. They are white, black, wealthy, middle-class, and welfare recipients (and a much smaller percentage fall into the "wealthy"

---

[1]Estimates vary so widely because there is no central location at which all homeschoolers register, and thus no easy way of counting them. Patricia Lines of the Department of Education (Office of the Assistant Secretary for Educational Research and Improvement, Washington, DC 20208) has made an effort to compile a current estimate. Figures for individual states are published in *Growing Without Schooling* magazine whenever they are available.

category than is often supposed). Among them are a good number of single parents, parents who work outside the home, and parents without traditional school credentials.

In 1988, as this is being written, the laws in many states are significantly more favorable to homeschooling than they were at the start of the decade. On one recent state survey of homeschooling families, several answered the question, "When did you first learn that homeschooling was an option?" by saying, "We always knew it was possible" (Plant, 1986). The first families who 10 years ago tested their state's compulsory education laws and began to pave the way for greater legal and social acceptance of homeschooling would not have been so sure.

Yet there are several new homeschooling bills pending before state legislatures. Court cases involving homeschoolers and school officials are still being argued all across the country. In states that leave the details of homeschooling arrangements up to the local superintendents, the specifics as well as the underlying principles of who is responsible for children's education—and who gets to make decisions about it—are still being negotiated.

It is the task of this chapter to argue that for those parents who wish to see the education of children as primarily the family's responsibility, there is much legislative and judicial support, as well as a sound educational basis, for such a view. This writer's intention is not to argue that all parents *ought* to exercise the choice and take on the responsibility that happens to be available to them. Rather, it is to make clear why legislatures and courts have consistently upheld this right, why they have been wise to do so, and what educational and social advantages there are—for those who engage in it and those who do not—in the educational alternative that then results.

HISTORY OF HOMESCHOOLING

Almost as soon as compulsory schooling was instituted in the United States, people began testing its limits. Was compulsory schooling meant only to ensure that no one who wanted to go to school could be prevented from going? Or was it designed to ensure that everyone received a particular type of education? What about those who preferred a different type? What ought to have happened when the state's interest in seeing people become educated and the individual's or family's interest in making choices about education came into conflict?

These are the sorts of questions that the institution of compulsory schooling raised, and continues to raise, and that the courts and legislatures have had to interpret and decide. Historically, legislative and judicial decisions have consistently favored people's right to choose over governmental monopoly of education, but this right, and the extent to which it may be exercised, continues to be tested.

When an Oregon statute that abolished private schools was challenged and eventually struck down in *Pierce v. Society of Sisters* (1925), the United States Supreme Court said in its ruling, "It is not seriously debatable that the parental right to guide one's child intellectually and religiously is a most substantial part of the liberty and freedom of the parent." The Court decided that the statute in question, by restricting parents' choices for their children so severely, was too great an infringement upon that liberty. The ruling continues,

> The fundamental theory of liberty upon which all governments in this Union repose excludes any general power of the State to standardize its children by forcing them to accept instruction from public teachers only. The child is not the mere creature of the State; those who nurture him and direct his destiny have the right, coupled with the high duty, to recognize and prepare him for additional obligations.

Two years later, in *Farrington v. Tokushige* (1927), the Court, having allowed for the existence of private schools in the *Pierce* case, now made it clear that the state (in this case, the territory of Hawaii) could not "standardize its children" by imposing uniform regulations on private schools, either. Once again, the Court affirmed that when the state said "education," it could not mean one kind of education only.

When, several decades later, families began testing these legal precedents to find out whether they applied to parents who wanted to teach their children at home rather than in *any* kind of school, judges—and later legislatures—overwhelmingly agreed that they did. In *Perchemlides v. Frizzle* (1978), argued in the Massachusetts Superior Court, Judge Greaney wrote in his ruling in favor of the Perchemlides family (a ruling that would later be looked upon as a model by judges elsewhere):

> The Massachusetts compulsory attendance statute might well be constitutionally infirm if it did not exempt students whose parents prefer alternative forms of education. And as to the scope of alternatives permitted by that statute, our Supreme Judicial Court has construed the "otherwise instructed" statutory exemption to include home education, given by the parents themselves, "provided it is given in good faith, and is sufficient in extent." *Commonwealth v. Roberts,* 159 Mass. 372 at 374.

Home education, then, was clearly an acceptable educational alternative. At the time of *Perchemlides v. Frizzle,* judges who wanted to affirm parents' right to educate their own children had to find the legality within such statutory phrases as "otherwise instructed," phrases that could be construed as allowing for home education but that did not explicitly state that as their intention.

As interest in home education grew, parents began to want statutory provisions for the alternative to be made explicit so that there could be no doubt in anyone's mind that homeschooling was a distinct and legal form of education and would not be confused with truancy. Laws that gave as the alternative to public or private schooling such options as "instruction by a properly qualified private tutor" left open the interpretation of that phrase, and seemed out of date by this time. Homeschooling in the late 1970s and early 1980s no longer meant bringing a tutor into the occasional wealthy home, as it had meant when such statutory phrases were written. New laws were needed for new situations.

During the 1980s, then, homeschoolers learned how to lobby their legislatures, how to present lawmakers with adequate information about something that was, for many, a new idea. At this writing, in 1988, laws making homeschooling explicitly legal have been passed in nineteen states since 1982. In no state is homeschooling explicitly prohibited, and in the three states that now require home schools to use a certified teacher—Iowa, Michigan, and North Dakota—court challenges to this requirement have put the situation in such flux that by the time you are reading these words, the requirement may have already been struck down.

Current state laws generally allow for home education in one of three ways: by allowing parents to register their home as a private school; by requiring parents to submit a "declaration of intent" form, usually annually, to their local school district or state department of education; and by requiring parents to seek approval from their local superintendents, who may or may not grant it.

As readers may suspect, this last option is least satisfying to parents who resent having to ask permission to do what they feel is already their right. In some instances, the approval process works smoothly, and parents and schools cooperate in what John Holt termed a "fruitful partnership," with the parents supplying the school with information about their children's progress and the school in turn giving the family access to school facilities and materials. Children in such situations may take an occasional class at the local school or, even more likely, participate in such extracurricular activities as band or after-school sports.

There are advantages to such an arrangement for schools as well. In an article for the educational journal *The Phi Delta Kappan,* John Holt (1983b) argued that schools would benefit from the involvement of students who had *chosen* to be there, for whatever reason. Holt said he sympathized with the frustration teachers experienced when working with a child who would clearly rather be somewhere else. He suggested that the presence of homeschooled children who were in school clearly because there was something that they wanted to do there would make other children consider the possibility that there was something in school worth getting.

But not all arrangements between schools and homeschoolers are as cooperative as those in this example. In states that require district approval, neighboring districts can vary widely in attitude and policy with regard to homeschoolers, and for this reason, many homeschoolers are eager to see such laws made more uniformly favorable.

When homeschoolers negotiate the extent of their right to teach their own children in the courts or legislatures, or with school officials, the questions are not only about who is responsible for education, but about who is to have control of it, who will get to define it. Courts, as we have seen, have consistently upheld the right of parents to control their children's education, but they have balanced it against the state's right to see that all children become educated. It is important to understand the ways in which courts—particularly the Supreme Court, when the challenge is on constitutional grounds—have interpreted this balance. When the Court has said that compulsory education is constitutionally allowable, it has done so on the ground that the state has the right to protect itself against children who might grow up so ignorant that they will become a burden to society. This, according to the Court, is the extent of the state's power over individual choices in education.

EDUCATIONAL EQUIVALENCE

One of the ways in which the questions inherent in this balance of an individual's and the state's rights are brought to bear is over the issue of educational equivalence. If a state law requires that education received in the home must be "equivalent" to the education that the child would be receiving in school, does this mean that such education should be identical to a school education? Similar to? "Comparable" to, as a couple of states word it? How are we to define *equivalence?*

Many schools would like to define it in terms of the number of hours and days per year on which instruction is given. Several state laws—including those that merely require parents to file an annual affidavit or declaration-of-intent form—ask parents to affirm that they are teaching their children for 900 hours or 180 days a year, or thereabouts. While many parents are happy to sign such a statement, believing that they are indeed fulfilling such a requirement, others have argued that such a definition of *equivalence* is misleading because it implies that children in school are in fact receiving direct instruction for 900 hours a year. Parents argue that this is impossible in a group setting, and thus that individual instruction cannot be subject to the same temporal guidelines.

Early in the homeschooling movement, parents began to address the question of time spent on instruction by researching the number of hours per week for which local schools sent a tutor to a child who was sick and temporarily unable to attend the regular classroom. Answers ranged from 2 to 7 hours per week, well under the 5 or 6 hours a day that children in school are actually in attendance (Holt, 1981). It was this latter figure that homeschoolers were being asked to duplicate, but they argued that if schools found that homebound students could keep up with their class by receiving only a couple of hours of instruction per week, parents should not be expected to provide several times that amount. Comparing individual to group instruction, parents said, was like comparing apples and oranges, and expecting home education to be an exact replica of school education misunderstood the nature of the former. "If I'm reading my child a bedtime story about the Indians and we get into a long discussion about American history, does that count as our history lesson for the day?" parents asked. "What about if my child sits and reads about history alone for an afternoon?"

Disputes about the meaning of equivalence sometimes had to be argued in court, as happened in 1978 when Iowa parents Robert and Linda Sessions were charged with failing to send their son to school or to "obtain equivalent instruction elsewhere." The court, ruling in favor of the Sessions family, held that the burden of proof fell on the school, rather than on the parents, to define *equivalent* and to show that what Robert and Linda Sessions proposed to do with their son was *not* equivalent

(Holt, 1981). This ruling set an important precedent, particularly, of course, for those states in which the law required schools and homeschoolers to come to an agreement. But perhaps because many people remain unaware of the significant and relatively recent rulings regarding home education, many homeschoolers are still being asked to prove that what they plan to do is equivalent to what is being done in school.

TEACHER QUALIFICATIONS

A second question that negotiations about the right to homeschooling raise concerns the definition of *qualifications.* Though, as mentioned earlier, only three states now require homeschooling parents to hold a teaching certificate, several others require them to be "competent," "qualified," or "capable of teaching." It must be evident even to those readers unfamiliar with these issues that such terms are vague at best, and are wide open to individual interpretation. Judges or school officials asked to determine whether a particular set of parents are qualified to teach often find it easiest to equate "qualified" with "certified," even when the law does not require them to make this equation.

For this reason, homeschooling parents have found it necessary to question the assumed relationship between certification and teaching. They ask whether certification always guarantees competence, and whether a certified teacher should always be assumed to be the better teacher for a particular child or in a particular situation. In posing this challenge, homeschoolers frequently point out that in most states in this country, private schools are not required to hire certified teachers, and tend to determine qualifications on the basis of interest in, and experience with, children, and skill in, and enthusiasm for, a particular subject. Parents argue that because home schools are classified as private schools in several states, homeschoolers should be allowed to determine teacher qualification in the same manner.

Though it is not within the scope of this chapter to discuss the nature of teaching, nor who may be best qualified to do it, in any detail, it must be pointed out that there is much reason to doubt the claim that only those who hold teaching certificates are qualified to engage in the activity. Though the National Education Association recently released a set of guidelines for homeschooling that included the recommendation that all home schools be required to use certified teachers ("Homeschooling," 1988), judges are increasingly making opposite rulings. In recent instances, these rulings have led to legislative proposals that would remove the certification requirement in the states that now possess it.

Thus, the nature of teacher qualification remains open to interpretation. In Massachusetts, a state that requires parents to seek the "prior approval" of their superintendent or school committee, parents must include in their proposal some explanation of why they feel themselves to be qualified to teach their children. It is up to the parents to determine the meaning of "qualified" and to argue that they fulfill the definition. Some discussion of the nature of teaching in the home setting, and by implication the kinds of things that make one qualified to do it, will follow later in this chapter.

EVALUATION

Finally, negotiations between homeschoolers and school officials also center around the question of how the home school will be evaluated: by what means, by whom, and with what consequences. The difficulty is that such questions immediately give way to other, trickier questions, which often demand that both sides make an effort to understand each other's way of thinking, and to compromise.

For many school officials, the easiest and best means by which to evaluate a home school is standardized testing. The appeal lies in the very notion of standardness, the idea of a common denominator that will allow an eight year old educated at home to be compared with third graders in the classroom. If such an eight year old scores at grade level on a standardized test, this seems to reassure the school officials that they are not negligent in their job of making sure that this child is becoming adequately educated. Likewise, if the child's test scores are low, this seems to give school officials adequate basis on which to doubt the effectiveness of the home school.

Homeschoolers have objected strongly to this latter claim. When a child in school scores badly on a standardized test, they argue, the effectiveness of the teaching, or of the institution of schooling, is not immediately called into question. More often *the child* is assumed to be in need of extra help in a particular area. In those cases in which low test scores do raise doubts about the adequacy of the teacher or the curriculum, the child is nevertheless allowed to remain in the same setting. In other words, standardized testing is not, for schoolchildren, a test of the value of the entire method of education. For homeschoolers, however, it has often been the case that low standardized test scores (though, as we will later see, high rather than low test scores are the norm for homeschoolers) call into question the value of the entire enterprise.

Thus, the question of means also leads to the question of the consequences of evaluation, or the uses to which that evaluation will be put. Many states, as a result of homeschoolers' lobbying efforts, now have written into the law the stipulation that test results are for parents' use only, or that a child cannot be required to stop homeschooling on the basis of low test scores.

But for many homeschoolers, the question of means is even more difficult, because they doubt that standardized testing is the most effective way to find out how much someone knows. Once again, this is a topic that is outside the scope of this chapter, but readers are encouraged to consult the references for further information on the topic. For the purposes of this discussion, it is enough to say that many, if not most, of the recently passed laws (and those currently being debated by state legislatures) list more than one (usually three) means of evaluating the home school, from which parents may choose. Commonly, the three options are standardized testing, evaluation by a third party (usually a certified teacher or licensed psychologist), and what has come to be known as the "portfolio method," a compilation of work samples, written descriptions, and so on, designed to give evidence of the student's progress.

In sum, the relationship between compulsory school laws and parents' right to home educate has been tested in many ways and in many arenas, and continues to be so tested. The questions, whether they are about statutory interpretation, local school district policy, or charges of truancy or educational neglect, all have at the root the larger questions of who is to have control of education, who will get to define it, and whether education should be seen as synonymous with schooling.

REASONS FOR HOMESCHOOLING

What has impelled the parents in the struggles just described? What is it about home education that seems to them so worth fighting for?

There are as many reasons for homeschooling as there are homeschoolers, so any brief analysis must necessarily be incomplete. Some parents come to homeschooling only after their child has been so miserable in school that the homeschooling alternative seems to them to be the only viable one. Others knew even before their children were born that they would not send them to school, or would offer them the choice of going or not going. Still others find that after living with their children for 5 or 6 years, watching and helping them learn about the world in so many ways, they don't want to give up the task, and the pleasure, to someone else.

Family closeness and cohesiveness tends to be among homeschoolers' top priorities ("family" is variously defined; as mentioned earlier, there are many single-parent homeschoolers). Homeschooling families probably spend more actual time together than the average American family. Home businesses are common, and some parents bring their children to a workplace outside the home. In both cases, the emphasis is on the family working together.

Perhaps above all else, homeschoolers like being with their children, find their growth and development interesting, and want to play an active part in their education. But this is not to say that only parents who don't send their children to school feel this way about them, or that feeling this way inevitably leads one to home education. It is simply an attempt at finding some characteristics that can be said to be common to most if not all homeschoolers.

Underlying these general feelings are often other beliefs. For a significant part of the homeschool population, these beliefs are religious, and involve a desire to determine which religious values will be passed on to one's children. For another significant part of the homeschool population (and these "parts" quite often overlap), motivation for homeschooling derives from a theory, or perhaps theories, about how children learn. We will devote some attention to these theories here, recognizing (again) that there is much more to be said than can be said in this space.

John Holt (1984) devised a metaphor for a common (though perhaps not consciously recognized) view of learning. The metaphor is of bottles in a factory, all waiting to be filled with the appropriate liquid.

> Down the conveyor belts come rows of empty containers of sundry shapes and sizes. Beside the belts is an array of pouring and squirting devices, controlled by employees of the factory. As the containers go by, these workers squirt various amounts of different substances—reading, spelling, math, history, science—into the containers. Upstairs, management decides when the containers should be put on the belt, how long they should be left on, what kinds of materials should be poured or squirted into them at what times, and what should be done about containers whose openings (like pop bottles) seem to be smaller than the others, or that seem to have no openings at all . . . . No one seems to ask the obvious question: How come so many of the containers, having had these substances squirted at them for so many years, are still going out of the factory empty? (pp. 32–33)

In contrast, Holt (and later, many homeschoolers) spoke of learning as active rather than passive. This theory, which Holt based on extensive observation of young children, saw children as scientists, taking in a vast amount of data about the world around them, forming hypotheses, and finally making knowledge out of their experience. Thus, babies learning to talk (and this is the one thing that we generally believe children can learn without being explicitly taught) are doing something extraordinarily complicated, and extraordinarily well. They figure out that the sounds people make are meaningful, not random noise but ordered, purposeful; the sounds *make things happen.* Babies then figure out what these sounds mean, and how to use them, and they do this, Holt said (and others have corroborated this), not simply by imitation but by active hypothesizing, testing, and making sense of their experience.

The easiest way to sum up this view of learning is to say that children are good at learning, and that learning is not separate from life. In this view, two of the most fallacious statements we can make are, "We must teach children how to learn," and "Children go to school to learn." The first implies that children would not know how to learn if we did not teach them; it is this writer's thesis that, on the contrary, human beings are born good at learning, and that the evidence for this lies, as described above, in the skill that every healthy baby exhibits.

The second fallacious statement implies that learning is something that can happen only in certain specifically designated places. "Children go to school to learn" says that anything that happens outside of school is not learning, and doesn't count. It is important to understand that school, in this analysis, is not simply the physical building but the way of thinking about learning that assumes that it is, or can be, separate from the whole human life.

Here is a thirteen year old who has never been to school talking about a life in which such distinctions are not made:

> Right now my main interests are weaving, writing, music and physics. I'm very interested in motors and machines, and I'm going to try to build one . . . . It seems

that whenever I do one thing, it leads me to something else. Sometimes it's hard to answer people's questions about the way we homeschool, because they're always asking, "Do you have PE? Does your mom teach you art?" and stuff like that. We don't break things down into categories. Take weaving for example. I have to figure out mathematically how to warp the loom, how much yarn I'll need, etc. So that's math. Then we have to warp the loom so that the pattern will come out right—more math. And then when I'm weaving, I'm having my craft lesson for the day. (Kopel, 1988, p. 29)

Is this child's life any less "educational" because it is not broken down into categories, because she would be hard pressed to say when she is learning and when she is not?

Some homeschooling families, to be sure, do "break things down into categories" to a greater degree than this one does, sometimes because the records they are required to keep necessitate this, sometimes because they themselves find something useful about the categorization. It is safe to say, however, that whatever the family's organizational and structural preference, there is in close to all cases a great respect for learning's incidental nature, and an ability to see learning in all sorts of situations.

Homeschoolers often emphasize that academic tasks can be learned in the process of engaging in real-world activities. One seven year old, for example, learned arithmetic through the measuring and record keeping necessary to the running of a home-based bakery (which she herself ran). Some homeschoolers refer to this type of learning as "organic"—that is, arising out of the interest of the learner, and the requirements of the task itself.

It may be helpful to look at how reading is commonly learned in the home school setting (though as the reader can perhaps by now imagine, it is difficult to say "commonly" when referring to the diversity of home school situations). First, it is important to recognize that reading in the home school does not automatically begin at age six. Some parents report that their children show an interest in reading at age four; others do not show this interest until age twelve, something that those accustomed to the uniformity of a school's reading curriculum may find difficult to accept. Yet studies, both formal and anecdotal, have shown that by, say, age fifteen (or even much earlier), it is impossible to tell who began reading when (Moore, 1975; Richman & Richman, 1988). Children who would have been described as having a serious reading problem in school (because they would have tested well below grade level at, say, age eight) are indistinguishable from their peers in this regard within a few years.

Second, homeschooling parents tend to give far less direct and formal reading instruction than is commonly thought to be necessary. Parents describe children who learn to read by being read to extensively, and by being given access to print in a variety of ways—signs, labels, messages, and letters, as well as books and magazines that the children see their parents enjoying and using for their own purposes. Gradually, the children start asking questions about what words say, and become interested in figuring out the stories in their favorite books. Some children seem to require more direct help than others, and parents adjust their responses accordingly.

Here is one eight year old telling the story, in *Growing Without Schooling* magazine, of how she taught herself to read, with her parents' help:

> When I was younger, I wanted to read but I couldn't. I was jealous because my older sister and brother could read hard books. When I looked at books I looked at the pictures and I got interested in what the words said. So whenever we passed a sign when we were riding in the car, I read it. I read signs like "STOP," "FREE," "BEST," "K-MART."
>
> One night as I was going to bed I wanted to look at books. I found *Hop On Pop* by Dr. Seuss. I started trying to read some of the words. I could read some of them, but I still couldn't read all of them and I asked Mom and Dad a lot of them like "mouse" and "wall." I felt very happy because I didn't know that I could read. I read the book out loud to Mom and Dad a lot . . . . Now I can read well and I love it (Murphy, 1988, p. 10).

This story makes many important points. The writer makes it clear that it was her own initiative that led her into reading; she sensed that reading was interesting, and she was eager to make sense of it. No one had to tell her that reading was important, or that it was time she got busy trying to master it. Furthermore, the jealousy that she experienced with regard to her older siblings' reading ability seems to have been inspirational as well. Had she had access only to models her own age, she would have missed the opportunity to envision herself a few years older, enjoying reading as her brother and sister did.

It is also interesting that the writer says, "I felt very happy because I didn't know that I could read." This suggests, as do many other stories of the same nature, that learning is not always a conscious process. Clearly this child's mind had been working to figure out the printed word in ways of which she was not totally aware.

Finally, this story suggests something important about the relationship between teaching and learning. In John Holt's words, "Unasked-for teaching prevents learning" (1983a, p. 68). Teaching that has not been requested, Holt argued, communicates the message, "I don't trust you to figure this out for yourself. You wouldn't be able to do it without my help." *Asked-for* teaching, on the other hand, seeks a response and deserves to get it.

The eight year old in the story was given the space, so to speak, to figure things out for herself, and so to get better at doing so, and to trust her own ability. When she decided that she needed specific help—as in the sounding out of a particular word—she was given it, but she was not given it until she asked. Her parents thus communicated to her the dual message, "We trust your ability to figure things out, and we are also available if and when you want our help."

Here, then, is a suggestion—by no means the only one—of what is necessary to be a successful homeschooling parent: responsiveness and accessibility. With regard to reading, this means answering a child's questions, making sure that print is available in a variety of ways, and setting an example by engaging in the activity oneself.

This last is also the beginning of an answer to the question, "What if the child wants to learn something and the parent doesn't know anything about it?" One parent wrote in John Holt's book *Teach Your Own* (1981),

> We never ask our kids to do things that we don't do ourselves, and consequently we inspire each other. We *all* read a lot, we *all* write a lot, we *all* speak very broken French, we *all* practice the piano, etc. People are often amazed at how "selfless" I am. They think they could never spend so much time with their kids, do all the necessary preparation it must take to "teach" all those subjects. Actually, I have never been so self-indulgent. I always wanted to learn French and take piano lessons, and when [my son] asked to do these things, I knew that here was my chance (pp. 113–114)!

One option, then, is to learn together. Another is to view oneself as a "general contractor," as one parent put it, and help find other adults who are interested in and knowledgeable about whatever it is the child wants to learn. Parents describe making use of relatives, friends, and members of the community in all sorts of ways, and as children get older they become able to seek out teachers themselves, to go beyond their immediate world. It is common to hear about homeschooled children involved in apprenticeships with older people, sometimes individually and sometimes in group situations (as in the case of the eight-year-old girl who became the youngest volunteer at her local nature center).

SUCCESSFUL HOMESCHOOLING

A question that may have arisen in readers' minds at this point is, "But what does all of this mean in terms of conventional academic success?" The following report describes conclusions that have been found repeatedly in other studies:

> Homeschooling seems to work. A single outstanding example was the admission to Harvard University last year of a young man who had been taught entirely at home [Note: There are now many examples of homeschoolers being admitted to college]. And from the broader pattern of available evidence one must conclude that, on average, children educated at home do well academically. Alaska and Arizona, two states that test homeschooled children, report that they perform at above-average levels as measured by nationally standardized tests. One study of children in a home tutorial network in Los Angeles showed that the children in the network scored higher on standardized tests than did the children in Los Angeles public schools. The "concern" about homeschooling, therefore, should be tempered by the knowledge that more children are failing academically in public schools than at home (Lines, 1985, p. 24).

A survey of Washington State homeschoolers found that "as a group, these 426 homeschoolers scored as well or better than their peers across the nation on virtually all of the six test scales measured by the Stanford Achievement Test series that were utilized in this research" (Wartes, 1987, p. 30). Other statewide studies offer the same conclusions.

Those who recognize that home education might provide sufficiently for a child's academic life often insist that regarding social life, it must surely be inadequate. Yet many homeschooling parents prefer the kind of social life that homeschooling offers to the kind available in school. John Holt (1981) writes,

> If there were no other reason for wanting to keep kids out of school, the social life would be reason enough. In all but a very few of the schools I have taught in, visited, or know anything about, the social life of the children is mean-spirited, competitive, exclusive, status-seeking, snobbish, full of talk about who went to whose birthday party and who got what Christmas presents . . . . Even in the first grade, classes soon divide up into leaders, . . . their bands of followers, and other outsiders who are pointedly excluded from these groups (pp. 44–45).

School's social life is also much more limited than we think. In many classrooms, talking, playing, whatever we think of as "socializing," goes on only during lunch, recess, and perhaps a few other specifically designated times. Much of a child's actual social life takes place after school, in the neighborhood or in Scouts, in after-school classes and the like, all of which homeschoolers have access to and often take part in.

There is a social life within the homeschooling movement as well. *Growing Without Schooling* magazine is full of stories of homeschooled children getting together for field trips, workshops, fairs at which they display and talk about their work, and, of course, much more informal times as well.

The social life of the homeschooler is, to be sure, *different* from the social life of the child in school, though how much and in what ways varies with each situation. Some people object that this difference deprives children of something important. John Holt (1981) writes,

> When I point out to people that the social life of most schools is mean-spirited, status-oriented, competitive, and snobbish, I am always astonished by their response. Not *one* person of the hundreds with whom I've discussed this has yet said to me that the social life of school is kindly, generous, supporting, democratic, friendly, loving, or good for children. No, without exception, when I condemn the social life of school, people say, "But that's what children are going to meet in Real Life" (p. 49).

A couple of things can be said about this. First of all, there is nothing particularly like "real life" about a situation in which thirty people of identical ages are gathered with one person who is considerably older. This situation is not found in the family, the workplace, or any other human grouping we can think of that children will later encounter; life, we might say, involves "vertical age grouping." Thus, homeschoolers who have a chance to be friends with younger children (often their siblings) and adults are in a very real sense better prepared for real life than their friends in school.

A ten-year-old homeschooler writes, "My view is that I have plenty of friends my own age, and also many younger friends. I also feel that I have some friends other kids don't have—adult friends" (Bergson-Shilcock, 1987, p. 3).

Second, it is perhaps unnecessarily defeatist to take the attitude that the nature of real life is beyond our control. Must it necessarily be "mean-spirited, status-oriented, competitive, snobbish"? How might we prepare children for a *different* kind of real life?

One way to do this is to encourage children to expect something different, to *make* a different kind of real life, not just in the future but right away. One sixteen-year-old homeschooler told *Growing Without Schooling* that in school, one is expected to hate one's brothers and sisters, but she and her younger brother were good friends, and she wasn't about to feel funny about that friendship just because it wasn't the way things were supposed to be (Keyes, 1988). If anything distinguishes home-schoolers with respect to social life, then, it is that they are not content to accept that how things are is the way things must necessarily be.

HOMESCHOOLING AND THE COMMUNITY

We have seen that some parents in this country prefer to educate their children at home, and have fought for the right to do so. The question that remains concerns the relationship between this small group's struggle and the educational community as a whole. Specifically, what is the effect of home education on this broader community?

According to legal studies professor Stephen Arons (1983), homeschooling brings to our attention the modern American conflict between public orthodoxy and private dissent. He says,

> The family that seeks permission to educate its children at home has unearthed a longstanding contradiction in American society. A history of individual autonomy and independent action has been all but buried by the inevitable institutionalization of life functions; yet individualism remains a central part of American consciousness . . . . The homeschooling family makes us aware of this painful contradiction between ideology and practice (p. 115).

It is not within the scope of this chapter to attempt to resolve this contradiction, or even to explore it at any length. What Arons makes clear, however, is that home education touches certain nerves in American society. It raises more questions than it might seem, at the outset, capable of doing. Perhaps this explains why the recent history of the homeschooling movement has been, as we have seen, in large part a history of court cases and legislative battles. Homeschooling seems to have to do with more than just the particular family in question at any given moment. Perhaps, then, we ought not to ignore the broader issues of choice, responsibility, and the definition of education that home education invites us to consider. Perhaps these are questions that *everyone* can benefit from thinking about.

In connection with this, a very strong case can be made for the value of having a right available even if, as is now the case, only a small percentage takes advantage of it. The availability of the right means that school does not have a monopoly on education. It means, increasingly, that people know that they do not *have* to send their children to school if school seems to them to be harmful, inappropriate for their particular child, or simply the less desirable alternative.

Those who know this, it can be argued, will not merely accept school as an unchanging institution. They will say, either by word or by deed (and of course the effect of the latter is stronger), "We know that we have other options, and we plan to exercise them if schools do not improve."

The rather harsh sound of this should not suggest that a confrontational stance is the only stance one can take in this regard. It does suggest that the power of available choices is real, and that home education ought not to be excluded from the broader educational community. That is to say, if people—even a very small number of people—choose home education over school education, it is in school's interest to understand why they made this choice, and to find out something about what home educators are doing. John Holt (1983b) writes,

> [The homeschooling movement] is—in effect, though certainly not by design—a laboratory for the intensive and long-range study of children's learning and of the ways in which friendly and concerned adults can help them learn. It is a research project, done at no cost, of a kind for which neither the public schools nor the government could afford to pay (p. 393).

Thus, home educators provide us with information about what happens when children are allowed to read at older ages, or to immerse themselves in one project for a very long time, or to choose their own course of study. At present, only a small minority of homeschoolers feel themselves to be on sufficiently good terms with their local school district that they willingly share this kind of information, in a spirit of mutual interest and shared enterprise. But it would be possible to work to change this, to make communication between schools and homeschoolers—in both directions—more positive and genuinely educational to all.

SUMMARY

Whenever there are institutions, it seems, there will always be people who question the need for them, or who prefer something different for their own lives. The individual's right to choose is as central to the American consciousness as compulsory schooling has come to be, and the home education movement is in many ways the story of the struggle for the peaceful coexistence of the two. This is indeed a *continuing issue,* worth following, worth thinking about, worth watching to see where it leads us.

REFERENCES

Arons, S. (1983). *Compelling belief: The culture of American schooling.* Amherst: University of Massachusetts Press.

Bergson-Shilcock, A. (1987). One homeschooler's answers [Flyer]. Cambridge, MA: Holt Associates.

Farrington v. Tokushige, 273 U.S. 284 (1927).

Holt, J. (1981). *Teach your own.* New York: Delacorte Press.

Holt, J. (1983a). *How children learn.* New York: Delacorte Press.

Holt, J. (1983b, February). Schools and homeschoolers: A fruitful partnership. *The Phi Delta Kappan,* pp. 391–394.

Holt, J. (1984, April). Why teachers fail. *The Progressive,* pp. 32–33.

Homeschooling. (1988, January). *NEA Now,* p. 1.

Keyes, E. (1988). Older homeschoolers. *Growing Without Schooling, 64,* 5.

Kopel, K. (1988). No categories. *Growing Without Schooling, 63,* 29.

Lines, P. (1985, May). States should help, not hinder, parents' homeschooling efforts. *Education Week,* p. 24.

Moore, R. (1975). *School can wait.* Provo, UT: Brigham Young University Press.

Murphy, C. (1988). Discovering she could read. *Growing Without Schooling, 61,* 10.

Perchemlides v. Frizzle, No. 16641 (Hampshire, Mass. Superior Court Civil Action, 1978).

Pierce v. Society of Sisters, 268 U.S. 510 (1925).

Plent, N. (1986). New Jersey unschoolers network 1986 survey.

Richman, H., & Richman, S. (1988). *The three R's at home.* Kittanning, PA: Pennsylvania Homeschoolers.

Wartes, J. (1987). Washington homeschool research project report from the 1986 homeschool testing and other descriptive information about Washington's homeschoolers.

3

The Origins and Significance of Employer-supported Child Care in America

MARY SALKEVER
Deputy Director, Maryland Committee for Children–Baltimore

JANET SINGERMAN
Deputy Director, Maryland Committee for Children–Baltimore

The work styles and life-styles of American families in the 1980s are quite different from those of 3 decades ago. The traditional roles of fathers and mothers have changed dramatically, with the result that fathers no longer devote their time exclusively to work, nor do mothers devote all of their time to their children and households.

Moreover, the realities of today's economy have induced both parents to enter and remain in the work force. The worker who is the sole supporter of a wife and children now represents less than 15% of the work force. Two-career families are here to stay. And women's careers, while they may be interrupted for pregnancy, are now resumed and continued.

Increasing divorce rates have also created many households headed by one working parent. In fact, the single-parent family, either male or female headed, is the fastest growing family type in the country.

All of these changes greatly impact the manner in which today's children are being raised. Consequently, quality child care has become a primary concern of parents, and population trends indicate that this concern is likely to intensify in the coming decade.

As working parents comprise an ever-increasing percent of the work force, innovative companies have begun to recognize that the availability of quality, affordable child care is not only a family concern, but also a corporate concern.

The provision of direct child care services by employers have been found to produce many benefits including reduced absenteeism, tardiness, and turnover;

increased employee productivity, morale, and health; and enhanced corporate community and public relations.

In this chapter, the evolving role of the employer in child care delivery will be explored from its first emergence in the United States in the early nineteenth century through the present day. The array of employer-supported child care options that have emerged to meet the ever-increasing work-force need will also be reviewed. Finally, the respective roles of business, government, and parents in helping this nation effectively address the tremendous need for child care will be examined.

HISTORY OF EMPLOYER-SUPPORTED CHILD CARE

While the history of formal employer-supported child care centers reportedly dates back to Scotland in 1816 and the history of child care in America dates back to Boston in 1828, the history of employer-supported child care in America dates back to 1863, when a day-care center was established for the children of mothers who were employed by hospitals, as well as mothers who made clothing for Civil War soldiers (Whipple, 1929).

Twenty-five percent of manufacturing was being done by women at the beginning of the war (Calhoun, 1960). However, the Civil War hastened the participation of women in general, and mothers in particular, into the labor force, and it was at this time that industrial and proprietary child care programs began to appear.

Proprietary programs included kindergartens, day-care centers, and nursery schools run as profit-making businesses. Industrial day-care centers, established for the children of employees of the sponsoring company, facilitated the recruitment of mothers to be employees, thereby indirectly benefiting the industry (Greenblatt, 1977).

Although not much is written on the matter, one could ascertain that the need for industrial day care diminished following the war and the number of day-care centers remained relatively low until World War I.

By World War I, women represented one-fourth of America's workers. The participation of women in the workplace increased by 1 million during the war and thus provided a stimulant to the expansion of industrial and proprietary day-care centers. By 1929, there were approximately twelve industrial day-care programs in the United States (Greenblat, 1977).

Although the number of day-care centers in America increased during the Great Depression, these programs were established as a means of creating jobs, rather than as a service for working parents. It was not until World War II that industrial day care expanded further as women again returned to work in factories and hospitals. The Lanham Act of 1941 paved the way for this expansion. Under this act, day-care centers were federally funded and were established to address the needs of "Rosie the Riveters" throughout the country. A total of $104 million of public funds went to support preschool programs under the Lanham Act. By July of 1944, 129,000 children were enrolled in 3,102 Lanham day-care centers (Greenblatt, 1977).

Two of the larger centers during World War II were established by Curtiss-Wright in Buffalo, New York, and by Kaiser in Portland, Oregon. A 1943 *New York Times* article by Dr. Lois Meek Stoltz, "The Nursery Comes to the Shipyard," described a new plan for child care launched at Kaiser's Portland yards. She wrote: "An outstanding undertaking for the care of American pre-school children in wartime is about to begin . . . . It seeks to . . . point the way toward putting a wartime job in line with the best practise in the field of child development . . . . Sixteen thousand woman now are helping build tankers and cargo ships at two of Portland's yards . . . . Two child service centers will be operated, one at each yard" (p. 20).

As mothers entered the yard, they left their children with teachers and nurses. When a mother picked up her child, she was able to buy dinner, at cost, to take home. The centers were open 24 hours a day, 364 days a year. In each center was an infirmary to care for sick children. Dr. James L. Hymes was resident director of the centers (Stoltz, 1943). A total of 4,000 children were served by the two centers. "Because the centers were considered a business expense, costs were included in the cost-plus-fixed-fee contractual arrangement with the government. In short, the federal government largely subsidized the industrial centers" (Greenblatt, 1977, p. 60). When the war ended, the Lanham Act was repealed, and most of these wartime day-care centers closed.

Still, the demand for day care continued, and although the repeal of the Lanham Act tremendously diminished the supply of child care, its value as a precedent for public and employer funding of day-care centers survived. Lanham Act day-care centers reflected a major national policy shift from the prevailing notion that the cost and provision of child care was exclusively a private, family responsibility to the notion that child care needs of workers were also the responsibility of government and employers.

The degree of employer interest in child care until the mid-1960s directly related to national interests, whether in response to the need for women workers during wartime or to stimulate the economy during periods of high unemployment, such as the depression.

In the midsixties and the following two decades, the feminist movement, high inflation, and increasing divorce rates resulted in record nonwartime female participation in the work force. By the mid-1980s, 71.5% of mothers with children under eighteen were in the labor force. Moreover, 68.8% of mothers with children under age six were in the labor force. Today, in what was once almost an exclusively male domain, women comprise 45% of the labor force and are represented in virtually every field and at all levels. Between 1986 and the year 2000, three-fifths (the majority) of the new entrants into the labor force will be women (*Child-Care: A Work Force Issue,* 1988).

The demographics of today's and tomorrow's work force, including the high rate of female participation, as well as an overall decreasing population of workers, necessitate employer interest in child care. Not surprisingly, such interest is tied primarily to the issues of maximizing corporate productivity and stimulating economic development.

It is this issue of corporate productivity that has challenged both employers and the child care community to develop creative models of assisting workers with their child care concerns. While the employer-assisted child care programs until the 1960s were primarily funded by government, similar programs today are funded primarily by the private sector.

In response, a wide array of employer-assisted child care options have evolved that can be classified in four categories: flexible personnel policies, informational programs, financial assistance, and direct services (Burud, Aschbacher, & McCroskey, 1984).

EMPLOYER-ASSISTED CHILD CARE OPTIONS

Direct Services

Direct services include all programs in which the employer is directly involved in providing care for employees' children whether such programs are located on site or near site and whether they are sponsored by an individual company or by a consortium of companies.

On-Site/Near-Site Child Care Centers

Typically, a good rule of thumb is that it takes approximately 1,000 employees to generate the 60–100 children necessary for a financially viable child care center.

Why so many workers for so few children? There are many reasons:

1. Not every employee will be of childbearing age.
2. Not every employee of childbearing age will have a child.
3. Not every employee of childbearing age with a child may have a preschool child (3–5 years of age), and most centers do not accommodate infants or school-age children.
4. Children's needs differ, and so parents with children within the age range served by the center may not elect to enroll the children in the center.
5. Parents' values differ, and what one parent may think is a high-quality program, another might think is unacceptable.
6. The cost of the program may be prohibitive for the parent, and employer subsidies are not necessarily available in such programs.

Beyond the sheer size of the work force, a key consideration is its composition and demographic makeup. Does the company have a relatively stable population, or is there a high amount of turnover? If the company has a stable work force, chances are that the years during which employees will need child care are very time limited, and without new workers from which to draw children, the child care center's life span is very short. If the company has a high amount of turnover due to working conditions, the provision of child care has been found to reduce turnover (a desirable goal). The question then becomes, Will there still be enough employees with children to make a center financially viable?

In terms of demographic makeup, issues to be considered include whether the company has employees located at several sites or only one. If the company is multisited, will the child care center be accessible to all employees, or will several centers be established to serve all employees?

These are just a sampling of the demographic questions to be asked. Ultimately, in order to determine whether an employer-supported child care program is a viable option, a company must develop, disseminate, and analyze a well-designed child care needs assessment survey to determine employees' level of interest. If sufficient interest is documented, there is a variety of factors to consider:

1. Cost: Does the company have the financial resources to develop a child care center (conservatively estimated at $250,000 for a sixty-child program)?

2. Space: Does the company have the indoor and outdoor space for the program on site, or will near-site space need to be identified?

3. Liability: Has the company considered its liability with regard to the direct provision of child care? Although there are a variety of ways to offset corporate liability (e.g., leasing space to a private child care provider), liability issues must be carefully considered.

Relatively few employers have actually established child care centers. A study conducted by Dr. Dana Friedman (1986, 1987) of the Conference Board indicated that there are fewer than 600 employer-supported child care centers in the United States and that many of these are operated by hospitals and government agencies. The major barriers to the expansion of such child care centers focus around cost and liability, and while there are a variety of ways to address these issues, they remain significant deterrents to the expansion of these programs.

Consortium-based Child Care

The primary alternative to on-site or near-site child care for small companies is the consortium-based child care center in which two or more employers, usually geo-graphically linked, jointly sponsored a child care program to serve their respective employees. In such programs, the start-up and operating costs are shared among consortium members, and center slots are usually reserved on a per-employer basis. These slots may then be made available to consortium members' employees on a subsidized or nonsubsidized basis.

The consortium-based child care center option offers employers the oppor-tunity to increase the work force from which to draw children over that which would be available within a single company and to share the costs and liability associated with a center.

Consortium-based child care is gaining popularity with the advent of light industrial parks across the country. These parks, usually located in rural or suburban areas, are particularly well suited to this care option. Consortium-based child care is also well suited to downtown business districts in which many employers are within close proximity and space is at a premium.

Financial Assistance

Child care is the fourth largest household expense in America after food, housing, and taxes. The typical yearly cost of full-time child care in major United States cities and suburbs was $3,000 in 1987 for one child (Children's Defense Fund, 1987). If a company's needs assessment survey indicates that the cost of care is a problem for employees and the company does not want to directly offer child care to employees, it may want to consider the development of a child care reimbursement program.

Child care reimbursement programs are established by employers to share the costs of care with employees. Sometimes known as child care voucher or vendor plans, reimbursement programs provide for the employer to pay for all or part of an employee's child care, on a fixed or sliding-fee-scale basis.

The parent selects the program in which to place the child, and submits child care receipts for reimbursement by the employer. Alternatively, an employer may issue a voucher for the parent to submit to the child care provider, and the provider can cash the voucher from the company.

There are key factors to consider when evaluating this option:

1. It is based on the premise that care is available within the community. If care is not available, a child care reimbursement program will not be as effective.
2. Moreover, the expense of this option, while tax deductible to the employer, is still considerable (although if the company is small, child care reimbursement programs would probably be less expensive to operate than on-site or near-site child care).
3. This option respects a parent's right to choose the form of child care that is most appropriate for the child and family. As employers using this option are neither directly providing child care nor directing employees to specific child care programs, child care reimbursement programs do not expose companies to liability lawsuits.
4. The employer is able to establish standards for the form of child care that is eligible for reimbursement and thereby may upgrade the quality of care received by employees' children.
5. For multisited companies, child care reimbursement programs are typically more equitable for all employees than direct service programs.

A variant of the vendor/voucher programs just described is a child care financial assistance program in which the employer purchases enrollment slots in specific facilities (child care centers and/or familiy day-care homes) and then makes the slots available on a subsidized basis to employees. Although the liability for offering such a program is higher than the typical vendor/voucher plan, such plans can guarantee the availability of care while reducing employees' cost for such care. One disadvantage to this plan is that the company may not be able to predict the exact number of slots to reserve, and as a result, slots may go unfilled or waiting lists may develop.

Informational Programs

There are two major forms of informational programs offered to working parents by employers: child care resource and referral counseling, and parenting education.

Child Care Resource and Referral Counseling

The primary purpose of a child care resource and referral (R&R) counseling service is to assist parents in selecting and locating child care that is well suited to their needs, preferences, and ability to pay. R&R's typically do not recommend specific child care programs; rather, they refer parents to a range of programs that are identified on the basis of the needs the parents present. In this way, a parent's right to select appropriate care is protected, and liability for child care choices rests with the parent.

Employers have found that by offering this form of assistance, they are able to effectively assist their employees whose child care plans are in flux by putting them in contact with experts who are aware of the availability of programs and the factors to consider when selecting care. Although the usefulness of R&R depends on the availability of child care, access to limited resources is usually eased through use of an R&R agency.

Although a company may establish a child care resource and referral service in-house, typically companies contract with community-based child care resource and referral agencies. In exchange, employees have access to information on a wide variety of child care programs, individualized counseling, educational materials, and follow-up assistance. Typically, resource and referral agencies will also offer companies the option of contracting for the R&R to perform vacancy checks before referring an employee to a specific program. When child care is in short supply, this assistance can greatly reduce the amount of time it takes an employee to find care.

Moreover, R&R agencies typically provide employers with utilization reports that document in aggregate form the child care needs of their work forces. This information is useful for planning further involvement in child care assistance.

Typically, the cost of replenishing the supply of child care depleted by employer contracts with resource and referral agencies is built into the cost of the R&R agency's contract. In this way, employers are not only protecting the availability of care for their own employees, but they are also stimulating the availability of care for the general community.

As a child care resource and referral service is relatively affordable, requires little involvement by the employer, makes a service available to the entire work force (whether the company is single sited or multisited, in one state or across the country), and helps to expand the availability of child care within a community, this option is one of the most popular among employer-supported child care options.

Parenting Education Programs

Employer-supported parenting programs are designed to help employees become more effective parents and employees. The premise behind parenting education at the workplace is that the better parent is the better employee because the parent will be able to focus on work at the office and the family at home. Workplace parenting programs usually address work/family issues like time management, conflict resolution, stress, latchkey alternatives, choosing child care, discipline, parent/provider communication, dual-career parenting, etc.

Parenting education may be offered on a weekly, monthly, quarterly, or annual basis. Some companies choose to focus on one topic throughout a series; others may choose a variety of topics within the series. Some parenting programs are conducted by company personnel, others are conducted by employees, and still others are conducted by volunteer or paid child-development professionals. Often held during the lunch hour, these programs offer employees information and the opportunity to interact with other working parents, share experiences, and find new ways to approach and resolve problems.

Responsive Personnel Policies

One of the most frequently overlooked areas of employer-assisted child care options is a company's personnel policy. Yet it is precisely within a company's personnel policy that corporate attitudes toward employees' family needs are reflected.

Any investigation into employer-assisted child care should begin with a review of the company's personnel policy to determine whether it is responsive to the needs of today's workers. Areas of focus should include work schedules, benefits, and leave policies. Revisions of corporate personnel policies are not always expensive and may produce significant results without adding, and perhaps saving, expenses. Creativity and creative management are the only prerequisites to responsive personnel policies.

Work Schedules

Numerous employers have found that by adjusting the typical 9:00 A.M.–5:00 P.M., Monday–Friday workweek, they have been able to recruit and retain more workers. There are many variants to the traditional workweek:

1. Flextime: Employees have core work hours with flexible starting and stopping times.
2. Compressed time: Employees work more hours per day, but have fewer workdays per week.
3. Task contracting: An employee is assigned tasks to complete within a given time frame, but need not specify hours or time worked.

4. Job sharing: Two or more employees share one position's work, salary, and benefits.
5. Flexiplace: The location where work is performed is flexible and can allow employees to work at home.
6. Peak time: Employees are hired for limited busy periods ranging from 1–25 hours per week and are paid higher wages than regular part-time staff.
7. Permanent part time: Blue-, white-, and pink-collar jobs are available on a permanent part-time basis with prorated benefits.
8. Voluntary reduced work time: An employee is able to request that a work-week be reduced with prorated salary and benefits.

Although some of these options might be inappropriate for certain employers, according to the February 1988 Bureau of National Affairs issue of *The National Report on Work & Family,* employers say cost, employee morale and productivity, and workers who would otherwise leave the work force are reasons for implementing flexible scheduling plans. During a labor-force shortage, alternative scheduling may induce some workers into the workplace who have traditionally not been able to work. Critics of alternative scheduling options, including unions and others, are concerned about potentially adverse effects, including wage and benefits reductions for part-time workers and the replacement of permanent full-time jobs with part-time jobs.

Flexible Benefits
Traditional benefits programs offered by companies provide employees with the opportunity to receive health insurance and are sometimes supplemented by life and dental insurance. These programs were typically designed to meet the needs of a one-paycheck family. As indicated earlier in this chapter, that worker represents a minute portion of today's work force, and yet many companies' benefits programs still provide for that family configuration. Today, it is much more the norm for the family to be headed by two wage earners. As such, the traditional benefits programs frequently provide for overlapping, duplicative coverage that is not advantageous to the worker.

In this era of spiraling insurance costs, many employers have found that the implementation of a flexible benefits program may actually save the company money while offering employees greater benefits flexibility. Most often called "cafeteria plans," these programs enable employees to choose from an array of benefits best suited to their needs.

A typical cafeteria plan offers employees a core of fixed benefits along with a group of optional benefits from which they may choose up to a prescribed dollar limit. Such benefits options include a variety of types of health insurance, life and dental insurance, extra vacation, cash bonuses, tax-deferred annuity plans, and child care reimbursement.

Employees are usually allotted a specific amount of benefits dollars and points, and each benefit option is ascribed a certain value. Employees may then choose to spend their benefits dollars or points in a manner that suits their specific situation.

The inclusion of child care reimbursement within a flexible benefits plan was made possible by the Economic Recovery Tax Act of 1981, which makes child care reimbursement a tax-deductible expense to the employer and nontaxable to the employee. Known as a Dependent Care Assistance Plan (DCAP), this provision enables an employee to set aside a portion of earnings (up to $5,000 per family) toward child or dependent care expenses, and the expenses become a tax-free benefit to the employee.

This set-aside portion can either be employer paid through a cafeteria benefits program or employee paid through a salary-reduction plan. In the latter situation, employees set aside a fixed portion of their pretax income for dependent care costs. As they incur expenses, they submit receipts for which they receive reimbursement. In this way, they pay for their dependent care expenses with pretax rather than after-tax income and increase their purchasing power.

The only caveat to the plan is that the amount an employee elects to set aside annually is subject to a "use it or lose it" provision. If any amount remains unexpended in an employee's account at the end of the calendar year, it reverts back to the employer. As payroll taxes are not paid on the amount employees set aside in DCAP accounts, employers pay less tax. While there are administrative costs to offering a DCAP, these costs are usually more than offset by tax savings.

In essence, the DCAP is a winner in three respects: it offers employers an inexpensive or cost-free way to be responsive to employees' child care costs, it enables employees to increase their dependent care purchasing power, and it frees up scarce day-care dollars and serves as a stimulant to supply. The Dependent Care Assistance Plan, whether within a flexible benefits program or a salary-reduction plan, is the fastest growing employer-supported child care option in America today.

Leave Policies

Enabling an employee to be away from work when a family's needs require absence is a technique that many employers have found results in retaining workers longer. While the establishment of some forms of leave may cost the employer money in the short run, when offset by the cost of recruiting and training new workers, such leave policies may be cost effective in the long run. Let's examine a few:

Sick leave. One innovation in this area is to include family illness and doctors' appointments as allowable absences within a sick-leave policy. Simply enabling employees not to lie about a family member's illness, when they must be absent from work regardless, is greatly appreciated and is not costlier to the employer.

Personal leave.   A policy that enables employees to take unpaid leave when family circumstances require (up to a proscribed limit) may result in retaining workers who would otherwise have to resign.

Maternity, paternity, or adoption leave.   Most employers who offer leave related to the birth of a new child do so on the basis of medical disability. Typically, such leave would allow 6–8 weeks' leave time to a birth mother following the birth of her child. This leave is sometimes paid through an employer's short-term disability insurance or a self-insurance fund and is based on the notion of physical impairment. Benefits and seniority typically continue throughout the leave period.

Adoption leave, typically granted only to adoptive mothers, is also increasingly becoming available and offers the same benefits as maternity leave. Some companies have implemented benefits whereby some of the costs related to adopting a child are reimbursed by the company.

Child-development experts agree that the first 3–6 months of a child's life are critical to the bonding that occurs between a parent and a child. As parents become better educated about child-development issues, many mothers and fathers would like leave time to share their child's first months of life. Family leave policies, based not on the disability of the mother, but rather on the needs of the child and the family, are increasingly being requested by workers. Fully or partially paid leaves for mothers and fathers, as well as unpaid leaves, are slowly entering company personnel policies.

As a result of the demand, a variety of legislation has been introduced on state and national levels to ensure workers the opportunity to enjoy protected leaves related to family needs.

Other Forms of Employer-Supported Child Care

In addition to all of the employer-supported child care options listed above, innovative employers have developed or subsidized a variety of special services to help working parents, including sick child care programs; summer, after-school, and holiday programs; family day-care networks; drop-in programs for emergency work hours; and more.

Employers have also helped the child care community and parents by donating both financial and in-kind resources to child care programs, thereby offsetting the start-up and/or operating costs of those centers.

Corporate philanthropy can take many forms. One outstanding example is that of the California-based Bank of America, which funded the development and implementation of a comprehensive campaign to increase the number of trained family day-care providers in California. Although the Bank of America was a primary supporter of this project, support was also attracted from a number of major California companies.

SUMMARY

This chapter has focused on the evolution and forms of employer-supported child care from its genesis in the United States. As working parents comprise an ever-increasing component of this nation's work force, and as work force demographics result in a labor shortage of workers in general and workers on the lower end of the salary scale in particular, employers and governments interested in economic growth will pay increasing attention to breaking down barriers to employment. The lack of affordable quality child care across America is a major barrier to the employment of parents with young and school-age children.

The challenge to our society is to provide a framework that will afford maximum work-force participation without sacrificing the emotional, physical, and social well-being of our children. Neither parents, employers, government, nor the child care community can effectively address this challenge alone. Together, the expertise of each community can achieve great strides toward the development of comprehensive child care resources on local, state, and national levels.

REFERENCES

Bureau of National Affairs. (1988). *The national report on work & family*. Washington, DC: Buraff.

Burud, S. L., Aschbacher, P. R., & McCroskey, J. (1984). *Employer-supported child care*. Boston: Auburn House.

Calhoun, A. W. (1960). *A social history of the American family* (university paperback ed.). New York: Barnes & Noble.

Child-care: A work force issue. (1988). Washington, DC: U.S. Department of Labor.

Children's Defense Fund. (1987). *Child care: The time is now*. Washington, DC: Author.

Friedman, D. (1986). *Child care makes it work—A guide to employer support for child care*. Washington, DC: National Association for the Education of Young Children.

Friedman, D. (1987). *Family-supportive policies: The corporate decision-making process*. New York: The Conference Board.

Greenblatt, B. (1977). *Responsibility for child care*. San Francisco: Jossey-Bass.

Stolz, L. M. (1943, November 7). The nursery comes to the shipyard. *The New York Times*, p. 20.

Whipple, G. M. (Ed.). (1929). *The twenty-eighth yearbook of the National Society for the Study of Education: Preschool and parental education*. Bloomington, IN: Public School Publishing.

PART TWO

When Should Early Education Begin?

T rain up a child in the way he should go; and when he is old, he will not depart from it" (Prov. 22:3). Since the beginning of recorded time, the importance of the early years for future growth and development has been extolled. Whether you start with the Bible, Aristotle, Plato, or Locke, the idea that what happens during the early years of life will affect later development is present. From birth through age six, the child learns all the rudiments of knowledge, wrote Comenius in *The School of Infancy* in the 1600s. In the early 1900s, McMillan, in *The Nursery School,* wrote that "at last the world seems to be awakening to the fact that human destiny is largely shaped by the nurture or neglect of early infancy and childhood" (p. v). The kindergarten, as well, was seen as a "child saver." Through experiences in the kindergarten, children, especially those who were children of the poor or immigrants, would learn the ways of democracy and develop the abilities necessary for citizenship.

Agreement as to the importance of the early years to later life is coupled with general consensus that learning begins early, at birth or even before. Nevertheless, there has never been universal agreement as to when education of the infant and young child should begin. It's not the idea of when humans begin to learn that is at issue, but rather when formal education should begin.

The work of Lorenz (1952) has guided researchers and educators in the search for the most efficient "when" to begin the process of education. Through his work on the imprinting in ducks and geese, Lorenz hypothesized the idea of critical periods. He believed that imprinting is the tendency of newly hatched geese to follow the first moving object they see during a critical period, which occurs shortly after hatching. The period is termed critical because exposure to the same moving object before or after this period does not ordinarily result in the appearance of the same imprinted behavior. Probably everyone is familiar with the photo in introductory psychology books of Lorenz, substituting himself for the mother duck during a critical period, being followed by a flock of baby ducks.

Others identified this type of critical period in animals. Scott (1962) demonstrated that for dogs, the period of critical socialization begins at 20 days of age and continues for a few weeks thereafter. If social relationships are not established during this period, it becomes increasingly difficult to do so later.

The human infant is clearly not a bird or a dog, but the search for critical periods for learning and education continued, and, although definitive times during which an appropriate stimulus must be presented if the relevant behavior is to appear have not been documented, research has supported the hypothesis that infancy is indeed a critical time.

Waddington (1975) suggested a theory of canalization. He described an epigenetic landscape, a graphic analogy depicting the interaction between environmental and genetic forces. Genetic forces are represented by the valleys and contours of the landscape; they make certain outcomes more probable than others. Environmental forces are represented by changes in the tilt of the landscape.

In this landscape, there are channels or canals. Genetic forces are represented by the canals that run down the landscape; the tilt of the figure represents environmental forces; and the ball represents some characteristic of the developing organism. Subtle environment forces are believed more likely to significantly affect the course of development early (at the top of the figure) rather than late in development (at the bottom of the landscape), where all channels are deeper.

Bowlby (1979) introduced the idea of a sensitive period. Instead of a critical period, he suggested, there are sensitive periods in the life of the human. For instance, the first 6 months of infancy seem to be a sensitive time for the infant to attach and bond to the mother. In general, a relationship between adequate social and affective stimulation in infancy and later personality growth development and intellectual functioning has been identified. This is what Erikson (1963) described as an attitude of basic trust.

Research documents the ideas of both Waddington and Bowlby. Schaeffer and Bayley (1963) demonstrated that the third quarter of the first year of life was critical for an infant's social attachment as a "feeling tone" about the social world. Others as well provided data supporting the importance of the early years of life (Goldfarb, 1945; Spitz, 1945).

BEGIN EARLY

If the research shows so clearly that the first years of life are the time most susceptible to environmental influences, and the time of most rapid growth, then all children should have an opportunity to experience the optimum environment during the early years of life. It is during the early years that deprivations could be most disastrous in their effects. Further, it may be more difficult to modify or compensate for neglect later in life. Optimal early education and care, a birthright of every child, would ensure that all children, regardless of the economic status and situation of the family, would:

- Develop a sense of emotional security that leads to later self-esteem and respect
- Have physical needs for nutrition and physical health met
- Experience a wide variety of sensory and cognitive experiences necessary for intellectual growth
- Develop social skills, learning to relate with others outside of the family circle

Discussing the idea that education should begin during the period of infancy, Alice Sterling Honig, in the chapter "Infant Toddler Education Issues: Practices, Problems, and Promises," explores the issue of beginning education during infancy. She makes the realities of the need for infant care clear and describes the values of early care and education for those who would be otherwise deprived of enriching and necessary educational experiences. Honig also makes it clear that whatever care and education are provided, they must be of only the highest quality.

The concern for early education has encroached upon the arena of public education and the role of the elementary school. Responding to the idea that early education can positively affect later academic achievement, younger and younger children are entering public schools. Now kindergartens are no longer only for five year olds, but are provided for three and four year olds. In the hopes of compensating for deprived backgrounds, school systems currently offer prekindergarten programs for three- and four-year-old children. Gayle Mindes points out in the chapter "Kinder-garten in Our Nation" that while 95% of all five year olds attend public kindergarten, more and more states are providing kindergarten for three- and four-year-old children. These programs are generally for children at risk and are designed to provide the educational experiences believed so critical for later intellectual and affective functioning.

Under the mandate of providing the foundation for all later learning and education, the kindergarten for five year olds has become the focus of a number of issues. The questions of what kindergarten education should consist of, the most appropriate method of instruction, and what can be expected of five-year-old children in the way of academic achievement are being widely discussed and argued. Mindes introduces these kindergarten issues in her chapter.

BETTER LATE THAN EARLY

The same theory and research on critical or sensitive periods is used by others to argue against early educational experiences. The fragility of young children, the sensitivity of the entire early childhood period, is used as a rationale to delay formal education as long as possible. So sensitive are these first years of life to environmental conditions, it is argued, that only the parents, within the security of the home, should educate the young. Providing early care and education is not only the parents' responsibility, but early separation of parents and child could be detrimental.

The idea that separation of infants and parents too early in life could lead to long-lasting developmental deficits has been supported by Yarrow and Goodwin (1973). They examined the critical period hypothesis applied to maternal separation and concluded that maternal separation before the age of 3 months is not nearly as harmful as separation at 9 months. Although there does not appear to be a critical period before and after which maternal separation will have no effect, there is a definite relationship between age at separation and disturbances in the infant. Honig reviews the research on the dangers of early separation in her chapter.

Even the experience of nursery school or kindergarten could be problematic. Young children, so susceptible to early environmental influences, would find early educational experiences difficult or even traumatic. Emotionally, the young child is ill prepared to relate with the many others found in a school setting. In a nursery school, children must share the attention of a single teacher with others, submit to a structured day and routines, and develop the skills of relating with numerous other children before they are developmentally able to do so.

Raymond S. Moore, with Dennis R. Moore, argues in the chapter "When Delay Isn't Procrastination" that early education of the young could result in irreversible damage. They cite research from a variety of fields to support their belief that formal education should be delayed until the child is at least seven or eight, or even older. Delay of education until later in life, when development is no longer so sensitive to environmental influences, would protect children from the potential hazards of inappropriate educational experiences and harmful peer pressures.

Perhaps the most critical reason children should not enter public school until later in life is the current failure rate of kindergarten children. It is not uncommon for school systems to fail as many as 10%, 15%, or even 39% of the total kindergarten population. It seems ludicrous that young children could fail at being children. The stress of early academic failure on fragile families, and on the susceptible young learner, is atrocious. In fact, kindergarten failure is the most sensitive predictor of high school drop-out rate. Until schools are better able to meet the needs of very young learners and their families, the cautions suggested by the Moores should certainly be given serious consideration.

Yet as Honig points out, care and education beginning early in life, during infancy or sometime during the first years of life, is a fact. The many families requiring child care in order to survive economically, the number of single parents, and the changing role of women all contribute to the fact of early education. Further, the benefits of early enriching educational experiences for those who might be otherwise deprived are clear. For this group of children, early enriching educational experiences are the first step in ensuring equality of educational opportunity, so vital to the continuation of a democratic society.

WHEN SHOULD EDUCATION BEGIN?

As you read the following chapters ask yourself these questions:

- What are the dangers of early education and care during infancy?
- How could these potential hazards be eliminated?
- What would be the result of delaying education until children are 8 or 9 years of age?
- How could our society provide for early education and care of all children without damaging effects?

REFERENCES

Bowlby, J. (1979). *The making and breaking of affectional bonds.* London: Tavistock.

Erikson, E. H. (1963). *Childhood and society.* New York: W. W. Norton.

Goldfarb, W. (1945). Emotional and intellectual consequences of psychological deprivation in infancy: A reevaluation. In P. Hoch & J. Zubin (Eds.), *Psychology of childhood* (pp. 234–344). New York: Grune & Stratton.

Lorenz, K. (1952). *King Solomon's ring.* London: Methuen.

McMillan, M. (1919). *The nursery school.* London: L. M. Dent & Sons.

Schaeffer, E. S., & Bayley, N. (1963). Maternal behavior, child behavior, and their intercorrelations from infancy through adolescence. *Monograph of the Society for Research and Child Development, 28*(3, Serial No. 87).

Scott, J. P. (1962). Critical periods in behavioral development. *Science, 138,* 949–958.

Spitz, R. A. (1945). Hospitalism: An inquiry into the genesis of psychiatric conditions in early childhood: Part 1. *Psychoanalytic Studies of the Child, 1,* 53–74.

Waddington, C. H. (1975). *The evolution of an evolutionist.* Edinburgh: Edinburgh University Press.

Yarrow, L. J., & Goodwin, M. S. (1973). The immediate impact of separation: Reactions of infants to a change in mother figures. In L. J. Stone, H. T. Smith, & L. B. Murphy (Eds.), *The competent infant: Research and commentary* (pp. 133–145). New York: Basic Books.

4

Infant/Toddler Education Issues: Practices, Problems, and Promises

ALICE STERLING HONIG

College for Human Development, Syracuse University

Infant/toddler care and education issues are often obscured by a web of mediating and intersecting factors, such as maternal affective state and attitude toward employment, responsivity toward the infant, social supports available to the parent, family socioeconomic status, quality care setting and degree of caregiver training, sex of infant, timing of entry, number of hours in care, security of attachment of infant with mother, and continuity of supports for learning that are provided along with infant other-than-mother care. In this chapter, historical issues and programs are reviewed, and a variety of tutorial and group-care models and their short- and long-term outcomes are presented. Suggestions are offered to mobilize legislators, parents, educators, directors of programs, and community agencies. Their cooperation can increase the probabilities of optimal outcomes for infant care and education and decrease potential difficulties that long day-care enrollments in the first year of life may entail for some infants.

Adult impacts on infant outcomes begin in the womb. The fetus whose mother smokes heavily, uses drugs, screams in angry fights with a partner, or is single, young, poor, and unsupported by loving intimates will have lower socioemotional and educational outcomes (Phipps-Yonas, 1980; Zuravin, 1988). Indeed, poor maternal nutrition or combinations of poverty and low education can result in infant retardation by 36 months unless strenuous educational intervention is provided (Ramey & Gowan, 1986).

RATIONALES FOR PRESCHOOL
VERSUS INFANCY EDUCATION

Bolstered by a variety of theoretical prescriptions and the results of carefully crafted researches in early childhood classrooms over the past decades, the value and rationales for *preschool* education have become coherent and clear-cut. For example, constructivists have demonstrated that provision of a rich variety of toys and materials allows preschoolers actively manipulating materials to acquire gradually the basic ideas of classification, seriation, numerosity, comparative size, etc. (Weikart, 1988; DeVries & Goncu, 1988).

Eriksonian theory adds subtle dialectic aspects to Piaget's concept that *peer interactions* are essential for learning social skills, such as gaining entry to a play group, responsible choosing among play partners and options, and taking reciprocal roles in fantasy play scenarios. Preschool educational settings with well-trained teachers are an ideal place for preschoolers to learn social problem-solving strategies that promote decentering and cooperative sustained play. Language research has shown the value of early writing experiences, as when a kindergarten child laboriously and triumphantly writes "HRS LV HR" (horses live here) over a drawing. Rich daily exposure to book reading and opportunities for discourse in everyday activities enhance later cognitive competence and school achievement.

Integrative and longitudinal studies (Berrulta-Clement, Schweinhart, Barnett, Epstein, & Weikart, 1984; Lazar & Darlington, 1982; Schweinhart & Weikart, 1988) testify clearly to long-term school achievement advantages of preschool education for poverty children in terms of fewer placements in special education and fewer students repeating grades, regardless of programmatic model. Issues related to preschool education, then, are perhaps more likely to arise with regard to more specifically focused variables, such as optimal staff/child ratio, the balance between child- versus teacher-initiated activities, promotion of nonsexist curricula, and pre-service versus in-service training requirements for teachers. Issues in preschool education, as contrasted with infant education, do not therefore challenge the fundamental premise of the positive value of such experiences for preoperational youngsters.

Economic issues are more acute for families making decisions about infant education and care. Where the "ideal" ratio of three infants to one caregiver prevails, then three "families of those infants must pay out of their own annual pay enough to support a staff person's full wage for a year . . . . Most parents who are at, just above, or just below the median income cannot afford to pay more than 10% of their total family income" (Morgan, 1986, p. 165) for child care.

Infant education issues do, of course, encompass some of the same sorts of problems, including optimal health care practices and staff-child ratios. But unlike the field of preschool education, fewer researches are available on the effects of ordinary *metropolitan* infant care/education compared with data from high-quality, university-based programs. This *modal versus model* issue (Wittmer, 1986) compounds the problems for public policymakers, as well as parents, in making choices regarding infant care. Furthermore, *pragmatic* issues become more salient when infant care is under consideration. Certain safety and health issues that require careful but routine solutions in preschool settings may pose serious problems in infant facilities. How staff safely evacuate children in case of a fire in an educational setting becomes an acute issue particularly in states that permit eight or more nonambulatory infants to be cared for by a single caregiver.

Political issues are often more intrusively introduced in addressing needs for infant care. The emphasis in providing preschool education is on optimizing educational advantages for the *child*. Political concern with infant care has often focused on family and societal needs rather than primarily on optimizing infant development. Thus, far less attention may be paid to the *quality* of infant care compared to preschool education experiences.

As an example, this writer visited a center for children of migrant worker parents where the preschool classrooms were run by Montessori-trained teachers. Well-programmed lessons and a profusion of educational materials testified to the high quality of educational goals and methods provided for the preschoolers. Upstairs, in a spacious and well-lit room, one caregiver (the infant teacher) sat and rocked herself. A beautiful elephant mural was painted high up on one wall. Each of twelve infants was lying on its back or side with a bottle propped close by on a rolled diaper. Silence (for the while) reigned. This caregiver, unlike the preschool teachers downstairs, had neither child-development or early childhood education training. In another newly built community facility, well-trained teachers engaged preschoolers in a variety of singing games with animated motions. In the nearby infant room, the latest plumbing facilities for diaper changing and rinsing were available. Yet three infants strapped into infant seats cried miserably, until beads of sweat formed on their faces, while across the room their assigned caregiver slowly diapered a fourth baby, concentrating on his bottom as she worked efficiently, cheerfully, and silently. Unlike the field of preschool education, the field of infant education is beset not only by programmatic and staff training issues, but by deeper value conflicts and genuine fear about possible negative as well as positive consequences. Theoretical considerations, pragmatic realities, and political pressures fuel some of the current polemics about infant care and education.

HISTORICAL CHANGES IN NEEDS FOR INFANT CARE/EDUCATION

Why are the issues regarding infancy care so particularly urgent for the decade of the 1990s? In the past few years, there has been a sharp rise in the needs for infant/toddler care but a singular dearth of teachers trained specifically for under threes and a scarcity of teacher/trainers specialized for the preparation of infancy teachers.

In the mid-1980s, more than half of married mothers of toddlers under 2 years were in the labor force—a "108% increase since 1970" (Children's Defense Fund, 1988, p. 6). The employment of mothers of children under 12 months increased 40.4%

in the United States between 1977 and 1985 (Klein, 1985). Near the end of the decade, almost one out of every two mothers of infants under 1 year was gainfully employed (Kamerman, 1986). This enormous growth rate in the need for developmentally appropriate facilities for infants and toddlers arose prior to the generation of abundant research knowledge about the long-term implications of *long* child care days for infants in other-than-mother care.

In addition, the fears, guilt, and worries of families who are forced to, or feel pressured to, search for quality educational programs for their infants are not assuaged by current attachment research data (to be discussed later) on the effects of full-time nonmaternal care for infants younger than 1 year.

Scenarios differ radically for babies in other-than-mother care. Overwhelmingly, most infants are cared for by someone in their own home. According to the United States Bureau of the Census (1987) figures on care arrangements, the percentages for infants under 2 years with employed mother are

Type of Child Care Arrangement	Percentage
Home-based	75.5
Day care center	16.3
Parent cares for baby while on job	8.2

For the different types of home-based care, the figures are

By relative in child's home	27.5%
By sitter or nanny in child's home	6.5%
By relative in another home	15.8%
In family day-care home	25.7%

Few data are available on outcomes for in-home settings. We do know a good bit about how *variable* the experiences of infants can be in family day-care settings. There may be less support for language development and yet perhaps more opportunities for nurturing body holding (Goelman & Pence, 1988; Golden et al., 1978). Only 10% of infants under 1 year in 1986 were being cared for in group settings where higher educational standards might be legally required. For example, we know from the Golden et al. work on infant/toddler day care in New York City that, although infant classroom aides were only required to have an eighth-grade reading level, in toddler classrooms for the older infants, head teachers were required to have a 4-year college degree. There were no minimal educational requirements for family day-care personnel with infants.

Some parents are obligated by employers and/or life circumstances to search for early infant care. Other mothers do not "have" to leave infants in care during the early months, yet their felt personal needs, fears about sociological data on the perils of possible divorce in later years, fears that their own professional training may become obsolete, lack of knowledge of infant needs, or lack of family support networks (or all of the above) lead them to choose infant care early in the first year. Cantwell (1989), a professional journalist, recalls how isolated she felt during the first months home alone with her first baby and far from relatives who might help:

> Whenever I read about some woman who has given up her job to tend the baby, I get nervous on her account. . . . I remember how isolated I was during the months that I stayed home with my first child, and how I boiled not only the nipples for her bottle but the plate on which I mashed her banana, the spoon with which I mashed it and the tongs with which I removed both plate and spoon from the pot. I was 200 miles from the network that had shared the responsibility of caring for pudgy, adorable me (as a baby) and frightened witless. If, soon, I returned to an office it wasn't for money, and it wasn't out of ambition. It was because raising a child in a country where families have shallow roots can be a desperately lonely business (p. C23).

Lest these fears seem exaggerated, it is instructive to note that Bowlby (1988) has pronounced that "looking after a baby, or toddler . . . is not only a skilled job but also a hard and exacting one" (p. 50). The problems of other parents may be even more acute.

A WORKING MOTHER

Andrea, a single parent, dreaded that if she did not find someone to care for her new baby right away, she might be late returning to work after the 3-week leave that her job allowed. In a nearby apartment building, Ms. Arbut "took in" babies and Andrea was grateful that there would be space for "just one more" in this unlicensed facility.

A few weeks later, Andrea felt frantic. Jonah cried so much at night. His bottom was raw and red, although Ms. Arbut assured Andrea that she changed the babies' diapers frequently. Over the next weeks, Andrea sought and tried other "sitters." She tried calling a day-care center, but they had space for eight infants and a long waiting list. A few months later, Andrea's supervisor warned her that she had no more personal days left. Andrea had been taking personal leave days whenever the baby had a fever and ear infecton. She worried that the hair on the back of his head seemed rubbed off, as if he lay on his back a lot. She worried because he did not smile and gurgle with bright eyes when she came to pick him up.

When Jonah was 8 months old and not babbling to her or saying "mama" as some babies do, she called around town until she found a family day-care home where Ms. Lasswell seemed genuinely interested in holding and cuddling and talking to the babies in her care. The new place meant getting up earlier every morning and getting home later, but Jonah seemed more alert and bright eyed now. A few months later, Ms. Lasswell's married daughter fell ill and needed her help, so she had to let all her babies go. Andrea desperately sought for friends or neighbors to keep Jonah while she started the round of calling once again.

Before Jonah was 1 year old, he had been left with several different people, few of whom had ever studied infant or child development, or knew about the fundamental needs of babies for leisurely body cuddling, turn-taking talk, and accurate responsive attunement and comforting to infant distress signals (Honig, 1981, 1983b, 1985a, 1985b, 1989).

Testimony from families speaks eloquently to the fact that not only has our nation failed to provide resources for the training of superb infant teachers and caregivers. It has also failed to remember that all parents, whether using infant care and educational facilities or not, are essentially in critical need of knowledge about infant growth and development and educational needs. This aspect of education for citizens has rarely been accorded the passion that car driving, macrame, and cheerleading courses can inspire in educational leaders who plan high school curricular offerings!

Questions and Issues in Infant/Toddler Care and Education

Because increased demand for infant education is so recent, many urgent questions and issues arise, for which we have sometimes more theoretical guidelines than abundant data for decision making. The complexity of issues stems partly from the fact that so *many* variables must be taken into account, such as parental social class, stress, educational level, available family supports, sex of infant, timing of entry into program, full- or part-time program participation, caregiver/infant ratio, caregiver training, and program quality. Richters and Zahn-Waxler (1988) have observed that answers to questions about infant day care may reflect the fact that "different combinations of parent, family and child variables may be relevant to particular subgroups of a given sample and not for others" (p. 332). Noting that *different* sets of variables in the family systems of employed versus nonemployed mothers of toddlers predicted different socioemotional outcomes, Weinraub, Jaeger, and Hoffman (1988) report that secure attachment and dependency were negatively related for toddlers of employed mothers and positively related in families of at-home mothers and toddlers. They suggest that the patterns of interrelationships among predictor family systems variables in looking at toddler outcomes may be very different. Thus, we "may need to develop different models of influence to explain family processes affecting child outcome" in families with different systems (p. 376).

In some cases, the current data base is conflicting and even confusing. What are some of the major questions posed? Some of the issues are essentially pragmatic and involve personal choices for families, while others will impact on public policy legislation and decisions to allocate community funds to support the training of child-development specialists and educators for children 0–3 years old.

For the fifteen questions below, the words *mother* and *parent* will be used, since data on fathers as primary infant educators are sparse.

1. Why have mental health professionals historically been so opposed to other-than-mother care for infants? Is other-than-mother care a positive or negative factor for the emotional development of infants?
2. Do educational achievement outcomes for babies depend on the delivery system for care, the caregivers' personalities, and how they are trained, or will any loving motherly figure do?

3. Do caregiver-infant ratios and group size make a difference in educational outcomes? As a corollary, how different are the educational and emotional outcome data for infants reared in high-quality educational settings versus ordinary, mostly custodial settings?

4. Does the long day-care day make a difference for babies' emotional well-being, or can they be comfortable in a high-quality educational setting despite the length of time they are left there? Specifically, will infants left in care settings for a major part of each day have as secure an attachment to mother (who still provides a great deal of child care) as do babies reared primarily by mother? If not, can a secure attachment to caregiver mitigate a less-secure attachment to mother?

5. If there are more insecure rather than secure attachments of infants to mothers as a result of full-time attendance in long day care, will the sequelae of insecure attachment to mother inevitably be associated with later dysfunctional socioemotional relationships of the child with peers, parents, and teachers, or will such untoward emotional outcomes prove transitory?

6. Is a more transactional view of infant development helpful (Sameroff & Chandler, 1975)? Specifically, are there differences in infants, such that some would be far more vulnerable *without* the delivery of early educational experiences, while some will be far more vulnerable with other-than-mother care, no matter how educationally facilitative, during the first year of life?

7. Is developmental continuity or discontinuity more characteristic of the effects of infant education on later academic achievement? Can we be more reassuring to parents that even if their infants have poorer-quality educational experiences in infancy, but high-quality educational supports for their learning at home, and in school later on, their cognitive attainments will be high? In other words, is infancy a critical period for educational achievements, or is *continuity* of support for learning and academic success more significant?

8. How important is status compared to personal variables in the family in determining outcomes of infant education experiences? What role does family socioeconomic status (SES) play? Maternal mental health? Parental education level? Parent stress?

9. Does the provision of long-day infant care, whether in a high-quality educational setting or not, dilute the emotional commitment and investment of the major caregiver? Will some parents of infants in care increase pressure for early child achievement of independence and cognitive milestones? Will an early educational boost for the baby in a facility be offset by a diminution of emotionally rich, leisurely, intense, pleasurable responsive interactions with the parent?

10. Can normally born babies in ordinary supportive family situations become superbabies through the provision of early and intense intellective programming and educational stimulation? Are superbaby programs "good" for babies and parents?

11. Does the degree (extensity and intensity) of early infant stimulation/education efforts significantly affect the outcomes for delayed or emotionally depressed or disturbed infants? Can intensive therapeutic/educational provision support adequate development for an infant in a severely dysfunctional relation with mother?

12. Does the "inoculation" hypothesis work? Does infant education, no matter how superbly well provided, permit an infant in a nonfacilitative home environment to catch up with and keep up with peers from more advantaged or favorable home environments, once the intervention is discontinued?

13. If infant education facilities seem to boost IQ in some children from at-risk or low SES families, are there other more negative social outcomes, such as noncompliance, aggression, and lack of ego control or ego resilience, or later difficulties with intimacy in adulthood that may still be associated with early infant group experiences?

14. How can expert teachers of infants and toddlers best be trained? What audiovisual materials, curricula, and learning models are currently available and efficacious for a director of an educational facility?

15. Can new alliances of businesses and families, or employee unions and families, change the current desperate shortage of high-quality infant/toddler education facilities and personnel?

Addressing the Issues

Programs that have tackled these issues make few distinctions between the terms *infant care* and *infant education*. In some service programs, a dichotomy may still linger. Caldwell (1986) has urged strongly that the terms be considered interchangeable:

> There is a false dichotomy between early childhood education and child care . . . child care operated within a social service orientation; the mother was the client. In early education programs, the client was the child. But the two fields have not been developing on parallel tracks; rather they have been on converging tracks that because of modern demographic realities have now merged. The resulting service is both educational and protective, and the client is the family unit (p. 7–8).

Some of the questions just presented are clearly addressed by clinical, experimental, and field studies. Others are answered more by predictions from theorists, such as Mahler and Erikson, than from extensive data. For some, cross-cultural studies provide insights into answers. For questions about superbaby programs or the long-term effects of long day-care educational settings on adult intimacy, there are no systematic prospective researches as yet.

The tide of societal change moves inexorably toward increasing need for quality infancy educational settings. Let us look at researches that can help us address some of the questions posed, or at least set them in perspective.

HISTORICAL ROOTS OF CONCERN WITH INFANT CARE

Findings that infants reared in institutional settings typically did poorly later on, both in school and life achievements, fueled some of the early concerns by psychoanalysts and others that any form of infant care would be harmful. Spitz's (1945) poignant research in South America showed that rich or poor babies flourished with normal developmental quotients in a wide variety of settings—whether upper middle-class homes (IQ = 131), poor fishing village (IQ = 108), or even prison nursery (IQ = 105), where matrons taught incarcerated mothers how to care for their babies and the inmates competed with each other to see whose baby was doing better. In contrast, however, Spitz measured a precipitous decline in infant IQ, from 124 at 4 months of age (when the babies were given up by their unwed mothers) in a foundling home down to 72 by 1 year of age. These babies were cared for in a custodial climate, yet provided with good hygiene and nutrition. Many of the foundling home infants died of infectious diseases. Spitz's film, *Grief: A Peril in Infancy*, documents severe delays in motor and communicative skill development and bizarre repetitive movements among the infants reared in a foundling home.

Early reported studies of the effects of institutionalization on infant development probably account for the shock and disapproval this author encountered from dozens of psychiatrists 2 decades ago at a professional meeting at which we were reporting initial data from the Syracuse Children's Center infant/toddler group care program (Caldwell et al., 1968). The Syracuse Children's Center was a pioneer effort founded by Drs. Caldwell and Richmond to provide educational and loving care for infants from 6 months onward. Half-day care was provided until 1½ years, full-day care thereafter. The psychiatrists 20 years ago were "shocked" that we were separating babies from mothers, even for a few hours per day, and even though many of the infants were from very difficult or chaotic family environments.

Risk Factors and Resilience in Infancy

How long lasting or serious are infancy risk factors? If infants are quite resilient, then infancy experiences, even if less than optimal or even if detrimental, might not pose such a worry for parents and educators. But the emotional developments of basic trust and trustworthiness, of hopefulness and optimism and drive to learn in cooperation with adult mentors, have theoretically and clinically been predicted and shown to be powerfully based in the earliest years of life (Erikson, 1963; Mahler, Pine, & Bergman, 1975). Moore (1975), in a longitudinal study of British youngsters, reported that boys who had been in other than maternal care during the first 3 years were less likely to read well, or pass their final examinations at age seventeen. Those raised primarily by their own families until school age were more likely to be trusted not to do things they should not do, and they expressed a stronger interest in academic subjects.

Stability and Predictability of Infant Ratings

Stability of early emotional and intellectual scores seems to differ in different studies. In studies of middle-class families, Waters (1978) reported very high stability of secure or insecure attachment of infants 12 to 18 months to mothers. Much lower stability has been found in more stressed families (Vaughn, Egeland, Waters, & Sroufer, 1979).

In the cognitive domain, Bayley (1955) has reported that there is zero correlation from infant developmental scores to intelligence scores in later life. Yet, for low-functioning infants, clinical plus developmental pediatric assessments correctly predicted over 70% of children who were performing below normal 10 years later (Illingworth, 1961). Thus, for infants at risk, early and developmentally appropriate education may be far more critical than for infants reared in more enriching homes.

In keeping with Bronfenbrenner's (1979, 1986) ecological theory, several classes of risk factors can be identified: biological/medical, personal/social, familial/parental, neighborhood, and societal. Where one risk factor is involved, long-term negative consequences may be negligible. But risk factors often come in clusters; they intersect and impact in multiplicative fashion on later developmental outcomes (Honig, 1984, 1986). Studies of *which* infancy risk factors potentiate long-term difficulties are therefore very important. Not all infants may be vulnerable if in poor-quality care settings; not all infants may thrive in high-quality settings.

Cross-cultural Researches

Cross-cultural researches have not only provided evidence of developmental delays in institutional infants, but some have also suggested the power of early educational enrichment opportunities to enhance the functioning of institutionalized babies (Dennis & Najarian, 1957).

In Teheran orphanages, J. McVickers Hunt (1980) varied the kinds of stimulation and personalized care provided to babies by untrained caregivers. Sometimes, he simply improved the ratio of caregivers to infants—from 1:10 down to 1:3. After several years, in one group (Wave V), Hunt assigned caregivers to specific infants, as well as improved the caregiver-infant ratio. He also taught Wave V caregivers how to *label their caregiving actions* with the babies, such as telling the babies while they washed an ear. Special toys were provided with instructions for use in enhancing Piagetian sensorimotor skills. Badger and Burns (1980) had shown in programs with low SES mothers that the use of such toys would promote earlier sensorimotor competence among the infants served. Further, Wave V babies were encouraged in vocal imitations and in semantic mastery. Previously, caregivers had not talked to the infants, since, they pointed out, the babies were not verbal yet! The orphans in this maximally educationally enriched group not only attained the earliest top scores for each of the Piagetian scales used, but they also looked brighter and more animated, and were subsequently adopted by families.

Poverty and Early Stimulation

Research findings with infants reared in poverty provided some of the early impetus for development of high-quality enrichment programs for under-threes. Over the past 3 decades, a predictable downward drift in infant developmental scores has been abundantly documented for infants growing up in low SES households. In a longitudinally followed sample of over 3,000 infants, there were infants who scored in the lowest quartile of Bayley mental scores (under 78) at 8 months, but who were reared in upper-class homes. These babies had IQ scores at age four that were superior to those of infants whose intelligence scores had been in the highest quartile at 8 months but who had been raised in low SES homes (Willerman, Broman, & Fiedler, 1970). Retarded infants were 7 times more likely to obtain IQs less than 80 at 4 years of age if they were reared in low SES homes compared to higher SES homes. These stunning data show the power of educational enrichment in a home setting to offset poor cognitive scores early in infancy. They also are encouraging in suggesting the noninevitabilty of poor prognosis from early cognitive lags in the first year of life into the preschool period if infancy and preschool enrichment and education are provided.

The classic longitudinal study of the reversibility of early infancy cognitive deficit, provided an enriched education setting could be offered and sustained, was a natural experiment in Iowa (Skeels, 1966). Thirteen orphanage babies, who at about 19 months of age seemed to be doing very poorly intellectually, were placed in an institution for retarded women. The ward inmates doted on the babies. Some acted as surrogate mothers, others as aunties. They vied with each other for helping "their" baby do best. Matrons, too, took a great interest in the tots. The average intelligence score of the transferred infants was 64 in contrast to the mean score of 87 of twelve infants left at the orphanage. One or two years later, the transferred toddlers who had been cherished and stimulated were found to have gained markedly in intellectual functioning (mean IQ = 96) and were subsequently adopted. Those left back at the orphanage plummeted in IQ, losing an average of 26 points. Thirty years later, Skeels and colleagues set out to find what had happened to the infants from their unique natural study. Those left in the orphanage had mostly become a burden on taxpayers for welfare, institutionalization, etc. Only half of this contrast group had completed third grade; none had completed secondary education. In comparison, the infants who had been given an educational and emotional boost, first by the retarded inmates and then by adoptive families, grew up to be productive citizens, many of whom had competed at least secondary education. When they had children, their children had a mean IQ of 103.9, none tested below 86, and they were performing at grade level in school.

In a less serendipitous, well-designed prospective longitudinal study on the Hawaiian island of Kauai, Werner (1989), beginning prenatally, followed the lives of poor at-risk infants to adulthood 32 years later. Among the 698 multiracial Kauai high-risk infants, some 25% developed into "competent, confident and caring young adults" (p. 72). Werner's analysis of 72 resilient children allows us to see what role infant temperament and demographic and family process variables played in the respective outcomes. First, resilient infants had been described at 20 months as more cheerful, friendly, responsive, and self-confident in interactions with both familiar and unfamiliar caregivers. They seemed more robust and assertive. Few had experienced prolonged separation from their primary caregiver during the first year of life. Significantly, *all of these resilient adults had had at least one significant caregiver from whom they had received a great deal of positive attention and nurturing during the first year of life.* Some of this nurturing came from significant parent substitutes, such as grandparents. More at-risk boys who had been firstborn turned out to be resilient. Interestingly, much of the risk literature suggests that male infants are more vulnerable in requiring early maternal nurturing for later emotional and scholastic achievement. More at-risk girls whose mothers were steadily employed were later in the resilient adult group.

What were the stressful life events in infancy that were more likely to predict a criminal record or a broken marriage 30 years later? At-risk babies who manifested coping problems as adults demonstrated these similarities:

1. Had a closely spaced younger sibling born less than 24 months after the study child
2. Were raised by an unmarried mother
3. Did not have a father present during infancy and early childhood
4. Experienced separations from mother during the first year of life, and prolonged disruptions, including parental illness, major moves, and unemployment of the major earner in the family
5. Did not have adequate substitute care during the first 20 months of life if the mother was employed

The Kauai study thus helps answer some of the questions raised earlier. Yes, the first year of life *does* seem to have special vulnerabilities. A secure and loving caregiver is critically important during this period. But no, the mother does not absolutely have to provide this relationship. Substitute caregivers who consistently provided tender responsive care were able to buffer the infant against stress. However, this means that if an infant in an educational care setting does not have a stable, attuned caregiver in the home environment, *then the profession of the infant caregiver/teacher is far more critical with respect to the socioemotional relationship and nurturance provided than might be the case for a preschool or elementary school teacher:*

> In a child care center, the teacher, a gentle and nurturing young man, was holding and cuddling a young toddler from a difficult and chaotic home situation. That morning, the baby had come into the center feeling rushed and miserable. The

director, endowed with an advanced education degree, spoke sharply to the caregiver: "Put him down. This is a *school*—and he knows how to walk."

Without thorough training in developmental needs of infants and toddlers, I fear that "degrees" may not provide ironclad guarantees of sensitive, tuned-in responsive caregiving that should be the birthright of every baby (Fraiberg, 1977).

Furman (1987), a psychoanalytic consultant to the Hannah Perkins Preschool, a therapeutic nursery, has written that the *role* of the preschool teacher is to help children learn how to learn in a safe group environment. She advises that sensual and intimate body aspects of caregiving belong firmly in the domain of the family. Katz (1980) too has noted that for preschool education the roles of teacher and parents are very different. Yet in infant/toddler care, the caregiver *must* often combine roles! If the caregiver does not minister to intimate bodily needs for sucking, diapering, comforting, and settling to sleep, then the emotional well-being of some infants may be seriously compromised. The roles of infant teacher and parent have many more characteristics in common than may be required for preschool educators, particularly if an infant is at developmental risk.

The 45% annual rate of turnover in child care settings that is common in the United States does not augur well for ensuring provision of stable, nurturing educators for infants vulnerable to multiple stresses and enrolled in educational facilities.

Infant Personality

Werner's findings (1989) also illuminate the lack of long-term importance of infant personality characteristics for later positive life outcomes. Infants who had a more outgoing positive temperment could indeed lure or recruit adults to attend to them and seemed to have better outcomes during the school years. But 30 years later, the major correlates of poor life coping were *not* infant characteristics, but depended more on parental characteristics and choices—too-close spacing of babies, prolonged disruptions of family, no father present, and poor-quality infant substitute caregiving.

Difficult infant temperaments (Thomas & Chess, 1977) might be considered sources of vulnerability for infants in care. But Crockenberg (1981) has confirmed that whether infants had easy, or triggery/intense, or suspicious, slow-to-warm-up temperament styles, there was no a priori reason for the irritable babies to be less securely attached to mother. Only when an irritable baby was reared by a mother who had been less attentive to the infant at 3 months and who had fewer adult supports, particularly spousal support, was there a greater chance that an irritable baby would be at risk for insecure attachment at the end of the first year of life. So it looks as if infant temperament, per se, cannot be blamed for poorer developmental outcomes. It is also clear that social supports for parents, in the form of outreach home visitors and in the form of superbly trained infant caregivers, may well be needed as *buffers* in some families in which babies have more difficult temperaments and parents have fewer people to count on.

INFANT EDUCATION MODELS

Infant education programs have been provided in a variety of models and settings, such as in home, agency, family day-care center, or elementary school (Honig, 1982). Does delivery system or locus of educational provision affect outcomes?

Tutorial Models

Tutorial models have been tried in home (Gordon, 1969; Levenstein, 1988; Olds, 1988; Painter, 1971; Schaefer & Aaronson, 1977) and out of home (Badger & Burns, 1980; Palmer & Siegel, 1977). Tutorial educational interactions in infancy have been found during, or right after, the end of program, to slow or reverse the intellective deficits so frequently documented in infants from low SES families. In most tutorial models, a trained paraprofessional or professional comes to the home and (1) provides appropriate activities for the infants, or (2) models such activities for parents to carry out with infants between home visits. Infants in the experimental groups typically gain about 10 IQ points more than control infants not in the educational tutorial program. In Palmer's tutorial program at a college site, black male toddlers received either a program of carefully sequenced concepts or a "discovery" variant where they could play with the same toys and have tutors respond to their queries, although they were not "formally" taught. The toddlers who were taught concepts scored higher on knowledge of polar opposites (such as heavy-light, tall-short). Ten years later, school achievements were higher for both concept and discovery youngsters compared with controls. Fewer tutored toddlers were left back or put into special education classes later in their schooling.

Levenstein's Mother-Child Home Visit (MCHV) Program (1988) raises additional issues relevant to the tutorial model. The conceptual basis of the MCHV, which has been replicated over the past 20 years nationally at many sites for about 5,000 families, was clear and simple. If rich language experience could be suggested to mothers and modeled for them with toddlers, around a basic core of appropriate books and toys provided biweekly as gifts for the low-income family, then mothers could enhance the school readiness of their youngsters through program participation for 1 or 2 years. In the initial years of this toddler education research program, first middle-class, highly educated volunteers, and later, mothers who had previously been trained to work as infant educators with their own toddlers, delivered the VISMs—Verbal Interaction Stimulus Materials. Toddlers in the initial tutorial program gained 17 IQ points, compared to 11 points for toddlers in the later program with home visits by paid parents formerly in the program. Later in elementary school, experimental children from the original project were significantly less likely than controls to be placed in special education classes (10.1% versus 39.1%).

Replication of the MCHV project in Bermuda has not been shown to benefit toddler cognitive scores significantly compared to a group of randomly assigned controls (Scarr & McCartney, 1988). Yet most of the Bermuda parents were high school graduates. In a fascinating analysis of MCHV research over a 20-year period,

Levenstein (1988) emphasized that there are differences in gain scores for toddlers whose mothers initially paid little attention to their own or their infants' learning needs. Some mothers were not involved in program goals and activities, as recorded in home visitor logs, until months or even a year after program initiation. Levenstein calls these mothers "Hesitators." Her data demonstrate that such families were especially good candidates for infancy education that made a difference, in comparison to control infants. Mothers whom she refers to as "Strivers" seemed already initially to be interested in further education, for themselves as well as their toddlers. They picked up on activities demonstrated; they were more likely to finish their own high school education; and they readily tuned in to the ideas that the MCHV program presented. Few differences were found for some of the MCHV replications between toddlers of Striver mothers in the program compared to controls whose mothers were also Strivers. When Hesitator mothers were "hooked in" to an educational program for their infants, then significant cognitive gains (pretest IQ = 85.3; post-MCHV IQ = 103.7) were indeed found for their children compared to control groups with large proportions of Hesitator mothers not enrolled in the program. In third grade, program children had normal reading and arithmetic scores, far above the untreated group's borderline scores.

Levenstein's (1988) findings are significant for the field of preventive infant education services. When economic resources are scarce for delivering infant education programs to families in a community, it may be wise to pinpoint longer-term resources, particularly for families of Hesitators. Other families may simply need toy and book provision and some ideas on how to teach tots and tune in to their developmental levels and needs. Not all families may need the same expensive long-term infant education program that Hesitator families may need. Sometimes those parents who volunteer their young ones for programs have the energy and opportunities to seek out and respond to program offers. They may not have infants as gravely at risk for later educational failure as families who require rigorous neighborhood canvassing and recruitment efforts before accepting educational enrichment opportunities for their infants and toddlers.

The state of Missouri is unique in offering the Parents as Teachers Project (PAT), a program of free home visits with enrichment materials and ideas for parents of under-threes. With the help of Dr. Burton White as senior project consultant, ongoing training was provided for program delivery staff 3 days per month for 3 years to 380 families expecting their first child ("New Parents," 1985). Blind testing when babies were 3 years old confirmed that project infants scored significantly higher than controls on intellective, achievement, and social measures. PAT parents became more knowledgeable about child development and more positive to educational institutions; 53% rated their school districts as very responsive to their children's needs compared with 29% of comparison parents.

Not all the tutorial educational model researches brought good news. In Schaefer's (1977) program, low SES toddlers received a year of carefully programmed weekly in-home tutoring that significantly raised their scores by 3 years of age. Yet when retested at age six, the experimental group had scores that had drifted downward and no longer differed from those of control children, whose scores rose after entry into elementary school. Educational inoculation in infancy does not "take." When in-home risk factors are multiple, the importance of continuity for infant/toddler education has been repeatedly demonstrated.

That the inoculation hypothesis must be discarded in favor of more sustained educational interventions with at-risk infants has been strikingly demonstrated in findings from Dr. Ira Gordon's (1969) home visitation project in Gainesville, Florida. Trained paraprofessionals brought carefully sequenced weekly lessons to poor rural mothers and modeled the use of Piagetian tasks with infants for either 1 or 2 years. Infants who had been in the experimental program for 1 year had higher Griffiths IQ scores at 12 months compared with control infants. Yet those infants who spent 2 years in program had Bayley mental scale scores (MDI) of 85.4—very similar to the MDI scores of control infants (86.6) after 2 years.

Even more disconcerting were the 2-year MDI scores of toddlers (79.5) who had first received 1 year of this parent-focused tutorial program and then served as one group of controls for the second year. Infant education at the level of a weekly 1-hour home visit for 1 year will not provide a quick permanent "fix" for infants seriously at risk for cognitive deficits.

Despite weekly in-service staff training, Gordon (1969) perceptively noted: "Tasks, when taught directly and by virtual rote methods, become tester evaluation items instead of instructional aids . . . . It is not the curriculum materials *per se* which make the difference; but the nature of the interpersonal relationship and the manner of delivery are of significant importance to learning" (pp. 60–62). *Who* the caregiver is and *how* the caregiver provides infant educational lessons may be far more crucial than locus of services for infants at educational risk.

Quality of Care

Caregiver and setting characteristics have been strongly implicated in child outcomes for infant care. Quality has been indexed particularly by caregiver-infant ratio, staff turnover, and child development training for caregivers (Honig, 1987; Howes, 1987; Howes & Rubenstein, 1985; Ruopp, Travers, Glantz, & Coelen, 1979). Toddlers with extensive center care during the first 2 years of life scored significantly poorer on cognitive and personality measures compared with children cared for either at home or in family day care. These results were particularly salient when center groups were large and when the number of infants per caregiver was large (Schwarz, Scarr, Caparulo, Furrow, & McCartney, 1981). Lower quality can also lead to poorer language outcomes as in the Bermuda day care study (McCartney, 1984; Phillips, Scarr, & McCartney, 1987).

Training and Stability of Care

Cummings (1980) compared the attachment of 12- to 28-month-old babies to stable caregivers who had worked at the center a long time versus unstable caregivers, there for a short time. In the day-care setting, infants preferred the stable caregivers, but this trend was not as marked in the strange and stressful setting of a laboratory. Building attachments with babies as a buffer against the stresses of daily separations from employed parents or as a buffer against inappropriate home interactions takes staff creativity, and stability.

How have caregivers been trained for education work with infants? Some investigators have not considered the variable of training particularly important. Almost any motherly person would do. Kagan, Kearsley, and Zelazo (1980) in setting up the Tremont Street group care for Chinese, black, and Caucasian infants, typified this position: "Women, especially those who have reared children, are probably best qualified for infant care" (p. 267).

Some infant caregivers are fortunate to live in communities where academic and practicum preparation is available. Some communities provide occasional infant caregiving workshops through affiliates of the National Association for the Education of Young Children (NAEYC) or the Southern Association on Children Under Six (SACUS) or community child care councils. The National Quality Infant/Toddler Caregiving Workshop at Syracuse University is a week-long intensive training experience available annually. In Washington, D.C., the National Center for Clinical Infant Programs disseminates excellent training resources, including their bulletin, *Zero to Three*.

That caregiver training is necessary has been made evident in studies of metropolitan care centers. Observing forty-three caregivers interacting with infants under 18 months of age in twenty-eight centers, Jacobson (1987) reported that there was low affect and little conversation. *Interactions* were defined as involving positive affect with lots of mutual eye contact and conversation. Levels of interaction were found to be low and lack variety. Educational interactions that involved infants with toys or language were rare.

Some infant education projects, such as Fowler's (1978, 1980) in Canada, have provided detailed reports on problems and progress in training paraprofessional staff to (1) carry out *elaborations* on kernal curricular ideas proposed by researchers and (2) invent flexible *changes* on such themes tailored to the particular infants who are served. Some projects have monitored in detail the changes in staff competence and transaction level pre- and postcaregiver training sessions. (See Honig, in press, for a survey on assessment of the preparation of infant/toddler caregivers in a variety of infant programs.)

The ABC (Assessing the Behaviors of Caregivers) scales have been used in some projects to monitor the effectiveness of in-service training to enhance the skills of infant/toddler caregivers in language and positive socioemotional, Piagetian, and physical caregiving interactions (Honig & Lally, 1981). Intensive training workshops using hands-on experiences, audiovisual materials, and demonstrations with babies have been shown to increase caregiver competencies in their transactions with infants and toddlers (Honig & Lally, 1988).

Therapeutic/Education Models

Intensity and extensity of education efforts vary widely in different programs and certainly may be potentially significant variables in program outcomes for some infants at risk. But for infants at *grave* developmental risk, infant education sometimes must become a full-fledged therapeutic endeavor or the baby may not only be socioemotionally and cognitively maladapted, but even suffer from physical failure to thrive.

Bromwich's (1981) parent-infant interaction model assigned two intervention staff members with graduate-level training for each preterm infant (ages 9 months to 24 months) served in a population where serious problems existed. Backup social worker and pediatric staff were also available. Empathic listening to parents, modeling for them, and experimenting with varieties of ways to interact effectively and positively with the infants in order to capture their interest in exchanges and activities were among the many techniques used. Thus, an intensive therapeutic/educational infant program may be called for when parents lack sensitive observation skills, cannot read baby's cues accurately, and are unaware of materials, experiences, and activities suitable for infant developmental stages.

Fraiberg, Adelson, and Shapiro (1975) have provided extraordinarily fine case studies of difficult, inspiring, and subtle therapeutic educational work in cases of severe infant failure to thrive. Unlike the preparation of professionals or paraprofessionals in other programs discussed earlier, the preparation of *therapeutic* change agents is necessarily meticulous, complex, and quite expensive in terms of advanced graduate training. To carry out this "kitchen therapy" model, intervenors need specialized training in making a cooperative therapeutic alliance with parents who have not known secure loving parenting in their own childhoods. The therapists provide ego strengths as well as models of good parenting. In San Francisco, this model is being carried out with low SES minority families by Dr. Jeree Paul and by Dr. Alicia Lieberman (in press), and in New Haven by Dr. Sally Provence (1983).

Particularly noteworthy too is the therapeutic work of Dr. Stanley Greenspan et al. (1987). In a triple thrust, they created therapeutic nurseries *plus* therapy individually for the infant and for the parent. Such procedures are surely expensive. Yet it may well be that for prevention of criminality, drug abuse, and educational failure, in some cases a straightforward educational model, whether tutorial or group, may not be sufficient to prevent later disturbances and deficits. The threats to infant development in such cases are so complex as to require professional attention to the needs of the parent and the mother-infant dyad. As well, the infant must be provided with opportunitites to learn more positive reciprocal interactions with a responsive therapist *and* in a play group of toddlers with parents present. The nursery provides opportunities for trained teachers to model and reinforce positive peer group interactions. Obviously, education for the infant educator in such cases will be far more intensive, extensive, and costly.

GROUP SETTINGS AS EDUCATIONAL
SUPPORTS FOR INFANT DEVELOPMENT

Among the programmatic models representing educational environments created during the early 1960s to prevent later cognitive and school deficits, none was more daring at the time than the concept of infant group care as an education intervention. Indeed, when Dr. Betty Caldwell established the Children's Center in Syracuse, New York, care of under-threes was illegal under state law (Honig, Caldwell, & Richmond, 1986). To compound the problem, theorists of disparate persuasions contributed ideas that pioneer project staff were aware might be interpreted as contrary to the possibility of positive outcomes for other-than-mother care. Thus, Keister (1970) in her early infant education research in North Carolina reported pointedly, in response to such anxieties, that infant group educational care had *not* decreased the intellectual function of the infants.

Theoretical Views Bearing on Infant Group Care

Freud (1940) described the early child-mother relationship as "unique, without parallel, established unalterably for a whole lifetime as the first and strongest love-object and as the prototype for all later love relations for both sexes" (p. 188).

Erikson's (1963) dialectical stage theory postulated a lifelong series of resolutions of emotional conflicts. For each of the eight nuclear conflicts, there is a life period of critical importance for establishing a favorable balance of positive to negative emotional polarities. Erikson sensitized caregivers to the vulnerability of *infancy* as a period for building an emotional balance in favor of basic confidence in others and trustworthiness in oneself and *toddlerhood* as a critical period for establishing a sense of the rightness of having a will of one's own. Through brilliant clinical and cross-cultural examples, Erickson demonstrated that caregivers must promote autonomy and initiatives of younger and older toddlers *without* diluting trust or engendering strong shame or crushing guilt. Interpretation of Eriksonian theory has made possible more-sensitive implementation of the role of the infant educator in group programs in promoting positive emotional development (Honig, 1987).

Piaget (1958), in his study of his own three infants, clarified the fundamental sensorimotor accomplishments that are necessary precursors for the development of preoperational intelligence. He provided perceptive and numerous examples of the gradual growth of cognitive milestones, such as object permanence, separation of means and ends, spatial and causal understandings, and representational capacity. Judicious interpretation of Piaget's work helps programmers clearly understand the importance of caregivers in priming an infant's interactions with materials and people in order that through equilibration struggles—the "matchmaking" process as the cutting edge of new learning—the baby can actively construct new developmental understandings and advances (Honig, 1974a, 1974b, 1978, 1983b).

Mahler's theory, too, although less cited by infant care specialists, has much to offer in the way of understanding the gradual transformation of the infant from a creature tuned into body molding and internal signals of distress or well-being to a creature whose strivings to practice and perfect early motoric and exploratory skills lead it to venture from the secure base of mother. Toddlers are involved in a dialectic seesaw. They want to be autonomous individuals with a will of their own, and yet they also yearn at some level for the lost paradise of "oneness" with the mother, when all problems were solved and all comforts provided by the caregiver. The crankiness that this conflict produces in the increasingly aware mind of the toddler in the "rapprochement" state (from about 1½ years to 3 years) is a masterful contribution of Mahlerian theory (Kaplan, 1978; Mahler, Pine, & Bergman, 1975).

Bowlby's (1958) ethological theory postulated that infants were biologically primed to become attached to their primary caregivers, their mothers. He conceived of attachment as a goal-corrected control system designed for the baby to obtain and maintain nearness and contact with the mother. Exploration urges will certainly take the cruising or walking baby away from the attachment figure. Yet, if the attachment figure gives help and comfort when needed, the baby will tend to develop a working model of the parent as loving and of self as a person worthy of such love. Bretherton (1985) notes further that "through continual transactions with the world of persons and objects, the child constructs increasingly complex internal working models of that world and of the significant persons in it, including the self" (p. 11). "However, it is only during the second 6 months of life that these proximity and interaction promoting behaviors are integrated into a coherent system around the mother" (p. 7). Sroufe and Fleeson (1988) conjecture that through this attachment process, children learn and internalize *both* sides of a relationship so that the complementary parental role is also learned. Thus, cycles of poor *or* optimal parenting can be perpetuated.

In the past few years, attachment theory research, inspired by Bowlby's ethological theory, has provided extensive understandings of the relationship (1) between early maternal caregiving styles and later infant attachment (Bretherton & Waters, 1985) and (2) between early attachment classifications and later socioemotional and cognitive functioning (Erickson, Sroufe, & Egeland, 1985; Farber & Egeland, 1982; Sroufe, 1985).

Ainsworth's (1982, 1983) work revealed that mothers who are averse to bodily contact are more likely to have infants who avoid them upon reunion in the Ainsworth "Strange Situation" procedure. In this standard series of eight brief 3-minute episodes, babies are left by and rejoined by mother, and/or stranger, in an increasingly stressful manner. Specifically in the second reunion episode, the infant is first left alone, then rejoined by a strange adult, prior to mother's arrival. Mothers who are responsive to infant distress, exhibit tender, careful holding, and feed infants sensitively in response to the baby's signals of need or satiety are likely to have *babies who actively accept comforting upon reunion* to the Strange Situation. These secure babies can settle into constructive play once the mother has returned. Mothers who have been affectionate but *insensitive* to, and *noncontingent* in response to, infant signals have anxiously resistive or ambivalently attached infants. Upon reunion, these babies may *seek* comfort from the mother's body, but cannot *take* comfort. Often they push her away or struggle to get down after wanting to be picked up.

Belsky (1988) notes that "incontestable patterns are evident in the literature regarding the future functioning of children with secure versus insecure infant attachment relationships" (p. 243). He expresses concern that *lengthy* participation in infant care/education facilities during the first year of life may be a risk factor for some infants. Using the Strange Situation paradigm, with infants from working-class and middle-class families, Belsky and Rovine (1988) found that if infants had 20 or more hours of nonmaternal care per week prior to 9 months of age, they were more likely to *avoid* mother in Ainsworth's reunion situation. Low-income infants who started nonmaternal care in the first year of life have also been found more likely to be classified as anxious-avoidant in their attachments (Vaughn, Gover, & Egeland, 1980). With upper-class families using nanny in-home care, Barglow, Vaughn, and Molitor (1987) noted an increase in avoidant responses upon reunion with mother if infant care had been 20 or more hours per week. Schwartz (1983) reported differential percentages of 82% versus 50% versus 35%, in moderate-to-high avoidance ratings for twelve-month old infants in full-time care versus part-time versus mother care. Moreover, even when secure attachment to mother had been demonstrated at 18 months, babies showed a deterioration in the quality of adaptation over the period from 18–24 months (Vaughn, Deane, & Waters, 1985) *if* there had been extensive nonmaternal care in the first year of life. In a difficult tool-using task, these early-day-care children tended to be more oppositional, less task persistent, more negative in their affect, and less compliant in following the mother's suggestions.

Translating Theory into Group Care Programs

Attuned to theoretical concerns, project directors of the earliest funded infant group educational experiences set up their research with questions framed to inquire whether or not such educational facilities posed a threat to the early emotional or cognitive development of babies (Honig, 1983a). Fortunately, the zeitgeist of the early 1960s permitted careful attention to provision of high-quality optimal environments for the youngest children in these pioneer day-care settings. For example, based on theoretical ideas described above, for the Syracuse Children's Center program, Caldwell and Richmond (1968) specified that caregivers need to provide the following:

1. A relatively high frequency of adult contacts involving a relatively small number of adults
2. A learning environment that is both stimulating and responsive in the interpersonal, experiential, and physico-spatial domains

3. An optimal level of need gratification
4. A positive emotional climate in which the child learns to trust others and self
5. An environment containing a minimum of unnecessary restrictions on a child's early exploratory attempts but a supply of natural restrictions that provide valuable feedback data helpful in refining movements and actions
6. Rich and varied but interpretable cultural experiences
7. A physical environment that separates figure from ground and contains modulated amounts and varieties of sensory experience
8. Access to play materials that will help accomplish specific educational objectives
9. New experiences that provide an appropriate match for the child's current level of cognitive organization. Stated in the language of Piaget's theoretical system, a new experience will be assimilated only if it is initially similar to previous experiences. Accommodation to the differences in the experience can occur only if it is not too different

These theoretical propositions were then translated into specific goals, interactions, and activities carried out by the teachers, whose backgrounds varied markedly. A "typical day" for the infants and toddlers was provided to illustrate this process.

The care and thoughtfulness with which these earliest research-based educational programs for infants were planned cannot be overemphasized. The Syracuse research staff and teachers, for example, met in ongoing study-group efforts to analyze theoretical and pragmatic writings with the constant goal of trying to interpret knowledge and ideas in order to create more appropriate advantageous environments for the infants served. This thoughtfulness permeated every aspect of program planning. Babies were not admitted until they were 6 months of age, lest early development of secure attachment or basic growth of trust in the mothering one should be attenuated, and they attended a half-day program for the first year. Caregivers held and cuddled babies a great deal, and responded promptly to distress cries. The ratio of caregiver to infants was kept low (1 to 4); each baby had a special person as an assigned caregiver. Whenever possible, Piagetian sensorimotor activities were carried out in naturally occurring, pleasurable interactions, and in the context of loving routines (Honig, 1974a, 1974b, 1977, 1987).

Three critical issues were the focus of research in the earliest published studies of the Syracuse Children's Center infant educational program. Using home observations and interview techniques, Caldwell et al. (1968) established that a mix of low SES with middle-class infants did not decrease the attainments of the latter. After 2 years in program, middle SES infants had gained 17 IQ points and infants from low SES families had gained 9 points. Second, after a mean duration of 18.8 months in attendance at the Children's Center, low SES infants showed a rise in developmental quotient (above 105) by 30 months, while matched, exclusively home-reared controls showed the IQ decrease from 12 to 30 months typical of infants from low-income families (Caldwell, Wright, Honig, & Tannenbaum, 1970).

Third, and most significant in the light of current concerns, this high-quality half-day infant education program did not dilute the attachment of mothers and babies. Using a nurturance/succorance interview created by Henry Murray, the Children's Center researchers found that whether infants had been in day care or not did not seem to make a difference in attachment scores. But if the home was characterized by lower intellectual stimulation and supports for infant/toddler learning, then attachment was attenuated, whether infants were exclusively home reared or in group care daily.

Longitudinal Studies of Infant Education Centers

Of the early university, research-based group education projects, three are of note because they provided long-term care until school age and were able to collect follow-up longitudinal outcome data.

The Milwaukee Project

Low-IQ (75) mothers living in dilapidated housing in poor Milwaukee neighborhoods were provided with one-to-one tutorial care for their babies at home from 3 months onward (Garber, 1988). When the mother trusted the tutor sufficiently, she allowed the infant to be brought to the learning center. Teacher-infant ratio remained at one to one until the baby was 12 months old. By 15 months, one teacher cared for two toddlers, and by 18 months, for three toddlers. Careful curricular planning characterized the education component during the entire preschool period. This extremely expensive and intensive effort to break the intergenerational cycle of poverty and school failure in families with retarded mothers resulted in mean preschool IQs of 121.6 for experimental children compared to control group IQs of 95.7. Children in this program scored 39 points higher (IQ = 118) than their older siblings (IQ = 79) had scored at the same age.

Initially, the effects of the infant education effort were impressive. However, the subsequent learning careers of these infants remind us of the crucial need for *continuity* of educational efforts for children at multiple risk. The high IQ scores achieved by infants dropped precipitously once the children entered low-achieving neighborhood elementary schools (Garber, 1988).

Age	Experimental IQ (*N* = 17)	Control IQ (*N* = 17)
72 months	109	87.6
120 months	104.2	86.3

Across the first four grades of school, teachers reported that the experimental children were more active, less compliant, and more in need of control than the control youngsters, although they played and worked well with peers. Thus, although the experimental children maintained a normal IQ level, superior to the control group, "their school behavior was poor and quite similar to the control children. Almost without exception, reports of lags in performance and discrepancies between potential and achievement were accompanied by reports of difficulties in attention span and motivation and/or attitude problems. As the children grew older, there were psychological reports of increasing conduct problems and absenteeism, which reflect negative attitudes toward school" (Garber, 1988, p. 307).

Somewhat mitigating these somber findings are differences in IQ performance for *siblings* of experimental versus control children, some of whose scores can be compared below:

	SIBLING IQ	
Age in Years	**Experimentals**	**Controls**
3	90.2	85.2
4	84	78.2
5	80.2	84.2
8	87.8	74.6
10	87.4	80.7
12–13	83.3	70.8
14+	86.1	74.1

The program mothers had been taught job and literacy skills for positions as entry-level dietitians and laundry workers. Garber (1988) suggests that the difference in performance for experimental siblings may be due to "diffusion from the maternal rehabilitation program's benefits into the family" (p. 300). In his overall assessment of the disappointing later educational findings for this intensive infant educational effort, Garber concludes: "The findings of the Milwaukee cross-sectional study and the longitudinal investigation supported the basic hypothesis that the most important environmental influence on cognitive development is the intimate interaction that takes place between the individual child and the parent or primary caregiver who mediates the environment for the child" (p. 405).

Garber might better have emphasized the critical need for *continuity* of educational efforts for many children in families and neighborhoods at high risk for educational failure. In a long-term study of Canadian twins, Lytton, Watts, and Dunn (1987) report that the highest correlations for school achievements were with *concurrent* parental supports, not those recorded for the parents during the children's infancy.

The Abecedarian Project

Dr. Craig Ramey and colleagues in Chapel Hill, North Carolina, provided a high-quality, cognitively oriented group program for poor black infants of low-education mothers (Finkelstein, Denta, Gallagher, & Ramey, 1978). From 3 months until the children graduated to elementary school, they attended the Frank Porter Graham Center. The effects of the Abecedarian program were particularly noteworthy for infants at biological risk, specifically those born with a low ponderal index (PI) (Ramey & Gowan, 1986). The PI is a neonatal weight-to-length ratio. When babies are long but skinny, their low PI at birth signifies fetal malnutrition prior to birth. Infants with normal and low PI scores were randomly assigned either to the experimental education group or to the control groups. Diaper service and pediatric and social work service as well as formula were provided to control families during the first year of infancy to ensure that differences that might be found in cognitive scores as a function of program could be definitively attributed to the infant education program and not to extraneous health or nutrition variables. The 3-year cognitive data shown below reveal to what extent risk factors intersect and how *bidirectional* infant-caregiver effects are:

	Fetal Malnutrition Status (Ponderal Index)	Stanford-Binet IQ
Experimental Infants	Low PI ($n = 5$)	96.4
	Average PI ($n = 17$)	98.1
Control Infants	Low PI ($n = 5$)	70.6
	Average PI ($n = 15$)	84.7

Immediately noticeable is the ameliorative effect of high-quality infant group educational care on cognitive scores at the end of the infancy period, *even* for babies born with low PI scores and therefore at biological risk. Note that normally born poverty infants *without* an educational infant program were already one standard deviation below the mean IQ score by the end of the infancy period.

The rationale for early infant education as *prevention* of cognitive deficit and as worthy of becoming an urgent social goal for infants at risk is highlighted by the retarded IQ score of 70.6 attained by low PI infants not enrolled in program. *Retardation may well be the outcome for vulnerable infants for whom early education is not provided.* Ramey and Gowan (1986) report that mothers of those low-functioning infants were not atttentive to their babies. Low-functioning infants may not elicit positive maternal interactions, and a grim cycle of increasing developmental deficits ensues. This confirmation of the *transactional* nature of development alerts us to how critically urgent high-quality caregiver training work and supports for staff stability must be. And yet many infant caregivers earn minimum wage. "The most poorly paid females are child care workers employed in private households. These women had median earnings of only $90 a week in 1986" (Rix, 1989, p. 347). The profession of child care center worker is listed in the Federal Register below that of parking lot attendant!

The Abecedarian program continued to follow children into elementary school years. Infants from the Abecedarian project, in comparison with low SES children who had community-based day care or minimal day care, scored higher on tests of cognitive development and "displayed less linear decline" (Burchinal, Lee, & Ramey, 1989, p. 132) in their intellectual scores four years later.

		Abecedarian	Community	Minimal
Bayley MDI	6 mo.	107.4	102.5	100.0
McCarthy	54 mo.	101.4	95.7	86.5

Note that community day care also may have stemmed the sharp decline in scores of children in attendance. What is *not* known was whether there was a difference among mothers who actively sought community-based care after they were assigned to control group randomly, and those who did not mobilize such efforts.

One of the project's disconcerting findings, however, was that program children in kindergarten and first grade were 15 times as likely as control group low-income youngsters (without early cognitively oriented, high-quality infant education) to act aggressively not only on the playground, but in corridors and classrooms (Haskins, 1985). These data jolt us into the realization that *purely cognitive goals are not sufficient for infant education facilities.* Once the American Guidance Service program "My friends and me" was introduced into the project, later program graduates did not show higher rates of antisocial behavior compared to the controls early in elementary school.

Prosocial curricular goals for infants and young children must be as carefully and conscientiously integrated components of early education programs as are cognitive, motoric, or language goals. Yarrow's research provided evidence that empathic, concerned toddlers were reared by mothers who modeled loving concern and categorically did not tolerate toddler use of aggressive actions as a means of solving social problems (Pines, 1979). Main and George (1985) observed that abused toddlers in day care evinced no empathy, but anger or indifference, to distressed peers. They refused friendly overtures, and were significantly more aggressive to adult caregivers as well as assaultive to peers.

The Syracuse Family Development Research Program (FDRP)

Omnibus models are rare in infancy research. An omnibus model not only provides high-quality infant education, but nutrition and health components are elaborately included, as are group meetings for parents and individual outreach home visitation and family support efforts. The Syracuse Family Development Research Program (Lally & Honig, 1977) was a long-term omnibus project whose major goal was to strengthen *family* functioning and to avert the "washout" effects that leave project and control youngsters functioning at a lower intellectual level several years after the program ends.

FDRP program goals were specified in detail for all staff members, including caregivers, director, cooks, bus drivers and riders, and home visitors. Home visitation staff, known as child development trainers (CDTs), were trained to bring positive discipline techniques, Piagetian sensorimotor games, and nutritional information to families and to serve as social supports for family problems (Honig, 1982). Such problems ranged from infant allergies to housing and boyfriend troubles. CDTs met weekly with their own supervisor as well as research staff.

None of the teenage mothers (mean age 18 years on entry to program) were initially high school graduates. Overwhelmingly, the parents were single mothers, with a firstborn or second-born child. Careful and elaborate control matches were found for each project family. FDRP classroom caregivers were extensively trained in intensive 2-week workshops every fall, in continuing staff conferences during nap times, and in case conferences devoted to specific infants with special problems, such as language delay, a vulnerability that may occur among young children in institutional settings (Tizard, Cooperman, Joseph & Tizard, 1972).

Program goals and professional requirements that flowed from these goals were specified in detail for all staff members. The CDTs visited pregnant mothers recruited into the program from the second trimester of pregnancy until the children graduated from the program into elementary school. From 6 months to 60 months, children attended the Syracuse Children's Center. This university-based, high-quality infant/toddler preschool facility provided half-day care from 6 months to 1½ years and full-day care thereafter. Younger infants were in small groups with one caregiver for four infants, and elaborate curricular offerings were programmed in a context of loving, body-cuddling interactions. Older toddlers attended a mixed-age, open-education program that permitted free choice of four major activitiy areas (sensory, fine motor, gross motor, and creative). Tutorial work was available daily in small group sessions with teachers targeting specific skills, such as colors or sound discriminations. Project manuals for teaching infant caregivers and parents were developed with generous feedback from staff (Honig & Lally, 1981; Lally & Gordon, 1982).

Interactions of caregivers with infants and toddlers were extensively monitored to ensure quality control and delivery of program goals. The checklist instruments used, "Assessing the Behaviors of Caregivers" (ABC I, II, III), were specifically designed for easy tallying of teacher interactions with tots (Honig & Lally, 1975a, 1975b, 1988). Process as well as outcome measures were administered, and ongoing assessments were routine for providers, parents, and children.

Longitudinal follow-up of the FDRP youngsters at age fifteen revealed some of the strengths of an omnibus educational program as well as some of the difficulties (Lally, Mangione, & Honig, 1988). About 75% of each group was located with no differences in attrition from experimental and control groups. FDRP youngsters exhibited far less social pathology. As teenagers, sixty-five children of the low-income families who participated in the program had a 6% rate of juvenile delinquency, compared to a 22% rate for fifty-four children in the control group. Not only was the control group rate almost 4 times greater, but the offenses of the twelve control youngsters were considerably more severe. Their recidivism rate was higher, and delinquencies included rape, robbery, and assault, compared to the complaint of "ungovernable" for three of the four delinquent experimental youths. The administrative and detention court costs for the FDRP youth were $12,000 compared with $107,000 for the control group.

Although the FDRP program had little impact on family income and career advancement, and many of the families were still living in poverty, *attitudes* significantly differentiated the families. Compared to control group youths, FDRP youngsters felt more positive about themselves, and were more likely to expect to be in school 5 years later (28% versus 53%). Program parents also reported feeling proud about the positive social attitudes and behaviors of their children, and were more likely to advise their children to try to reach their full potential. Control parents were more likely to advise their children not to expect too much.

Academic outcomes were mixed and depended markedly on sex of child. Three-quarters of the girls from the FDRP program had *C* averages or better; none was failing. More than half the controls had averages below *C*, and 16% were failing. Teachers rated program girls as having more-positive attitudes about themselves. Program boys, by contrast, were doing as poorly as contrast youth in school. Thus, educational facilitation during infancy and preschool years, even when combined with outreach to families, did not seem to overcome the fact that, overwhelmingly, program males were brought up in single-parent homes *without strong male role models for educational achievement.* The power of negative neighborhood mores with respect to male school achievement and the lack of continuing supports for families during the transition into school years may also account for these educational findings.

PROGRAMMATIC RESEARCH: TIMING OF ENTRY, LENGTH OF DAY, SEX OF INFANT

Infant-care researchers are struggling to untangle the large and subtle array of variables that are implicated in infant education outcome data.

From group-care research programs initiated as part of President Johnson's Great Society policies and from second generation projects, the first practical issues were addressed. Could early education settings be organized and staff trained in order to facilitate infant learning and provide a positive emotional climate for babies without detriment to infant-mother attachment? The answer for half-day high-quality programs was surely a resounding "Yes, if." *If* included careful attention to staffing, training, few infants per adult, and family support provision. These findings hold for family day care as well as center care. Caregivers in family day-care homes that were officially sponsored or regulated tended to provide a safer physical environment, and to be more actively involved and talk more with the children than caregivers in unregulated family day-care homes (Stallings, 1980).

The proportion of securely attached infants among employed and nonemployed mothers may not differ, but a greater preponderance of avoidant insecure attachment has been found among those babies whose mothers returned to employment *full time* during the first year of life (Vaughn et al., 1980). For premature infants, developmental scores are higher for babies whose mothers did not leave them for more than 20 hours per week (Cohen, 1978). No compromise of infant-mother attachment has been reported for infants in high-quality *part-time* care during the first year of life (Belsky, 1988).

Can school failure or social dysfunction be prevented by high-quality infant care? Here again, the answer is "Yes if." *Continuity* and quality of care are critical. However, families with increased stresses tend to place their infants in *poorer*-quality child care centers (Howes & Olenick, 1986). Family support and guidance may be needed to increase parental understanding of appropriate educational settings for infants.

For male infants, the answers are more troubling. Boys are more vulnerable; the early timing of maternal return to full-time employment may have differential negative effects for males (Hoffman, 1984).

Effects of timing and sex of child on infant attachment were examined for a sample of ninety-seven two-parent, middle-class families, with forty employed mothers and fifty-seven nonemployed mothers (Chase-Lansdale & Owen, 1988). "Boys were significantly more likely to be insecurely attached when their mothers were employed than when their mothers were not employed, and there were almost twice as many resistant as avoidant infant-father attachments within the employed-mother group" (p. 1507). A subanalysis of the families indicated that there were higher rates of insecure attachments to both mother and father for infants in families recruited *prenatally* compared to those recruited near 1 year of age. Families with insecure year-old infants *may* have been more likely to refuse project participation. Future researches on outcomes of infant education will need to be aware of, and control for, outcome differences due to *time* of recruitment of families to be studied.

These researchers speculate whether infant boys in employed-mother families are treated with appropriate sensitivity and responsiveness by their fathers, who may consider that boys are "supposed" to be sturdier than girls. In early-mother-employed families, more may be expected of boy babies (due to this presumed hardiness) and fewer efforts made to compensate for the stresses of the dual-career family with responsive tenderness to baby's needs. Instead, parents may expect early maturity despite infant needs, because parents' hectic lives increase the pressures on the family for children to grow up fast. Superbaby pressures may be particularly deleterious for males.

Timing of entry into infant care and extent of care during the first year of life have been related to the vulnerabilty of infants who may develop insecure attachments whether avoidant *or* resistant. Chase-Lansdale and Owen (1988), speculate:

> It is just as likely that insecurely attached infants experience maternal absence as a source of unpredictability (commonly viewed as an antecedent of resistant attachments) as much as a source of unpredictability (commonly viewed as a source of rejection and an antecedent for avoidant attachment) . . . . Maternal employment may place boys, but not girls, at risk for socioemotional difficulties (p. 1510).

Negative effects of infant care on males may, however, be mediated by maternal emotional maturity. Benn (1986) interviewed thirty *well-educated full-time* employed mothers of eighteen-month-old firstborns. In the Strange Situation, secure attachment was more frequent for boys who had been left earlier in care. But *maternal personality integration was correlated with infant security.* More highly integrated mothers left their sons with a sitter, whereas poorly integrated mothers chose to place their sons in family day-care arrangements. Thus, mother's affective qualities intersected with sex of infant. "When the mother-son relationship is characterized by warmth, acceptance, and freedom of emotional expression—a pattern characteristic of highly integrated mothering—it appears that the male infant can remain reassured of maternal availability even in her absence" (Benn, 1986, p. 1230). Some male infants may be more vulnerable than others, with maternal characteristics *mediating* the risk factors. Such findings underscore how important family supports are for families *across* the socioeconomic spectrum. Coordination between mother-infant pairs in teaching-learning situations is strong by 18 months. *Joint* attention to tasks helps babies learn better (Maccoby, Snow, & Jacklin, 1984).

Clarke-Stewart (1984) examined variations in setting for an older group of toddlers (two to four year olds) from mostly two-parent, middle-class families. She studied babies across a wide variation of part-time or full-time maternal or other-than-mother care. One of the clearest findings in this complex sample, where child care arrangements changed from year to year, was that higher cognitive outcomes for the children were "significantly correlated with caregiver training, knowledge, and stability; with structure, materials, and order in the program; and with the proportion of children in the class who were of high SES" (p. 93).

The long day-care day may not be best for babies. Clarke-Stewart reported that social competence with an adult stranger was higher for children when caregivers were more highly trained and knowledgeable and mothers worked fewer hours. Social competence with a peer in year one of the study was predicted by a higher level of caregiver training and knowledge, a more favorable caregiver-child ratio in day care, and also when the child spent more time with mother. Thus, variables *both from day care and from the home* seem to be implicated in the cognitive gains of children in this study, which dealt only with toddlers and preschoolers and not with infants younger than 2 years, who may be even more vulnerable to deprivation of time with mother.

SOCIOEMOTIONAL FUNCTIONING AND INFANT DAY CARE

Data on social and emotional functioning of children who have attended day care in infancy are confounded often by family social class, marital status, parent-child relationships, number of hours daily in care, and quality of care (McCartney & Galanopoulos, 1988). Noncompliance and aggression have been reported often for children who experience extensive day care as infants (Melhuish, 1986; Rutter, 1981; Sroufe, 1988).

The earliest investigation of socioemotional outcomes was for a group of low SES preschoolers who had participated in university-based, high-quality infant day care. They were compared at 4 years of age with peers cared for exclusively at home during infancy (Schwarz, Strickland, & Krolick, 1974). The children were observed 4 months after they had entered a preschool program together. The infant care group was observed to be more physically and verbally aggressive with adults and peers, less cooperative, and less tolerant of frustration.

Howes and Olenick (1986) compared toddler compliance for families using either low-quality day care (determined by adult-child ratio, staff training, and staff continuity). Children were more demanding in high-quality day care, and at home they were more skilled negotiators over compliance issues. They resisted temptation better in a laboratory task compared with peers from low-quality centers, who were less compliant at home. Of interest is the finding that toddlers who had more hours per week alone in interactions with their fathers were *less* noncompliant, both at home and in the center. Fathers who generously provide focused attention for, and responsive interactions with, infants may also buffer them against possible negative socioemotional effects of lower-quality day care.

Negative socioemotional outcomes do not seem to depend on family social class. Social difficulties with peers may show up even when programs provide high-quality day care and serve children from college-educated, high-income intact families (Field, Masi, Goldstein, Perry, & Silker, 1988). Field and colleagues report no differences in parent-child reunion behaviors observed at pick-up times at the end of the day for advantaged preschoolers who had attended infant day care compared with nonattenders. However, teachers rated the advantaged preschoolers who had attended *full-time* infant care as more aggressive and assertive than advantaged preschoolers who had attended infant day care *part time*. Answers to questions regarding effects of infant care may well depend on how *long* the infant's daily separation from mother lasts.

In a group of 3½ year olds who had been in a community-based day care since infancy, no differences were found in overall level of behavioral problems in comparison with an exclusively home-reared control group (Rubenstein, Howes, & Boyle, 1981). However, the infancy day-care group were verbally less compliant with their mothers during a boring sorting task in comparison with an exclusively home-reared control group (50% versus 8%). The infant day-care group had more temper tantrums as preschoolers and more separation distress with mothers.

A meticulous retrospective study, controlling for marital status and social class, has revealed "sleeper" effects of full-time infant care (Vandell & Corasaniti, 1989). Suburban middle-class third graders who had been in full-time infant care were less compliant, had poorer work habits and grades, and were less likely to be chosen as preferred playmates by peers compared with schoolmates who had been in part-time infant care or full-time maternal care during the first year of life.

Secure attachment to caregiver can be helpful to an infant insecurely attached to mother. Howes, Rodning, Galluzzo, & Meyers (1988) assessed, via a Q sort technique, infant security of attachment to mother and also to the toddler caregiver in day care. Toddlers were categorized as either secure or insecure with *each* adult. Children insecure with mother *or* with caregiver engaged in less high-level play with their caregivers than those rated secure with *both* the parent and the caregiver. Toddlers categorized as *insecure* with both mother and caregiver had the lowest level of adult play scores and spent the least time engaged with peers.

The future wave of researches into day care and early education will need not only to look at transactional variables between infants and adults who care for them, but to look for the historical and interactive effects of conjoint family *and* child care variables on child outcomes.

The importance and need for further researches into socioemotional outcomes of extensive and part-time care in early infancy lie in the findings that early positive outcomes are associated later on with children's more optimal socioemotional functioning. The Blocks (1983) have demonstrated positive correlations between ego control and ego resiliency at 3 years (the end of the infancy period) and a variety of positive social skills and positive peer popularity ratings at age seven.

REFLECTIONS AND CONCLUSIONS

"A crucial task for many mothers of newborns is to find a balance between their own desires for employment and what they think is best for their infant" (Bower, 1988, p. 221). Yet, care situations for infants currently reflect a range running from awful to superb, from inexpensive to over $200 per week. A great deal of advice is being written for employed parents (Brazelton, 1986). What *can* be done by parents, educators, legislators, and public policy advocacy groups to help this situation?

Ongoing political struggle is needed for a generous national policy for parental leave with infants. During the early months of life, infants and their primary caregivers begin a delicate dance, a dyadic dialogue that fine-tunes their mutual intimacies, initiatives, and adjustments to lead them to fall deeply and delightedly in love with one another. It takes *time* to learn the beloved's body styles, tempos, and signals. Such attunements would certainly be clinically presumed to predict attunement decades later in intimate spousal relationships. Kaplan (1978), from extensive clinical work with infants and mothers, writes:

> The first, or core experience of wholeness comes from the dialogue of oneness, the dialogue of unconditional love . . . . The second experience of wholeness comes after the achievement of separateness from which arises constancy, . . . the capacity to unite love and aggression, . . . the reconciliations of oneness and separateness . . . . Constancy confirms our sense of personal wholeness (pp. 30–31).

Without an initial leisurely time to dialogue and fine-tune their love relationship, both parent(s) and infants are cheated. The disgrace is that other civilized nations, such as Denmark, Israel, and Sweden, have provided legal means to protect these precious months required for the building of a foundation of basic secure attachment, while the United States has yet to enact such legal safeguards.

Infant/toddler workers need professional training and status. Nationally and at the state level, a strong fight is needed to upgrade the status and professionalization of infant/toddler caregiving. Preschool education in many colleges means teaching students about children from 3 years of age onward. It is as if one were to teach a course on human sexuality from the stomach up! Quality caregivers of infants and toddlers require finely honed skills that need to be and can be impervious to late-afternoon or Friday fatigue (Honig, Caldwell, & Tannenbaum, 1973) Teaching toddlers to *share*, to touch *gently*, even to keep hands held in a circle game takes noble and patient efforts and ingenuity. Talking to young toddlers all day in order to enhance, lure, confirm, and expand their early linguistic decodings and encodings is a formidable task. Rare is the infant teacher who has been trained in detail to recognize and support the emergence of prosocial skills, syllogistic reasonings, or receptive and expressive language. The adult with diapering skills but without language and sociable communication skills brings infant care down to an unaccept-able, routine custodial level. The educational risks for infants not lured and chal-lenged by talented "matchmakers" are too great.

Directors need financial and community supports for training infant *educarers* (a term Magda Gerber and Betty Caldwell have both promoted). Without support, many directors may not feel equipped to teach theoretical understandings of Mahler, Winnicott, Erickson, Piaget, or Bowlby. Without training, some caregivers with at-risk infants may fall into the trap of *re-creating* the negative interactions that stressed or abused toddlers are accustomed to receive and elicit (Wittmer & Honig, 1988).

Access to researches that illuminate optimal caregiving practices adds intellec-tual "ammunition" to the caregiver's armamentarium of knowledge. An admirable example of important research for infant educators is Matas, Arend, and Sroufe's (1978) work detailing the intricate way in which the *securely attached* infant may be an "ornery" toddler in a routine situation in which toy cleanup is required, but is revealed as a zestful, persistent problem solver, cooperative with maternal sugges-tions in trying to solve difficult tool-using tasks. In contrast, an insecurely attached toddler gives up easily, is oppositional, and falls apart when task demands are difficult. Training provides *theory, researches, clinical evidence* (such as Brazelton's work on lowered enuresis rates when toilet training is started later and carried out in support-ive and gentler ways), and of course *pragmatic skills* in responsive caregiving, health, safety, nutrition, and room arrangements.

Fortunately, materials are available for training—books, articles, and short informative summaries of researches and of clinical findings (Honig & Wittmer, 1982). Videotapes and filmstrips exist in abundance for infant caregivers (see Honig and Wittmer, 1988, for an annotated bibliography of audiovisual training materials for infant caregivers). Without direct *targeted training monies*, most directors will not be able to afford to send their staff to courses or workshops. State and community funds and college tuition credits, given in exchange for student access to observe in centers, can support caregiver participation in sources and workshops. Turkey raffles and sales of roses at Mother's Day are simply too chancy as techniques for generating training funds—though they may be sufficient to buy some sorely needed new toys for toddlers.

Wages must adequately compensate infant educators. Political work is not enough. Economic supports must be given if teachers of infants and toddlers are to be paid an honorable wage for professional work. Since the ideal ratio for infants in groups is one caregiver for three or four infants, this means that the costs of quality care will be beyond the means of all but affluent parents. State and federal monies are required to subsidize training courses and salaries for well-qualified infant teachers, even when preschool educators in the same facility are able to be paid from fees and some community funds. Tax monies have been spent on airplane company cost overruns, on tobacco subsidies, and on savings and loan bailouts; surely the education of our youngest citizens requires no less a response to crisis.

State and federal legislative mandates are required to keep infant and toddler ratios within the limits that will permit high-quality educational experiences. Sustained turn-taking bouts with a perceptive teacher boost cognitive, language, and reasoning skills, and in-depth thinking through a problem about the physics of liquids at the water table or solids in the block corner. When there are dozens of toddlers for one teacher and one aide to care for, then this educationally clarifying type of dialogue becomes logistically impossible.

Family day-care quality needs to be upgraded. We need to designate some centers as training resources to upgrade family day-care quality. Since, overwhelmingly, infants are cared for in family day care, centers should be supported to become *magnets* in communities. Family day-care workers should be able to come to centers to learn more about babies. "Star" quality centers could serve as models with family day-care homes as satellite centers. Vans serving several satellite centers could solve logistic problems of transportation between the family day-care homes and centers.

Modeling by excellent center infant staff, kits of materials available on loan, and special workshops are integral components for such a system. In a recent visit to a family day-care home known for tender cuddling of babies and a tight budget, this writer found only three plastic chewable baby books available, with complex pictures of a beribboned chick, dogs as fire chiefs, and schematic faces. None of the available reading material was suitable for showing and labeling pictures to infants. *Important* pictures—such as a baby, a puppy, a kitty, or a banana—are necessary book ingredients for infants. It is critical (and easy!) to hook babies on books so that they become book lovers very early (Honig, 1985a). Caregivers need more than familiarity with available materials; they need access to supplies of appropriate books for babies.

Formative assessments in centers can build in assurances of quality care. Directors, perhaps with the help of local colleges, need to learn to use available assessment tools as *formative evaluation* to evaluate areas of strengths and need among infant educators. For example, in one center, the director commented to me, "We have used your ABC scales and of course our caregivers came out wonderfully high on body loving—we do a lot of back rubs at nap time and a lot of cuddling. But I had not realized that we were not singing to or reading to the babies as much at all." Easy-to-use checklists, such as ABC, can pinpoint *specific* caregiver interactions that need a boost or a commendation. The new Infant/Toddler Environmental Rating Scale being developed by Dr. Thelma Harms specifically for infant centers will boost the abilities of directors to assess the overall quality of their infant programs.

Industry and workplaces can give support for building high-quality centers.

More employee unions, more industrial parks, and more large corporations are beginning to work with organizations that have expertise in developing, staffing, and monitoring program quality for child care from infancy onward. For example, Resources for Child Care Management in New Jersey has worked with Campbell Soup Company and Johnson & Johnson's world headquarters to initiate on-site child care with quality control from first spadeful in ground breaking to last detail in staff hiring and supervision.

High schools and colleges need to promote child-development courses. For young adults, schools can glamorize and promote courses on parenting and the mysterious lives of those small nonfurry, and nonverbal primates known as human babies. Many well-educated parents and parents-to-be are terrified of a new baby. They may flee back to employment early because they are afraid. All parents need to know how to sink deeply into that rich pool of bodily sensations, in leisurely feeds, tender snuggles, and inspirations of mutual gazing, where bonding, attachment, and the joy of love can be learned.

Pediatric and nursing education can augment supports for optimal infant education. Obstetric and pediatric offices are ideal places to provide pamphlets for parents that explain what parents need to look for in a quality care setting (Honig, 1988). Infancy slide shows in office waiting rooms give parents-to-be and new parents access to materials that reassure, enlighten, and strengthen their abilities to become what Winnicott (1965) has felicitously called "ordinary devoted" or "good enough" parents. Medical school intern and residency requirements in child development can be integrated into the training of pediatricians (Wittmer & Honig, 1987). As professionals, pediatricians and nurses are often in the front line of action to *help parents empathize with infant neediness.* Fears of their needy baby can impel parents to withdraw strong positive emotions for their babies and even lead to anger or emotional unavailability. Some parents need help to tune in to and overcome what Fraiberg et al. (1975) have so arrestingly conjured as "Ghosts in the Nursery"—ghosts from the family's past who haunt and distort relationships so that ancient unresolved griefs, rages, and jealousies are interposed between the parent and the real baby needing to be nurtured in the present.

Learning role-switching skills can increase optimal parenting. Professional parents need to recognize and tackle what I clinically call the "armored parent" or the "Gucci shoe syndrome" in more flamboyant terms. Parents who work in the professional world for long days—and sometimes nights—can find it hard symbolically and literally to take off the fancy clothes that shield them as professionals. Stress-reduction techniques may make it easier for parents to relax, kick off the expensive shoes, get into comfortable clothes, and cuddle with infants at the end of a long day. Genuine encounters with a real parent, *not* an armored professional still clinging to official facets of the self, are imperative for the baby. In an optimal scenario, Bowlby (1988) suggests that "a mother's intuitive readiness to allow her interventions to be paced by her infant" is matched by the infant's readiness to shift rhythms "gradually to take account of the timing of his mother's interventions. In a happily developing partnership each is adapting to the other" (p. 8). Babies need to drape and mold. Winnicott has advised that "the main thing is the physical holding" (1965, p. 54). *Babies need dominion over the caregiver's body.* "Cuddling, lap nuzzling, and lap snuggling give babies the courage to go forth and tackle some of the more difficult early adventures of learning, such as eating solids with a spoon" (Honig, 1983b, p. 4).

Professional polemics abound on the "meaning" of increased avoidance of mother by full-time day care infants (Clarke-Stewart, 1988; Clarke-Steward & Fein, 1983). Avoidant babies in the Ainsworth Strange Situation *may* be adapting reasonably to daily separation rather than reflecting emotional maladjustment, as has been suggested. *They may instead be providing a danger/alert signal for child-development specialists and for parents.* We cannot assume that infant indifference to the specialness of the parent in a reunion situation can be considered more "mature" behavior by an infant in day care. Clinically speaking, we can suggest that the adult who takes off the invisible "armor" of the professional and becomes the "good enough" parent every evening is less likely to have an insecurely attached baby. Cinderella needed a fairy godmother for her transformatoins; modern parents too may need outside supports for becoming unarmored.

Hospitals that have prebirth classes for expectant parents can offer postbirth classes in "Becoming a tuned-in partner with your infant." Parents need to learn about how to be lovers and educators of babies *outside* the womb, not only inside. They need to be prepared for colic, for waking interminably at night for feedings, for differences in temperament styles, for the ways they can use a diapering table for intensive language lessons as well as extensive bottom cleaning.

It is hard to empathize with infant needs unless you know *who* babies are. Thus, familes particularly need to be tuned in to ages and stages. Are they prepared to enjoy the great cusp of joy when, at about a year, a newly locomoting baby cruises off to explore and has a "love affair with the world" (Kaplan, 1978)? Are caregivers prepared for that conflicted period of toddlerhood, the gray period of Mahlerian rapprochement, when the emotionally wildly seesawing toddler wrestles with new needs for autonomy and old needs for merging? Only with the support of insightful and patient adult partners can toddlers and young children make their way toward inner constancy and eventual sturdy independence. Insights and empathy can boost the morale of both the baby and the adult through those difficult times.

Realization is needed that "big" is not best for babies. Small infant/toddler centers are calmer and more homelike for babies. On many kibbutzim in Israel, once there are too many babies in a baby house, another baby house is built. Infants do not thrive in warehouse educational institutions. The challenge to provide quality infant care demands attention not only to ratio and group size, but to the ambiance of the education facility.

This means that the profession of family day-care worker may become even more important as increasing members of infants need early care. Usually, social service agencies are responsible for the licensing of such facilities. Often, training monies are nonexistent for such personnel. Advertisements for adults to run a family day-care facility are often accompanied by no training prerequisites—but by a requirement that the adult have an outside income available! More attention to organizational changes in how family day-care facilities are licensed and how training is provided (through visiting vans? through satellite affiliation with a quality center as previously described?) is urgently needed. The strengths and sensitivities of family day-care workers to serve cultural minorities or non-English-speaking parents are often overlooked in planning for future community needs for child care.

Day-care centers need permanent parent-liaison persons. Some centers are fortunate to have a social worker on staff. Some child care staff actively and competently involve parents. They hold spaghetti suppers, discuss aspects of development, and show slides of children to parents. Other centers have a write-in book in which a parent who has been up all night with a teething baby can write down his or her concerns as the infant is brought in. If child care is to be a true partnership with parents, then there will have to be parenting experts on staff. Parenting experts can handle parent worries, run workshops, give private consultations, and advise caregivers, particularly when a baby is listless, screaming, dull-eyed, or unresponsive over time to the lures and loving overtures of professionally competent staff. Zigler and Turner (1982) suggest that to date, parents and day-care workers have "a failed partnership." In their study, parents spent an average of 7.4 minutes per day in the center, and 10% of the parents did not even enter with their children in the morning.

Funds for a parent-educator troubleshooter/consultant in education facilities will need to be supplied by the community. Parent fees rarely cover the costs of infant care; deficits are frequently made up by using tuition earned from preschoolers' families. Preventive mental health facilities or even a pastoral counseling agency providing family therapy in a community can "adopt" the infant-care setting as a domain where they can take responsibility for staffing and/or provision of consultations in case of need.

In Chicago, supports for parents are provided by the Family Resource Coalition (Weissbourd, 1981). A family drop-in center provides direct help with child rearing, health, housing, and education problems. Family advocacy and community linkages are stressed and relief child care is provided.

SUMMARY

With a concerted effort to train and retain staff, enlighten and empower parents, and compensate adequately those who rear the youngest of our citizens, we shall be able to make a breakthrough in education. From the earliest cradle days, small persons known as infants are entitled to the highest-quality education that parents and caregivers in partnership can provide.

REFERENCES

Ainsworth, M. D. S. (1982). Early caregiving and later patterns of attachment. In M. H. Klaus & M. O. Robertson (Eds.), *Birth, interaction, and attachment* (pp. 35–43). Skillman, NJ: Johnson & Johnson Baby Products.

Ainsworth, M. D. S. (1983). Patterns of infant-mother attachment as related to maternal care. In D. Magnussen & V. Allen (Eds.), *Human development: An interactional perspective* (pp. 35–55). New York: Academic Press.

Badger, E., & Burns, D. (1980). Impact of a parent education program on the personal development of teen age mothers. *Journal of Pediatric Psychology, 5,* 415–422.

Barglow, P., Vaughn, B., & Molitor, N. (1987). Effects of maternal absence due to employment on the quality of infant-mother attachment in a low risk sample. *Child Development, 58,* 945–954.

Bayley, N. (1955). On the growth of intelligence. *American Psychologist, 10,* 805–818.

Belsky, J. (1988). The "effects" of infant day care reconsidered. *Early Childhood Research Quarterly, 3,* 235–272.

Belsky, J., & Rovine, M. J. (1988). Nonmaternal care in the first year of life and infant-parent attachment. *Child Development, 59,* 157–167.

Benn, R. (1986). Factors promoting secure attachment between employed mothers and their sons. *Child Development, 57,* 1224–1231.

Berrulta-Clement, J. R., Schweinhart, L. J., Barnett, W. S., Epstein, A. S., & Weikart, D. P. (1984). Changed lives: The effects of the Perry Preschool Program on youths through age 19. *Monographs of the High/Scope Research Foundation, 8.*

Block, J. H., & Block, J. (1983). The role of ego-control and ego-resiliency in the organization of behavior. In W. Damon (Ed.), *Social and personality development: Essays upon the growth of the child* (pp. 282–320). New York: W. W. Norton.

Bower, B. (1988). From here to maternity. *Science News, 34,* 220–222.

Bowlby, J. (1958). The nature of the child's tie to his mother. *International Journal of Psychoanalysis, 39,* 350–373.

Bowlby, J. (1988). *A secure base: Parent-child attachment and healthy human development.* New York: Basic Books.

Brazelton, T. B. (1986). Issues for working parents. *American Journal of Orthopsychiatry, 56*(1), 14–25.

Bretherton, I. (1985). Attachment theory: Retrospect and prospect. In I. Bretherton & E. Waters (Eds.), *Growing points of attachment theory and research* (pp. 3–35). *Monographs of the Society for Research in Child Development, 50* (1–2, Serial No. 209).

Bretherton, I., & Waters, E. (Eds.). (1985). *Growing points of attachment theory and research. Monographs of the Society for Research in Child Development, 50*(1–2, Serial No. 209).

Bromwich, R. (1981). *Working with parents and infants: An interactional approach.* Baltimore: University Park Press.

Bronfenbrenner, U. (1979). *The ecology of human development: Experiments by nature and design.* Cambridge, MA: Harvard University Press.

Bronfenbrenner, U. (1986). Ecology of the family as a context for human development: Research perspectives. *Developmental Psychology, 22,* 723–742.

Burchinal, M., Lee, M., & Ramey, C. (1989). Type of day care and preschool intellectual development. *Child Development, 60,* 128–137.

Caldwell, B. M. (1986). Professional child care: A supplement to parental care. In N. Gunzen-hauser & B. M. Caldwell (Eds.), *Group care for young children: Considerations for child care and health professionals, public policy makers, and parents* (pp. 3–13). Skillman, NJ: Johnson & Johnson Baby Products.

Caldwell, B. M., & Richmond, J. (1968). The Children's Center in Syracuse, New York. In L. L. Dittman (Ed.), *Early child care—the new perspective.* New York: Atherton Press.

Caldwell, B. M., Richmond, J. B., Honig, A. S., Moldovan, S. E., Mozell, C., & Kawash, M. B. (1968). A day care program for disadvantaged infants and young children—observations after one year. In G. A. Jervis (Ed.), *Expanding concepts in mental retardation* (pp. 103–115). Springfield, IL: Charles C. Thomas.

Caldwell, B. M., Wright, C. M., Honig, A. S., & Tannenbaum, J. (1970). Infant care and attachment. *American Journal of Orthopsychiatry, 40,* 397–412.

Cantwell, M. (1989, January 5). Close to home. *The New York Times,* p. C23.

Chase-Lansdale, I., & Owen, M. T. (1988). Maternal employment in a family context: Effects on infant-mother and infant-father attachment. *Child Development, 58,* 1505–1512.

Children's Defense Fund. (1988). *A call for action to make our nation safe for children: A briefing book on the status of American children in 1988.* Washington, DC: Author.

Clarke-Stewart, K. A. (1984). Day care: A new context for research and development. In M. Perlmutter (Ed.), *Parent-child interaction and parent-child relations in child development: The Minnesota Symposia on Child Psychology* (Vol. 17, pp. 36–58). Hillsdale, NJ: Erlbaum.

Clarke-Stewart, K. A. (1988). The "effects" of infant day care reconsidered. *Early Childhood Research Quarterly, 3,* 293–318.

Clarke-Stewart, K. A., & Fein, G. (1983). Early childhood programs. In M. M. Haith & J. J. Campos (Eds.), *Handbook of child psychology: Vol. 2. Infancy and developmental psychology* (pp. 917–999). New York: Wiley.

Cohen, S. E. (1978). Maternal employment and mother-child interaction. *Merrill-Palmer Quarterly, 24,* 189–197.

Crockenberg, S. (1981). Infant irritability, mother responsiveness, and social support influences on the security of mother-infant attachment. *Child Development, 52,* 857–865.

Cummings, F. (1980). Caretaker stability and day care. *Developmental Psychology, 16,* 31–37.

Dennis, W., & Najarian, P. (1957). Infant development under environmental handicap. *Psychological Monographs, 71* (7, Whole No. 436).

DeVries, R., & Goncu, A. (1988). Interpersonal relations in four year old dyads from constructivist and Montessori programs. *Early Child Development and Care, 33* (1–4), 11–28.

Erickson, M. F., Sroufe, L. A., & Egeland, B. (1985). The relationship between quality of attachment and behavior problems in preschool in a high risk sample. In I. Bretherton & E. Waters (Eds.), *Growing points of attachment theory and research* (pp. 147–166). *Monographs of the Society for Research in Child Development, 50* (1–2, Serial No. 209).

Erikson, E. (1963). *Childhood and society.* New York: W. W. Norton.

Farber, E. A., & Egeland, B. (1982). Developmental consequences of out-of-home care for infants in a low-income population. In E. Zigler & E. Gordon (Eds.), *Day care* (pp. 102–125). Boston: Auburn.

Field, T., Masi, W., Goldstein, S., Perry, S., & Silke, P. (1988). Infant day care facilitates preschool social behavior. *Early Childhood Research Quarterly, 3,* 341–359.

Finkelstein, N. W., Dent, C., Gallagher, J., & Ramey, C. T. (1978). Social behavior of infants and toddlers in a day-care environment. *Developmental Psychology, 14,* 257–262.

Fowler, W. (1978). *Day care and its effects on early development: A study of group and home care in multi-ethnic, working-class families* (Research in Education Series 8). Toronto: The Ontario Institute for Studies in Education.

Fowler, W. (1980). *Infant and child care.* Boston: Allyn & Bacon.

Fraiberg, S. (1977). *Every child's birthright: In defense of mothering.* New York: Basic Books.

Fraiberg, S., Adelson, E., & Shapiro, V. (1975). Ghosts in the nursery: A psychoanalytic approach to the problems of impaired infant-mother relationships. *Journal of the American Academy of Child Psychiatry, 14,* 387–421.

Freud, S. (1940). *An outline of psychoanalysis (SE 23,* 144–207). London: Hogarth Press.

Furman, E. (Ed.). (1987). *What nursery school teachers ask us about: Psychoanalytic consultations in preschools.* Madison, CT: International Universities Press.

Garber, H. L. (1988). *The Milwaukee Project: Preventing mental retardation in children at risk.* Washington, DC: American Association on Mental Retardation.

Goelman, H., & Pence, A. R. (1988). Children in three types of day care: Daily experiences, quality of care and developmental outcomes. *Early Child Development and Care, 33*(1–4), 67–76.

Golden, M., Rosenbluth, L., Grossi, M. T., Policare, J. J., Freeman, H., Jr., & Brownlee, E. M. (1978). *The New York city infant day care study.* New York: Medical and Health Research Association of New York City.

Gordon, I. J. (1969). *Early child stimulation through parent education* (Final Report No. PHS-R-306). Washington, DC: Children's Bureau, Department of Health, Education, and Welfare.

Greenspan, S. I., Wieder, S., Lieberman, A. F., Noren, R. A., Lourie, R. S., & Robinson, M. (Eds.). (1987). *Infants in multirisk families: Case studies of preventive intervention* (Clinical Infant Reports No. 3.). Madison, CT: International Universities Press.

Haskins, R. (1985). Public school aggression among children with varying day-care experience. *Child Development, 48,* 806–819.

Hoffman, L. W. (1984). Maternal employment and the young child. In M. Perlmutter (Ed.), *Parent-child interaction and parent-child relations in child development: The Minnesota Symposia on Child Psychology* (Vol. 17, pp. 240–298). Hillsdale, NJ: Erlbaum.

Honig, A. S. (1974a). Curriculum for infants in day care. *Child Welfare, 53,* 633–643.

Honig, A. S. (1974b). The developmental needs of infants: How they can be met in a day care setting. *Dimensions, 2*(2), 30–33, 60–61.

Honig, A. S. (1977). The Children's Center and the Family Development Research Program. In B. M. Caldwell & D. J. Stedman (Eds.), *Infant education: A guide for helping handicapped children in the first three years* (pp. 81–100). New York: Walker.

Honig, A. S. (1978). Training of infant care providers to provide loving, learning experiences for babies. *Dimensions, 6*(3), 33–43.

Honig, A. S. (1981). What are the needs of infants? *Young Children, 37*(1), 3–10.

Honig, A. S. (1982). Intervention strategies to optimize infant development. In E. Aronowitz (Ed.), *Prevention strategies for mental health* (pp. 25–55). New York: Neale Watson.

Honig, A. S. (1983a). Evaluation of infant/toddler intervention programs. In B. Spodek (Ed.), *Studies in educational evaluation* (Vol. 8, pp. 305–316). London: Pergamon Press.

Honig, A. S. (1983b). Meeting the needs of infants. *Dimensions, 11*(2), 4–7.

Honig, A. S. (1984). Research in review: Risk factors in infants and young children. *Young Children, 39*(4), 60–73.

Honig, A. S. (1985a). The art of talking to a baby. *Working Mother, 8*(3), 72–78.

Honig, A. S. (1985b). High quality infant/toddler care: Issues and dilemmas. *Young Children, 41*(1), 41–46.

Honig, A. S. (Ed.). (1986). *Risk factors in infancy*. London: Gordon & Breach.

Honig, A. S. (1987). The Eriksonian approach: Infant/toddler education. In J. Roopnarine & J. Johnson (Eds.), *Approaches to early childhood education* (pp. 49–69). Columbus, OH: Merrill.

Honig, A. S. (1988). Choosing quality care. *Early childhood update, 4*(1), 1, 7–8.

Honig, A. S. (1989). Quality infant/toddler caregiving: Are there magic recipes? *Young Children, 44*(4), 4–10.

Honig, A. S. (in press). Assessing the preparation of infant/toddler caregivers. In S. Kilmer (Eds.), *Advances in early education and day care,* Greenwich, CT: JAI Press.

Honig, A. S., Caldwell, B. M., & Richmond, J. B. (1986). Infancy interventon: Historical perspectives. *Early Child Development and Care, 26,* 89–93.

Honig, A. S., Caldwell, B. M., & Tannenbaum, J. (1973). Patterns of information processing used by and with young children in a nursery school setting. *Child Psychiatry and Human Development, 3,* 216–230.

Honig, A. S., & Lally, J. R. (1975a). Assessing teacher behaviors with infants in day care. In B. Friedlander, G. Kirk, & G. Sterritt (Eds.), *Exceptional infant: Assessment and intervention* (Vol. 3, pp. 528–544). New York: Brunner/Mezel.

Honig, A. S., & Lally, J. R. (1975b). How good is your infant program: Use an observation method to find out. *Child Care Quarterly, 1,* 194–207.

Honig, A. S., & Lally, J. R. (1981). *Infant caregiving: A design for training*. Syracuse, NY: Syracuse University Press.

Honig, A. S., & Lally, J. R. (1988). Behavior profiles of experienced teachers of infants and toddlers. *Early Child Development and Care, 33,* 181–199.

Honig, A. S., & Wittmer, D. S. (1982). *Infant/toddler caregiving: An annotated bibliography*. Urbana, IL: ERIC Clearinghouse on Early Childhood and Elementary Education. (Catalogue No. 195)

Honig, A. S., & Wittmer, D. S. (1988). *Infant-toddler caregiving: An annotated guide to media training materials*. Sacramento, CA: California State Department of Education.

Howes, C. (1987). Quality indicators in infant and toddler child care: The Los Angeles study. In D. A. Phillips (Ed.), *Quality in child care: The education of young children* (pp. 81–88). Washington, DC: National Association for Young Children.

Howes, C., & Olenick, M. (1986). Family and child care influences on toddler compliance. *Child Development, 57, 202–216.*

Howes, C., Rodning, C., Galluzzo, D. C., & Meyers, L. (1988). Attachment and child care. *Early Childhood Research Quarterly, 3,* 403–416.

Howes, C., & Rubenstein, J. (1985). Determinants of toddlers' experiences in daycare: Age of entry and quality of setting. *Child Care Quarterly, 14,* 140–151.

Hunt, J. M. (1980). *Early psychological development and experience*. Worcester, MA: Clark University Press.

Illingworth, R. S. (1961). The predictive value of developmental tests in the first years, with special reference to the diagnosis of mental subnormality. *Journal of Child Psychology and Psychiatry, 2,* 210–215.

Jacobson, A. L. (1987). Infant-caregiver interactions in day care. *Child Study Journal, 40,* 197–209.

Kagan, J., Kearsley, R. B., & Zelazo, P. R. (1980). *Infancy: Its place in human development.* Cambridge, MA: Harvard University Press.

Kamerman, S. (1986, February). *Infant care usage in the United States.* Report presented to the National Academy of Sciences Ad Hoc Committee on Policy Issues in Child Care for Infants and Toddlers, Washington, DC.

Kaplan, L. (1978). *Oneness and separateness: From infant to individual.* New York: Simon & Schuster.

Katz, L. (1980). Mothering and teaching: Some significant distinctions. In L. Katz (Ed.), *Current topics in early childhood education* (Vol. 3, pp. 47–63). Norwood, NJ: Ablex.

Keister, M. E. (1970). *The "good life" for infants and toddlers.* Washington, DC: National Association for the Education of Young Children.

Klein, R. (1985). Caregiving arrangements by employed women with children under one year of age. *Developmental Psychology, 21,* 56–68.

Lally, J. R., & Gordon, I. (1982). *Learning games for infants and toddlers.* Syracuse, NY: New Readers Press.

Lally, J. R., & Honig, A. S. (1977). The Family Development Research Program. In R. Parker & M. Day (Eds.), *The Preschool in action* (pp. 149–194). Boston: Allyn & Bacon.

Lally, J. R., Mangione, P. I., & Honig, A. S. (1988). The Syracuse University Family Development Research Program: Long-range impact of an early intervention with low-income children and their families. In D. R. Powel (Ed.), *Parent education as early childhood intervention: Emerging direction in theory, research, and practice* (pp. 79–104). Norwood, NJ: Ablex Publishing Corporation.

Lazar, I., & Darlington, K. (1982). Lasting effects of early education: A report from the Consortium for Longitudinal Studies. *Monographs of the Society for Research in Child Development, 47*(2–3, Serial No. 195).

Levenstein, P. (1988). *Messages from home: The Mother-Child Home Program and the prevention of school disadvantage.* Columbus, OH: Ohio State University Press.

Lieberman, A. (in press). What is culturally sensitive intervention with parents? *Early Child Development and Care.*

Lytton, H., Watts, D., & Dunn, B. E. (1987). Early mother-son relations and son's cognitive and social functioning at age 9: A twin longitudinal study. *Early Child Development and Care, 27,* 343–358.

Maccoby, E. E., Snow, M. E., & Jacklin, C. N. (1984). Children's dispositions and mother-child interaction at 12 and 18 months; A short-term longitudinal study. *Developmental Psychology, 20,* 451–492.

Mahler, M., Pine, R., & Bergman, A. (1975). *The psychological birth of the human infant: Symbiosis and individuation.* New York: Basic Books.

Main, M., & George, C. (1985). Responses of abused and disadvantaged toddlers to distress in age-mates: A study in a day-care setting. *Developmental Psychology, 21,* 407–412.

Matas, L., Arend, R. A., & Sroufe, L. A. (1978). Continuity of adaptation in the second year: The relationship between quality of attachment and later competence. *Child Development, 49,* 547–556.

McCartney, K. (1984). Effects of quality of day care environment on children's language development. *Developmental Psychology, 20,* 244–260.

McCartney, K., & Galanopoulos, A. (1988). Child care and attachment: A new frontier the second time around. *American Journal of Orthopsychiatry, 58*(1), 16–24.

Melhuish, E. C. (1986). *Infant day care and social behavior: An analysis of home individual and group care effects.* Urbana, IL: ERIC Clearinghouse on Elementary and Early Childhood Education. (ED No. 277 464)

Moore, T. (1975). Exclusive early mothering and its alternatives: The outcome to adolescence. *Scandinavian Journal of Psychology, 16,* 255–272.

Morgan, G. (1986). Supplemental care for young children. In M. W. Yogman & T. B. Brazelton (Eds.), *In support of families.* Cambridge, MA: Harvard University Press.

New Parents as Teachers Project. (1985). *Executive evaluation summary.* Jefferson, MO: Missouri Department of Elementary and Secondary Education.

Olds, D. (1988). The prenatal/early infancy project. In R. H. Price, E. I. Cowen, R. P. Lorion, & J. Ramos-McKay (Eds.), *14 Ounces of prevention.* Washington, DC: American Psychological Corporation.

Painter, G. (1971). *Infant education.* Los Angeles: Dimensions.

Palmer, F., & Siegel, R. (1977) Minimal intervention at ages two and three and subsequent intellective changes. In M. C. Day & R. K. Parker (Eds.), *The preschool in action* (2nd ed., pp. 3–26). Boston: Allyn & Bacon.

Phillips, D. A., Scarr, S., & McCartney, K. (1987). Dimensions and effects of child care quality: The Bermuda Study. In D. A. Phillips (Ed.), *Quality in child care: What does research tell us?* (pp. 43–66). Washington, DC: National Association for the Education of Young Children.

Phipps-Yonas, S. (1980). Teenage pregnancy and motherhood: A review of the literature. *American Journal of Orthopsychiatry, 50,* 403–431.

Piaget, J. (1958). *The origins of intelligence in children.* New York: International Universities Press.

Pines, M. (1979). Good samaritans at age two? *Psychology Today, 13,* 66–74.

Provence, S. (1983). *Clinical case reports: Infants and parents.* Washington, DC: National Center for Clinical Infant Programs.

Ramey, C., & Gowan, J. W. (1986). A general systems approach to modifying risk for retarded development. In A. S. Honig (Ed.), *Risk factors in infancy* (pp. 9–26). London: Gordon & Breach Science.

Richters, J. F., & Zahn-Waxler, C. (1988). The infant day care controversy: Current status and futrue direction. *Early Childhood Research Quarterly, 3,* 319–336.

Rix, S. E. (1989). *The American woman 1988-1989: A status report.* New York: W. W. Norton.

Rubenstein, J., Howes, C., & Boyle, P. (1981). A two year follow-up of infants in community-based day care. *Journal of Child Psychology and Psychiatry, 22,* 209–218.

Ruopp, R., Travers, J., Glantz, F., & Coelen, C. (1979). *Children at the center: Final results of the National Day Care Study.* Cambridge, MA: Abt.

Rutter, M. (1981). Socioemotional consequences of day care for preschool children. *American Journal of Orthopsychiatry, 51*(1), 4–28.

Sameroff, A. J., & Chandler, M. J. (1975). Reproductive risk and the continuum of caretaking casualty. In F. D. Horowitz (Ed.), *Review of child development research* (Vol. 4, pp. 187–244). Chicago: University of Chicago Press.

Scarr, S., & McCartney, K. (1988). Far from home: An experimental evaluation in Bermuda. *Child Development, 59,* 531–543.

Schaefer, E., & Aaronson, M. (1977). Infant education research project: Implementation and implications of a home tutoring program. In M. C. Day & R. K. Parker (Eds.), *The preschool in action* (2nd ed., pp. 51–72). Boston: Allyn & Bacon.

Schwartz, T. (1983). Length of day-care attendance and attachment behavior in eighteen-month-old infants. *Child Development, 54,* 1073–1078.

Schwarz, J. C., Scarr, S. W., Caparulo, B., Furrow, D., & McCartney, K. (1981, August). *Center, sitter, and home day care before age two: A report on the first Bermuda infant care study.* Paper presented at the annual meeting of the American Psychological Association, Los Angeles.

Schwarz, J. C., Strickland, R. G., & Krolick, G. (1974). Infant day care: Behavioral effects at preschool age. *Developmental Psychology, 10,* 502–506.

Schweinhart, L. J., & Weikart, D. B. (1988). The High/Scope Perry Preschool Program. In R. H. Price, E. L. Cowan, R. P. Lorion, & J. R. McKay (Eds.), *14 Ounces of prevention* (pp. 53–65). Washington, DC: American Psychological Association.

Skeels, H. M. (1966). Adult status of children with contrasting early life experience. *Monographs of the Society for Research in Child Development, 31*(3, Serial No. 105).

Spitz, R. A. (1945). Hospitalism: An inquiry into the genesis of psychiatric conditions in early childhood. *Psychoanalytic Study of the Child, 1,* 53–74.

Sroufe, L. A. (1985). Infant-caregiver attachment and patterns of adaptation in preschool: The roots of maladaptation and competence. In M. Perlmutter (Ed.), *Minnesota Symposium on Child Psychology* (Vol. 16, pp. 41–81). Hillsdale, NJ: Erlbaum.

Sroufe, L. A. (1988). A developmental perspective on day care, *Early Childhood Research Quarterly, 3,* 283–292.

Sroufe, L. A. & Fleeson, J. (1988). Attachment and the construction of relationships. In W. Hartup & Z. Rubin (Eds.), *The nature and development of relationships.* Hillsdale, NJ: Erlbaum.

Stallings, J. A. (1980). An observational study of family day care. In J. C. Colbert (Ed.), *Home day care: A perspective.* Chicago: Roosevelt University.

Thomas, F., & Chess, S. (1977). *Temperament and development.* New York: Brunner/Mazel.

Tizard, B., Cooperman, O., Joseph, A., & Tizard, J. (1972). Environmental effects on language development: A study of young children in long-stay residential nurseries. *Child Development, 43,* 337–358.

United States Bureau of the Census. (1987). *Who's minding the kids? Current population reports, Series P-70.* Washington, DC: U. S. Government Printing Office.

Vandell, D., & Corasaniti, M. A. (1989). *Variations in early child care: Do they predict subsequent social, emotional, and cognitive differences?* Unpublished paper, University of Texas, Dallas.

Vaughn, B. E., Deane, K. E., & Waters, E. (1985). The impact of out-of-home care on child-mother attachment quality: Another look at some enduring questions. In I. Bretherton & E. Waters (Eds.), *Growing points of attachment theory and research* (pp. 110–135). *Monographs of the Society for Research in Child Development, 50*(1–2, Serial No. 209).

Vaughn, B., Egeland, B., Waters, E., & Sroufe, L. A. (1979). Individual differences in infant-mother attachment at 12 and 18 months: Stability and change in families under stress. *Child Development, 50,* 1203–1214.

Vaughn, B. E., Gove, F. L., & Egeland, B. (1980). The relationship between out-of-home care and the quality of infant-mother attachment in an economically disadvantaged population. *Child Development, 51,* 1203–1214.

Waters, E. (1978). The reliabilty and stability of individual differences in infant-mother attachment. *Child Development, 49,* 483–494.

Weikart, D. (1988). A perspective on High/Scope's early education research. *Early Child Development and Care, 32,* 29–40.

Weinraub, M., Jaeger, E., & Hoffman, L. (1988). Predicting infant outcome in families of employed and nonemployed mothers. *Early Childhood Research Quarterly, 3,* 361–378.

Weissbourd, B. (1981). Supporting parents as people. In B. Weissbourd & J. Musick (Eds.), *Infants: Their social environments* (pp. 169–183). Washington, DC: National Association for the Education of Young Children.

Werner, E. (1989). High-risk children in young adulthood: A longitudinal study from birth to 32 years. *American Journal of Orthopsychiatry, 59*(1), 72–81.

Willerman, L., Broman, S. H., & Fiedler, M. (1970). Infant development, preschool IQ and social class. *Child Development, 4,* 69–77.

Winnicott, D. W. (1965). *The maturational processes and the facilitating environment: Studies in the theory of emotional development.* Madison, CT: International Universities Press.

Wittmer, D. S. (1986). Model versus modal child care for children from low-income families. *Zero to Three, 6*(5), 8–10.

Wittmer, D., & Honig, A. S. (1987, March). *Implementing a child development model for training pediatricians.* Poster presented at the 64th annual meeting of the American Orthopsychiatric Association, Washington, DC.

Wittmer, D. S., & Honig, A. S. (1988). Teacher re-creation of negative interactions with toddlers. *Early Child Development and Care, 33,* 77–88.

Zigler, E., & Turner, E. (Eds.). (1982). *Day care: Scientific and social policy issues.* Boston: Auburn.

Zuravin, S. J. (1988). Child maltreatment and teenage first births: A relationship mediated by chronic sociodemographic stress? *American Journal of Orthopsychiatry, 58*(1), 91–103.

5

Kindergarten in Our Nation

GAYLE MINDES
Roosevelt University–Chicago

Kindergarten is the focus of great interest in schools and society today. This interest can be viewed from a variety of perspectives: elementary school teachers and administrators, parents, legislators, and the public. Values and attitudes influence the formulation of each perspective. From each perspective, a variety of strategies have been used to accomplish a specific, advocated role for the kindergarten in American society.

HISTORICAL BACKGROUND

Differing perspectives on the kindergarten have determined its nature throughout history. Frederick Froebel, who originated the kindergarten in Germany during the 1800s, perceived the kindergarten as a way of achieving freedom for the individual. Self-activity, self-control, and play were to enable children to develop freely and be at one with God. However, the authoritarian Prussian government of Germany did not view this perspective well, and the kindergarten never flourished in its native land (Weber, 1984).

In contrast, the kindergarten found fertile soil in America. Numerous individuals and agencies adopted the perspective of freedom, of self-activity, and of gentle treatment of children. Churches and social agencies set up "free" kindergartens for the poor to offset the conditions of poverty and to provide a "proper moral focus" in the lives of young children. In order to foster their particular values, individuals and private schools started tuition-based programs (Ross, 1976).

By the 1890s, women's groups were lobbying for kindergartens in public schools so that programs would be available for all children. Nevertheless, only 12% of the nation's preschoolers were enrolled in kindergarten by the mid-1920s (Shapiro, 1983). In the 1930s, the federal government sponsored early childhood education through the Works Progress Administration to relieve unemployment as well as to enrich the lives of children. The 1940s found a continued federal involvement through the Lanham Act, which provided employed women with day care for their children. Following *Sputnik* in 1957 and the ensuing critiques of American education, "achievement began to replace adjustment as the highest goal of the American way of life" (Dowley, 1971, pp. 17–18).

Approximately 95% of all children today are enrolled in kindergarten (Sava, 1987). Most five year olds, therefore, are educated in public schools. Indeed, this trend is highlighted by six states that have lowered mandatory school entrance to age five (Robinson, 1987). Those responsible for public education develop and agree upon curriculum goals. A growing number of four year olds are entering public school. States are developing programs to supplement special education, Head Start, and Chapter 1 programs. These programs are being directed to the families of the poor, who have less access to preschool education. Whereas 67% of four year olds from families with incomes greater than $35,000 receive preschool education, only 33% of young children whose families earn less than $10,000 per year were enrolled in prekindergarten programs (Marx & Seligson, 1988). Twelve states have legislation to provide programs for the at-risk four year old (Neuweiler, 1988).

This chapter will examine the various perspectives toward the kindergarten. A description of each will be presented and the convergence of the several perspectives discussed. The early childhood educator's role will be assessed. In conclusion, this chapter suggests directions for the future of the kindergarten as well as the role of the early childhood educator in determining these directions.

PERSPECTIVES

Elementary School Perspective

From this perspective, kindergarten is the first rung on the academic ladder of formal school. The curriculum taught in formal school often is determined from the top down (Shepard & Smith, 1986). Goals are portioned downward from the outcomes expected at the top. This viewpoint has impacted the kindergarten curriculum. A kindergarten curriculum revolving around mastery of top-down academics is the result. Children complete workbooks and worksheets. Direct instruction is the typical teaching method. Teachers deliver formal teacher-proof lessons to young children, who must achieve mastery of the content.

A lockstep, direct instruction curriculum is the result of the perspective that the child is an empty vessel to be filled. The teacher's role in such a kindergarten is to deliver the curriculum into the child. The elementary school classroom is a place of large group instruction and so then is the kindergarten classroom (Hatch & Freeman, 1988a). Copying from the chalkboard is an integral part of the whole class activity. Identical worksheets are distributed to each child for coloring, cutting, and pasting. Packaged curriculum assignments are completed. Individualization of instruction rarely occurs in these classrooms—that is, all children must complete all worksheets. Modification of assignments, selection of certain papers for certain children, rarely occurs. Individualization only refers to when the assignment is completed.

Teachers using this perspective frequently implement ability grouping. They conduct assessment, usually with standardized instruments accompanying the commercial curriculum materials, to determine which children have absorbed the required learning. Those who cannot demonstrate mastery frequently either are retaught using the same methods, are referred out of kindergarten, or are failed. In some cases, the children who fail kindergarten are placed in developmental kindergartens or developmental first grades, giving them an extra year to catch up with their peers (Peck, McCaig, & Sapp, 1988).

Because large numbers of children fail to achieve the prescribed curriculum material (Uphoff & Gilmore, 1985), some school systems conduct screening procedures prior to kindergarten.

> As a result, more and more 5 and 6 year olds are denied admission to school or are assigned to some form of extra-year tracking such as "developmental kindergarten," retention in kindergarten, or "transitional" first grade (Meisels, 1987, Shepard & Smith, 1988). Such practices (often based on inappropriate uses of readiness or screening tests) disregard the potential, documented long-term negative effects of retention on children's self-esteem and the fact that such practices disproportionately affect low-income and minority children; further, these practices have been implemented in the absence of research documenting that they positively affect children's later academic achievement (Gredler, 1984; Shepard & Smith, 1986, 1987, Smith & Shepard, 1987) (National Association for the Education of Young Children [NAEYC], 1988, p. 42).

Many children are denied entrance into kindergarten on the basis of a test score (Peck et al., 1988). This practice occurs regardless of whether the instruments used to screen children out of kindergarten are valid or not (Meisels, 1987).

In some instances, the elementary school community has changed the entrance age for kindergarten in response. This change requires a child to be five prior to August 1 rather than prior to December or January (Peck et al., 1988). The school views this requirement as a way to protect the younger, and perhaps unready, children from potential failure.

School systems also have responded to the large numbers of children unable to master the top-down academic curriculum by lengthening the day. Pressured with numerous competencies and goals for the five year old to master, teachers and school administrators believe that a full, rather than half-day, program will give more time on task (Fromberg, 1987).

Parent Perspective

The elementary school regards parents as consumers of information and implementers of school-determined goals. That is, the school plans parent education programs to deliver what the school has decided is important or missing from parenting in their communities (Schlossman, 1976). The school seeks parental involvement on its own terms (Kagan & Zigler, 1987). This involvement customarily means dropping the child at the door of the classroom, attending two yearly parent conferences, attending whole-school parent meetings, and occasionally volunteering for a special classroom project or field trip organized by the teacher.

As a special population of the public, parents maintain high expectations for the kindergarten experience. This experience is regarded as the first "real year" of school, a beginning of the first publicly funded no-cost day care, in some cases. For the parent and the child, it is an emotionally significant milestone (Galinsky, 1987). From their memories of school, many parents believe that young children learn to read, to write, and to compute with books, papers, and pencils during the kindergarten year. Parents have learned from the media that today's children are smarter. Children watch educational television, read with their parents, and may have had day-care and preschool experiences. In the parents' view, then, their five year old should be particularly ready for school experiences. Many parents look at academic experiences for their children as the next logical step from preschool (Hatch & Freeman, 1988b; Hills, 1987). Most accept the notion of assessment for the purpose of categorization of children. Such categorization experiences are part of their own school memories. They are dismayed, however, when services are withheld because of eligibility criteria, that is, when their children are "not ready" on the basis of a screening measure or are short of the established entrance age.

Parents look to the school for guidance regarding their children, but they come as educated customers. They view their children as bright, capable learners and expect the school to teach their children what they need to know.

Legislator and Public Perspective

The various state legislatures want action on the part of local schools (National Governors' Association, 1986, 1987). Particularly in large cities, schools have failed to prepare children for society (National Council on Excellence in Education, 1983). Legislators now believe what the professionals have long known—that the early years are learning years in the child's life. In this regard, perhaps one of the most widely read studies in recent years is the High Scope Longitudinal Study (Schweinhart, Weikart, & Larner, 1986). Based on the media interpretation of this study and a report by the Committee for Economic Development in *Children in Need: Investment Strategies for the Educationally Disadvantaged* (1987), legislators found the impetus to draft legislation for permissive and mandated programs in early childhood education and kindergarten. They believe that these programs will prevent the future failure of our public schools. In response to past failures and to the various concerned educational communities, legislative mandates have been drawn for improvements in public education—for change of age of entry dates and for full-day kindergarten to deliver more programs earlier in the child's life (Blank, 1985). These include special programs for the child of poverty circumstances, for the academically at-risk child, and for the handicapped child, including children of ages three and four. In some cases, legislators have attached special funding to these mandates, e.g., Head Start and special education (Morado, 1986, 1986b). In Georgia, legislation requires young children to sustain an exit test from kindergarten, before first grade. If a young child fails the test, the child must be retested and may be placed in a "developmental" first grade to "catch up." Since a similar testing program began in Minneapolis in 1984, 11–14% of kindergartners have failed (O'Neil, 1988).

Legislatures also have addressed the competency of the entire educational profession through proposals for testing of teachers and changing educational requirements for certification. The public now wishes to more firmly control entry to the profession. In some cases, legislators sought professional input for the definition of these changes. Unlike other professions, educators are not in control of the entry process for teachers. State legislatures in recent years have firmly determined that for the "public good," certification will be a publicly determined procedure (American Association of Colleges for Teacher Education, 1988).

PERSPECTIVE CONVERGENCE

Many parents, elementary school teachers, administrators, legislators, and the public view kindergarten as the beginning of formal schooling. Formal schooling from their perspectives connotes books, papers and pencils, and serious learning. However, the convergence of views breaks down over issues of screening, school entry age, and length of school day. Parents customarily want their children to enter school as soon as possible and certainly by age 4.5 or 5 years. Frequently, they do not perceive the differences between four and five year olds or believe that teachers should cope with the differences. As more of the academic content of the K–12 curriculum has been pushed down to kindergarten, elementary school teachers have urged that children be older before they attend school (Shepard & Smith, 1986, 1988). Thus, parents and teachers are at odds. There is some congruence, however, on the issue of whole-day experience.

Many parents want kindergarten to be an all-day experience. A full-day program provides parents with day care for their children. Administrators in elementary school are concerned about the space and budgetary implications of the whole-day delivery system (Peck et al., 1988). Legislatures are encouraging such programs. They do so in the interest of providing more education to young children to make up for perceived deficiencies in the family environments, which may then offset the potential problems of the future (Kagan & Zigler, 1987; Zimiles, 1986).

As the demographics of our society change, parents have increased interest for programs to serve younger children in the public school, that is, a junior kindergarten experience. Part of this demand is rooted in the desire for more day care; part is the desire for academic advancement (Zimiles, 1986). Some administrators in elementary schools seek to be responsive to expressed parent needs. These individuals may also have extra space in buildings due to declining enrollments. They accordingly have developed programs for three- and four-year-old children. Sometimes these programs are on a fee-for-service basis and usually are viewed as different than the regular elementary program. In the past, some programs in public schools have existed for four year olds. These programs are the exception, rather than the norm (Hymes, 1987). For example, New York state has permissive legislation for public school programs for all four year olds (Campbell, 1987). During the depression and World War II, federally supported programs existed for four year olds in schools. These programs always have been for limited purposes and of limited duration (Takanishi, 1977).

There is a long history of special programs for young children regarded to be at risk, such as handicapped children or those involved in the Head Start program (Bricker, 1986). These publicly funded programs generally have been regarded as separate entities serving special populations. As the issues affecting kindergarten are addressed, these special programs for younger children must be kept in mind so that policies addressing common issues can be developed and implemented.

Considering the perspectives of elementary school teachers, administrators, parents, legislators, and the public, what is the appropriate role for early childhood educators in this process of determining appropriate practices in kindergarten education? How should early childhood educators respond? In the next section, responses of these educators and recent collaborative efforts will be described.

EARLY CHILDHOOD EDUCATION PROFESSIONAL RESPONSE

As professionals, early childhood educators have been extremely active in asserting their knowledge and right to be responsible for kindergarten. From the early childhood point of view (Bredekamp, 1987; Moyer, Egertson, & Isenberg, 1987), kindergarten is part of the same developmental stage as preschool or nursery school programs. The five year old in kindergarten learns and behaves in similar ways to three and four year olds. Three-, four-, and five-year-old children learn through experience with concrete objects and through interaction with their peers and teachers. Young children acquire knowledge at school that builds on the foundations established at home. From birth, infants learn through playing with their primary caretakers and significant others. As they grow, young children use small toys in their playful interactions with others to enlarge their understanding of the world. In this way, young children form cognitive understandings and develop social relationships and emotional competence (Biber, 1984).

With this perspective in mind, curriculum for kindergarten is most appropriately child centered (Chicago Association for the Education of Young Children, 1984). The emphasis is on the child's active exploration and discovery of the environment. Teachers facilitate the child's learning by providing experiences that will be stimulating and nurturing. Workbooks are not a part of this environment. The curriculum is individualized because "developmentally appropriate" implies accommodation to individual variation among the group of children. Teachers consider individual child background and experience as well as individual learning style when planning the learning activities (Bredekamp, 1987). Evaluation of children and their programs is conducted to assist in refining the management of the curriculum. Activities are varied in response to evaluation of individual children. Only unusual cases and situations warrant a referral for a child to be moved from one program to another. These referrals only follow the interpretation of multiple sources of information about the child (NAEYC, 1988). From the early childhood perspective, parents are partners in the educational process. They are involved in the teaching, the assessment, and the educational decision making regarding their children (Bredekamp, 1987).

In the early 1980s, professional associations began publishing position papers that described and emphasized the early childhood perspective regarding best kindergarten procedures and practices. These papers were written in response to practices that early childhood educators observed as they had contact with public schools, teachers, and parents. The culmination of this grass-roots effort resulted in the publication of *Developmentally Appropriate Practice in Early Childhood Programs Serving Children From Birth Through Age 8* by the National Association for the Education of Young Children in 1987 (Bredekamp).

Some collaborative efforts, beginning in the early 1980s, were directed toward the assertion of the responsibility of early educators for programmatic control of kindergarten. These early efforts include the *Joint Statement on Literacy Development and Pre-First Grade* (Early Childhood and Literacy Development Committee of the International Reading Association, 1986). This statement emphasizes the role of active learning in the development of early literacy in young children. Young children learn to read by writing and talking about their own experiences. Later, pictures and books become important tools for learning to read. Partners in this statement were the Association for Supervision and Curriculum Development, the International Reading Association, the National Association for the Education of Young Children, the National Association of Elementary School Principals, and the National Council of Teachers of English. These efforts continue now and hopefully will continue into the 1990s with the efforts of major educational professions leading the way. Collaboration between the National Association for Elementary School Principals and the National Association for the Education of Young Children resulted in dialogue and joint press conferences about the best practices for young children (Elkind, 1987; Sava, 1987).

The Association for Supervision and Curriculum Development (ASCD) sponsored an Early Education Study Institute in 1987 to bring together public schools working with early childhood education issues and prominent early childhood educators. A book (Warger, 1988) of the proceedings further disseminates the issues to the membership, a membership composed largely of educational administrators and curriculum supervisors. A 1988 Kindergarten Trends Conference along similar lines was planned in response to ASCD member interest. Early childhood educators were the keynoters for this conference directed toward public school personnel. In 1988, ASCD chose early childhood education programs to participate in a network. The Early Childhood Network is a process to identify the best principles and practices. This affirmation tends to put quality programs into the observable realm. Although these programs are broader than kindergarten, the practice of including early childhood educators in the selection of program models serves to highlight the important role that early childhood educators have in the supervision and authority for such programs, including kindergarten.

Because the position papers, conferences, publications, and collaborative efforts have been successful in highlighting the key responsibility for early childhood educators in kindergarten education, the efforts must continue. Nevertheless, the idea that early childhood educators should determine goals and procedures for kindergarten is not universally accepted. Many classroom teachers report that they have little or no part in decisions that determine curriculum and instructional methodology. Instead, those decisions are made by administrators, influenced by public demand for more stringent educational standards and the ready availability of commercial, standardized tests (National Association of Early Childhood Specialists in State Departments of Education, 1987).

Many elementary school personnel believe that elementary school curriculum already is organized for kindergarten-age children. This belief stems from the notion that curriculum can be broken into small pieces and absorbed by the learner at any age (Carnine, Carnine, Karp, & Weisberg, 1988). Curriculum specialists develop the end goal for the twelfth grader and extend it back to include activities for the kindergartner. This material, simplified and watered down for young children, can be successfully "spoon-fed" to four and five year olds.

The early childhood profession has not completely reached the legislators or the public either. Legislators in recent years have accepted monitoring responsibility for all of education. Some of these legislative mandates have impacted program practice. Testing of children and the setting of standards for achievement are among the mandates that are diametrically opposed to appropriate developmental practice (Peck et al., 1988).

The justification for early childhood educators' responsibility in kindergarten needs to be publicly and clearly stated. Early childhood educators can make contributions to the understanding of the complexities of kindergarten education. These contributions include a clear notion of development, an interpretation of the role of play in the young child's life, and the collaborative role of parents in early childhood education. Early childhood education must articulate these contributions to elementary school teachers and administrators, to parents, to the legislators, and to the public. Points to be included in this articulation are out lined in the following section.

EARLY CHILDHOOD EDUCATION PROFESSIONAL CONTRIBUTION

The clear *notion of child development* stemming from the early childhood education perspective specifically impacts four issues. These issues directly related to kindergarten are (1) age of entrance to school, (2) screening measures, (3) appropriate curriculum, and (4) length of school day.

Developmental principles impact upon the age at which children should be when entering kindergarten. Because children develop at different rates, a wide variation exists in typical behavior, making the appropriate age for entering school an arbitrary question (Shepard & Smith, 1987). What kind of program a child enters is the more crucial variable. Elkind (1987) has stated that if the program is developmentally appropriate, then it will accommodate the variation in growth patterns. If, however, the program is paper-and-pencil based, the age for appropriate kindergarten entrance may be closer to age seven. At this age, most children are developmentally ready for paper-and-pencil tasks. Due to precedence, desire for child care, and the focus on early academic achievement, this recommendation is unlikely to be acceptable to parents, elementary school teachers, administrators, legislators, and the public. Thus, early childhood educators must continue to articulate the developmentally appropriate kindergarten curriculum.

An appropriate curriculum is one rooted in the philosophy that young children are curious, active learners whose view of the world is different from adults'. Primary goals of the kindergarten experience are the fostering of social competence and the capacity to function and learn in groups (Bredekamp, 1987).

Developmental principles also impact on the question of screening measures. If assessment is developmentally based, it serves as a guide for appropriate programming for young children. If the principle of variation in development simply serves as a justification for eligibility into programs, then programmatic decisions are made that cannot be supported with the instruments used (Meisels, 1985; NAEYC, 1988).

The question of the length of the school day—half day or whole day—is another arbitrary issue (Puleo, 1988). If the curriculum is child centered and developmentally appropriate, a whole-day experience can be beneficial. It may contribute to a less fragmented day with fewer transitions from school to day care. It also may enhance academic performance for children who are at risk of academic failure (Fromberg, 1987). If, however, the curriculum is paper-and-pencil based or fragmented by many special subject teachers, then the whole day may be inappropriate for kindergartners (Peck et al., (1988).

These four issues—age of entrance, screening for entrance, curriculum practices, and length of school day—are intertwined with developmental principles. They require continued, informed articulation on the part of early childhood educators.

The *role of play* in the young child's life demands particular attention. Early childhood educators must continue to advocate for a curriculum including this crucial area. Some educators misunderstand the role of play as a learning medium. Many elementary school teachers and principals characterize play as an "extra," a nonessential activity. Parents perceive play as "messing about," an activity that can be performed at home. However, through play, children develop their real understanding of the world. They develop cognitively, physically, and socially/emotionally through the active, happy pursuit of self-selected activities (Rubin, Fein, & Vandenberg, 1983). Joyful participation in school sets the stage for the expectation that school is fun, a worthwhile place to be, and a place to be successful. In this way, the child maintains what Katz (1988) has called a disposition to learn. The child maintains his curiosity.

Contrast this experience to that of the young children who fail in their first experience in kindergarten. They cannot complete the worksheets. Their motor coordination is not fully enough developed. They have not "passed" the test and are sent to a "developmental" program, away from their peers. Although the effect of such practices is still being clearly documented, it seems that the practice of retaining children has been largely detrimental to children (May & Welch, 1984; Shepard & Smith, 1986, 1988; Walker & Madhere, 1987). In the long term, early retention resulted in dropping out at the high school level (Chicago Public Schools, 1987).

Parents as partners is the principle by which early childhood educators have operated (Honig, 1979). This results in shared decision making about program implementation strategies for individual children. Parents and teachers establish goals for learning experiences at school and at home that mesh. Parents are welcomed into the classroom as meaningful participants on a regular basis. Respect for individual family contributions to the curriculum is fostered. This partnership viewpoint is one that recognizes the contribution of parents to the educational process. The parent is not treated as an external consumer who must be "educated" by the experts at school. With the parent as partner in the child's education, self-esteem is fostered for the child and his family. Academic goals can be understood by the parent and reinforced at home. The climate is established for mutual respect and mutual problem solving.

Although early childhood educators may be convinced of the legitimacy of their position regarding expertise in kindergarten, the other important participants—parents, elementary school teachers and administrators, and the legislators and the public must be convinced (Karweit, 1988).

THE TASK FOR EARLY CHILDHOOD EDUCATION PROFESSIONALS

Early childhood educators need to continue to publicize the contributions that they can make to kindergarten education. Important contributions can be made by early childhood educators because they have special knowledge that comes from early childhood education research: (1) a clear notion of child development, (2) an awareness of the role of play in the young child's life, and (3) an understanding of the collaborative role of parents. Early childhood educators, as the experts, must present facts, illustrations, and a firm commitment to best practices in kindergarten. Elementary school teachers, administrators, parents, legislators, and the public need to read and hear the "knowledge base" as outlined by Spodek (1986) and others (Bredekamp, 1987; Peck et al., 1988).

> Early childhood is clearly one of the most crucial periods of development in the entire life span. It is characterized by rapid development, major shaping influences, and vulnerability, with long-term consequences. All of us who are concerned with the early years are searching for ways to prevent the heavy casualties that are taking place and to minimize the grave disparities that still persist in this country in opportunities for development, education, and health. These issues, indeed, go to the very heart of our future as a people. They have consequences not only for the individual but for the fabric of our entire society (Hamburg, 1987, pp. 6–7).

SUMMARY

Early childhood efforts at communicating with elementary school teachers, administrators, parents, legislators, and the public are particularly important when early childhood practices may be different than the common perspective and conventional wisdom (Hatch & Freeman, 1988b). If books, papers, and pencils are not appropriate curriculum for kindergartners, then what is appropriate and why, and how does it work? If entrance to school and length of school day are essentially arbitrary decisions, then what kind of program is needed to create a "teachable" group? What is necessary to avoid failure for young children? If current screening procedures are being misused, then what kinds of procedures are appropriate for making decisions about group placement for kindergartners?

It is imperative that these and other questions be discussed, in both the professional and public arena. It is through such action that best practices can be assured in kindergarten so that the convergence of perspectives of the elementary school teachers, principals, parents, legislators, and the public is influenced by early childhood educators, who are the real professionals in kindergarten education.

REFERENCES

American Association of Colleges for Teacher Education. (1988). *Teacher education policy in the states*. Washington, DC: Author.

Biber, B. (1984). *Early education and psychological development*. New Haven: Yale University Press.

Blank, H. (1985). Early childhood and the public schools. *Young Children, 40*(4), 52–55.

Bredekamp, S. (Ed.). (1987). *Developmentally appropriate practice in early childhood programs serving children from birth through age 8*. Washington, DC: National Association for the Education of Young Children.

Bricker, D. (1986). *Early education of at risk and handicapped infants, toddlers, and preschool children.* Glenview, IL: Scott, Foresman.

Campbell, B. (1987). From national debate to national responsibility. In S. L. Kagan & E. F. Zigler (Eds.), *Early schooling: The national debate* (pp. 65–82). New Haven: Yale University Press.

Carnine, D., Carnine, L., Karp, J., & Weisberg, P. (1988). Kindergarten for economically disadvantaged children: The direct instruction components. In C. Warger (Ed.), *A resource guide to public school early childhood programs* (pp. 73–99). Alexandria, VA: Association for Supervision and Curriculum Development.

Chicago Association for the Education of Young Children. (1984). *Kindergarten: What should be.* Chicago: Author.

Chicago Public Schools, Department of Research and Evaluation. (1987). *High school dropouts, 1981–85.* Chicago: Author.

Committee for Economic Development. (1987). *Children in need: Investment strategies for the educationally disadvantaged.* New York: Author.

Dowley, E. M. (1971). Perspectives on early childhood education. In R. H. Anderson & H. G. Shane (Eds.), *As the twig is bent* (pp. 12–21). Boston: Houghton Mifflin.

Early Childhood and Literacy Development Committee of the International Reading Association. (1986). Joint statement on literacy development and pre-first grade. *The Reading Teacher, 39,* 822–824.

Elkind, D. (1987). Superbaby syndrome can lead to elementary school burnout. *Young Children, 42*(3), 14.

Fromberg, D. P. (1987). *The full-day kindergarten.* New York: Teachers College.

Galinsky, E. (1987). *Thre six stages of parenthood.* Reading, MA: Addison-Wesley.

Gredler, G. (1978). A look at some important factors for addressing readiness for school. *Journal of Learning Disabilities, 11,* 284–290.

Hamburg, D. A. (1987). *Fundamental building blocks of early life.* New York: Carnegie Corporation.

Hatch, J. A., & Freeman, E. B. (1988a). Kindergarten philosophies and practices: Perspectives of teachers, principals, and supervisors. *Early Childhood Research Quarterly, 3,* 151–166.

Hatch, J. A., & Freeman, E. B. (1988b). Who's pushing whom? Stress and kindergarten. *Phi Delta Kappa, 70,* 145–147.

Hills, T. W. (1987). Children in the fast lane: Implications for early childhood policy and practice. *Early Childhood Research Quarterly, 2,* 265–273.

Honig, A. S. (1979). *Parent involvement in early childhood education* (2nd ed.) Washington, DC: National Association for the Education of Young Children.

Hymes, J. L. (1987). Public school for 4 year olds. *Young Children, 42*(2), 51–52.

Kagan, S. L., & Zigler, E. F. (Eds.). (1987). *Early schooling: The national debate.* New Haven: Yale University Press.

Karweit, N. (1988). A research study: Effective preprimary programs and practices. *Principal, 67*(5), 18–21.

Katz, L. G. (1988). Engaging children's minds: The implications of research for early childhood education. In C. Warger (Ed.), *A resource guide to public school early childhood programs* (pp. 32–52). Alexandria, VA: Association for Supervision and Curriculum Development.

Marx, F., & Seligson, M. (1988). *Public school early childhood study: The state survey*. New York: Bank Street College.

May, D. C., & Welch, E. L. (1984). The effects of developmental placement and early retention on children's later scores on standardized tests. *Psychology in the Schools, 21,* 381–385.

Meisels, S. J. (1985). *Developmental screening in early childhood: A guide* (rev. ed.). Washington, DC: National Association for the Education of Young Children.

Meisels, S. J. (1987). The uses and abuses of developmental screening and school readiness testing. *Young Children, 42*(2), 4–6 + .

Morado, C. (1986a). Prekindergarten programs for 4 year olds: Some key issues. *Young Children, 41*(5), 61–63.

Morado, C. (1986b). Prekindergarten programs for 4 year olds: State involvement in preschool education. *Young Children, 41*(5), 69–71.

Moyer, J., Egertson, H., & Isenberg, J. (1987). The child-centered kindergarten: Position paper of the Association for Childhood Education International. *Childhood Education, 63,* 235–242.

National Association of Early Childhood Specialists in State Departments of Education. (1987). *Unacceptable trends in kindergarten entry and placement*. Distributed by state departments of education.

National Association for the Education of Young Children. (1988). NAEYC position statement on standardized testing of young children 3 through 8 years of age. *Young Children, 43*(3), 42–47.

National Council on Excellence in Education. (1983). *A nation at risk*. Washington, DC: Author.

National Governors' Association. (1986). *Time for results*. Washington, DC: Author.

National Governors' Association. (1987). *Results in education*. Washington, DC: Author.

Neuweiler, H. (1988). State briefs. *AACTE Briefs, 9,* 8 + .

O'Neil, J. (1988). Failure at age five? New Georgia testing policy draws fire. *ASCD Update, 30,* 1 + .

Peck, J. T., McCaig, G., & Sapp, M. E. (1988). *Kindergarten policies: What is best for children?* Washington, DC: National Association for the Education of Young Children.

Puleo, V. T. (1988). A review and critique of research on full-day kindergarten. *Elementary School Journal, 88,* 427–437.

Robinson, S. L. (1987). The state of kindergarten offerings in the United States. *Childhood Education, 63,* 23–28.

Ross, E. D. (1976). *The kindergarten crusade: The establishment of preschool education in the United States*. Athens: Ohio University Press.

Rubin, K., Fein, G., & Vandenberg, B. (1983). Play. In P. Mussen (Ed.), *Manual for child psychology: Social development* (pp. 694–774). New York: Wiley.

Sava, S. G. (1987). Development, not academics. *Young Children, 42*(3), 15.

Schlossman, S. L. (1976). Before home start: Notes toward a history of parent education in America, 1887–1929. *Harvard Education Review, 46,* 436–467.

Schweinhart, L. J., Weikart, D. P., & Larner, M. B. (1986). Consequences of three preschool curriculum models through age 15. *Early Childhood Research Quarterly, 1*(1), 15–45.

Shapiro, M. S. (1983). *Child's garden: Kindergarten movement from Frobel to Dewey*. University Park: Pennsylvania State University Press.

Shepard, L. A., & Smith, M. L. (1986). Synthesis of research on school readiness and kindergarten retention. *Educational Leadership, 44,* 78–86.

Shepard, L. A., & Smith, M. L. (1987). Effects of kindergarten retention at the end of first grade. *Psychology in the Schools. 24,* 346–357.

Shepard, L. A., & Smith, M. L. (1988). Escalating academic demand in kindergarten: Counterproductive policies. *Elementary School Journal, 89,* 135–147.

Smith, M., & Shepard, L. (1987). What doesn't work: Explaining policies of retention in the early grades. *Educational Leadership, 45,* 129–134.

Spodek, B. (1986). Using the knowledge base. In B. Spodek (Ed.), *Today's kindergarten: Exploring the knowledge base, expanding the curriculum* (pp. 137–143). New York: Teachers College.

Takanishi, R. (1977). Federal involvement in early education (1933–1973): The need for historical perspectives. In L. Katz (Ed.), *Current topics in early childhood education* (Vol. 1, pp. 139–163). Norwood, NJ: Ablex.

Uphoff, J. K., & Gilmore, J. (1985). Pupil age at school entrance—How many are ready for success? *Educational Leadership, 43,* 86–90.

Walker, E. M., & Madhere, S. (1987). Multiple retentions: Some consequences for the cognitive and affective maturation of minority elementary students. *Urban Education, 22,* 85–102.

Warger, C. (Ed.). (1988). *A resource guide to public school early childhood programs.* Alexandria, VA: Association for Supervision and Curriculum Development.

Weber, E. (1984). *Ideas influencing early childhood education.* New York: Teachers College.

Zimiles, H. (1986). The social context of early childhood in an era of expanding preschool education. In B. Spodek (Ed.), *Today's kindergarten: Exploring the knowledge base, expanding the curriculum* (pp. 1–14). New York: Teachers College.

6

When Delay Isn't Procrastination

RAYMOND S. MOORE
Moore Foundation–Washougal, WA

with DENNIS R. MOORE
Moore Foundation–Washougal, WA

Frequent presumptions these days in use of early childhood education (ECE) research remind me of an experience in 1950 while picking boysenberries on a crowded trellis in California's Napa Valley. I reached out to push away a small green branch, only to be startled as it moved slightly by itself. I looked closer to discover that it was a baby rattlesnake! As a California native, I had encountered many rattlers, but they had always been on or near the ground and in subdued grayish, green, brown, and black hues. This dangerous little fellow was a bright green with almost undetectable markings, a dead ringer for the berry vine. Just so, educators often assume faulty practices are productive, and misinterpret sound research to be against children's welfare.

Our title for this chapter in no sense suggests delay for educating young children. "Education" here isn't synonymous with schooling. It involves parental precepts, example, and leadership at least as much as the teacher at school. We believe youngsters should be educated from birth and their parents helped to understand their likely needs even before conception. Our chief concern here is about the relative accountability and skills of the family and the state in rearing and educating them.

We are particularly interested in correct interpretation and application of ECE research that (1) stands the test of replicability and selfless interpretation and (2) is cross-fertilized with reliable findings in ECE-related disciplines. We will illustrate these two points to show how and why ECE research must be carefully examined and interpreted. Then we will provide research evidence for delaying school entrance and early formal schooling. And finally we will show how the home fits best in the educational pattern as it seeks a harmonious balance of the mental, physical, moral, and social powers in its children.

THE EXAMINATION AND INTERPRETATION

Take Head Start as a prime object of ECE research. For over 20 years, the United States Department of Health and Human Services (HHS) and the old Department of Health, Education, and Welfare (HEW) have depended primarily on one unreplicated study in Ypsilanti, Michigan, to justify spending billions of taxpayer dollars.

Was the research sound? Was it properly used? HHS staffers privately declare that because it reaps the votes of the underprivileged, Head Start has become a political football in a costly congressional game. Somehow, early on, HHS discarded Home Start—the program some researchers thought was HHS's most productive child-care arm and that is enjoying new respect. Despite its productive service to homes and close similarity to the present highly successful Ypsilanti experiment, members of congress somehow found it less politically viable than Head Start.

Head Start money not only gets out votes, but also puts butter on researchers' bread and gives comfort to vested interests like the NEA, which want mandatory all-day kindergarten and all children in school by ages three or four. Similar interests have been carried so far that in 1972, California State School Superintendent Wilson Riles declared readiness "outmoded" ("Getting Smarter," 1971). He greased the legislative skids to authorize schooling for all California children down to age two and a half (Moore, Moon, & Moore, 1972). Fortunately, alert researchers saw its dangers, and wise legislators voted it down.

We speak of "vested interests" because, as we shall shortly see, such educators and educational groups have hardly a research leg to stand on. They seem less concerned with children than dollars and jobs. In our analysis of more than 8,000 ECE studies under federal grants, we could not find one replicable study that suggests that day care or kindergarten is desirable for a child who can have a normal home (Moore, R. S., & Moore, D. N., 1975, 1979).

Nevertheless the Ypsilanti study was well done. They began by studying "storefront" Head Start operations under the direction of skilled professionals and well-trained paraprofessionals. Yet in a few years, it became apparent to these perceptive specialists that they would serve children and families far better if they spent more of their time with target children and families in their homes instead of in institutional settings (L. J. Schweinhart, personal communication, April 28, 1981, May, 1988; Schweinhart & Weikart, 1986). Thus they became parent educators in a fuller sense, teaching home management and insuring that their influence spread out to other children in each family—along lines pioneered by Phyllis Levenstein (1971) in New York, L. G. Daugherty (1963) in Chicago, Mildred Smith (1968) in Flint, Michigan, and in the South, Susan Gray (1969, 1971, 1974) and Barbrack and Horton (1970), where results were unusually cost effective and consistently satisfying.

There are wide differences between typical lay-oriented Head Start operations and the sophisticated, highly professional Ypsilanti program, which has prospered in well-financed continuity for over 20 years. In fact, it has been so well financed that to replicate it nationally would break the government bank. HHS and the Congress have either deliberately ignored or astonishingly overlooked this vast difference between highly professional, home-oriented Ypsilanti Head Start and conventional Head Start, which for years were at least as diverse as Rolls Royce and Yugo.

The unique Ypsilanti study rightly reported positive results, especially after centering its efforts more in the home. Typical Head Start has never consistently survived similar scrutiny. University of Chicago's Benjamin Bloom (1980), Head Start "father," along with Westinghouse Learning Corporation (1970) and others, has long considered Head Start a failure.

Yet HHS uses Ypsilanti data to justify standard Head Start operations. HHS apparently pays little heed to its critics, including some of its own staffers, who dare not press the matter. So HHS promotional literature and appeals to Congress have been largely based on deliberately or ignorantly skewed rationales, i.e., on expensive and unique Ypsilanti rather than typical Head Start. The HHS sales pitch is so convincing and pervasive that even conservative Republican Senator Jeremiah Denton, for a while a key figure in HHS matters, told us he was convinced of Head Start's viability (although perceptive Democratic Congresswoman Edith Green deeply doubted HHS claims).

But the sequel here is as interesting and perhaps even more potentially damaging than the main feature. HHS stands by while educational associations and other vested ECE interests use the Ypsilanti data on disadvantaged children to suggest that Head Start should be applied in principle to all normal children. This is much like saying that if hospitals help ill children, all healthy youngsters should be hospitalized, too. In all these plans, no consideration is given to possible damage to families.

So much for misinterpretation and misapplication of ECE research. Another striking example demonstrates the lack of cross-disciplinary interest and activity among researchers themselves, which ultimately insures that only a skewed or partial picture will be offered to those on educational frontiers.

Outstanding researchers like David Elkind (1970, 1981, 1987) correctly determine that we are rushing our children into school and burning them out. Yet Elkind, president of the National Association for the Education of Young Children (NAEYC), appears to be unaware of the findings of Urie Bronfenbrenner (1970) and others that parents are more positive socializers of children than are peers, or of Stanford's Albert Bandura that peer dependency (and its social contagion) is pervasive among preschoolers (Bandura & Huston, 1961; Bandura, Ross, & Ross, 1961; Bandura & Walters, 1963). Nor yet that there is fifteen times the likelihood of communicable disease (United States Communicable Disease Control Center, 1984) and fifteen times the incidence of negative aggressive acts (Farran, 1982) among day-care children as in a normal home. So Elkind, a scientist who fears burnout, strangely advocates day care, loaded as it is with serious risks.

American educators in general demonstrate an indifference to sound research when it's uncomfortable or inconvenient or confronts their vested interests. Nor are they alone. Our studies in Japan and northern and central Europe have found educators there also well set in their ways (Moore, Kordenbrock, & Moore, 1976). Among the few exceptions we have seen are Alaska, when that state found that early schooling endangered the vision of Eskimos; Norway, when its kindergarten experiment did not turn out as expected; and the Philippines, when educators learned the value of work education.

Speaking specifically of ECE research, University of North Carolina Professor Earl Schaefer (1971), former head of ECE research for the National Institutes of Health, lamented that "although much [ECE] research data has been generated . . . they have as yet had minimal impact on educational planning . . . " (p. 14). When I was graduate research and programs officer for the United States Office of Education, Morvin Wirz (personal communication, July 19, 1972), head of our Division of Handicapped and Rehabilitation, insisted, "So many of our programs . . . operate from the gut level—without basis in research. Drawers are full of research, but they are ignored."

Such indifference to the mental and emotional health of children is not new. The pages of history outline great cycles—e.g., Chaldean, Medo-Persian, Grecian, and Roman—that began with vigorous cultures awake to the needs of children and ended with families surrendering to the state—on advice of Plato, Aristotle, and others. Yet stronger familial societies inevitably won ("Education vs.," 1941; Zimmerman, 1947).

Research provides links from past to present and offers moving perspectives on children today, like Greece and Rome and their persuasive examples of reasons for declining literacy, academic failure, widespread delinquency, and rampant peer dependency. These four problems act in concert to deny our goal of happy, confident children—healthy in body, mind, and spirit.

Whether or not we can be conclusive about causes, America's decline from an estimated 90% literate population in the last century to today's 50% who have survival literacy parallels our scramble to institutionalize children earlier (*The Adult Performance,* 1983). By "survival" literacy, we mean the ability to keep a bank account or complete a job or a driver's license application.

DELAYING FORMAL SCHOOLING AND INSTITUTIONAL LIFE

Instead of studying how best to meet their needs, we often put our little ones out of the home, away from environments that best produce secure, outgoing, healthy, happy, creative children. Both in our research analyses and our basic studies at Stanford (Forgione & Moore, 1973) and the University of Colorado Medical School (Metcalf, personal communication, March 22, 1974, 1975), we were forced to conclude that America is rushing its little ones out of the home and into school long before most, particularly boys, are ready (Moore, R. S., & Moore, D. N., 1975, 1979), and that no children should be confined in formal, structured classrooms before age eight or ten, and for some, even age twelve.

The effect on mental and emotional health is deeply disturbing, so much so that boys, whose maturity lags behind girls about a year at normal school entry, outnumber girls thirteen to one in learning-failure classes and eight to one among the emotionally disturbed (Soderman, 1984). It is apparent that most educators have little understanding of the depression, sense of failure, and disaster bred by forcing youngsters to repeat a grade. Yet our Stanford team found that no state in America makes provision in its school laws for this late maturing of boys (Forgione & Moore, 1973)!

University of California, Berkeley, learning psychologist William Rohwer, basing his conclusions in part on investigations in twelve countries by Sweden's Torsten Husen (1967) offers a solution much like thousands of home-teaching parents have found:

> All of the learning necessary for success in high school can be accomplished in only two or three years of formal skill study. Delaying mandatory instruction in the basic skills until the junior high school years could mean academic success for millions of school children who are doomed to failure under the traditional school system (Rohwer, 1971, p. 314).

Dr. James T. Fisher, who in his prime was considered by many to be the dean of American psychiatrists, would also agree (Fisher & Hawley, 1951). At age eight, instead of to school, his wealthy father sent him west to learn how to punch cattle and work with his hands. He returned home to Boston at age thirteen unable to read or write, and was "the most bowlegged boy in Boston" (Fisher & Hawley, p. 14). He graduated well from a Boston high school 3 years later, convinced that he was something of a genius until he found that any normal child could do it if he "could be assured of a wholesome home life and proper physical development" (Fisher & Hawley, p. 14). Dr. Fisher added that such a plan "might provide the answer to . . . a shortage of qualified teachers" (Fisher & Hawley, p. 14).

Rohwer and Fisher's solution would delay school entrance at least until the child is eleven or twelve—ages that in our research picture become critical. Urie Bronfenbrenner (1970) and his Cornell University team, for instance, found that children who spend more of their time with their peers than their parents until at least the fifth or sixth grades (about ages eleven or twelve) become peer dependent. They knuckle under to peer values, which Bronfenbrenner calls "social contagion." Listed here could be almost any habit, manner, obscenity, finger sign, rivalry, ridicule, drug, alcohol, or sexual practice, and even kinds of music that conflict with normal family values. Such peer dependency brings losses of self-worth, optimism, and respect for, and even trust in, peers. Surprisingly, attractiveness of peers does less to force this dependency and these losses than children's feelings of parental indifference or rejection.

No wonder then that consistent, warm parental responsiveness leads the Smithsonian Institution's formula for genius and leadership (McCurdy, 1960). Harold McCurdy, the study's chief investigator, adds two other ingredients to the recipe: (1) very little time spent with peers, and (2) much free exploration in which parents encourage children's interests, motivations, and creative bents in working out their own fantasies (in contrast to adult-contrived videos, comic characters, and other learning crutches). McCurdy noted:

> The mass education of our public school system is, in its way, a vast experiment on reducing . . . all three factors to a minimum; accordingly, it should tend to suppress the occurence of genius (1960, p. 33).

Another reference to the 11–13-year age range is the Bar Mitzvah transition for Jewish children—when they are considered to reach the age of responsibility at about twelve for girls and thirteen for boys. This is particularly interesting not only in terms of Bible references to the age of Christ when he first went to Jerusalem and reportedly outwitted the rabbis at age twelve, but also in terms of current cognition research at Oklahoma University (Quine, 1965).

There David Quine (1965), until recently a counselor and math and science specialist from the Richardson, Texas, public schools, is studying the differences between conventionally schooled children and youngsters taught at home primarily through informal methods—with a great deal of warm parental responsiveness and considerable freedom to explore and create on their own. Working with Professors Ed Merrick and Jack Renner, Quine is confirming Jean Piaget's findings that average conventionally educated children reach the period of "formal operations" (consistent, adult-level reasoning) at about ages fifteen to twenty. But home-taught children, who are taught informally and responsively and given freedom to explore, develop adult-level cognition between ages ten and eleven or twelve.

Here we have a sound guide for parents who are willing to make the effort to build truly thoughtful children. When mothers and fathers respond often and warmly, using more and more *whys* and *hows* in their conversations as their children mature, when they identify their offsprings' interests and capitalize on them, when they lay down consistent precepts and set sound examples in values and manners, they build children of great mental, physical, and spiritual stability and power. And parents are badly needed in this role for a much longer period of their children's lives.

Sociability

It is well known that children are generally not sound role models, particularly in groups outside the family. Little wonder that the Smithsonian found that the history of genius consists largely of children who were reared at home.

The average owner of a fine dog is more careful in obedience training him than most parents are of their children. The owner would laugh you to scorn or answer angrily if you suggested that he send his young dog down to the kennel or pound daily in a yellow group cage to receive some socializing by his peers. He knows that a dog's manners and normal restraint go out the window the moment he moves in with the pack. Yet that is precisely the exercise most American early schoolers go through each school morning, beginning in the school bus.

The sociability developed via peers, which is so prominently hailed by most school officials and parents, is in fact an undesirable, negative quality embracing *narcissism*—the "me-first" ethic—instead of the more positive trait of golden-rule *altruism.* It builds *age-segregation,* as children are virtually caged with their peers, instead of the far more desirable quality of *age-integration,* where children get along well with all ages, colors, and creeds. Bronfenbrenner (1970) and colleagues lay the blame for this social contagion primarily at the door of our schools.

CONFRONTING READINESS

Whether or not the child is desirably socialized, top learning psychologists warn that early formal schooling is burning out our children. Many teachers who attempt to cope with these youngsters are also burning out. *The learning tools of the average child who enrolls today between the ages of four and six or seven are neither tempered nor sharp enough to cope with the academic litter that increasingly is tossed at them.*

During the 1950s and 1960s, Paul Mawhinney (1964), Director of Pupil Personnel, and other psychologists in Michigan's elite Grosse Pointe School District decided on an experiment to enroll four and five year olds in school. Money was never a problem in this wealthy district. For fourteen summers, a testing program was carried out to select early entrants for kindergarten. Parents fought to have their children accepted and were often angered if the children were rejected. Yet after 14 years, Mawhinney found:

1. Nearly one-third of the entrants became poorly adjusted.
2. Only about one out of twenty was judged to be an outstanding leader at the end of the experiment.
3. Nearly three out of four were lacking in leadership.
4. About one in four of the very bright entrants was either below average in school or had to repeat a grade.
5. The experiment was a failure, and for many, a personal experience in failure, destroying their self-respect.

After only 5 or 6 years of this experiment, Grosse Pointe psychologists had misgivings. Yet they were forced to continue the experiment for nearly 9 more years because of pressures from the parents, who insisted on the superiority of their young children. Sadly, these children felt incapable of doing what was expected of them, when if they had been allowed to develop normally, their prospects were in virtually every case outstanding. Even worse for many, they appeared to sense that they had not lived up to parents' expectations and had disappointed them in a significant way.

Similarly in Montclair, New Jersey, Principal John Forester (1955) studied 500 children from kindergarten through high school. He found that those pupils who were very bright but very young at the time of school entrance did not realize their potential. They tended also to be physically less mature, emotionally less stable, and less likely to exercise leadership than those who were not rushed. Forester feared that early school entry and formal kindergarten—as demanded by the NEA, other vested interests, and uninformed laymen today—not only may result in maladjustment in school, but that it may have "an adverse effect on adult life."

RESEARCH EVIDENCE

We have already offered enough research evidence, we believe, to satisfy the average objective thinker about delaying formal studies. Yet there is much of a specific nature to be told, for regardless of the overwhelming evidence, unobjective thinkers daily demonstrate political power and ability to lead us down education's primrose path. They may need more evidence.

We find that we risk national survival when we realize what we ignore: All replicable evidence, as far as we can tell, points in one direction, namely toward letting little children grow naturally and in balance mentally, physically, spiritually, and socially so that their values are established before they are institutionalized. All developmental aspects in children's lives point in this natural direction, e.g., their senses, cognition, neurophysiology, maternal attachment, and other readiness factors.

Their Senses

Vision

Children's senses are tools they use to convey facts and acts into their mental mixers—their brains. Whether we speak of vision, hearing, taste, touch, or smell, the senses generally mature on an intersensory basis. That is, they average out in maturity for most children between the ages of eight and ten, with some stabilizing later, but little, if any, earlier.

More than 3,000 studies have been made along these lines by the Optometric Extension Program of the American Optometric Association, with consistent findings that young children's eyes should not be put upon with much reading at least for the first 6 to 8 years (Moore, R. S., & Moore, D. N., 1975, 1979). During the first 8 to 10 years, their reading should be limited to 15 or 20 minutes at a time, for they need rest through refocusing their eyes on distant objects—which is a much more natural activity for those ages than close-up reading or drawing.

Vision is a broad-based neuropsychological process; that is, it involves the brain as well as the eye (Krippner, 1971). Even though a single, clear visual image may be received by the eye, a child still may not be able to decode printed material because of deficiencies in organization and interpretation in the central nervous system (CNS) due to lack of maturation. Though it is generally accepted that the newborn's eye is as fully functional as the adult's, other factors affect overall vision—from the differences in plasticity due to age to the developmental advancement of the visual cortex and related CNS factors.

Development of the eye itself corresponds somewhat with that of the nervous system as a whole. During the first 3 years of life, the eye increases in size (Robinson & Tizard, 1966). Yet there is no drastic change in refraction (Young, 1970). Then there is a clear visual progression from 3 to 7½ years of age, on the average, with visual perception disabilities virtually disappeariang after age ten in the normal child (Frostig, Lefever, & Whittlesey, 1963). By the age of thirteen or fourteen, the eye usually reaches its maximum growth (Young, 1970). At the time when most children enter school, the visual-perceptive mechanisms are still incomplete, compared to the development of adult mechanisms (Dyer & Harcum, 1961). So myopia is frequently the result of prolonged looking at near objects at an early age (Young, 1970).

Two Texas ophthalmologists, Henry Hilgartner, M.D., (1962) of Austin, and Frank Newton, M.D., (personal communication, October 24, 1972) of Dallas, independently reached the same conclusions. They found that as school entrance ages moved from a relatively unpressured age eight around 1908 to a strictly enforced age six in the early 1930s, the incidence of myopia (abnormal nearsightedness) changed from one in seven or eight in 1910 to one out of five by 1962.

Similar reports came from Francis Young (Young & Lindsley, 1969) of Washington State University, who evaluated older Eskimos who had little or no formal schooling before Alaska became a state. He then examined Barrow, Alaska, preteen children who had been in school since age six. He found, depending on their ages, that 58% to 68% of all the children were already visually crippled. He later told us personally that by late teens, the figure rose to 88%.

W. Ludlum (1974) supports Young's findings, suggesting that while the cornea is fully developed at birth, growth of other parts of the human eye continues to the ages of nine to eleven. He warned against formal reading programs or any extended voluntary reading by children earlier than ages six or seven. A few years ago, Dr. Hilgartner told us he seldom sees a twelve year old with normal vision anymore.

Hearing

Auditory accuity and perception is similarly a broad-based neuropsychological process and is also a function of age, although most children seem to achieve it somewhat earlier than visual maturity (Marty & Scherer, 1964; Stevenson & Siegel, 1969). Fairly satisfactory auditory perception is generally achieved by age eight (Wepman, 1960, 1968). This follows consistent increase in auditory perceptual ability from age five, so that there is a clear difference between the interpreting and ordering of auditory stimuli in the average third grader and in the first-grade child (Impellizzeri, 1967; Riley, McKee, & Hadley, 1964).

Nearly every family has "hearing" experiences that create consternation, impatience, or trouble because parents don't understand. Others are often comical. For example, Saralee Rhoades of Missouri found her children pledging allegience to the American flag, then throwing themselves down in great hilarity and commotion. When she investigated, she found that they heard "fall" instead of "for all" at the end of the pledge, so thay thought they were simply following orders. Others have been heard to pray, "Our Father, which art in heaven, Howard [instead of 'hallowed'] be thy name." Many never do get over these early auditory discrimination errors—such as saying, "I axed him" for "I asked him" or "keep tract" for "keep track." President Carter always said "new-kew-ler" when he meant "nuclear" (new-clear).

When integrating vision and hearing with taste, touch, and smell, none of which are mature in most children before ages eight to ten, you can understand why many children under classroom teachers and peer pressures do poorly in reading. Add to this the failure of many teachers to understand that there is no special reason why immature children should not see letters backward (mirror imaging) or that they should not naturally read in any particular direction. Japanese script, for example, runs from left to right or right to left, or very often from top to bottom.

We know a lot about reading, but no one knows exactly how we read! We agree with the Michigan Reading Association's bumper sticker that proclaims, "The child who reads is the child who was read to." But, we repeat, no one knows exactly how this all happens. We do know, however, that when children's learning tools are not yet sharp and tempered by maturity, there will be delays in reading and other skills.

Now put yourself in the place of this otherwise bright and creative five year old, faced with pressures to perform, but with a "shovel" yet in the tinfoil stage. It may not turn into sharpened steel for a year to 5 or 6 years. Yet you give the child a task as hard as shoveling snow or gravel from your driveway! Richard and Penny Barker's Britt learned to read at age four and her sister, Maggie, at eleven. Yet by the time Maggie was twelve, she was reading at least as skillfully as Britt did when she was twelve. Early reading doesn't necessarily suggest greater brilliance!

On the other hand, this all does suggest that our mandating little kids into formal, scheduled, structured work before they have had a chance to grow up naturally can, from one perspective, be considered a form of child abuse. The emotional lashing they take from their peers and often from teachers, while trying to lift an unbearable load, is akin to ancient torture, only it might be much more damaging than the lashes once given to village sluggards. The sheer dereliction of states who mandate little boys into school and subject them to the same constraints as they lay on the more mature little girls says something about the ignorance or selfishness of those who make laws. Are we afflicted with madness? What do we have against our children?

It has been clearly demonstrated that a late-starting child, given time to mature, will quickly catch up to and usually pass children who have entered school earlier, and with much less likelihood of insecurity, depression, neurosis, failure, and failure's twin—delinquency. This freedom to grow in the family nest is particularly crucial to handicapped or "exceptional" children, who usually suffer from the cruelty of which groups of children are capable—as sure as a pack of dogs will mercilously humiliate a young newcomer and quickly destroy the obedience and manners so carefully trained into him. Rivalry and ridicule become shafts of barbed steel in the hearts of children who are immature, slow, or otherwise exceptional.

The practice of special education that has flowered in the last generation is often one of the cruelest jokes of all. Many, if not most, of the children exiled to what many kids consider the garbage pile are basically bright and creative youngsters who haven't been given time to grow up. We have found that so-called dyslexia, in at least ninety-nine out of a hundred cases, is not true dyslexia at all. For dyslexia is by definition "an impairment of the ability to read due to a brain defect" (*Random House Dictionary,* 1966, p. 446). True dyslexia is actually rare. But misdiagnosis of learning disability is rampant. We seem somehow compelled to fill up our "special-ed" classes. Honest educators say that "somehow" to a greed for dollars and jobs, including federal subsidies, that has no relationship whatsoever to true professionalism, which holds the developmental needs and welfare of the child paramount to all other considerations. Some are frank to say that if they don't go after their share of federal dollars, taxpayers may see that they lose their jobs.

Cognition

We have already referred to the Quine studies and to Piaget. Suffice it to say, Piaget called the rushing of little children "the American thing." When some of us spent time with him and his assistant, Barbel Inhelder, at Geneva in the 1970s, he seemed neither alarmed nor desperate about the American rush. He simply seemed dismayed, stoical, and rather helpless at Americans' disregard for sound research. This has also been noted by Piagetian authority John L. Phillip (1969).

If Americans want thoughtful children, they must be concerned about their thought processes. The Quine study should be a warning here. Piaget (1962) pointed out that decisions involving a combination of several ideas are not easily made until eleven or twelve years of age. Hans Furth (1970) adds that these general concepts of the developing intelligence evolve whether the child goes to school or not.

It is popular these days to point to Japan's educational system as a model. Having lived there for a number of years and having come close to many of Japan's leading educators, we know well of their lament at their historic lack of creativity. They readily admit that they can pick up others' inventions and improve on them. They consider themselves a rigidly disciplined society, but do not claim to be a creative people. Their astonishing success may well derive more from their self-discipline and their close family ties—two areas in which America pretty well trails the industrial world. Yet despite Japan's strong family closeness, educational pressures are felt by many of their leaders to be responsible for the highest child suicide rate in the world.

You almost certainly have noted by now that these various maturity levels— senses, cognition, brain development, sociability, etc.—come together or integrate roughly between the ages of eight and twelve. We call this the children's IML or integrated maturity level—the approximate time they are ready for formal, structured learning (Moore, R. S., & Moore, D. N., 1975, 1979). One child, even a twin, may develop rapidly in vision, and his sibling more rapidly in auditory discrimination, but most children will level out in these maturational levels and be far more ready for institutional life by ages ten to twelve than by five or six. The IML may be as important—or more so—for school readiness as IQ and other inventories have been for school counseling; it offers a clear and impressive planning base for parents and teachers.

If children appear to have no physical sensory deficiencies, educators often assume that their senses are ready to accomplish the usual school tasks. However, Morency and Wepman (1973) found that the child who enters school perceptually unready (visually, auditorily, intersensorily, etc.) will have difficulty in school achievement and will unlikely be able to catch up even after the perceptual processing ability is fully developed. When academic pressures are imposed before the IML, there is genuine risk that the sensory avenues may be damaged or closed or immature and the child will be learning handicapped. This is one explanation why astonishing increases in special education enrollments have paralleled lowering of school entrance ages.

Jensen (1969), McCarthy (1955), Kohlberg (1968), Olson (1947), and Brenner and Stott (1973) are among the many researchers who insist that readiness involves experience as well as sensory readiness and/or that children may differ 4 or 5 years or more in reaching both sensory and cognitive maturity. Brenner and Stott's 15-year study on children's readiness led them to generalize that the older children are, the better they will function and structure their environments and the more they will have in experience and understanding of the world. And the greater their body of knowledge before they go to school, the more successful they will be at the beginning and in subsequent school years. Joseph Halliwell's (1966) examination of all the available studies comparing early and late school entrants brought the same conclusions (Halliwell & Stein, 1964). This is also a clear reason why children who start later, and usually in a higher grade, will shortly be well ahead of early starters in achievement and leadership.

Neurophysiology: The Brain

This is far too vast an area to treat fairly as a small segment of this chapter. A decent synopsis may be found in our book *School Can Wait* (Moore, R. S., & Moore, D. N., 1979), or, for lay reading, in *Better Late Than Early* (Moore, R. S., & Moore, D. N., 1975). Yet let it be said that brain development (neurophysiological readiness—reasonable maturity of the central nervous system, including the ability to coordinate perceptual processes) is a variable frequently overlooked in evaluating school readiness.

The central nervous system (CNS) is not structured to mature as a single unit or organ, but rather as a complex interworking of many highly sophisticated lesser elements. Each separate functional area has its own timing and sequence of development. We speak here of myelination (sheathing of nerve fibers), lateralization (melding of the hemispheres of the brain), brain weight, etc.

Furthermore, and importantly, *the structure and the function of the human brain appear to move along together in the learning process* (Ellingson & Wilcott, 1960; Huttenlocher, 1966; Moore, R. S., & Moore, D. N., 1975, 1979; Rabinowicz, 1974; Scherer, 1968; Yakovlev, personal communication, July 25, 1972; Yakovlev & Lecours, 1967). Yet we are cautious about specifically limiting any of these and about relating one to another. At birth, the brain is about one-quarter of the adult weight, possessing virtually all its brain cells and all major brain regions. By 6 months, its weight has doubled, but thereafter growth slows down; from 2 years until adolescence, it is relatively uniform. The brain continues to grow in mass until about age twenty-five, but CNS maturation is not necessarily uniform. It is generally useless, even dangerous, to presume upon or toy with this process in the young child by overloading the CNS.

While we are only at the threshold of understanding brain growth and maturation, we repeat neurophysiologists' findings that CNS function becomes possible as structure develops. There are qualitative breaks in the unfolding of intelligence and conscious experience. From our current understanding of brain development, these also follow the growing capacity simultaneously to process multisensory information. Replicated research evidence suggests this capacity is not fully accomplished until ages eight to ten or even later (Moore, R. S., & Moore, D. N., 1975, 1979).

This helps us understand the conclusions of Elkind (1970, 1981, 1987), Rohwer (1971), and Husen (personal communication, November 23, 1972)—who (with Rohwer's help) found from his studies of twelve or thirteen foreign countries that the earlier children enter school, the more likely they are to hate it. Once again we use the analogy of tempering and sharpening of tools: Young children's tasks often become more frustrating to them than being told to cut down a good-sized tree with a dull ax or knife.

Maternal Attachment

If there is any area of child development on which researchers agree, it is on the crucial importance of maternal attachment. This does not deny the need for paternal attachment, but recognizes the mother as generally closest to the child in the early years. Leading students such as Mary Ainsworth (1969, 1972), Sylvia Bell (1971; personal communication, September 10, 1975), John Bowlby (1952, 1969, 1973), Marcelle Gerber (1958), J. L. Gewirtz (1972a), R. A. Spitz (1949), L. J. Yarrow and F. A. Pederson (1972), and others are alarmed at the movement away from mother and the home. Dr. Bowlby (1952), then ECE head of the World Health Organization and acknowledged dean in the maternal attachment arena, suggested that a home must be very bad before it is bettered by a good institution. He was concerned about breaks in maternal attachment before age eight.

The sum of the thinking of these authorities is that attachments and quality of care influence learning from birth into the school years. The strength and quality of attachment is principally determined by the amount and kind of care given by the mother or mother figure. For those mothers who suggest that they give quality time in lieu of quantity of time, we feel constrained to ask if they or their husbands may do that at the office. The affectional bond gives stability to children's uncertain world and contributes to a healthy independence.

An attachment is an affectional bond that gives stability in a world full of uncertainties. The mother or mother figure to whom the child has become attached affords a safe base from which to explore the unknown, a place to which one can return when things "out there" become too threatening. An emotional stability evolves that builds a desirable independence and makes possible a child's persevering in spite of frustrations—to stay with a task until a goal is reached (Gewirtz, 1972b).

Anxiety, fear, and stress generated by separation from parents may move beyond the creation of emotional problems or neuroses to develop serious learning and behavior problems. When anxiety becomes acute or chronic as it does with children who are given jobs for which they do not have adequate tools, it may result in low performance, erratic conduct, and personality disorders as a result of what Ruebush (1963) calls "disorganization of cognitive responses."

Parental attitudes are powerful in this process. Children are quick to discern parental indifference, as previously noted from Bronfenbrenner (1970). Martin Engel, director of America's National Day Care Demonstration Center in Washington, D.C., observed:

> The motive to rid ourselves of our children, even if it is partial, is transmitted more vividly to the child than all our rationalizations about how good it is for that child to have good interpersonal peer group activities, a good learning experience, a good foundation for school, life, etc., etc. And even the best, most humane and personalized day-care environment cannot compensate for the feeling of rejection which the young child unconsciously senses (1970, p. 5).

Yet educator demands for earlier schooling largely ignore parental attachment.

The standard rebuttal here, of course, is that these days, women must go to work so the family can financially survive. There are at least two appropriate questions for this rationale (bearing in mind that we do not condemn those mothers whose circumstances compel them to work or whose psychological makeup makes mothering difficult or impossible): (1) Who works harder than good mothers at home, many of whom have home industries in which their children share responsibility and rewards? (2) What do we do with *Fortune* magazine's recent questioning of the assumption that times are harder on families today, moneywise, than a generation ago?

> It is said to be no longer economically feasible for Mommy to stay home with the kids as she routinely did a generation ago. Proportion of married women with children under 6 who worked in 1956: only 16%. Proportion today: 54%.

Government aid is needed, the argument goes, because families today are in a cruel bind. They need Mom's paycheck but also need somebody to take care of the kids . . . .

Are American families today really under more economic pressure to generate two incomes than they were in, say, the Fifties? No way. Women today may be under new social pressures to get out there and work: they are also looking at job opportunities not available to their counterparts 30 years ago. But America's Daddies today are on average more able to support the Mommies than they were in the Fifties. In 1956 the average male head of household with a nonworking wife earned $4833. Adjusting for 30 years of inflation that's $22,000. The equivalent figure for 1986 was $25,803 (Seligman, 1988, p. 124).

So the conventional wisdom seems to the editors of *Fortune* to be neither good reasoning nor common sense. It appears logical that families must decide—and schools must acknowledge their constitutional right to decide—whether to give precedence on the one hand to conventional wisdom and extra family "needs" or to the welfare of their children on the other (*Cantwell v. Connecticut*, 1940; *Farrington v. Tokushige*, 1927; *Martin v. Struthers*, 1943; *Meyer v. Nebraska*, 1923; *Pierce v. Hill Military Academy*, 1925; *Pierce v. Society of Sisters*, 1925; *Roe v. Wade*, 1973; *Wisconsin v. Yoder*, 1972).

A PRACTICAL ALTERNATIVE: THE HOME SCHOOL

At least forty-five of the fifty United States have changed policies or laws to accommodate those parents who wish to delay schooling, and there is optimism in the remaining five that they will fall in line. Constitutional provisions were not highlighted in American history until the last 65 years. Until the public school became dominant in American education, there were no confrontations between parents and the state.

For the first three centuries or more of American history, the home school dominated the educational scene. There were of course church, private, and "common" schools, but few educators these days realize that many or most of these institutions operated only for 8 to 12 weeks or so out of the year. So children remained at home for most of the time. Even in school, the school days were usually short enough to let children out early to do real home work—their chores.

Two other observations may be in order here: First, as public education has become dominant and the family influence has decreased in education, illiteracy and delinquency have increased. We have earlier presented reasons for this dilemma from the research of Bandura (1961, 1963), Bronfenbrenner (1970), McCurdy (1960), and others. Second, throughout history, the home has excelled in fostering achievement, behavior, sociability, and creativity. And for good reasons.

First, we must concede that home schools are advantaged by concerned parents. Public and other schools would not be in as deep perplexity today if parents of their children were as concerned as home-teaching parents.

Second, home schools provide many times more responses per day than are heard in the average classroom. Goodlad (1983) found that teachers averaged about 7 minutes altogether all day in personal dialogue with their students. There is also the chance that those receiving the most attention are the misbehaved. This seldom allows more than a response or two per child daily unless a child is naughty, while in an average home school, a youngster receives upwards of a hundred responses. And in the adult example and response is great educational power.

Third, the tutorial situation has proven in virtually every study on this topic to be far more effective than the classroom.

And fourth, the application of the Smithsonian formula or findings for informal instruction in the 8-Year Study (see below) are far more likely to be applied at home than in the conventional school. When combined with the Hewitt-Moore plan for balancing study with entrepreneurial work and service for the less fortunate neighbor, this builds strong children.

Achievement

Every state that has made comparative studies of its home schools and public schools has found that home-taught children excelled (e.g., Alaska, Arkansas, Oregon, Tennessee, and Washington). That this was even true in Alaska where parents were teaching the same curricula at home as teachers used in classrooms is of special interest. The only possible exception might be math teaching in Tennessee, where in the two tests given there was a toss-up between home and classroom teaching (B. W. Long, personal communication, February 10, 1987). Yet when we reported this in our seminar, Tennessee teachers told us that they were given advance copies of tests and told to teach from them. In reading, the home schooler scores ranged to 93 percentile on Stanford tests, thirty-one points higher than Tennessee public schoolers' score of sixty-two—itself twelve points higher than the national norm.

Although we do not have a national sampling of achievement figures, we did study thirty-one families taken to court across the nation, and found that the average child scored 81.1 percentile on standardized tests. And among the Hewitt-Moore Child Development Center's 5,000 or more students, the current average is well above 80 percentile, including students transferring from public schools.

We give must credit here to the Smithsonian formula and lessons learned from the famed 8-Year Study undertaken in the twenties and thirties, in which it was found that informally taught children excelled over those in conventional classrooms, and those with no formal teaching at all excelled above all (Aikin, 1942). And, although we don't suggest license, we remember conclusions like Rohwer's (1971) that suggest waiting for formal education until about junior high age, and studies like Mermelstein and Shulman's (1967) that demonstrate that at least until age nine, unschooled children do at least as well as those in classrooms.

Additional credit must go to experimental techniques and materials that are now available to conventional schools as well as home schools through the Moore

Foundation (P.O. Box 1, Camas, Washington 98607), including *Math-It* and *Winston Grammar,* which have proven respectively that they can turn a math failure around, usually within a week, and can make most students enjoy grammar. Such programs do rely on readiness. For instance, *Basic Math-It*'s readiness measure asks a concentration level that insures that students be mature enough to count from 20 to 1, with eyes closed while tying a bowknot.

And credit also is due work-study balance in which children become entrepreneurs and helpers to those less fortunate than they. This can also help conventionally schooled children by making them officers in the family industry—making and selling bread, muffins, cookies, and wooden toys, or performing lawn services, baby-sitting, old-folk care, or any of hundreds of services. Children can take over responsibility for writing checks for monthly bills and otherwise, as part of their math, and become involved in contriving to save on utilities and food. Self-worth and creative achievement flourish here.

Behavior

We have no recorded evidence of delinquency among children who have been exclusively home taught. Generally, they are considered model citizens. In one Arkansas trial that we witnessed, the judge said he wished that we could have many more such models as the student who stood before him. This scene has been repeated many times in courts and legislatures.

Socialization

The same principles and evidence apply in the home as we cited earlier. Additionally, John W. Taylor V (1986) completed a national sampling of home-schooled youngsters based on the Piers-Harris Children's Self-Concept Scale in cooperation with several universities. Among the findings: 77.7% of the children ranked in the top quartile, with over half of them in the top 10%. Only 10.3% of the home schoolers scored below the norm. And parents' educational level seemed to make no difference in the children's performance (Gustafson, 1987; Wartes, 1988).

Those who are prejudiced because of groupthink or vested interests may argue against the home and for the school as a sanctuary for young children. But even in the harassed family nests of our troubled times, the proof of the pudding is delicious in the eating. Not only do home-taught children average significantly higher than those classroom taught, but they are producing disproportionate numbers of geniuses of classical quality from Virginia and Florida to Washington and California, and from Mississippi and Texas to Michigan, Wisconsin, and Idaho.

These include top GED and SAT students, Merit Scholars, and entrepreneurs from ages six to eighteen, who make and sell everything from lemonade to computer ROMs and make from $.25 an hour to more than $20,000 yearly. They range from full-scholarship Ph.D. candidates to a fourteen-year-old middle child of a family of eleven children, who is whizzing on a $10,000 consultancy at his state's largest chemical corporation, potentially saving the company millions of dollars a year. Some of these youngsters are operating several successful businesses before age eighteen. Others are already successful free-lance writers and editors of articles and books. If the all-American goal is good citizenship and the ability to make a living, family schools on the average are excellent laboratories and showcases for education.

These are citizens whose children know many warm responses and a great deal of freedom to explore while remaining much closer to home than to their peers. The most productive of them do not know what it is to have their brains squashed into the conventional lecture-textbook-test extrusion process dumbed down for the "average student," whomever that may be. The textbook becomes a resource more than a prison; the child reads directly from great biographies instead of swallowing predigested, secondhand textbook food. This may be necessary in college, but not in basic education. Children do not need parental confrontation or drill after they have learned their basic skills. They dwell more on whys and hows than on whats, wheres, and whens. They become thinkers rather than mere reflectors of others' thoughts, creators rather than peer dependents.

Every study that has faced the issue of parent teaching ability has concluded that home education flourishes regardless of parent education level. Interestingly, home teachers who are certificated teachers generally admit they have more trouble than those who aren't—ostensibly because they have more to forget and have no place to pass the blame if students don't achieve. Nor should this be surprising, for every authority or study we can find on certification suggests that it's a doubtful, unproductive demand in basic education (Conant, 1963; D. Erickson, personal communication, April 27, 1988; Medley & Coker, 1987; Orlans, 1975).

One of the most important factors of all is the integrity of the family. If we are to take our research seriously (and we invite anyone who can provide replicable data to the contrary to produce it), and if we are interested in the survival of our culture, it is time to take seriously Zimmerman's (1947) challenge that something radical must be done. Our educational system is already considered totalitarian by some overseas authorities (Suviranta, 1973).

One of the principal problems, as we have noted, is that we have plenty of research, but don't apply it (1) when it confronts our vested interests or traditional practices and (2) when a very strong personality or powerful group makes it embarrassing for us to disagree. On this second factor, Irving Janis (1971) observes that this is precisely what obtained at some of America's greatest failures, e.g., the Bay of Pigs, Pearl Harbor, and Vietnam. He declares that however fine a group we have (scientists, educators, politicians, etc.), and assuming "its humanitarianism and its high-minded principles, [it] might be capable of adopting a course of action that is inhumane and immortal" (p. 44). He concludes poignantly in the spirit of Parkinson's law:

> The more amiability and esprit de corps there is among the members of a policy-
> making ingroup, the greater the danger that independent critical thinking will be

replaced by groupthink, which is likely to result in irrational and dehumanizing actions directed against outgroups (1971, p. 44).

These days, many families find themselves to be in the out-group, facing with trepidation the in-group of school officials and social workers who frequently are hailing them into court for teaching at home, and in some cases are taking their children. Fortunately, the in-group constitutes only a small percentage of these officials, but they are ominous enough to scare many parents out of the family tranquillity they cherish. Delay here is not procrastination, but rather the disciplined view.

SUMMARY

We feel forced to conclude that our only reasonable chance for survival as a free democratic society is to educate parents on the value of cherishing their children longer in their homes. So much for institutions. Yet this is personally threatening, too! As we look at modern trends, with millions both in day care and in nursing homes, we are compelled to conclude—as the Greeks and Romans did when their societies were collapsing—that the earlier you institutionalize your children, the earlier they will institutionalize you![1]

REFERENCES

The adult performance level project (APL). (1983). Austin, TX: University of Texas.

Aikin, W. M. (1942). *The story of the eight-year study* (Vols. 1–4). New York: Harper.

Ainsworth, M. D. S. (1969). Object relations, dependency, and attachment: A theoretical review of the infant-mother relationship. *Child Development, 40,* 969–1025.

Ainsworth, M. D. S. (1972). Attachment and dependency: A comparison. In J. L. Gewirtz (Ed.), *Attachment and dependency* (pp. 97–137). Washington, DC: V. H. Winston & Sons.

Bandura, A., & Huston, A. C. (1961). Identification as a process of incidental learning. *Journal of Abnormal and Social Psychology, 63,* 311–318.

Bandura, A., Ross, D., & Ross, S. A. (1961). Transmission of aggression through limitation of aggressive models. *Journal of Abnormal Psychology and Social Psychiatry, 62,* 575–582.

Bandura, A., & Walters, R. H. (1963). *Social learning and personality development.* New York: Holt, Rinehart & Winston.

Barbrack, C. R., & Horton, D. M. (1970). *Educational intervention in the home and paraprofessional career development* (DARCEE Papers and Reports, Vol. 4, No. 4). Nashville, TN: Peabody College.

Bell, S. M. (1971). *Early cognitive development and its relationship to infant-mother attachment: A study of disadvantaged Negro infants* (Final report, Project No. 508, Johns

---

[1]If any scholars, legislators, or others are interested in research data or home-school methodology or ways of helping school systems, send an SASE to Moore Foundation, P.O. Box 1, Camas, Washington 98607.

Hopkins University). Washington, DC: U.S. Department of Health, Education, and Welfare.

Bloom, B. S. (1980). *All our children learning*. Washington, DC: McGraw-Hill.

Bowlby, J. (1952). *Maternal care and mental health*. Geneva, Switzerland: World Health Organization.

Bowlby, J. (1969). *Attachment and loss* (Vol. 1). New York: Basic Books.

Bowlby, J. (1973). *Attachment and loss: Vol. 2 Separation, anxiety, and anger*. New York: Basic Books.

Brenner, A., & Scott, L. H. (1973). *School readiness factor analyzed*. Detroit: Merrill-Palmer Institute.

Bronfenbrenner, U. (1970). *Two worlds of childhood: U.S. and U.S.S.R.* New York: Simon and Schuster.

Cantwell v. Connecticut, 310 U.S. 296 (1940).

Conant, J. B. (1963). *The education of American teachers*. New York: McGraw-Hill.

Daugherty, L. G. (1963). Working with disadvantaged parents. *NEA Journal, 52*(2), 18–20.

Dyer, D. W., & Harcum, E. R. (1961). Visual perception of binary pattern by preschool children and by school children. *Journal of Educational Psychology, 52*, 161–165.

Education vs. Western civilization. (1941, Spring). *The American Scholar*, pp. 184–193.

Elkind, D. (1970). The case for the academic preschool: Fact or fiction? *Young Children, 24*, 180–188.

Elkind, D. (1981). *The hurried child*. Reading, MA: Addison-Wesley.

Elkind, D. (1987). *Miseducation: Preschoolers at risk*. New York: Knopf.

Ellingson, R. J., & Wilcott, R. C. (1960). Development of evoked responses in visual and auditory cortices of kittens. *Journal of Neurophysiology, 23*, 363–375.

Engel, M. (1970). *Rapunzel, Rapunzel, let down your golden hair: Some thoughts on early childhood education*. Unpublished manuscript, National Demonstration Center in Early Childhood Education, United States Office of Education, Washington, DC.

Farran, D. (1982, September). Now for the bad news . . . . *Parents Magazine*, p. 80.

Farrington v. Tokushige, 273 U.S. 284. 71 L. Ed. 646 (1927).

Fisher, J. T., & Hawley, L. S. (1951). *A few buttons missing*. Philadelphia: J. B. Lippincott.

Forester, J. J. (1955). At what age should children start school? *School Executive, 74*, 2–3.

Forgione, P. D., & Moore, R. S. (1973). *The rationales for early childhood policy making* (Research Grant No. 50079-G-73-01). Washington, DC: U.S. Office of Economic Opportunity.

Frostig, M., Lefever, W., & Whittlesey, J. (1963). Disturbances in visual perception. *Journal of Educational Research, 57*, 160–162.

Furth, H. G. (1970). *Piaget for teachers*. Englewood Cliffs, NJ: Prentice-Hall.

Gerber, M. (1958). The psycho-motor development of African children in the first year, and the influence of maternal behavior. *Journal of Social Psychology, 47*, 185–195.

Getting smarter sooner. (1971, July 26). *Time*, p. 38.

Gewirtz, J. L. (1972a). *Attachment and dependency*. Washington, DC: V. H. Winston & Sons.

Gewirtz, J. L. (1972b). Attachment, dependence and a distinction in terms of stimulus control. In J. L. Gewirtz (Ed.), *Attachment and dependency* (pp. 139–177). Washington, DC: V. H. Winston & Sons.

Goodlad, J. I. (1983). A study of schooling: Some findings and hypotheses. *Phi Delta Kappan, 64*, 465.

Gray, S. W. (1969). *Selected longitudinal studies of compensatory education—A look from the inside.* Nashville, TN: George Peabody College.

Gray, S. W. (1971 , December). The child's first teacher. *Childhood Education,* pp. 127–129.

Gray, S. W. (1974). Children from three to ten: The early training project. In S. Ryan (Ed.), *Longitudinal evaluations of preschool programs* (pp. 113–124). Washington, DC: Office of Child Development.

Gustafson, S. (1987). *A study of home schooling: Parental motivations and goals.* Unpublished thesis, Woodrow Wilson School of Public and International Affairs, Princeton University, Princeton, NJ.

Halliwell, J. W. (1966). Review the reviews on entrance age and school success. *Journal of Educational Research, 59,* 395–401.

Halliwell, J. W., & Stein, B. W. (1964). Achievement of early and late school starters. *Elementary English, 41,* 631–639.

Hilgartner, H. (1962). *The frequency of myopia found in individuals under 21 years of age.* Unpublished manuscript.

Husen, T. (Ed.). (1967). *International study of achievement in mathematics: A comparison of twelve countries* (Vols. I and II). New York: John Wiley & Sons.

Huttenlocher, P. R. (1966). Development of neuronal activity in neocortex of the kitten. *Nature, 211,* 91–92.

Impellizzeri, I. H. (1967). Auditory perceptual ability of normal children aged five through eight. *Journal of Genetic Psychology, 111,* 289–294.

Janis, I. L. (1971, November). Groupthink. *Psychology Today,* pp. 43–46, 74–76.

Jensen, A. R. (1969). Understanding readiness: An occasional paper. Urbana, IL: Educational Resources Information Center. (ERIC Document Reproduction Service No. ED 032 117)

Kohlberg, L. (1968). Early education: A cognitive-developmental view. *Child Development, 39,* 1013–1062.

Krippner, S. (1971). On research in visual training and reading disability. *Journal of Learning Disabilities, 4*(1), 65–76.

Levenstein, P. (1971, December). Learning through (and from) mothers. *Childhood Education,* pp. 130–134.

Ludlum, W. (1974, December 12). Young readers may harm eyes. *South Bend Tribune,* p. 34.

Martin v. Struthers, 319 U. S. 141 (1943).

Marty, R., & Scherer, J. (1964). Criteria for the maturation of the cortical system. *Progressive Brain Research, 4,* 222–236.

Mawhinney, P. E. (1964). We gave up on early entrance. *Michigan Education Journal, 1*(4), 25.

McCarthy, D. J. (1955). Pre-entrance variables and school success of underage children. *Harvard Educational Review, 25,* 266–269.

McCurdy, H. G. (1960). The childhood pattern of genius. *Horizon, 2*(1), 33–38.

Medley, D. M., & Coker, H. (1987). How valid are principals' judgments of teacher effectiveness? *Phi Delta Kappan, 68,* 138–140.

Mermelstein, E., & Shulman, L. S. (1967). Lack of formal schooling and the acquisition of conservation. *Child Development, 38,* 39–52.

Metcalf, D. R. (1973). *An investigation of cerebral lateral functioning and the EEG* (Report of a study under Research Grant No. 50079-G-73-02-1). Washington, DC: U.S. Office of Economic Opportunity.

Meyer v. Nebraska, 262 U.S. 390, 43 S.Ct. 625 (1923).

Moore, D. R., Kordenbrock, D. K., & Moore, R. S. (1976, November, December). Lessons from Europe. *Childhood Education,* pp. 66–70.

Moore, R. S., Moon, R. D., & Moore, D. R. (1972). The California report: Early schooling for all? *Phi Delta Kappan, 53,* 615–621.

Moore, R. S., & Moore, D. N. (1975). *Better late than early.* New York: Readers Digest Press.

Moore, R. S., & Moore, D. N. (1979). *School can wait.* Provo, UT: Brigham Young University Press.

Morency, A., & Wepman, J. M. (1973). Early perceptual ability and later school achievement. *Elementary School Journal, 73,* 323–327.

Olson, W. C. (1947). Experiences for growing. *NEA Journal, 36,* 502–503.

Orlans, H. (1975). *Private education and public eligibility.* Lexington, MA: Lexington Books.

Phillip, J. L. (1969). *The origins of intellect: Piaget's theory.* San Francisco: H. W. Freeman.

Piaget, J. (1962). The stages of the intellectual development of the child. *Bulletin of the Menninger Clinic, 26*(3), 120–145.

Pierce v. Hill Military Academy, 268 U.S. 510, 45 S.Ct. 571 (1925).

Pierce v. Society of Sisters, 268 U.S. 510, 45 S.Ct. 571 (1925).

Quine, D. (1965). *The intellelctual development of home taught children.* Unpublished manuscript.

Rabinowicz, T. (1974). Some aspects of the maturation of the human cerebral cortex. In S. R. Berenberg, M. Caniaris, & N. P. Masse (Eds.), *Pre- and post-natal development of the human brain* (pp. 212–235). Basel, Switzerland: S. Karger.

The Random House Dictionary of the English Language [unabridged]. (1966). New York: Random House.

Riley, D. A., McKee, J. P., & Hadley, R. W. (1964). Prediction of auditory discrimination learning and transposition from children's auditory ordering ability. *Journal of Experimental Psychology, 67,* 324–329.

Robinson, R. J., & Tizard, J. P. M. (1966). The central nervous system in the newborn. *British Medical Journal, 22*(4), 49–55.

Roe v. Wade, 410 U.S. 113 (1973).

Rohwer, W. D. (1971). Prime time for education: Early childhood or adolescence? *Harvard Educational Review, 41,* 316–341.

Ruebush, B. E. (1963). Child psychology. *Yearbook of the National Society for the Study of Education, 62*(Pt. 1), 460–515.

Schaefer, E. S. (1971, October). Learning from each other. *Childhood Education,* pp. 13–17.

Scherer, J. (1968). Electrophysiological aspects of cortical development. *Progressive Brain Research, 22,* 480–490.

Schweinhart, L. J., & Weikart, D. P. (1986). *Preschool experiences affect juvenile delinquency rate, 15-year study finds.* Ypsilanti, MI: High/Scope Educational Research Foundation.

Seligman, D. (1988, February 15). The day care follies. *Fortune,* p. 124.

Smith, M. B. (1968). School and home: Focus on achievement. In A. H. Pasow (Ed.), *Developing programs for the educationally disadvantaged* (pp. 68–103). New York: Teachers College, Columbia University.

Soderman, A. K. (1984, March). Schooling all 4-year olds: An idea full of promise, fraught with pitfalls. *Education Week,* pp. 19–20.

Spitz, R. A. (1949). The role of ecological factors in emotional development in infancy. *Child Development, 20,* 145–155.

Stevenson, H. W., & Siegel, A. (1969). Effects of instructions and age on retention of filmed content. *Journal of Educational Psychology, 60,* 71–74.

Suviranta, A. (1973). Home economics answer to the problems raised in industrialized countries. In *XIIth Congress of the International Federation for Home Economics, Final Report* (pp. 92–99). Boulogne, France: Federation internationale pour l'economie familiale.

Taylor V, J. W. (1986). *Self-concept in home schooling children.* Unpublished doctoral dissertation, Andrews University, Berrien Springs, MI.

United States Communicable Disease Control Center. (1984, September 5). Researchers say day-care centers are implicated in spread of disease. *The Wall Street Journal,* p. 4.

Wartes, J. (1988, April). *Homeschooler outcomes.* Symposium conducted at the American Educational Research Association's National Conference, New Orleans.

Wepman, J. M. (1960). Auditory discrimination, speech, and reading. *Elementary School Journal, 60,* 325–333.

Wepman, J. M. (1968). The modality concept. In H. K. Smith (Ed.), *Perception and reading* (pp. 1–6). Newark, DE: International Reading Association.

Westinghouse Learning Corporation/Ohio University. (1970). The impact of Head Start: An evaluation of the effects of Head Start on children's cognitive and affective development. In J. L. Frost & G. R. Hawkes (Eds.), *The disadvantaged child* (2nd ed., pp. 197–201). Boston: Houghton Mifflin.

Wisconsin v. Yoder, 406 U.S. 205 (1972).

Yakovlev, P. I., & Lecours, A. R. (1967). The myelogenetic cycles of regional maturation of the brain. In A. Minkowski (Ed.), *Regional development of the brain in early life* (pp. 34–44). Oxford, England: Blackwell Scientific Publications.

Yarrow, L. J., & Pedersen, F. A. (1972). Attachment: Its origins and course. In W. W. Hartup (Ed.), *The young child: Reviews of research* (pp. 54–66). Washington, DC: National Association for the Education of Young Children.

Young, F. A. (1970). Development of optical characteristics for seeing. In F. A. Young & D. B. Lindsley (Eds.), *Early experience and visual information processing in perceptual and reading disorders* (pp. 35–61). Washington, DC: National Academy of Sciences.

Young, F. A., & Lindsley, D. B. (1969). The transmission of refractive errors within Eskimo families. *American Journal of Optometry and Archives of American Academy of Optometry, 46,* 676–685.

Zimmerman, C. (1947). *Family and civilization.* New York: Harper and Brothers.

PART THREE

Who Will Teach
Young Children?

We all want the best for our children—the best of food, clothing, health care, housing, and especially the best in education. As the quality of any early childhood program ultimately depends upon the teacher, any attempt to provide the best in early education logically focuses on the teacher.

Who is the best teacher of young children, and how this person should be trained, however, is a question of long standing in the field of early childhood education. Can anyone be an effective teacher of young children, or should that person be a parent before being considered competent to teach the children of others? Would a background of supervised work with children be enough to prepare a person to be an early childhood teacher? Or are high school diplomas or college degrees sufficient preparation?

Historically, there have been differing opinions as to who is the best teacher of children. John Amos Comenius in the *School of Infancy* advocated that mothers are the first and primary teachers of the young. Certainly, few would argue with the fact that learning begins at birth. And the person closest to the child, the mother, is the child's first teacher.

Mothers, the principal source of nourishment and comfort, are integral to infants' early learning (Lefrancois, 1988). They are the base that infants and young children use for exploration, the object of security, attachment, and love.

So critical to the child's cognitive, emotional, and social development are mothers, that it was once believed that only women could be effective teachers of young children. Female teachers would be closer to the mother figure the child attached to during infancy and would serve to protect and maintain this emotional attachment believed necessary for emotional health.

Females, however, were historically considered better teachers of young children for other reasons. Women would better be able than men to find the nose wiping, mess cleaning, comforting, and protecting—essential components of teaching young children—satisfying and rewarding. "As the cliche goes, just love little children" wrote Almy (1975, p. 75).

On the other hand, Frederick Froebel, the father of the kindergarten, rejected women as teachers. He hypothesized that men were the best teachers, for only men had the ability to think clearly, to study and understand philosophy, and to see the principles of the universe presented in the gifts and occupations of the kindergarten curriculum (Froebel, 1912). Women, regardless of whether or not they were mothers, would not be suited for the intellectually demanding task of teaching kindergarten.

Piaget (1969), while not specifying gender, was most specific in his belief that the best teachers of the youngest of children were highly intellectual. He, as Froebel, believed the study of philosophy and psychology, and much more, was necessary preparation for teaching. In *Science of Education and the Psychology of the Child* (1969), Piaget stated:

> The future primary-school teacher should begin by acquiring his baccalaureate and then go on to spend three years receiving his specialized training. During the first of these three years, the candidates take practical courses that enable them to become acquainted with the problems, and then, in the third year, they again return to practical work. The second year, on the other hand, is spent at the university where the candidates take courses in psychology, pedagogy, and special courses in education (pp. 128–129).

Still, today there is little agreement as to who is the best teacher of young children. What knowledge, skills, or attitudes teachers should have, or how teachers are to gain the necessary prerequisites, is an issue that has yet to be resolved.

Nita Barbour, in the chapter "Issues in the Preparation of Early Childhood Teachers," traces the history of, and discusses the issues surrounding, the field of early childhood teacher preparation. She describes a number of programs of teacher preparation, and documents the lack of agreement as to what intellectual knowledge, procedural skills, or attitudes are considered necessary for the teacher of the very young.

AGREEMENT THROUGH CERTIFICATION AND ACCREDITATION

Accreditation procedures do, however, offer the field some basic agreement as to the minimal essential knowledge base and skills for teachers who do enroll in 4-year baccalaureate early childhood teacher education programs. In 1982, the National

Association for the Education of Young Children (NAEYC) developed the *Early Childhood Teacher Education Guidelines for 4- and 5-Year Institutions*. These guidelines have been accepted by the National Council for the Accreditation of Teacher Education (NCATE). NCATE provides a mechanism for voluntary peer regulation of professional education and a process by which the profession of education declares its expectations for professional education and then applies these to the program units.

To date, the guidelines have been applied to well over one hundred early childhood teacher education programs. Elliott, Lessen-Firestone, and Federlein (1984) suggest that the guidelines have been effective in defining the nature of early childhood teacher education. Nevertheless, the impact of the guidelines on the field of early childhood teacher preparation is limited by a number of factors.

Multidisciplinary Nature of the Field

The first factor is the multidisciplinary nature of early childhood education. Young children cannot be educated without concern for their health, safety, and physical care. The NAEYC guidelines only minimally address disciplines other than that of education. Further, because the field is multidisciplinary, teacher preparation takes place in diverse settings. Teacher preparation programs are located in departments of home and family, child development, psychology, or child care. Teachers receiving their degree in other than a college of education are unaffected by the NAEYC guidelines.

Diversity of the Field

The second factor negating full implementation of the guidelines is the diversity within the field of early childhood education. Programs for young children may be under the auspices of the federal, state, or local government. Many programs are sponsored by churches, industry, private associations, or for-profit franchised business chains.

Generally, only those teachers under state or local requirements for certification and accreditation are required to have any formal education or preparation. These are usually teachers of public school kindergarten programs, or of the primary grades. Under the auspices of state or local governments, these teachers must meet certification requirements that usually begin with the completion of a 4-year baccalaureate university program within departments of education of human development (Spodek & Saracho, 1982).

REQUIREMENTS IN OTHER SETTINGS

Teachers not under state or local requirements, such as those working in church-related, charitable, or privately run child care programs, may not be subject to any certification or accreditation program. Thus, it must be recognized that there is a large population of people teaching young children not subject to any certification or accreditation procedures at any level.

Because so many teachers of young children have no formal training or preparation, nor are under any certification or accreditation programs, many have tried to identify personality characteristics believed associated with teacher effectiveness. Among the many listed are truthfulness, sensitivity, curiosity, understanding, patience, lovingness and kindness, sincerity, a sense of humor, the ability to be reflective, and respect for children and their families (Almy, 1975).

In an attempt to go beyond vague descriptions of ideal personality traits without requiring a baccalaureate, other ideas for the preparation and credentialing of teachers have been developed. One of these, primarily designed for teachers of Head Start, is the Child Development Associate (CDA) program. Announced in 1971 as a large-scale effort to establish a new category of child care workers, the Child Development Associate program trains men and women to be more than aides, yet not to replace teachers with 4-year college degrees. Combining some college course work at either a community college or a university with actual work with children, the CDA program offers a new form of credential for teachers of the very young. Gail Perry, in the chapter "Alternate Modes of Teacher Preparation," describes the theory, history, and nature of the CDA program. Its strengths, weaknesses, and directions for the future are discussed.

The question of who will teach our children, and how best to prepare them, is not answered in the following chapters. Although theory and research, as an understanding of history, guide the development of programs in teacher education, the realities of the field of early childhood education will continue to impact, and in part determine, who will teach young children.

Currently there are over 18 million preschool children in the United States, more than at any other time in the past 20 years (Center for Educational Statistics, 1985). Nearly half of all infants have mothers employed outside the home, and 59% of mothers of three and four year olds are employed outside the home. In 1985, there were 9.6 million children under six with mothers employed outside the home, and by 1995, there will be 14.5 million children under six with mothers employed outside the home (Children's Defense Fund, 1987).

These trends mean a tremendous increase in the numbers of children enrolled in some form of child care or early educational program and a corresponding increase in the numbers of persons needed to work in these programs.

Add to the increasing and immediate need for large numbers of teachers of young children the reality of finances, and the question of who will teach becomes confounded with that of who will pay. Twenty-five percent of all four and five year olds are poor (Children's Defense Fund, 1987). The poor are unable to afford certified, degreed teachers from accredited programs. The limited numbers of those holding the CDA certificate may not even be affordable by the very poor as teachers of their children.

Who will teach then becomes an issue of who is responsible for the care and education of the very young in our nation. Will the federal, state, or local government subsidize teacher salaries and training? Will industry better be able to support certified and accredited teachers? Or will the family, especially the mother, whether trained or not, be given the full responsibility for the education of the young?

Under the Constitution's mandate of providing for the general welfare of our society, in the past the government has assumed responsibility for special programs and policies directed toward young children. General welfare has typically included ensuring equality of educational opportunity. This equality may begin in the early years with the provision of teachers who all hold baccalaureate degrees and are certified in early childhood education for all children. Thus, all children, whether enrolled in private, for-profit, employer-based, or any other type of early child-care or educational program, would have the right, under the Constitution, to be taught by teachers who all have the same high quality of education and training.

WHO WILL TEACH?

As you read the following chapters, ask yourself

- Who is the best teacher of young children?
- What should early childhood teacher-education programs consist of?
- What are the issues surrounding the 4-year teacher-education programs?
- What effect will the Holmes Group, the Carnegie Report, and other organized demands for improvement of the quality of teacher preparation have on the field of early childhood teacher preparation?
- How can the standards of NCATE be applied to those not involved in 4-year baccalaureate programs?
- Should all teachers of children—those in child care and nursery schools and those working as aides, assistant teachers, and teachers—be required to have the same level of training?
- What are the major values of the CDA program? What are its weaknesses?
- How could links be built between the CDA program and the 4-year teacher-preparation training programs?
- Who should be responsible for the funding, monitoring, and standard setting for programs of early childhood teacher preparation?

REFERENCES

Almy, M. (1975). *The early childhood educator at work*. New York: McGraw-Hill.

Center for Educational Statistics. (1985). *Conditions of education*. Washington, DC: U.S. Government Printing Office.

Children's Defense Fund. (1987). *A children's defense fund budget: FY 1988*. Washington, DC: Author.

Elliott, S., Lessen-Firestone, J., & Federlein, A. (1984). Early childhood teacher education guidelines for 4- and 5-year programs: A preliminary survey of their relevancy and impact. *Young Children, 39*(2), 54–56.

Froebel, F. (1912). *The education of man* (D. Hallmann, Trans.). New York: Appleton.

Lafrancois, G. (1988). *Of children.* Belmont, CA: Wadsworth.

National Association for the Education of Young Children. (1982). *Early childhood teacher education guidelines for 4- and 5-year institutions.* Washington, DC: Author.

Piaget, J. (1969). *Science of education and the psychology of the child.* New York: Viking Press.

Seefeldt, C. (1988). Teacher certification and program accreditation in early childhood education. *The Elementary School Journal, 89,* 241–252.

Spodek, B., & Saracho, O. (1982). The preparation and certification of early childhood personnel. In B. Spodek (Ed.), *Handbook of research in early childhood education* (pp. 399–426). New York: Free Press.

7

Issues in the Preparation of Early Childhood Teachers

NITA BARBOUR
University of Maryland–Baltimore County

Whenever quality of teaching in American schools is questioned, then the level of education for classroom teachers becomes a part of the concern. Though the educational level for teachers-in-training has gradually increased from a basic elementary education to 4 years of college education, there have been persistent accusations throughout 3 centuries of American education that teachers are "semi-literate and poorly educated people" (Haberman, 1983, p. 102). Issues regarding training may have had different emphases throughout history, but similar concerns continue to be raised as each new generation tries to understand why schools are failing to fulfill for citizens the great American dream.

The issues of quality in training, at various times and with different levels of intensity, have revolved around assorted programs: Who are the candidates? How much education is required to train competent teachers? What should the educational content be? Is one philosophical orientation preferable to another? Should a teacher have technical training or a liberal education? How much and what quality of apprenticeship should there be? At different times, universities and colleges have developed experimental programs to try to address the concerns for quality teacher education. Though the programs might have been deemed successful or partly successful, little extensive research of the total education program or even extended support for these programs has been provided (Houston & Newman, 1982).

In this chapter, I shall give a brief historical overview of the teacher-education issues noted above. A description of three programs with differing philosophical orientations, but designed to address the concerns about quality teacher education, will also be presented.

WHO ARE THE TEACHER CANDIDATES?

Though there have been some changes in characteristics of teaching candidates over the years, many of the same social and economic conditions of the nineteenth century relating to teachers persist today. Teachers of young children in the nineteenth century were mostly single women with an elementary school education and limited, if any, professional training. Teaching was viewed as an appropriate temporary job for a young woman until one could marry and start raising a family. The few men who applied for jobs as teachers of young children were from working-class parents or genteel poverty and viewed teaching as a temporary position until they could complete training for other professions or, as schools developed into large organizations, could move up the school hierarchy as administrators (Lanier & Little, 1986). Though there were many teachers of young children who were bright and caring individuals, the majority viewed teaching as something to do until something better came along.

In the early twentieth century, with the expansion of high schools, the educational level of teacher candidates greatly increased. As normal schools became teachers' colleges in the 1930s and 1940s, the educational level of teacher candidates made another leap forward. However, as we move into the twenty-first century, the pool of candidates for teachers of young children, in spite of the increasing level of education, has remained much the same as throughout the history of American education. The candidacy pool is, and has been, dominated by women who view teaching as a temporary position until marriage or until opportunities open up in administrative positions. Though married women now stay in teaching, the position is often viewed as a good occupation to combine with marriage and raising a family, rather than as a career profession in which both economic and intellectual advances can occur. It is not surprising that Lortie (1975) found teacher candidates to be very conservative in their outlook. He maintains that teachers do not enter the field to be innovative or creative in their teaching, or to challenge traditional practice. Instead, they tend to believe in those techniques or practices that they have internalized from their own schooling experience, in spite of any training to the contrary.

The woman's movement has not been advantageous to the teaching profession. There have been advances made in other fields of endeavor that are deemed more prestigious than teaching, so that bright and ambitious young women, often barred from these fields in the past, now find job openings and advancement. Lanier and Little (1986) point out that the movement has not helped to make teaching young children, traditionally viewed as woman's work, a more prestigious or more lucrative position, nor has the movement helped the teaching profession provide greater opportunities for upward mobility.

Because of the numbers of teachers needed and the small pool of academically talented persons, there aren't enough students, of both sexes, in that pool to meet the demands. Unfortunately, even more of the talented are seeking other fields of endeavor. Research studies indicate that education departments are not only attracting fewer of the academically talented, but also are admitting more of the lowest-ranked students into their courses (Vance & Schlechty, 1982). Sarason, Davidson, and Blatt (1986) blame university faculties for providing too-few programs that could attract quality teacher candidates or programs that would enable their graduates to stimulate children's intellectual skills.

Moving toward the twenty-first century, the American commitment for improvement of teaching as a profession seems enervated. Advancing candidate qualifications is still an open agenda.

HOW MUCH TRAINING IS NEEDED?

The education of teachers in this country has evolved from teachers being trained by serving an apprenticeship under an experienced teacher to requirements of certification for 4 years of education, including training in one's specialty. Early childhood teachers who teach in public schools have been similarly educated. However, the required 4-year programmatic training has been slow in coming.

In the early years of American education, little education was required of a teacher. Girls who had completed what would be the equivalent of an elementary education were deemed capable and able to teach. If they received any additional training, it would have been as an apprentice under an already-practicing teacher.

The first private normal school in America was opened in Concord, Vermont, in 1823 and the first public normal school in Lexington, Massachusetts, in 1837. These 3-year training programs required an elementary school education for admission, and graduates, thus trained, had the equivalent of a high school education with some pedagogical courses. However, these normal schools were slow in expanding. By the turn of the century, only about 11,000 of the 400,000 practicing teachers had either public or private normal-school training (Haberman, 1983). By 1914, many cities began to provide teacher-training programs in order to provide training for their own elementary school teachers. These programs became normal schools, as the requirements for entrance expanded to a high school diploma and the length of the program expanded from 1 to 2 to 3 years. Though as late as the 1950s there were teachers with only a high school diploma and a few weeks of normal-school education, the number of years required to become a teacher had expanded. Between 1911 and 1940, normal schools were expanding into 4 years of training and becoming teachers' colleges. Even as this was happening, there was concern that some teachers needed at least 5 years of education. With the intent of providing secondary schools with academically more-capable candidates, the first master of arts in teaching degree was offered at Harvard in 1936 (Houston & Newman, 1982). The program met with only modest success, as there was little demand for such an expensive training program in a field that offered such low remuneration (Woodring, 1957).

After the Second World War, with a large influx into American colleges and universities, teachers colleges again underwent a change, becoming multipurpose state colleges and universities with education departments responsible for teacher training, though the major academic work was completed in other departments

(Bone, 1980; Haberman, 1983; Woodring, 1976). In the late 1950s and early 1960s, precipitated by the advent of *Sputnik,* the quality and quantity of teacher education came under attack for its lack of rigor. At that time, there was strong support for 5-year training programs, including programs for elementary and early childhood teachers. Experimental programs for master of arts in teaching, master in education, and bachelor's degrees that required 5 years for certification were developed. The Fund for the Advancement of Education supported many of these programs in an effort to improve the quality of education, to attract more qualified persons into teaching, and to relieve a growing teacher shortage (Woodring, 1957). In the 1970s, as the teacher shortage abated, the scholarship funds dwindled, and teacher salaries leveled off, many of these programs ceased to exist. However, experienced teachers wishing to continue to be certified were required to continue their education. Thus, many teachers in today's schools have the equivalent of 5 years of postsecondary education.

Today, early childhood public school teachers (pre-K–primary), to be certified, are required to have 4 years of education with special training in early childhood curriculum and human development and the equivalent of a master's degree in order to renew certification. But no such consistency exists for teaching in nursery schools, private kindergartens, day-care centers, and Head Start programs that house a large number of children who receive early schooling from less-trained individuals.

Historically, programs for the very young child were founded by women of great zeal in order to provide care, nurture, and stimulating experiences for children of the poor, of immigrants, or of working parents (Snyder, 1972). Though there were prominent educators advocating and arguing about the type of education these young children should have, the teachers who cared for and taught these children had varying levels of education and training. The situation is the same today. One of the major questions continuing today regarding training for the very young is whether a 4-year liberal education beyond high school is needed and how much technical training should be required. Since the advent of Head Start in 1965, the United States government has provided monies to train Head Start teachers. The early programs were summer sessions to retrain experienced teachers so they could work with very young children who were "educationally handicapped" (Houston & Newman, 1982). The funded programs for training Head Start teachers has changed since then. The present CDA competency training program funded by the United States government, described by Gail Perry in chapter 8 of this boook, requires candidates to have a high school diploma for admission and provides the equivalent of 1 to 2 years of professional and technical training. The head teacher in the Head Start classroom is required to have *either* a 4-year degree in early childhood education, *or* a CDA credential. One can see that there are still discrepancies in the amount of education teachers of young children are required to have.

Nationally, there are continued demands that teachers of young children have increased years of education. Two early childhood organizations, the National Association for the Education of Young Children (1982) and the Association of Childhood Education International (1983), have prepared position papers with the hope of improving education for all teachers of young children. Though they do not state a 4-year college requirement, both recommend that all early childhood teachers have a liberal education, as well as professional and technical courses in early childhood education.

The Carnegie Forum on Education and the Economy (1986) and the Holmes Group (1986) recommend that 5 or even 6 years of training are needed in order to prepare competent teachers. Both groups recommend abolishing undergraduate degrees in education and requiring teacher-preparation programs to be on a graduate level. A liberal arts education would be required of all teacher candidates with either an academic major or enough study in multiple areas of concentration to constitute several academic minors. The pedagogical studies, offered only at the graduate level, would prepare teachers to make appropriate curriculum decisions, and these would be accompanied by clinical or internship experiences under the supervision of a head teacher or a career professional. Research activity would also be a part of the training. Recommendations have some similarities to the master of arts in teaching and master in education innovative programs of the 1950s and 1960s. However the new reports differ in that they recommend changing the teaching profession by developing a career ladder with intellectual and monetary incentives for teachers. Teachers would progress up this ladder by demonstrating expertise in teaching and by continuing their education to the doctoral level.

WHAT SHOULD THE CONTENT BE?

The notion of what a teacher needs to know to be a competent teacher has changed over the years as length of training has increased. However, the debate regarding the importance of a liberal education in relationship to a technical education still rages. According to Woodring (1983), the debate about the importance of a liberal education versus the need for professional studies originated as the result of differing philosophies. One faction held to the idea that stressed the importance of enculturating the young into the wisdom of great thinkers and classical studies. The antithesis of that idea stressed the importance of understanding the nature of children and that the goal of education was the growth of individuals. Sarason et al. (1986) maintain that universities themselves have been responsible, at least in part, for this dichotomy. While local educational agencies and state agencies were recognizing the need for trained teachers, faculties at universities viewed elementary school teaching as requiring only skill training and did not feel that such courses should be part of a liberal arts college curriculum. The early normal schools thus developed outside the intellectual influence of liberal arts colleges and universities.

In the 1800s, when teachers needed only early childhood education to be accepted in normal schools, it was not deemed important that teachers have a great deal of knowledge. The teaching curriculum they studied consisted of teaching under supervision in the morning and taking methods courses in the afternoon. The academic content was only slightly more difficult than the content they needed to teach to their pupils. Haberman (1983) points out that there was great relevance between the subjects taught the prospective teachers and the subjects they in turn taught the children. Emphasis for learning to be a teacher was on the skill of imparting knowledge, and this could be learned as one watched a model teacher. Even the first principal of the first public normal school, Mr. Cyrus Pierce, noted that he taught his students by his "own example" and had four methods of recitation—question and answer, conversation, calling on first one and then another to give an oral analysis of the lesson, and written analysis (Norton's study, cited in Haberman, 1983).

As normal schools developed into 2-, 3-, and eventually 4-year programs, more knowledge both of a technical and liberal arts nature was required of teachers. The great expansion of knowledge, related to child development, learning theory, and strategies of teaching, meant that teachers needed to be educated in the new theories. As more Americans became better educated, teachers needed more intellectual content in their own schooling. Woodring (1976) reports that normal schools in 1851 were offering such liberal arts courses as algebra, geometry, astronomy, philosophy, history, English language, literature, and geography, besides professional education courses and practice teaching. He suggests that the content may not have been pursued in any great depth, since all these subjects were to be completed in a 2-year period. More content knowledge required from teachers meant more education was necessary.

In spite of increased education, the specter, in the 1950s, of poorly educated teachers again was raised, and so continued the debate of the professional education of teachers as opposed to the liberally educated teacher. No longer could the limited normal-school education be considered adequate. These schools became the multi-purpose colleges and universities, and a new emphasis was placed on general knowledge and academic background for prospective teachers. Some colleges required a liberal arts major in addition to general education and professional training.

In the 1970s and 1980s, in addition to a continuing concern for liberally educated teachers, other curriculum changes were taking place. From data gathered in the Preservice Education Study, Howey (1983) notes that less than 40% of a prospective teacher's total undergraduate study was in professional training, with less than 15% of that time in some sort of supervised practice. According to Howey, this hardly seemed enough time to adequately prepare teachers, especially in view of the fact that new technology was being developed and concern for minorities and handicapped children required that departments of education change their curricula to include such technological and professional courses as microteaching, computer instruction, individualized instruction, specialized reading courses, multicultural education, and techniques for mainstreaming handicapped children into the classroom. Method courses changed to include such techniques as microteaching, simulation, protocol materials, and reflective teaching (Houston & Newman, 1982).

In an attempt to influence the content of teacher-training programs, the premier early childhood organizations, the Association of Childhood Education International (1983) and the National Association for the Education of Young Children (1982), have published recommendations for both broad liberal education and professional courses in order that teachers be adequately trained. The list includes academic study in philosophy, sociology, anthropology, math, science, social studies, language, and literature; professional study in educational philosophy, learning theory, child psychology, early childhood curriculum, and human relations; technical study in methods of teaching early childhood education; and several practical experiences.

As knowledge expands, and demands that teachers be more and more knowledgeable increase, one can well understand why reports on schooling recommend that schools develop different steps for becoming an expert teacher and at the top the career professional be required to obtain a Ph.D. and have several years of experience (Goodlad, 1986; Holmes Group, 1986). Haberman (1983) reminds us that we need to resolve the dilemma of the academic and professional content needed in teacher-preparation programs as there is a limited amount of time, even if training were extended to 5 or 6 years, to include everything that many critics feel is needed for one to become an expert teacher. Certainly, in spite of continued controversies, there is a consensus that all teachers should be liberally educated with in-depth knowledge and understanding of the range of subjects they are to teach, and that teachers need a professional education that includes knowledge of the problems of universal education, understanding of learners and the learning process, methods and materials for instruction, and some practice in the skills of teaching (Woodring, 1983).

IS ONE PHILOSOPHICAL ORIENTATION BETTER THAN ANOTHER?

As knowledge about child growth and development and different learning theories has developed, nineteenth- and twentieth-century debates have ensued regarding the basic philosophical orientation to be expected of teachers of young children.

Early childhood education has been traditionally rooted in Rousseauian philosophy of nurturing young children. In his book, *Emile,* Rousseau (1762/1947) stated the importance of educating children without restrictions in nature and allowing them to unfold naturally through play and developing their senses, a romantic notion for educating children of the rich. Though Rousseau greatly influenced ideas about education, he never put them into practice. It was Pestalozzi who translated these ideas into practical programs for all young children, rich or poor. He stressed the dignity, worth, and individuality of all children, and he devised materials and object lessons that developed the child's oral language and sensory perception (Weber, 1984). In the mid 1800s, Pestalozzi's method became known in this country through a normal school established at Oswego, New York. Teachers of pedagogy urged their students to use these methods recognizing the individuality of children and instructing them by using materials that lead from concrete to abstract concepts, from particular to general ideas (Woodring, 1976). At the same time, Frederick Froebel's ideas, following Rousseau's and Pestalozzi's philosophies, were making great impact on the kindergarten movement in this country, through such educational leaders as

Henry Barnard, Susan Blow, and Elizabeth Peabody. Froebel developed carefully designed materials, called gifts and occupations, that teachers could use with children. These were intended to develop children's creative self-expression and sensory perception, and the materials were later developed so that other teachers could follow instructions and use them in their classrooms. They represented the first "programmed" materials available to all teachers anywhere (Weber, 1969). Unfortunately, these materials that were so influential in establishing the notions of the importance of play and of nurturing children came to be used in ritualistic and uninteresting ways.

At the beginning of the twentieth century, G. Stanley Hall and John Dewey exerted influence on early childhood educators, stressing that the scientific method of child study should be the base of the teacher's curriculum. Though Dewey and Hall stressed the importance of play and activity for children's learning, the role of the teacher in providing the child's education was to change. Previously, the early childhood teacher was expected to be a nurturer and dispensor of carefully designed materials. She was now to become a person who could study, analyze, and evaluate the growth and learning of children so that she could determine appropriate learning goals and provide appropriate activities for children in her classroom (Weber, 1984).

At the same time that Dewey's ideas were influencing education, so were the writings and research related to the behaviorism of William Thorndike. Thorndike theorized that learning was the result of responses and connections that the organism makes to stimuli that are received. Since he believed that change was a result of a change in habits of thought and action, then it was the teacher's responsibility to establish worthy habits for children, and thus to help them behave in predetermined ways. Skinner expanded these theories of learning to include operant conditioning as a way children learn. Gestalt psychologists influenced concepts of education in relation to closure and insight. Psychoanalysis theory of personality development moved educational theory away from academic learning, as the only goal of schools, to responsibility for the development of the whole child. Arnold Gesell's theories of maturation and readiness influenced the child-study movement also. His normative ages and stages were presented to teachers in training as ways of determining children's levels of maturation and readiness for certain types of instruction. Piaget's theories of intellectual development became very current in this country in the 1960s and challenged the notion of fixed intelligence. His developmental theories of children's growth emphasized the role environment plays in the child's intellectual development.

By the mid 1900s, there were a number of conflicting theories about child development and learning. Teacher candidates' curriculum expanded to include the various theories, and teachers were expected to integrate this knowledge into their own personal philosophy (Borrowman, 1956). As a result, what children could learn and how that learning should be taught became a great controversy. In the 1960s, the federal government funded a large research project in an effort to determine effective models of early childhood education. Structured program models emphasizing academic content and basically behavioristic in theory were compared to open education models emphasizing the child's total development and basically following the teachings of Piaget and Dewey. The theories and the movements, as well as research related to these theories, are all part of the continuing controversies in teacher-education programs today.

Though most teacher-education programs tend to follow the more eclectic approach of presenting all the theories, some programs have been designed in response to a particular theory. The competency-based teacher-education models were developed on the behavioristic notion that learning can be structured in a sequential manner and that activities can be developed to assure that learning takes place. Other programs have a strong basis in the psychoanalytic theory of personality development. In these programs, students are to be in charge of their own learning, and the development of one's own personality becomes an important focus.

HOW IMPORTANT ARE THE PRACTICAL EXPERIENCES?

Practical experiences have been a hallmark of teacher training since the beginning of teacher education. Most candidates for teaching in the 1700s and into the 1800s were first apprenticed to experienced teachers. They learned how to become teachers by observing another teach and by teaching themselves. As normal schools developed, the same principle of apprenticeship continued. In the first normal school in Massachusetts, a model elementary school for thirty boys and girls of ages six to ten was established. The students at the normal school were the children's teachers, and the principal of the normal school, Mr. Pierce, was the students' supervisor and instructor. Pierce believed that his students would learn to be good teachers by observing him model different practices with children and subsequently practicing the techniques with the children (Haberman, 1983). The general philosophy of the direct teaching experience was that this experience should be at the very heart of the preservice training program and that improved technique in teaching children should be the goal of the program (Borrowman, 1956).

In the first part of the twentieth century, Dewey was concerned that this viewpoint of field experiences relied too heavily on students learning only technical skills and not analytical skills. Dewey advocated a college laboratory school in which teacher-education students could participate in teaching children with methods reflecting current research as well as theoretical, social, and ethical principles of learning (Dewey, 1940). Critics of this approach maintained that students trained in this fashion had not learned to deal with the "real world of teaching." The arguments in the 1940s and 1950s regarding the importance of student teaching experiences revolved around these two issues: Should these student teachers be versed in the techniques of teaching, or should they be developing into thoughtful and independent teachers, able to make decisions about curriculum practices? The debate continues today.

In the 1970s and 1980s, field experiences in most teacher-training programs expanded so that programs include early experiences. This concept is based on the sociological notion that there is a school culture that teacher candidates must master if they are to become successful teachers. The persons deemed most capable of presenting this culture are the experienced and expert teachers who have amassed a great deal of knowledge about what works in particular classrooms (Berliner, 1986). It is felt that the student teacher's learning, to be effective, must take place in the school setting, where the candidate can learn the tools of the trade in the reality of day-to-day class events (Zeichner, 1983). Most programs of teacher education have some field experiences beginning in the freshman or sophomore year, where teacher candidates progress from limited experience with classroom teaching and management to full-time teaching under expert supervision (*State of Teacher Education,* 1977).

There is a tendency today to increase the number and length of these classroom experiences, and this perspective raises the question in teacher education as to whether teacher candidates should be trained to fit into existing school patterns, thus learning to become good technicians, or whether trainees should be educated to effect changes in the schools. Do more experiences in the classroom tend to encourage prospective teachers to support the status quo, or can these varied and different experiences help to give trainees an understanding of how change can be effected? Can these experiences have a liberating effect on their thinking? In spite of the increases, there is not clear evidence of the beneficial nature of such experiences (Waxman & Walberg, 1986).

Extended field experiences are developed in connection with the theoretical college courses with the intent that as students examine different practices, witness varying socioeconomic conditions, and study theories of development and learning, they will develop the analytic and problem-solving skills necessary to become thoughtful and independent teachers. Schon (1987) suggests that practical experiences can produce reflective students if the program of studies provides students with opportunities to connect university knowledge with prior experiences, practice at a point when students are ready to try out new ideas and methods learned in university classrooms, and, most important of all, time for reflection. Haberman (1983) points out that research examining the efficacy of field experiences indicates that in reality students are more concerned with the technical aspects of teaching. With cooperating teachers exerting much more influence over their behaviors than college instructors or supervisors, students tend to believe that development of the skills of a technician and a classroom manager is most important. Zeichner (1980) concludes that "field based experiences seem to entail a complicated set of both positive and negative consequences" (p. 46).

Today, educators continue to insist on the importance of practical experiences for teacher candidates. Yet, if university training programs are to prepare future teachers able to move beyond the status quo, then field experiences must provide students with opportunities to compare and contrast techniques and methods, observe children's actions or learning as a result of these practices, and then analyze and criticize their own and others' actions in relationship to current sociological and psychological theories of development and learning.

MODEL PROGRAMS

Do teacher educators respond to the demands for change and excellence that are mounted every few years? At times, it would seem that they do not, since too many teachers seem unable to educate all young children so that the American dream is fulfilled. However, many changes have taken place over the years with regard to teacher education. The length of training has increased, and the content of curriculum has extended to include both liberal arts and professional courses. As different learning theories and developmental theories have been espoused, course content has been adapted, and field experiences have been extended and varied in content.

Philosophical Orientation

Certainly change is slow, but there have been many changes in teacher-education programs that strive to incorporate into teacher training certain elements of what critics suggest needs to be improved. During the reform movements of the 1960s and 1970s, many teacher-education programs were revised (Joyce, Yarger, Howey, Harbeck, & Kluwin, 1977; National Commission on Teacher Education and Professional Standards, 1963; Razik, 1980). The United States Office of Education in 1968–1969 funded ten institutions to develop innovative teacher-education programs that could then be tested out (Houston & Newman, 1982). Besides specific technical differences, the innovative programs reflected different philosophical orientations. In analyzing these varying programs, Zeichner (1983) describes four different philosophical approaches: behavioristic, traditional-craft, personalistic, and inquiry-oriented teacher education. Razik similarly organizes the model programs he describes into four categories—developmental, behavioral, humanistic, and behavioristic/humanistic. Houston and Newman categorize similar models of teacher education into competency-based, personalized, and humanistic.

Behavioristic or competency-based teacher education focuses upon the technical aspect of teacher education and has its foundation in the behavioral viewpoint of conditioned learning. Advocates maintain that there are specific competencies that a teacher must master and that these competencies can be sequenced and mastered in a predetermined fashion. The goals and objectives of such a program are stated in behavioral terms, pretests are often given to determine the level of competency of candidates, standardized procedures for accomplishing the goals are established, and means for objective evaluations of the stated competencies are developed. The belief of advocates of such a viewpoint is that there is a predetermined body of professional content to be learned, as well as specific types of teaching skills to be mastered. In the 1970s, the movement gained much support. Sandefur and Westbrook (1978) reported that out of 686 institutions studied, 84% were involved in or exploring competency-based education. A follow-up study indicated that interest waned in the 1980s as those involved in this type of training dropped to 59% (Sandefur & Nicklas, 1981).

The personalistic or humanistic approach is based upon perceptual and developmental psychologies. Teacher-education programs are developed to provide for the psychological maturity of the teacher candidates. The programs are responsive to the needs of teacher candidates, who become active participants in their own learning. Students are encouraged to try out a number of different approaches and techniques and to discover the method of teaching that best suits their unique personalities. Combs and his colleagues (1974) implemented a program of teacher education at the University of Florida based on humanistic principles. In other programs, courses for self-understanding and personality development are offered as important components of the teacher-training program, as in the Syracuse University program (Razik, 1980). Sometimes infusion of the concepts, skills, and attitudes necessary for self-understanding is the model used (Cole, McCormick, & Hayes, 1985). Some programs have experimented with a special seminar group in which students share problems and build a personal educational belief system (Goodman, 1982).

The inquiry-oriented perspective educates the teacher candidate to be a critical thinker. As the candidate studies both the content of professional education and the skills of teaching, the prospective teacher is taught to relate the theory of the college classroom to the reality of the school classroom. A questioning attitude is encouraged regarding school curriculum, teaching practices, and the knowledge, skills, and attitudes, plus the social culture, children bring to the classroom. The prospective teachers' course of study should require them not only to examine and question these issues, but to determine the consequences of their own and others' actions. The inquiry-oriented perspective advocates that teachers should become decision makers in their own classrooms and thus must have not only the skills for teaching and knowledge of curriculum and development, but also the ability to question and to analyze.

Zeichner and Tabachnick (1982) point out that though these differing perspectives are found in various practices, a total program for training teachers in any given institution tends to be eclectic in nature and would use more than one orientation. This situation is due, in part, because, even though a particular orientation is the prime focus of a certain program, different instructors in the same institution offer differing perspectives.

Models of Specific Programs

The teacher-education programs that are described next would function with more than one philosophical orientation—however a different major focus or orientation undergirds each described program. Though all three programs were developed with the intent to improve students' academic knowledge and improve the quality of practical experiences, they differ in their strategies for effecting change.

Competency-based education became a byword of the 1970s. Though many teacher-education programs adopted varying forms of this type of instruction, there are programs developed around the basic tenents of behaviorism. The content, skills, and attitudes essential for teacher education are identified and then criteria-referenced objectives are established. Experiences are designed to meet these objectives, and evaluation procedures are developed to assess learning.

Weber State College's Individualized Performance Based Program is an example of the competency-based program (Burke, 1972). Though the academic component of the program is an important part of the student's program for certification, the professional component is the focus of this description. Modules developed to include all the components deemed essential for teacher preparation are the main focus of instruction. Each module is consistent in its format but varies greatly in content, type of learning experience, and evaluation procedures. All the modules, however, contain a preassessment tool, behavioral objectives for the particular competency sought, and a variety of learning experiences to enable students to achieve the competency and procedures for student's self-evaluation, as well as evaluation by others. Students sign out modules and are responsible for carrying out the requirements of the learning modules, seeking advice and consultation from a faculty member, and completing the assessment requirement. The faculty, besides developing and revising the modules as needed, conduct certain lectures and seminars pertinent to specific modules, advise and counsel students, and direct the assessment of the students' progress and completion of the modules. Though students basically can proceed at their own pace and study in a variety settings, i.e., college, home, or school, 2-hour blocks of time are set aside for some of the modules that are dependent upon group lectures or seminars.

An interaction laboratory provides for human-relations training for the students. A practicum center approach to student teaching provides the practical experiences for the students. A team-teaching approach is used to place and supervise the students. The team consists of a master teacher, another certified teacher, and three or more students. The master teachers work in cooperation with the college faculty to provide the trainees with experiences of observing children and for planning and conducting lessons in accordance with the aims and objectives of the teacher-education program.

Though the model is heavily behaviorist in its approach, there are also elements of the personalized approach. Students make many decisions about their own pace and style of learning. Students develop self-awareness through the human-relations training labs. The craft of teaching is demonstrated by experienced and expert teachers in the fields, as students learn the "culture of schooling" from those who should know it best.

In contrast, the philosophical perspective of the University of Missouri-Columbia program is based on a personalized, humanistic approach (Leake, 1981). This program, developed to impact on the personal life and behavior of its participants, emphasizes the importance of human uniqueness and the development of participants' competencies in intrapersonal and interpersonal relationships. The HIP program—an acronym for "humanizing, individualizing, and personalizing"—consists of three 16-semester-hour blocks, including both field experiences and university course work. Students usually take one of the blocks per year, thus pursuing their university academic requirements in the off semesters. In this manner, the students are totally immersed in teacher training during the semesters that they are enrolled in the program.

Each participant in the HIP program is a member of both a learning community in the participating school and a learning community at the university, which includes an interdisciplinary team of professional educators. Students spend one-third of each day in their assigned classrooms and the rest of the day in an open-space university classroom. The faculty integrates the professional content so that daily learning in the university classroom correlates with daily learning from field experiences. The professional content is integrated into didactic activities, which are usually offered in 2- or 3-week time slots and are usually competency based with behavioral objectives, instructional alternatives, and alternative assessment procedures.

Specialized topics, such as values clarification, humanistic education, discipline strategies, drug education, media techniques, and career education, are emphasized throughout the entire program. Ongoing planning and evaluation of the instructional program by the faculty takes place at weekly design meetings. Students have input into the curriculum at the biweekly learning community meetings attended by both students and teachers. Students also select the topics for the special topic seminars planned each semester.

While students are involved in their assigned field experiences, they are closely supervised by university faculty, and conferences between cooperating teachers, students, and university faculty are held on a regular basis. Usually the students' advisors are their university supervisors and are the same persons for all 3 years of involvement in the program.

A good deal of individualizing and personalizing of the program is further provided by the low advisor-advisee ratio, not more than one to ten. Advisors meet weekly with their advisees to discuss and evaluate both successes and problems students are encountering. These meetings, at times formal, are often held on a more informal basis, such as over dinner or lunch. The various types of formal and informal group meetings required in the program provide trainees the opportunities for developing important intrapersonal and interpersonal skills and for helping them define their unique teaching strengths.

The University of Maryland Baltimore County Early Childhood Developmental Program was developed using a process approach to education (Barbour & Webster, 1987). The intent is to develop teachers who approach teaching as young children approach the world, "always asking questions, becoming completely absorbed in the search for the truth" (Torrance, 1970, p. 3). The content of professional study is reorganized around the processes of perceiving, knowing, creating, feeling, valuing, communicating, decision making, and problem solving (Berman, 1968). Child development, learning theory, curriculum concepts and practices, and self-awareness are studied and practiced in courses that integrate the content with the processes. All candidates are required to fulfill general academic requirements, but must also complete an academic major in a discipline of the student's choice.

Four components were designed to integrate the students' professional and academic knowledge, understanding of self, and practical application:

1. Conferencing processes
2. Direct instruction in early-childhood content
3. Experiences in observing and recording child behavior and in organizing instruction for young children
4. Processes for examining one's own feelings and beliefs regarding issues and experiences related to children.

Conferencing Process

Formal conferences with college instructors, as well as with classroom teachers, are ongoing throughout the students' experiences. An initial interview/information session informs candidates of the program and acquaints the early childhood staff with students' interests, experiences with young children, and academic areas of interest. As students are observed working with young children, conferences are held with student, classroom teacher, and college supervisor to encourage students to analyze events. Each semester, two formal, regularly scheduled conferences are conducted with each student and the early childhood staff to evaluate the student's progress in academic, professional, and practical knowledge.

Direct Instruction

Students are required to attend lectures and seminars related to professional content organized around the processes. Students study learning, curriculum, and developmental theories, then observe children and plan instruction according to pertinent theories. Students compare and contrast their experiences with each other, as well as with certain theorists.

Experience

During each semester that students take early-childhood courses, they are required to work two mornings a week under the direction of skilled classroom teachers. Students thus have a variety of school experiences, working with children from infancy to 8 years, with principals and directors with different philosophies, with teachers of different classroom management and organizational styles, with children from different cultural and socioeconomic backgrounds, and with parents who have different expectations and involvement in their children's education.

Examination of Feelings and Beliefs

The process of examining one's beliefs, attitudes, and values occurs informally in many settings during the students' program, i.e., in class, in schoolrooms, in conferences, in dorm life, and at home. Formally, there are process seminars organized around such content as children's literature, creative media, math, and science. In these seminars, students examine their own feelings of joy, fear, frustration, anxiety, and love in relation to the content and compare these feelings with what they witness or study regarding children's feelings. The seminars are aimed at helping students understand how feelings and sense of self-worth affect teaching and learning.

As students progress through the program, particular skills and competencies are emphasized at each level. In the final semester, students are expected to integrate their knowledge and experiences in order to plan and make decisions for children's learning. During this time, they expand their concept of a teacher's role in society and examine the political and social forces that affect education in America.

Though the basic focus of the program is to enable students to analyze and question theories of child development and curriculum, considerable emphasis is placed on developing one's own style and craft of teaching. While there are some particular behavioral skills required of students, most of the listed competencies are developmental.

SUMMARY

Throughout the 1900s, college training programs have continually responded and reacted to society's demand for improved instruction in schools. Education requirements for teachers of young children have increased from a high school diploma with a few weeks of normal-school training to a requirement of a bachelor's degree from an accredited college or university. The early normal schools expanded their years of required study until they eventually became multipurpose universities. Teacher educators have experimented with, and tried, in various ways, to resolve, the issues that seem to plague the profession. Liberal arts requirements have been upgraded, and professional studies have broadened to include new technologies and new emphases for changing populations. Requirements to enter teacher-education programs have been changed in efforts to attract more capable students. Required field experiences, which allow for gradual introduction as well as a variety of experiences with observation and practice, are in nearly every teacher-training program. Innovation, change, and experimentation have taken place in teacher education in the twentieth century. However, it has not been extensive or intensive enough to eliminate the controversies that surround teacher education.

Some educators suggest that in order to address improvement in the teaching profession, it is necessary to upgrade the rewards system. One way, often suggested, is to provide a career ladder for outstanding classroom teachers, who would be specially trained as career professionals to assume responsibility for curriculum innovation and for supervision of program neophytes. This newly created position would require not only expertise in teaching, but additional study plus collaboration with university specialists to conduct research projects on teaching and on the conditions surrounding teaching (Carnegie Forum on Education and the Economy, 1986; Goodlad, 1986; Holmes Group, 1986).

If America is to continue its leadership in the twenty-first century, then change and improvement in teacher preparation must continue. Most likely this means that controversy, as well as experimentation, will be with us for some time to come.

REFERENCES

Association of Childhood Education International. (1983). *Childhood education's guidelines for teacher preparation.* Washington, DC: Author.

Barbour, N. H., & Webster, M. T. (1987). *Theory into practice: Field based education programs do work.* Urbana, IL: Educational Resources Information Center. (ERIC Document Reproduction Service No. ED 286 620)

Berliner, D. (1986). In pursuit of the expert pedagogue. *Educational Researcher, 15*(7), 5–13.

Berman, L. M. (1968). *New priorities in the curriculum.* Columbus, OH: Merrill.

Bone, T. (1980). Current trends in initial training. In E. Hoyle & J. Megarry (Eds.), *Professional development of teachers: World yearbook of education 1980* (pp. 57–70). London: Kogan Page.

Borrowman, M. L. (1956). *The liberal and technical in teacher education: A historical survey of American thought.* New York: Teachers College Press.

Burke, C. (1972). *The individualized competency-based system of teacher education at Weber State College.* Washington, DC: American Association of Colleges for Teacher Education.

Carnegie Forum on Education and the Economy. (1986). *A nation prepared: Teachers for the 21st century.* New York: Author.

Cole, D. J., McCormick, T. E., & Hayes, D. G. (1985). *Institutional change: The infusion of human relations into preservice teacher education programs.* Urbana, IL: Educational Resources Information Center. (ERIC Document Reproduction Service No. ED 258 942)

Combs, A. W., Blume, R. A., Newman, A. J., & Wass, H. L. (1974). *The professional education of teachers: A humanistic approach to teacher preparation* (2nd ed.). Boston: Allyn & Bacon.

Dewey, J. (1940). *Education today.* New York: G. P. Putnam's Sons.

Goodlad, J. I. (1986). *A place called school: Prospects for the future.* New York: McGraw-Hill.

Goodman, J. (1982). *The role of the university: The seminar experience in a humanistic teacher education program.* Urbana, IL: Educational Resources Information Center. (ERIC Document Reproduction Service No. ED 213 685)

Haberman, M. (1983). Research on preservice laboratory and clinical experiences: Implications for teacher education. In K. R. Howey & W. E. Gardner (Eds.), *Education of teachers: A look ahead* (pp. 98–118). New York: Longman.

Holmes Group. (1986). *Tomorrow's teachers.* East Lansing, MI: Author.

Houston, W. R., & Newman, K. K. (1982). Teacher education programs. In H. E. Mitzel (Ed.), *Encyclopedia of educational research* (5th ed., pp. 1881–1894). New York: Macmillan.

Howey, K. R. (1983). Teacher education: An overview. In K. R. Howey & W. E. Gardner (Eds.), *The education of teachers* (pp. 6–37). New York: Longman.

Joyce, B. R., Yarger, S. J., Howey, K., Harbeck, K., & Kluwin, T. (1977). *Preservice teacher education*. Washington, DC: Office of Education, Department of Health, Education and Welfare. (ERIC Document Reproduction Service No. ED 146 120)

Lanier, J. E., & Little, J. W. (1986). Research on teacher education. In M. C. Wittrock (Ed.), *Handbook of research on teaching* (3rd ed., pp. 527–569). New York: Macmillan.

Leake, J. B. (1981). *Excellence at a new level for teacher education*. Urbana, IL: Educational Resources Information Center. (ERIC Document Reproduction Service No. ED 200 578)

Lortie, D. (1975). *Schoolteacher*. Chicago: University of Chicago Press.

National Association for the Education of Young Children. (1982). *Early childhood teacher education guidelines*. Washington, DC: Author.

National Commission on Teacher Education and Professional Standards. (1963). *Changes in teacher education*. Washington, DC: National Education Association.

Razik, T. A. (1980). *Innovation in teacher education: The challenge to prepare teachers as agents of change*. Urbana, IL: Educational Resources Information Center. (ERIC Document Reproduction Service No. ED 202 858)

Rousseau, J. J. (1947). L'Emile ou l'education. In O. G. Tellows & R. R. Tarrey (Eds.), *The age of enlightenment* (pp. 416–513). New York: F. S. Crofts. (Original work published 1762)

Sandefur, W. S., & Nicklas, W. L. (1981). Competency-based teacher education in AACTE institutions: An update. *Phi Delta Kappan, 62,* 747–748.

Sandefur, W. S., & Westbrook, D. (1978). Involvement of AACTE institutions in CBTE: A follow-up study. *Phi Delta Kappan, 59,* 633–634.

Sarason, S. B., Davidson, K. S., & Blatt, B. (1986). *The preparation of teachers: An unstudied problem in education* (rev. ed.). Cambridge, MA: Brookline Books.

Schon, D. A. (1987). *Educating the reflective practitioner: Toward a new design for teaching and learning in the professions*. San Francisco: Jossey-Bass.

Snyder, A. (1972). *Dauntless women in childhood education*. Washington, DC: Association of Childhood Education International.

State of Teacher Education. (1977). Washington, DC: National Center for Education Statistics. (ERIC Document Reproduction Service No. ED 164 487)

Torrance, E. P. (1970). What it means to become human. In M. M. Scoby & G. Graham (Eds.), *To nurture humanness* (pp. 1–17). Washington, DC: Association of Supervision & Curriculum Development.

Vance, V. S., & Schlechty, P. C. (1982). The distribution of academic ability in the teaching force: Policy implications. *Phi Delta Kappan, 64,* 2–27.

Waxman, H. C., & Walberg, H. J. (1986). Effects of early field experiences. In J. D. Raths & L. G. Katz (Eds.), *Advances in teacher education* (Vol. 2, pp. 165–185). New Jersey: Ablex.

Weber, E. (1969). *The kindergarten*. New York: Teachers College Press.

Weber, E. (1984). *Ideas influencing early childhood education: A theoretical analysis*. New York: Teachers College Press.

Woodring, P. (1957). *New directions in teacher education*. New York: Fund for the Advancement of Education.

Woodring, P. (1976). The development of teacher education. In K. Ryan (Ed.), *Teacher education* (pp. 1–25). Chicago: University of Chicago Press.

Woodring, P. (1983). *The persistent problems of education*. Bloomington, IN: Phi Delta Kappa Educational Foundation. (ERIC Document Reproduction Service No. ED 245 366)

Zeichner, K. M. (1980). Myths and realities: Field-based experiences in preservice teacher education. *Journal of Teacher Education, 31*(6), 45–55.

Zeichner, K. M. (1983). Alternative paradigms of teacher education. *Journal of Teacher Education, 34*(3), 3–9.

Zeichner, K. M., & Tabachnick, B. (1982). The belief systems of university supervisors in an elementary student teaching program. *Journal of Education for Teaching, 8*(1), 34–54.

8

Alternate Modes of Teacher Preparation

GAIL PERRY
University of Massachusetts–Amherst, MA

One belief has remained constant through the years—that good programs for young children rely on competent staff, and central to the development of competent teachers are good teacher-preparation programs. It has never been more imperative than now, as we near the end of the century with the world population growing at 150 a minute (Hymes, 1988), to meet the child care challenge with innovative and effective systems for producing qualified teachers. These past 3 decades have seen a struggle within, and a reexamination, of the teacher-preparation system as teacher educators have attempted to respond to the accelerated social changes and their own standards. This chapter will examine the emergence of several viable alternatives to traditional 4-year campus-based college preparation.

In the late 1960s, bolstered by Ford, Carnegie, and Conant's study, *The Education of American Teachers* (1963), teacher-preparation programs came under a mantle of criticism, prompting reform movements. Early childhood programs of teacher education as well became targets of the popular school-bashing trend. The criticism most frequently leveled at these institutions was that of offering programs irrelevant to the real work of teachers. Changes in the way we prepare persons to teach young children were influenced by several factors in the environment: the growing demand for more preschool teachers than existing teacher-education schools were able to produce; the emergence of greatly diversified child care settings serving both younger and older children and their families for longer hours; more children from diverse ethnic groups attending preschools, as well as handicapped youngsters—all of whom required many different kinds of early-childhood staff; and a profusion of research and literature that contributed to an expanded understanding of the teaching process of both adults and children.

NEW PERSPECTIVES OF THE ROLE OF
THE NURSERY SCHOOL TEACHER

Since the nature of teacher preparation must perforce be governed by current understanding of the teaching process, this next section will highlight some of the newer concepts of the teaching role. These views of teaching both guided and took form in the best of the alternative modes of teacher preparation. Many of these perspectives were elaborations and modifications of the role of the nursery school teacher set forth in the beginnings of the early childhood movement.

Early childhood educators began to see the child through different lenses. One of those lenses was that of competency. There was a new respect for young children as competent human beings, capable of setting directions for their own learning. As infancy research grew and became more sophisticated, even a month-old infant was viewed as having many capabilities (Bower, 1974; Horowitz, 1975). Child-development researchers began to ask what preschoolers could do and to describe their competencies—children with memory and math skills and creative intelligence, with ideas of their own—rather than the previous deficit model, which described what young children could not do in relation to older children (Donaldson, 1978; Gelman, 1978; Nelson & Gruendel, 1981; Wellman & Somerville, 1978). This led to helping the teacher learn to listen more sensitively to what the young child was saying and doing; to see the young child as a source of ideas and a participant in shaping the curriculum, as well as the recipient of curriculum. "The child must be a fully involved participant in his own learning" (Hawkins, 1974, p. 1). The idea of the teacher as a "facilitator" became popular, and teachers were urged to focus on a child's self-concept as well as autonomous behavior. The child should be helped "to grow in awareness of self: who he is, what he can do, what his place in the world can be . . . (and the teacher) encourages children's awareness of selves as persons with unique interests, abilities, and characteristics; accepts and values the natural individuality of children and children's trust in their own ability to cope with the world" (Mallum, 1970, p. 15).

Another lens through which the teaching role was viewed was the emphasis on providing the right learning environment and classroom setting. Many diversified materials and equipment became key provisions for fostering curiosity and learning (Hawkins, 1974). These provisions were often raw materials, discarded items that were turned into creative, imaginative learning centers or activities. Emerging from this view was the widely popular "hands-on" movement. Through the proliferation of Piagetian theory and its many interpretations (and misinterpretations) and translation to the early childhood classroom, the concept of the child as an active learner gained new meaning. Although this idea was certainly not new to the early childhood establishment (Johnson, 1934), the notion that "intelligence will not develop fully unless children have the chance to test themselves against and come to terms with, all sorts of chunks of the world of experience" (Wiles, 1973) gained recognition throughout the child care network and prompted a profusion of preschool literature designed to assure that the teacher of young children first and foremost gave children opportunities to manipulate, play, and explore. "Free play" (which later gave way to work/play to make explicit the distinction that play was children's work) still dominates schedules of early childhood programs. Aside from providing an environment rich in stimulating materials, the teacher's role during free play was not clearly defined, or else was stated in ambiguous terms, such as "letting the children explore" or "helping them problem solve."

A view through a third lens portrayed new thinking about the role of context in the young child's learning. A body of developmental literature emerged that emphasized the role of context in cognitive as well as social activities, and suggested that children's skills fluctuate as a function of the situation (Barker & Wright, 1954; Brofenbrenner 1979; Rogoff & Lave, 1984). These developmental psychologists portrayed cognition as an everyday affair that takes shape in the course of individual participation in socially organized practices. "Cognitive development takes place as children gradually make their way toward a system of adult existence in a community" (White & Siegel, 1984, p. 253). The concepts of the socialization of children into the larger society, and concurrently parent/teacher relationships, have been valued for many years by early childhood educators. However, in many ways, the socialization has been treated as a "universal process through which all children acquire a common stock of knowledge, attitudes, beliefs and customs . . ." (White & Siegel, 1984, p. 239) producing the generic three, four and five year old. Head Start gave the early childhood field an intense experience with children who operate in widely varying contexts. The terms *multicultural education* and *cultural and cognitive conflict* became more evident in the literature as implications for the teacher were defined. The preschool teacher was asked to become sensitive to these behavior settings that influence children's thinking and development in order to adapt curriculum and interactions with children appropriately.

A fourth way our view of the teaching role was sharpened was in magnifying the actual teacher/child encounter. Teaching came to be seen less as a one-way process—what teachers do to and for children. Teaching as a reciprocal process that changes from minute to minute as the teacher/child interaction proceeds was illuminated by sociolinguists (Cazden, 1984; Cazden, John, & Hymes, 1972; Green, 1983). The curriculum was seen as much more than what teachers plan in advance. As teacher-child interactions were analyzed in the actual process of implementing activities and group times, it became clear that children's and teachers' responses to each other during classroom discourse often determined what was taught and what was learned, regardless of what was in the curriculum plan for that day.

> On the basis of the cues people in interaction develop an idea of what the context is at the moment; in a sense they define the context. Because in the course of the on-going interaction, the context may change from moment to moment, their

definition of context may also change. It is partly because of these momentary definitions that people are able to know and decide what is going on. How they shape their discourse shows what they really understand the task to be; what they do shows what they understand is going on. (Guthrie, 1976, p. 3)

Curriculum, within this perspective, is an evolving process created through reciprocal teaching interactions, as the teacher attempts to make the child a true partner in the discourse. Videotape feedback, interaction analysis patterns, and microteaching techniques all helped teachers examine, define, and refine their teaching behavior as good teaching was seen in the microcosm of the dynamic teacher-child exchange.

FEATURES OF THE ALTERNATIVE TEACHER-EDUCATION MODELS

As an artifact of the much-described era of the sixties, the alternative teacher-education movement was a revolution—not only marked by the proverbial "bucking of the establishment," but also carrying the banner for children and teachers as human beings first and foremost. The doors of teacher education were opened to persons from a wide ethnic and socioeconomic background. The commitment to change, innovation, and relevance resulted in curricula that were characterized not by preconceived answers, but by a dynamic development as the program grew. Most programs were informal in ethos, small in scale, and anxious to try out the new ideas about teaching. While alternative programs were created to meet specific teacher-education needs, some common threads emerged that were related to the newer perspectives of the teaching role.

Integration

The first thread that seems to tie the teacher-education alternatives together was the priority placed on the integration of theory and practice. Traditional modes of teacher education still expected the student to master theoretical concepts of child development in relative isolation, without ongoing opportunities to integrate this content into their own lives and work with children. While lip service was given to the importance of early and extended fieldwork, with the exception of a limited number of institutions, few chances were offered to students for practical application until the end of their 4 years of campus study. Often, it was many years before the students' course work became relevant to their intended goal—to learn how to teach. Therefore, the alternative teacher educator was most often located at or near teaching sites and developed specific techniques designed to make the theoretical implications come alive in practice with children.

A second aspect of the integration principle addressed by alternative teacher education was the coordination between preschools and teacher-training programs. Student teachers at traditional institutions often had to face discrepancies between the idealized textbook world of teaching portrayed in the college classroom and the real world of children confronting them when they entered their teaching sites. Directors, cooperating teachers, and college faculty frequently criticized each other's views of teaching and disagreed about appropriate learning experiences for young children. The student teacher was thus caught in the middle, with few resources from whom to seek guidance. Most of the alternative models of teacher education sought to move away from placing all responsibility on the college for preparation for educational service. Instead, they developed collaborative models in which teacher preparation was accepted as a mutual responsibility of colleges, schools, professional organizations, and the students themselves. Vehicles were established for discussing needs and differing philosophies and for reaching compromises—in general, making the teacher preparation more responsive to local communities and the students themselves. Alternative teacher education was not seen as a set of common experiences of all students as in the traditional mode, but rather as a set of common objectives with varied and unique experiences. Professional organizations also became more actively involved in the teacher-preparation process, such as the development of the *Early Childhood Teacher Education Guidelines for Four- and Five-Year Programs,* which were established by the National Association for the Education of Young Children (NAEYC) (1982).

Autonomy/Reciprocal Relationships

A second unifying feature of the alternative teacher-preparation models was the promotion of autonomy and reciprocal relationships between teacher and learner. Just as the research on teaching as a reciprocal process sharpened our insight into the teacher/child dialogue and relationship in the preschool, so, too, did it cast a shadow on the unidirectional relationship in the college classroom. On traditional campuses, professors dominated the classroom discourse through lecture and examination, and students listened, took notes, and studied for exams. As older, more experienced child-care providers entered college classrooms, they were unsatisfied with the passive, subordinate roles they were expected to play and wanted more active participatory roles as learners. Teacher-education alternatives responded by treating students as autonomous and competent, trusting them to take more responsibility for generating their own curriculum projects and direction of study. Students' life experiences were respected as an important contribution to the understanding of early childhood education subject matter. Teacher-education settings were characterized by a two-way exchange between instructors and students: both were viewed as teacher/learner.

One example of an innovative strategy used by teacher educators to promote autonomy was the scaffolding model that emerged from the work of Vygotsky and Bruner (Vygotsky, 1962; Wood, Bruner, & Ross, 1976). Scaffolding is based on Vygotsky's notion of the "zone of proximal development," which is defined as the distance between a child's actual developmental level as determined by independent problem solving and the higher level of potential development as determined through problem solving under adult guidance or in collaboration with more capable peers. Bruner used the scaffold metaphor to describe the ideal teaching process whereby initially the teacher carries the major responsibility for activity, erecting a scaffold. As the child's development progresses, the scaffold gradually diminishes—roles of the teacher and child become increasingly equal—until the child can finally do alone what formerly could be done only in collaboration with the teacher. Teacher educators used this supportive model to help students learn the skills of teaching.

"Hands-on" Activities

A third feature of the alternative teacher-preparation models was the priority given to "hands-on" activities in class, and the concomitant emphasis on creating an interesting physical space for children. This was a distinct move away from learning primarily through text and lecture. Following the Katz (1975) principle of congruity—that adults be treated according to the developmental principles they must follow when they themselves teach young children—efforts were made by teacher educators to reduce the anxiety and tension often associated with traditional teacher-education programs. Teacher training classrooms were relaxed settings amply supplied with materials, where students could work and reflect on that work. Student teachers were invited to "mess about" with materials—to invent and construct learning materials, role-play potential teaching events, and generally practice and refine the roles they play in the classroom.

TEACHER-EDUCATION ALTERNATIVES

Teacher-education reform took on many faces, including the proliferation of consultants and advisors, training offered by specific preschool curricular models, on-the-job training, training and internships designed specifically for the paraprofessional, teacher centers, innovative nontraditional programs offered by colleges themselves, and federally initiated programs such as supplementary training and the Child Development Associate (CDA) program. These will be described briefly, with a greater emphasis on the more extensive teacher-preparation alternatives of teacher centering and the CDA program.

Consultants and Advisors

As crash preschool programs were launched, the need for immediate, on-site training was filled by consultants—experts who could travel quickly to a community and conduct workshops, visit teachers in their classrooms, and advise administrators on a variety of problems, including the development of further training. The consultant was able to individualize training based on on-site evaluations or requests and to respond specifically to the particular program needs. Contracts were arranged fairly easily, and training was usually cost efficient, as it could be designed to fit the program budget and time constraints and conducted without drawing the teaching staff away from their jobs. The quality of the training was directly related to the competency of the consultant, although by and large the core of early childhood educators serving in this capacity were the most experienced and competent. Many excellent materials, such as the booklet *Helping Others Learn to Teach* (Katz, 1979), were developed to offer techniques and principles to guide teacher educators in general, but were especially apt for consultants who had the flexibility and autonomy to innovate. One of the real problems of this form of teacher preparation was the inconsistent and short-term nature of the training. Different consultants would begin to develop ideas and competencies, but leave the program before training goals had been accomplished or trainees were able to successfully apply the new strategies or integrate new understandings into their own knowledge base.

Training by Curricular Models

As new preschool curriculum models gained popularity—and spurred on by the Office of Child Development's project, Planned Variation, which was designed to measure the impact of these approaches to early education—curriculum sponsors began to engage more actively in the role of teacher preparation (Klein, 1973). Approximately half of these sponsors were universities that had lab schools and campus training programs; the remainder were educational laboratories and research facilities, such as the Far West Lab for Research and Development in California and High/Scope Foundation in Michigan. The training was conducted through a combination of bringing trainees to the sponsor's facility for a concentrated period of time and sending staff members from the curriculum sponsors into the community where the model was being implemented. The strength of this form of teacher education lies in the clear delineation and specificity of teaching roles and philosophy of learning, thereby enabling the students to develop in-depth skills in these areas. Also, the learners are provided with a continuing evaluation and support in implementing teaching strategies with children over the year following the initial training. However, the strength of this teacher preparation is also its weakness. The potential preschool teacher experiences only the narrow domain of one perspective of learning theory, teaching role, and curriculum development associated with the particular model. "In all models, for successful curriculum implementation, the teacher must not only be fully aware of his role as prescribed by the model, but must be willing to carry out that role at all times" (Klein, 1973, p. 362). Even the exposure to the child-development literature is constrained by the modeler. Early childhood education students in this situation thereby learn only to do some things well as dictated by the curriculum model, rather than become a decision maker and develop a philosophy of teaching—to choose a curriculum and methodology best suited to an individual teaching situation.

On-the-job Training

As preschool enrollment continued to soar, and working conditions led to the highest rate of turnover in any occupation, directors were forced to hire untrained staff or those who were often ill-prepared for the diversified settings and teaching roles they were expected to perform. On-the-job training thus became a reality for many preschools. The success of on-the-job training depends on supervision by a staff member who models exemplary teaching, coupled with on-site personnel who have the time and skills to conduct adult education. In optimal settings, where these two criteria are met, on-the-job training can provide invaluable preparation for teaching because the training is truly individualized, paced to meet the trainees' demonstrated progress as they learn to adjust their teaching behavior in rhythm with the ebb and flow of classroom life. Expectations for the trainees can be clear and realistic. Even child development is best learned in a direct relationship with children, in which theory and reading can come alive in the actions of the young children with whom they work.

Unfortunately, the very impetus for on-the-job training—high numbers of untrained teachers—was also its downfall. It is, even today, difficult to find enough exemplary models from whom prospective teachers can learn. Many child care settings are ineffective places to acquire teaching skills. Some colleges offered courses in adult education, and "training of the trainers" sessions were sponsored by the government, producing a small core of skilled education coordinators. These resources, however, were too few, and most child care settings still do not have personnel who have the necessary time or skills to devote to teacher preparation. On-the-job training is most often sporadic and inconsistent.

Paraprofessional Training

Training for paraprofessionals was developed in response to two movements in the field. First was the recognition that the needs of young children in classrooms could be better addressed by employing a diversified staff—"persons of widely differing skills, training, work experience, socioeconomic background, and life histories on the teaching team" (*New York State Guidelines,* 1969, p. 4). The early manpower training programs emerged from the idea of a teaching team to perform the many and varied preschool functions (Pearl & Reissman, 1965). Teacher guidelines began to specify the role of paraprofessionals. "Some tasks could be performed by a teacher with a 2-year degree and 3–5 years practical experience; some tasks could be performed by a teacher aide with a specified amount of training and a year of experience; and some classroom functions could be carried out by an entry level classroom aide with appropriate personal qualities and a minimal orientation" (*New York State Guidelines,* 1969, p. 4). The participation of paraprofessionals on teaching teams became a reality, enriching the classroom life and facilitating the individualization of learning for children. Also, employing paraprofessionals from the child's community, especially parents, was seen as a way to provide a link to the community, creating a knowledgeable classroom resource about the child's culture and commensurate needs.

Another factor contributing to the development of paraprofessional training was the concept of career development. New access could be gained to the teaching profession for those usually unable to enroll in college programs. Persons trained as auxiliary personnel, once hired, would be eligible to receive further training and education, enabling them to master the skills and knowledge necessary to move up through the ranks into teaching positions. The paraprofessional training programs were largely federally funded through the Economic Opportunity Act (Head Start), Education Professions Development Act, Manpower Development and Training Act, Demonstration Cities, and Title I, so enrollment preference was given to low-income persons and the unemployed. At issue was the question of the real purpose of paraprofessional training. This issue—"to create jobs for the poor or to improve the quality of education?" (Davies, 1968)—was hotly debated at a conference on auxiliary personnel sponsored jointly by Bank Street College and the Philadelphia public schools. The overriding reply was that the prime concern was for the child as a learner. The rationale given for this argument was that a child's learning comes as much from the social milieu as the school setting: therefore, educating members of a child's community or home will contribute immeasurably to the child's overall growth and development. The training was carried out in intensive summer sessions and follow-up supervision on the job. Although the programs were developed by colleges outside their regular 4-year programs, these training programs resulted in one of the first collaborations between middle-class and working-class persons to conduct teacher preparation. They served together on committees set up to direct the selection and recruitment of trainees and to assist in the planning of the training, as well as jointly participate in the training and ultimately teaching or home/school roles.

Teacher Centers

Teacher centers were labeled as one of the "hottest educational concepts on the scene" in the 1970s (Schmeider & Yarger, 1974), although historically their prototype began with the teacher institutes of the mid-1800s serving as preservice teacher training facilities (Ritchie, 1957). The impetus for teacher centers came from a wide variety of sources, such as the open-education movement in this country, the National Commission of Teacher Education and Professional Standards, and renowned educational spokespersons and teachers at the grass-roots level. Like open education, the precedent for teacher centers was in England, where they were set up as "local facilities and self-improvement programs organized and run by the teachers themselves for purposes of upgrading educational performance" (Bailey, 1971). The American centers, however, were mostly established by federal funding to state departments of education or educational laboratories and private consulting firms and universities (Spodek, 1974). Their overall purpose was to integrate educational constituencies—children and teachers, administrators, supervisors, college and university staff, and interested community members—in order to improve the quality of the teaching/learning situation (Schmeider & Yarger, 1974). Those centers whose main constituency was preschool teachers were diversified and unique in their structure and functioning, responsive to the needs of the communities which they served. Descriptions of three different teacher centers will illustrate the content and range of this kind of teacher preparation (Pilcher, 1973).

Learning Institute of Early Childhood Education (LIECE)

The Learning Institute of Early Childhood Education (LIECE) was conceived by a well-known private school, National Child Research Center, whose board of trustees concluded in their examination of large numbers of preschools arising in the Washington, D.C., area that only a small number offered quality settings, because they were staffed by poorly trained teachers. They stated that the major reason for the continuing shortage of professionally skilled nursery school teachers was not only a shortage of schools specifically oriented to preparing such teachers, but also the inflexibility of most existing schools to adapt to the urgent needs of those already in the field and those waiting to enter it by a shorter or less time-demanding route than a 4-year college program. Further, they argued that there was a need to reduce the scale of teacher education programs—"Following the lead of mass production economy, where cost is reduced as volume is increased, almost all institutions have grown larger, to the point that even colleges and hospitals are giants: and they are not the efficient giants of business and industry, but the clumsy giants of human services. We have only recently realized that where the product is human services, mass-production methods do not reduce the cost, they reduce the quality of human relations, at the great cost of human wholeness.... There is urgent need for small institutions, where human beings deal directly with a few other human beings, not with pieces of paper" (National Child Research Center, 1972, p. 2). Lastly, they argued that the small college programs that did exist were exclusive in their admission, and they saw the need to serve students from all races and a wide variety of cultural and economic backgrounds. The Learning Institute of Early Childhood Education was thus launched by a small grant from a private foundation, as well as affiliation with a local college. The goal was to offer a flexible teacher-training program using the facilities and staff of an exceptional nursery school as the foundation of a program of nursery education. The creation of the teacher center was reminiscent of the special energies and improvisation that characterized so much of the nursery school movement in this country. "The rambling grounds of the Research Center with its huge old trees became a hive of activity. With hard work, a coat of paint and much imagination a large trike shed was changed into a creative space for adult learning and the adjacent porch became the office and library" (Perry, 1973, p. 2). The training program was centered in the philosophy that just as children must have a wide array of materials to explore and manipulate, so must teachers have the opportunity to work with materials and solve problems in unique and original ways. The teacher center was stocked with tools, art supplies, all sorts of scrounge materials, and triwall for constructing children's equipment. It was hoped to create the kind of environment in the teacher center that teachers would in turn create for children. The 9-week seminars met in the evening, allowing students to keep daytime teaching positions. The seminars were participatory democracies, with the emphasis on discussion and sharing of ideas in an atmosphere in which students were free to express opinions, articulating continually the bridge between the seminar topics and what they were experiencing in their classrooms. The commitment to addressing the needs of the teachers was seen as the faculty traveled all around the city to observe and use videotape conferencing to support each teacher's learning in the classroom. Students were asked to conduct learning experiences with small groups of children based on their own interpretation of the literature. Students were thereby helped to translate into action some of the theories being discussed in the seminars. In addition to the seminars, teachers could visit the center to use the resources, including a professional library. LIECE offered consultative services, sponsored professional symposia, and conducted research in which teachers were involved.

The Peabody Early Childhood Education Project (PERCEPT)

The Peabody Early Childhood Education Project was housed in a large prefabricated extension of a private school and during the year operated a preparation for novice teachers of children ages three to eight. The students were college graduates from fields other than education, primarily mothers of school-age children, and were selected on a basis of commitment to teaching and the open-education principles practiced in the school. Teacher preparation occurred through participation with a "focal class" of multicultural children, seminars, workshops, and conferences with teacher trainers. Emphasis was on promoting professional, personalized teaching through (1) structuring the curriculum to promote individualization of instruction; (2) guiding the child's learning processes toward self-motivated learning; and (3) performing a variety of roles supportive of effective optimal learning (Procopio, 1971). The focus of teacher preparation in PERCEPT was in constant change, moving within an orbit controlled by the evolving needs of each child, developing new curriculum emphases, and building specific teaching strengths in accord with the increasing confidence of neophyte teachers. Student teachers learned by becoming part of a daily web of subtle learning and teaching in an atmosphere of respect and trust on the part of teachers and learners at all the different levels. Students teachers were accepted as members of the school staff from the beginning of their preparation for teaching and joined the professional staff in planning and implementing the curriculum and in firsthand contacts with parents. Collaboration with the public school system enabled PERCEPT students to use other practice-teaching stations with kindergarten and primary-school children. Closed-circuit television recordings were often used to give feedback to the students. Their progress as teachers was measured largely through self-evaluation using an extensive questionnaire designed by an outside professional team for the purpose of looking at the program through the eyes of the student-teacher participants.

The Early Childhood Education Study (ECES)

The Early Childhood Education Study in Newton, Massachusetts, served primarily as a resource laboratory for teachers of young children, with the goal of extending the involvement of teachers in decision making concerning classroom programs and materials and the physical environment of schools (Leitman, 1969). ECES documented the growth of teachers and children to share with peers and, as new attitudes about teaching evolved, shared these findings with teachers through films, written materials, and slides. The center was well stocked with materials and a helpful center staff to aid teachers and architects to create better places for children to live and learn. Teachers were not given answers, but rather the raw materials to discover for themselves the methods and style right for them, their children, the school, and the community.

The greatest success of teacher centers was the energy and creative spark they contributed to the teacher-education movement. Through innovative teaching strategies and badly needed teacher-support systems, teacher centers breathed fresh life into preschool teaching and collaborative teacher education. The problem was lack of ongoing funding bases. Those centers that were collaborations with educational systems were able to transfer programs when federal funding was no longer available.

Supplementary Training

While nonprofessionals were used as assistants in private nursery schools and parent cooperatives prior to 1960, Head Start was the first to use paraprofessionals from the poverty community as auxiliary staff in the classroom (Flynn, 1969). Employment of Head Start parents was another step in the effort to break the cycle of poverty from which disadvantaged children came. The first attempt to prepare this group for work in the Head Start centers, initiated by the Office of Economic Opportunity, included a 1-week orientation for summer Head Start personnel. This was extended later to 8 weeks, and both programs were conducted by universities. They offered a unique blend of supervised work experience with basic courses in child growth and development. These programs proved to be too short in duration to develop the necessary skills and knowledge, and did not provide for the career interest of staff since they did not lead to marketable degrees. In July 1967, Head Start embraced the concept of career development and implemented the Head Start Supplementary Training Program, designed to provide postsecondary education for Head Start staff, leading to 2- and 4-year degrees. This training program became the first nationwide effort of educational institutions to offer an alternative system for the preparation of early childhood teachers. By 1970, 207 institutions were involved in training 7,000 potential teachers across the country, often in localities where early childhood teacher training was unheard of in the past (Flynn, 1969). Although supplementary training was only offered to Head Start staff, because it was conducted by university faculty, this training program influenced teacher-preparation programs generally. Examples of institutional change include the following:

1. The training was conducted on site, with faculty traveling into the communities to teach courses and supervise the implementation of the course work.
2. Course content was modified to relate to students' work experience.
3. Specialized curriculum was designed for on-campus junior and senior students who were interested in teaching in poverty areas.
4. Several institutions without departments of early childhood education used the supplementary training program to initiate early childhood programs.
5. Admission policies were modified to accept life experience credits and students who could prove their competence during the first year of study.
6. Compressed course offerings were established in shortened time periods at times when working child-care staff could attend.
7. Consortia of institutions were established to serve a cluster of trainees in a region.
8. Positions of professional and nonprofessional career development specialists were established, who helped the teacher educators bridge the gap between theory and practice. These specialists attended classes and guided trainees' on-site progress between classes (Flynn, 1969).

The strength of this program was the continuity, accessibility, and relevance. Each trainee could continue in the training program over a period of years, progressing at a personal rate of learning. At the same time, participants could continue in their jobs at the Head Start centers. Federal guidelines mandated that programs be developed that would address the needs of the students. Therefore, the supplementary program was contextualized in two ways. First, classes were designed to be responsive to students' life experiences and understandings. Second, career development specialists bridged the gap between the local community and the university through regular observations and conferences in which the students' questions, misconceptions, or problems could be discussed and brought to the attention of college professors.

The weakness of the supplementary training program was the high cost, incurred in paying for faculty to travel regularly into communities (*An Assessment of Head Start,* 1978). In rural regions, this might involve great distances. As a consequence, institutions without federal funding were not likely to duplicate the program. A second drawback occurred because of the admission restriction to Head Start personnel: the program gained its reputation as good teacher education for low-income students or those working in child care, and many of the innovations were not spread into the broader teacher-education community.

THE CHILD DEVELOPMENT ASSOCIATE PROGRAM[1]

In 1972, in response to the demand for competent child-care personnel, the Office of Child Development launched a new program—the Child Development Associate. With the Child Development Associate (CDA) program, the most pronounced and well-defined alternative for teacher preparation was born. The early conceptualization of the CDA program, in 1970, centered on improving the quality of care provided in child-care settings by increasing the competence of the program staff. The program was designed to serve newcomers seeking entry into the child care profession, experienced center staff who may have had little or no formal training, or personnel credentialled to work with older children, who wished to gain the skills neeeded to work with preschoolers (Klein & Weathersby, 1973). A lofty projection of the CDA program was to "develop a middle level professional group to care for our nation's children . . . and put into place a mechanism whereby our society could develop, in fairly large numbers, a body of individuals who were trained and psychologically equipped to be caretakers of young children" (Zigler, 1971, 1983). The basic purpose was to design and promote a system of training and credentialling individuals based on their demonstrated competency with children rather than course work taken at a university. A CDA was defined as a person who will be able to assume full responsibility for the daily activities of a group of young children in day-care centers, Head Start programs, private nursery schools, and other preschool programs (Zigler, 1971). Unlike some hastily improvised programs of the past, serious thought and careful planning went into the development of the CDA program. Milton Akers and Marilyn Smith (1971) of NAEYC, engaged to conduct a feasibility study for the program, hailed the idea as a "courageous step in endeavors to insure competent personnel" (p. 3) and commented on the generally warm reception to the concept by the early childhood education community.

Developing the Competencies

The success of this national effort rested in the defining of teacher competencies that would undergird the system. A task force of respected early childhood educators and child-development specialists was engaged to develop a preliminary set of competencies in collaboration with the Office of Child Development. A basic premise that guided the work of the task force bore a semblance to the ideas of Lucy Sprague Mitchell in the founding of Bank Street College—that of a "whole child" approach. A child's psychological functioning cannot be extrapolated from his total functioning

---

[1]I wish to thank Donna Horowitz and Kim Sincox for their assistance in making available the Child Development Associate Research Institute at the Childlife Archives of the Please Touch Museum, 210 N. 21st St., Philadelphia, PA 19103. The materials in the archives provided a rich insight into the history and development of the CDA program.

(Biber, 1973). This premise was exemplified by the following statement in the preliminary draft of the competencies:

> For children, the acquisition of skills and knowledge, the development of attitudes and feelings towards themselves and others, the ability to solve problems and to experience life as satisfying and meaningful occur "simultaneously" throughout development (Biber, 1972, p. 8).

Likewise, there was general agreement to a "whole teacher" approach. Competency could not simply be represented by lists of isolated teaching behaviors to be checked off, but was seen as an integrated pattern of skills, attitudes, and feelings that provide meaning to the discrete behaviors (Biber, 1972). "Competent teaching is not just the ability to perform skills according to a formula; it involves decisions that combine judgment and skill" (Broudy, 1972, p. 12). The task force maintained this qualitative view, that teaching was a distinctly human, intrinsically complex art, rather than the quantitative view that constituted so much of the performance-based education movement in the elementary school with its shopping lists of easily measurable teacher behaviors (Bentley, 1975). The latter perspective, which departed from the humanistic trend, stood in contrast to the CDA program philosophy. Bentley exemplified that tone regarding performance-based education with his beliefs that a comprehensive taxonomy of teacher competence is urgently needed; that the proliferation of lists of competency statements, in most cases not even rank ordered in importance, is appalling, with almost 300 behavioral objectives in one model; and that too few programs have proceeded with sufficient care to identify competencies that derive from clearly delineated conceptual frameworks about teaching, available research, or experience of the profession (1975).

The CDA task force further differentiated between competence and competencies, the singular and the plural (Lightfoot as cited in Biber, 1972), with the thrust of the CDA program on the composite development of competence. Much effort went into assuring that the competencies represented a distinct point of view about teacher-child interaction as well as specific expectations of what the optimal experience for both teacher and children in an educational setting should be. Thus, the content of the competence definition was relevant and representative of competent caregiver performance.

Over a period of 2 years, the competencies were refined, examined, and researched by approximately 1,200 child development experts in culturally, philosophically, and administratively diverse child care programs (Williams, 1975). Professionals funded to develop training and assessment procedures for the CDA program were also charged with the responsibility of defining and validating the competency statements. The competencies were subsequently reviewed by the CDA Consortium, a nonprofit corporation composed of organizations and individuals concerned with quality care for young children (Klein, 1973).

Although many problems arose in the development of the competencies, the greatest challenge was the need to keep the competencies general enough to become a universally accepted competence, yet detailed enough to be observed and evaluated. The following phrase was often quoted throughout the deliberative papers between the Office of Child Development and the early childhood group: "[While] the substance of life as lived is seamless, the structure of scholarship is necessarily compartmentalized" (Bruner, 1971, p. 32). The challenge was to establish a broad ideology that would incorporate a variety of thinking and formulations about how children learn and grow best, and would be sensitive to the diverse contexts that constitute good early childhood settings—"the kind of underlying competence that makes it possible for performance to vary as a reflection of varying situations and dispositions" (Shapiro, 1973, p. 523). At the other end of this issue was the demand to incorporate the specificity that would communicate clearly the expected attitudes, understandings, and skills that were to be exhibited by a competent caregiver.

Of special concern to the task force was the question of pluralism. The nursery-school teacher prototype had been, to date, that of a middle-class teacher. There was a strong sentiment that the competencies should address the diversity of children and families encompassed in preschool settings. Yet, "there exists no single ideal program or teaching style which meets all children's motivations, developmental needs and problems, styles of thinking, expectations and sources of gratification, parental values and preferences even when consensus of overall goals is reached" (Biber, 1972, p. 6).

The generated set of competencies, stated as child-development processes rather than IQ or achievement scores, has not changed measurably over the past 14 years the system has been in use. The competencies are divided into six general goals, which are then subdivided into thirteen specific functional areas (*Preschool Caregivers,* 1987):

I. TO SET UP AND MAINTAIN A SAFE AND HEALTHY LEARNING ENVIRONMENT
  A.. *Safe*—Candidate provides a safe environment to prevent and reduce injuries.
  B. *Healthy*—Candidate promotes good health and nutrition and provides an environment that contributes to the prevention of illness.
  C. *Learning Environment*—Candidate uses space, relationships, materials, and routines as resources for constructing an interesting, secure, and enjoyable environment that encourages play, exploration, and learning.

II. TO ADVANCE PHYSICAL AND INTELLECTUAL COMPETENCE
  A.. *Physical*—Candidate provides a variety of equipment, activities, and opportunities to promote the physical development of children.
  B. *Cognitive*—Candidate provides activities and opportunities that encourage curiosity, exploration, and problem solving appropriate to the developmental levels and learning styles of children.

    C.   *Communication*—Candidate actively communicates with children and provides opportunities and support for children to understand, acquire, and use verbal and nonverbal means of communicating thoughts and feelings.

    D.   *Creative*—Candidate provides opportunities that stimulate children to play with sound, rhythm, language, materials, space, and ideas in individual ways and to express their creative abilities.

III. TO SUPPORT SOCIAL/EMOTIONAL DEVELOPMENT AND PROVIDE POSITIVE GUIDANCE

    A.. *Self*—Candidate provides physical and emotional security for each child and help each child to know, accept, and take pride in self and to develop a sense of independence.

    B.   *Social*—Candidate helps each child feel accepted in the group, helps children learn to communicate and get along with others, and encourages feelings of empathy and mutual respect among adults and children.

    C.   *Guidance*—Candidate provides a supportive environment in which children can begin to learn and practice appropriate and acceptable behaviors as individuals and as a group.

IV. TO ESTABLISH POSITIVE AND PRODUCTIVE RELATIONSHIPS WITH FAMILY

Candidate maintains an open, friendly, and cooperative relationship with each child's family; encourages their involvement in the program; and supports the child's relationship with the family.

V. TO ENSURE A WELL-RUN, PURPOSEFUL PROGRAM RESPONSIVE TO PARTICIPANT NEEDS

Candidate is a manager who uses all available resources to ensure an effective operation. The candidate is a competent organizer, planner, record keeper, communicator, and cooperative worker.

VI. TO MAINTAIN A COMMITMENT TO PROFESSIONALISM

Candidate makes decisions based on knowledge of early-childhood theories and practices, promotes quality in child-care services, and takes advantage of opportunities to improve competence, both for personal and professional growth and for the benefit of children and families.

The functional areas were illustrated with specific examples, or competency indicators, which served to amplify, in a prototypic sense, the competency rather than act as an arbitrary indicator.

    The CDA competencies were respected as an important contribution to the field of early childhood education (*Interview with Rebecca Shuey,* 1983). There is some evidence that the competencies define what a qualified caregiver of young children does in that work (Pettygrove, 1980). Researchers in the National Day Care Study (Ruopp, Travers, Glantz, & Coelen, 1979) found the CDA competencies to be significantly related to a child's performance on some developmental indices in the programs studied. However, there was also recognition by the CDA developers that competence cannot be totally represented by any finite set of behaviors, and when ascertaining teaching competence, consideration must be given to knowledge, skills, or attitudes less easily identified or measured objectively (Williams, 1975).

Developing the CDA Assessment and Credentialling System

One unique aspect in the conception and implementation of the CDA system was the active collaboration between private and public sectors and all the many facets of the early childhood community. The vehicle for this collaboration was the CDA Consortium, which was organized in 1972 to develop the assessment and credential award system. The consortium, a private nonprofit corporation funded by the Office of Child Development, was composed of thirty-nine national associations and two public members, who represented a wide range of interests in early childhood education/child development. These members were divided into nine separate categories, such as organizations representing ethnic-minority populations and organizations concerned with training and improvement of teacher education.

The consortium's basic goals following the establishment of the competencies were to

- establish methodologies for assessing such competencies (CDA) and issue appropriate credentials to persons possessing such competencies
- develop and disseminate principles and advise on programs for training to obtain such competencies
- promote an understanding and acceptance among professionals, governmental bodies, and the general public of the credential and of the competencies on which it is based (Child Development Associate Consortium, 1976, p. 2).

Complementing its own powerful membership and staff, the consortium further involved the early childhood community by contracting with forty-four researchers and sponsoring task forces and colloquies to provide the expertise needed to develop assessment instruments and design the credentialling procedure (*The Child Development Associate,* 1976). Two national field tests were launched to evaluate and test the system.

The resulting credentialling system had six phases, which have now been collapsed into five steps.

Registration Process
During this stage, applicants send documentation of their interest and eligibility. To be eligible, the candidate must be eighteen or older; be able to speak, write, and read well enough to fulfill the CDA responsibilities; identify a child-care setting where the applicant can be observed; have three formal or informal educational experiences; and have 640 hours of experience working with children age three to five in a group,

home-based, or infant/toddler setting, depending on the particular CDA credential the applicant is seeking.

Team Formation/Information Collection

The second stage of the assessment involves organizing a team of people—the local assessment team (LAT)—who will assess the candidate's competence, illustrating the consortium's viewpoint that a team assessment is more likely to produce competence than one person who oversees the prospective teacher's student teaching. Two of the team members are chosen by the CDA candidate—an advisor, who has had professional responsibility for the candidate's training, and a parent/community representative, who has had a child in the applicant's class. They observe and prepare documentation as to the candidate's teaching ability. The applicant also prepares a portfolio that contains written evidence of competency in the thirteen functional areas and how present work relates to the developmental level of children in the applicant's care. The last member of the LAT is the CDA representative, an early childhood professional who is selected and trained in the credentialling process by the CDA National Credentialling Office. This representative constitutes the outside member of the team and goes to the local community to observe and interview the candidate just prior to the assessment meeting.

Team Meeting

During this stage, the four members of the LAT meet and present their information regarding the candidate's teaching ability. The candidate is included as a full voting member in the assessment, based on the following three reasons: (1) the candidate is the source of information available only from a personal perspective; (2) the candidate can clarify questions about performance that other team members may have; and (3) since the candidate will be implementing suggestions for improving competence, which are requisite for each functional area, the candidate is better able to understand the suggestions if present when they are discussed during the meeting. After the team reviews and discusses the information from all four LAT members, the LAT members vote on the candidate's competence in each of the thirteen functional areas and overall competence, using a vote of "competent" or "needs more training." Therefore, the competence decision represents the judgment of the diverse team members representing the community and parents of children in the candidate's class, the professional growth of the candidate over an extended period of time as experienced by the candidate's trainer, and the outside perspective of the CDA representative who represents the national professional perspective. An overview of the team's discussion is compiled into a profile of the candidate.

Although the meeting is kept informal and open to promote discussion, the CDA representative follows guidelines established by the CDA National Credentialling Office to insure that standard procedures are maintained. Certain principles guide the LAT meeting during which the candidate is ultimately judged as "competent" or "needs more training." Each of the LAT members is equally important. The parent's rights to speak and vote are equal to those of the professional members of the team.

All assessors must cite the supporting evidence for their votes in legible and clear language. The team members are expected to reach a consensus through sharing and discussing the information they have brought to the meeting. While a candidate can receive votes of "needs more training" in some of the thirteen functional areas, an overal "competent" vote must be given by all LAT members in order for the candidate to be credentialled. The assessment is verified by strict adherence to a standard format set by the consortium for collecting data about the candidate and in conducting the team meeting (Ward, 1974).

In the fourth step, all materials from the LAT meeting are sent to the CDA National Credentialling Office, and if all members of the LAT have voted the candidate competent, the CDA credential is awarded for a period of 3 years. The fifth step entails renewing the credential based on an updated statement of the candidate's professional development in each of the thirteen functional areas, conjointly with a professional early childhood reviewer and parent/community reviewer. Currently the credential can be attained by teachers in a group setting, home visitors, family day-care providers, and those who work in bilingual settings or with infants and toddlers (*CDA Competency Standards,* 1984).

The CDA approach to evaluating competence includes both theoretical formulations of the prospective teacher about child growth and learning that are tapped in the interview, portfolio, and advisor's observations, and the style of interpersonal relations by which these are interacted. The CDA is expected to demonstrate certain personal qualities, such as sensitivity to children's feelings and ideas or protection of orderliness without sacrificing childish spontaneity and exuberance. The objective of the CDA Consortium was to incorporate a mutual training and teaching experience into the assessment process.

COMPETENCY-BASED TRAINING

As work on the CDA program progressed, it became apparent that new strategies and systems were needed to supplement already-existing settings for training persons to become CDAs. The Office of Child Development assumed major responsibility for evolving new training programs and guidelines for the training. They used the previously established principles and excellent ongoing Head Start supplementary training sites, as well as funding thirteen pilot training programs to develop approaches to training for competence. The goals of the CDA training programs were to help candidates develop concepts of their own work roles; understand and refine their interpersonal styles in relating to children, parents, and colleagues; acquire specific teaching techniques; and acquire a broad background in the field of early childhood education, including relevant theories, principles, and the social issues and contexts of programs for young children (*CDA Program,* 1973).

Competency-based teacher education was framed in part by the ongoing national movement of Performance-Based Teacher Education (PBTE). PBTE was fortified by the increasing public interest in accountability of teachers and schools, new concepts of management, relevance, and individualization of instruction (Elam, 1971). "Performance Based Teacher Education, as in the CDA training, is a program which specifies the competencies to be demonstrated by the student, makes explicit the criteria to be applied in assessing the student's competencies, and holds the students accountable for meeting those criteria" (Cooper & Weber, 1973, p. 14).

But while the roots of the PBTE sprang from behavioral psychology with its focus on programmed learning, operant conditioning, and quantifiable teaching behaviors, CDA training preserved the basic tenets of the pioneers of its own field—early childhood education. Foremost in the CDA training was the conviction that the best preparation for becoming a good teacher is through guided *focused* experiences with children. CDA training guidelines required that 50% of each trainee's time be spent in field settings where good teachers serve as appropriate models. In essence, the training was seen as a two-way process—watching a good teacher organize a day and discussing that observation with an advisor. The student implements the principles with the children, which is again analyzed with the advisor. "Provision is thus made for discussion, feedback self evaluation, and practice, to help the students understand their own teaching relationships and the children's behavior. These insights are then incorporated into daily activities that promote children's growth and learning" (Klein, 1973, p. 361).

These sentiments are echoes of the words of Lucy Sprague Mitchell (1979) in *On Teachers and Teaching* reflecting on her work with preparing early childhood teachers in the 1920s:

> Learning that comes through firsthand experiences has a smiting quality quite unlike the intellectual comprehension which comes through learning from hearing about someone else's experiences. . . . *The study of child development,* if based entirely on the complicated analysis of children's behavior found in books, may become so theoretical as to give teacher little guidance when faced with a particular child. . . . This means that a teacher's education must be based upon direct experiences with both children and the world around him. . . . Second, merely being with children however, does not teach one to observe their growth, nor does it necessarily reveal the hidden springs of children's behavior. If it did all teachers and parents would really understand children! No. Teacher Education must include a technique of observation (which is gather *evidence*), and a background which will enable him to *interpret* the behavior he observes (p. 9).

Other CDA training criteria that drew from the wisdom of early teacher preparation were the requirements to individualize training and organize it so that academic work and fieldwork were an integrated set of experiences (*CDA Program,* 1973). Based on the policies established by Head Start supplementary training, instructors achieved this integration by going to the CDA trainee's own community and workplace to conduct the majority of the training. This enabled instructors to capitalize on the trainee's own life and work experiences as a basis for understanding theoretical assumptions. Both initial appraisals of a student's knowledge and skill level and ongoing evaluations of trainee progress guided the content of the training. So, too, did Mitchell, in establishing the Bureau of Educational Experiments, form liaisons with publicly funded educational enterprises so that students could experience a program integrating child-development knowledge and curriculum, and establish a pattern of workshops and individual consultation, adapting theory to the natural constraints of the classroom and students' lives (Mitchell 1979).

Competency-based teacher education stands in contrast to traditional 4-year teacher preparation in several distinct aspects (Bentley, 1975; Cooper & Weber, 1973; Houston, 1974; Howsam & Hymes, 1976):

Competency-based Education	**Traditional Teacher Education**
Competence seen as an ability to perform	Competence seen as a set of credentials
Communication about preparation in a language of objectives and subsequent performance	Communication in a language of courses and credits
Teacher education primarily in field	Teacher education primarily on campus
Feedback on preparation given after each experience in a language of objectives and performance	Feedback on preparation experience given at the end of the semester in the form of grades
Preparation viewed as helping people—ways to include people not normally accepted in teacher training to help them become teachers	Preparation viewed as screening—ways to exclude people without proper credentials from the teaching profession
Oriented to the individual	Oriented to the group, the class
Participation as aides, interns	Student teaching
Flexible, nonlinear time for training everyone according to demonstrated needs and abilities	Four-year time frame treats everyone the same regardless of experience or skill with children
Placement on the learner of the accountability for meeting the competency criteria	Placement on the institution for student learning

In both the CDA and traditional teacher-preparation systems, child-development knowledge and practical skill with children are counted as important. Further, both believe that theory and practice should be integrated. It is a matter of emphasis. In the CDA system, the priority is set on demonstrated skill with children, and in the traditional system, priority is set on mastery of a body of knowledge about children and the world. Proponents of competency-based teacher education believe that the competencies should "drive" the system—that theory can best be learned while engaged in dynamic interactions with children.

University-based proponents contest that students cannot become skilled teachers of children until they have demonstrated an understanding of their growth and development.

CDA has been successful in meeting its major goal—to improve the quality of child care for large numbers of children and their families. Researchers (Granger, Lombardi, & Gleason, 1984; Pettygrove, 1980) have found the CDA program contributes to improved job performance and desirable child outcomes. While the goal of establishing a midlevel professional has not been reached, the career development goals of providing caregivers with greater access to training and credentialling have been accomplished and have resulted in a body of competent child-care workers. As of May 1988, CDA credentials have been awarded to 25,165 candidates (Phillips, 1988). Furthermore, 70% of this group of child-care workers continue their formal education and join professional organizations, demonstrating a commitment to professional growth after becoming credentialled.

One of the most far-reaching benefits has been the psychological effect on child-care workers who have received the CDA credential. CDA candidates often live in depressed environments where high unemployment and deteriorating social conditions leave little to bolster self-esteem and are likely to engender harsh behavior with children. After earning the CDA credential, these workers have increased confidence, testify to a sense of achievement and efficacy, and generally exhibit a "take charge" attitude toward their lives (Granger et al., 1984). This personal gain has increased morale and motivation on the job with direct positive effects for the children in their care.

Perhaps one of the great advantages of the CDA program was focusing the collective wisdom of a large number of professional early childhood educators on the pragmatic problems of staff shortage, low morale, etc. Not only has teacher education benefited, but child care in general has been served by bringing the thinking of this group to the frontlines of child care.

The CDA program has endured for almost 2 decades, but has often been, and is currently, in a state of flux. The CDA program is not without its critics. While much of the criticism has come from the ranks of the professional educational establishment, innovators and administrators of the program itself have sought to address the weaknesses of the system. The most outspoken attacks have focused on the competency-based curriculum—teaching skills and their practice—and its emphasis on technical, practical, and management concerns. "Practical training at the expense of liberal education sacrifices resourcefulness, imagination, and versatility, and transforms teaching from a complex process into a technical trade" (Berk & Berson, 1981, p. 9). Broudy (1972), decrying the philosophical vacuity and lack of a clearly delineated knowledge base, states that the basic unit of competency-based teacher education becomes not the course designed to impart knowledge, but the teaching act itself, frequently dealing with only the most easily understood and transmitted behaviors. Katz (1988) cautions against curriculum that trivializes the course of study and shortcuts the students—they need to wonder, reflect, examine, and analyze pertinent phenomena in the process of becoming competent.

A second major criticism aimed at the CDA program was that the credential was driven by an overriding need to adapt to diversity and by political and economic concerns that catered to one segment of the potential teaching population (Berk & Berson, 1981). The focus on providing access for the low-income worker has led to a procedure of self-selection into CDA training that does not specify any prerequisites, such as personal qualities like warmth, patience, humor, flexibility, and openness to learning, that might dispose the trainee to become a good teacher of young children. Admittedly, the CDA assessment system, or any means of ascertaining teaching competence, does not protect the general public (especially the clients, young children and their families) from possible incompetence that could result from lack of these characteristics. Opponents fear the replacement of professionals by child-care workers whose preparation shortcuts the more extended and valid 4-year program.

The cornerstone of competency-based teacher education, which is primarily conducted on site, is the presence of good models and effective on-the-job supervision and training. Finding good models for practice teaching has long been a problem in our profession. This problem has undermined good CDA training, especially since trainers could not even select the sites for their trainees. Further, the CDA training system did not incorporate a thorough preparation for the teacher educators involved, most of whom had little experience in their own professional preparation in the skills of on-the-job training and supervision.

A problem that continues to plague the CDA system is the question of degree of competence. What level of mastery constitutes competence? The reply varies with both the CDA instructor and the assessment team, and across the competencies themselves. Each CDA training program and members of the LAT have their own standards for acceptable level of performance and understanding that they bring to the CDA process. In some competency areas, such as making sure the classroom is safe and free from hazardous conditions, it is easier to expect 100% perfection. But establishing 100% perfection would be unreasonable, if not unsound, for most of the more complex teaching competencies. Teachers at all levels should keep on growing! In the judgment-referenced system that underlies the CDA program, the decision of degree of competence rests with the individual trainer and the LAT in what Katz terms their "best judgment." The result is that CDAs are credentialled with varying degrees of competence.

Lastly, a complaint that has come from both the ranks of CDAs themselves and researchers evaluating the CDA system is that the credential does not "admit recipients to the ranks of the profession" (Benson & Peters, 1988; Granger & Marx, 1988; Peters, 1988). These researchers found few extrinsic benefits, such as promotion and pay raises, and by and large, the CDA credential only guarantees entree to the lowest-paying positions in the field, rather than giving CDAs access to the mainstream of teaching in the United States (Benson & Peters, 1988).

SUMMARY

The CDA program, and the teacher-education alternative movement in general, has made an important contribution to teacher preparation in early childhood education. The debate and exploration of the questions of teaching competency, relevant teacher education for the job, and the optimal contextualization/decontextualization of teacher preparation have enlightened the issues and the answers. Institutions involved in early childhood teacher preparation have incorporated new course content, provided greater flexibility and access to their programs, and begun to make more productive links with the community as they engage in joint enterprises to prepare future teaching personnel. Hopefully the fight for professional status will not obliterate the need in the future development of teacher preparation for a *variety of steps and alternative systems* to educate *a diversified early childhood staff* to meet the complex needs of young children, while at the same time preserve the unique roots from which this field emerged.

REFERENCES

Akers, M., & Smith, M. (1971). *CDA feasibility study*. Washington, DC: National Association for the Education of Young Children.

An assessment of Head Start supplementary training program in providing CDA competency-based training. (1978). Report by Kirschner Associates, Inc., prepared for ACYF, HEW, Vol. 1, Executive Summary National Survey.

Bailey, S. K. (1971). Teachers' centers: A British first. *Phi Delta Kappan, 53,* 146–149.

Barker, R. G., & Wright, H. F. (1954). *Midwest and its children: The psychological ecology of an American town*. Evanston, IL: Row, Peterson.

Benson, M. S., & Peters, D. L. (1988). The child development associate: Competence training and professionalism. *Early Child Development and Care, 38,* 57–68.

Bentley, B. (1975). *Some views on competency-based education*. New York: Bank Street College of Education.

Berk, L. E., & Berson, M. P. (1981). A review of the CDA credential. *Child Care Quarterly, 10*(1), 9–42.

Biber, B. (1972). *CDA task force report*. Washington, DC: Child Development Associate Consortium.

Biber, B. (1973). *Child development associate: A professional role for developmental day care*. Washington, DC: Office of Human Development/Child Development.

Bower, T. G. R. (1974). *Development in infancy*. San Francisco: W. H. Freeman.

Bronfenbrenner, U. (1979). *The ecology of human development*. Cambridge, MA: Harvard University Press.

Broudy, H. S. (1972). *A critique of performance-based teacher education*. Washington, DC: American Association of Colleges for Teacher Education (AACTE).

Bruner, J. (1971). Overview of development and day care. In E. Grotberg (Ed.), *Day care: Resources for decisions* (pp. 28–43). Washington, DC: Office of Economic Opportunity.

Cazden, C. B. (1984). Classroom discourse. In M. C. Wittrock (Ed.), *Handbook of research on teaching* (3rd ed.). New York: MacMillan Press.

Cazden, C. B., John, V. P., & Hymes, D. (1972). *Functions of language in the classroom*. New York: Teachers College Press.

CDA competency standards and assessment system. (1984). Washington, DC: National Credentialling Program, National Association for the Education of Young Children.

CDA program: A guide for training. (1973). (No. (OCD) 73–106). Washington, DC: Department of Health, Education and Welfare.

The child development associate. (1976). (Report on program development). Washington, DC: CDA Consortium.

Child Development Associate Consortium. (1976). *The Child Development Associate Consortium's credential award system*. Washington, DC: CDA Consortium Research Report.

Conant, J. B. (1963). *The education of American teachers*. New York: McGraw-Hill.

Cooper, J. M. & Weber, W. A. (1973). A competency based systems approach to education. In J. M. Cooper, W. A. Weber, & C. E. Johnson (Eds.), *Competency-based teacher education: A systems approach to program design* (pp. 7–18). Berkeley, CA: McCutchan.

Davies, D. (1968, April). *Where are we all headed?* Address before the Conference on Auxiliary Personnel sponsored by the Philadelphia public schools and Bank Street College of Education, Philadelphia.

Donaldson, M. (1978). *Children's minds*. New York: W. W. Norton.

Elam, S. (1971) *Performance-based teacher education: What is the state of the art? Performance-based teacher education series: No. 1*. Washington DC: American Association of Colleges for Teacher Education.

Flynn, J. C. (1969). *Head Start supplementary training: From aloofness to commitment* (Prepared for the National Conference on Career Development). Washington, DC: Project Head Start, Office of Economic Opportunity; Bureau of Work Training Programs, Department of Labor; Bureau of Educational Personnel Department, Department of Health, Education and Welfare.

Gelman, R. (1978). Cognitive development. *Annual of Psychology, 29,* 297–332.

Granger, R. C., Lombardi, J., & Gleason, D. J. (1984, April). *The impact of the child development associate program on CDAs: Results of a national survey*. Paper presented at the annual meeting of the American Education Research Association, New Orleans.

Granger, R. C., & Marx, E. (1988). *Who is teaching?* New York: Bank Street College of Education.

Green, J. (1983). Research on teaching as linguistic process. In E. Gordon (Ed.), *Review of Research in Education*. (pp. 151–252). Washington, DC: American Education Research Association.

Guthrie, L. F. (1976, November). *Young children make sense: An ethnographic account of interaction*. Paper presented at the annual meeting of the American Anthropological Association, Washington, DC.

Hawkins, D. (1974). *The informed vision: Essays on learning and human nature*. New York: Agathon Press.

Horowitz, F. D. (1975). *Review of child development research* (Vol. 4). Chicago: University of Chicago Press.

Houston, W. R. (1974). *Exploring competency based education*. Berkeley, CA: McCutchan.

Howsam, R. B., & Hymes, J. L. (1976). *Educating a profession*. Washington, DC: American Association of Colleges.

Hymes, J. L. (1988). *Early childhood education. The year in review: A look at 1987.* Carmel, CA: Hacienda Press.

Interview with Rebecca Shuey. (1983). Washington, DC: Office of Child Development.

Johnson, H. (1934). *Children in the nursery school.* New York: John Day.

Katz, L. G. (1975). *Second collection of papers for teachers.* Urbana, IL: College of Education, University of Illinois.

Katz, L. G. (1979). *Helping others learn to teach: Some principles and techniques for inservice educators.* Urbana, IL: ERIC Clearinghouse of Early Childhood Education.

Katz, L. (1988, January). *Early childhood teacher education: Traditions and trends.* Comments at National Association for the Education of Young Children Colloquium, Miami.

Klein, J. W. (1973). Making or breaking it: The teacher's role in model (curriculum) implementation. *Young Children, 28,* 359–366.

Klein, J. W., & Weathersby, R. (1973, September-October). Child development associates: New professionals, new training strategies [Reprint]. *Children Today.*

Leitman, A. (1969). Early childhood education study. In C. Rathbone (Ed.), *Occasional papers.* Newton, MA: Early Childhood Education Study.

Mallum, M. A. (1970). *California children's centers curriculum guide.* Torrance, CA: California Children's Centers, Directors and Supervisors Association.

Mitchell, L. S. (1979). Making real teachers. In C. B. Winsor (Ed.), *On teachers and teaching* (pp. 8–18). New york: Bank Street College of Education.

National Association for the Education of Young Children. (1982). *Early childhood teacher education guidelines for four- and five-year programs.* Washington DC: Author.

National Child Research Center. (1972). *Teacher training at National Child Research Center* (Report to the Board). Washington DC: Author.

Nelson, K. A., & Gruendel, J. (1981). Generalized event representations: Basic building blocks of cognitive development. In M. Lamb & A. Brown (Eds.), *Advances in developmental psychology* (pp. 131–157). Hillsdale, NJ: Erlbaum.

New York state guidelines for career development of auxiliary personnel in education. (1969). Albany: State Education Department.

Pearl, A., & Reissman, F. (1965). *New careers for the poor: The nonprofessional in human service.* New York: Free Press.

Perry, G. (1973). *Learning institute of early childhood education.* Washington DC: National Child Research Center.

Peters, D. L. (1988). The child development associate credential and the educationally disenfranchised. In B. Spodek, O. N. Saracho, & D. Peters (Eds.), *Professionalism and the early childhood practitioner* (pp. 93–104). New York: Teachers College Press.

Pettygrove, W. B. (1980, March). *Competency for children's sake.* Summary report of a research program on the Child Development Associate credential, Davis, CA.

Phillips, C. (1988, January). *Summary of the council model for training and assessment.* Paper presented at the Teacher Education Colloquium sponsored by the National Association for the Education of Young Children, Miami, FL.

Pilcher, P. S. (1973, Autumn). Teacher centers: Can they work here? *Outlook,* pp. 13–19.

Preschool caregivers in center-based programs. (1987). Washington, DC: Child Development Associate National Credentialing Program.

Procopio, M. A. (1971). *Teacher preparation in open education Peabody early childhood education project.* Lakeville, MA: Advisory for Educational Environments.

Ritchie, H. G. (1957). Growth of the modern conception of in-service education. *The fifty-sixth yearbook of the National Society for the Study of Education* (pp. 35–66). Chicago: University of Chicago Press.

Rogoff, B., & Lave, J. (1984). *Everyday cognition: Its development in social context.* Cambridge, MA: Harvard University Press.

Ruopp, R., Travers, J., Glantz, F., & Coelen, C. (1979). *Children at the center* (Vol. 1). Cambridge, MA: Abt.

Schmeider, A. A., & Yarger, S. J. (1974). Teacher/teacher centering in America. *Journal of Teacher Education, 25*(1), 5–10.

Shapiro, E. (1973). Educational evaluation: Rethinking the criteria of competence. *School Review, 81,* 523–549.

Spodek, B. (Ed.). (1974). *Teacher education of the teacher, by the teacher, for the child.* Proceedings from a conference sponsored by NAEYC, Washington, DC.

Vygotsky, L. S. (1962). *Thought and language.* Cambridge, MA: MIT Press.

Ward, E. (1974). the making of a teacher. In B. Spodek (Ed.), *Teacher education* (pp. 45–54). Proceedings of a conference sponsored by the National Association for the Education of Young Children, Washington, DC.

Wellman, H. M., & Somerville, S. C. (1978, September). *Everyday memory performance of toddlers.* Paper presented at the annual meeting of the American Psychological Association, New York.

White, S. H., & Siegel, A. W. (1984). Cognitive development in time and space. In B. Rogoff & J. Lave (Eds.), *Everyday cognition: Its development in social context* (pp. 238–277). Cambridge, MA: Harvard University Press.

Wiles, K. (1973). Piaget, materials, and open education. *Head Start Newsletter,* Regional Training Center, University of Maryland, College Park.

Williams, R. (1975). *Report to the consortium.* Unpublished paper.

Wood, D. J., Bruner, J. S., & Ross, G. (1976). The role of tutoring in problem solving. *Journal of Child Psychology and Psychiatry, 17,* 89–100.

Zigler, E. (1971). A new child care profession: The child development associate. *Young Children, 27,* 71–74.

Zigler, E. (1983). *Interview with Roberta Bouverat.* Philadelphia: CDA Research Institute, Child Life Archives, Please Touch Museum.

PART FOUR

What Should the Curriculum Contain?

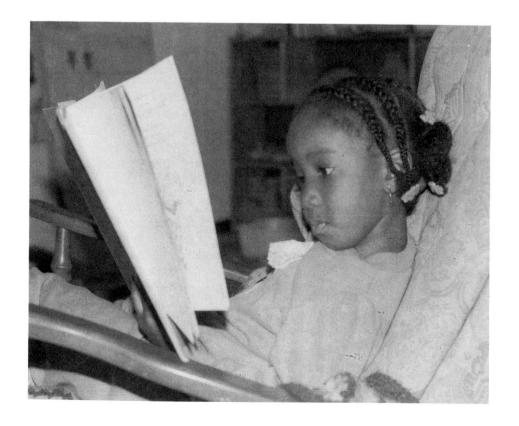

Curriculum—a word that evokes many images in the minds of parents, teachers, and administrators (Williams, 1987)—has long been a controversial issue in the field of early childhood education. Whether the childish nature of children, their play and pleasurable activity, should be respected as the foundation for the curriculum, or whether the adult should determine the curriculum is a conundrum that has "persisted unabated since the earliest days of formal educational thought" (Evans, 1982, p. 115).

In our nation, controversy over the early childhood curriculum raged as soon as the kindergarten became widespread. When first established in America, the kindergarten curriculum consisted of gifts and occupations. The gifts—cubes and balls, beads and pebbles—and the occupations—paper weaving or perforating and bead stringing—were "the center around which revolved all the concentric circles of the kindergarten curriculum" (Blow, 1894, p. 164). It wasn't long, however, before changes in these prescribed gifts and occupations were suggested. In 1890, Anna Bryant, speaking at a conference of the National Education Association, openly criticized the rigid adherence to the prescribed gifts and occupations, and Patty Smith Hill (1902) argued that purposeful activities might hold more learning. For example, she suggested giving the children "little problems designed to promote practical solutions; give paper dolls and ask them to make a bed to fit them using the blocks in the fourth gift" (1902, p. 51). Their suggestions were met with hurt feelings, anger, and even hostility.

Nor did curriculum in the nursery school escape squabbles. Many of the nursery schools of the 1920s and 1930s based their curricula on the principles of John B. Watson. These schools focused on teaching children proper habits of hand washing, toileting, dressing, and eating. At the other end of the continuum were those nursery school educators who used psychoanalytic theory as the source of curriculum. These educators encouraged children's self-expression through free play, finger paints, stories, music, and dance. The more behavioral habit-training nursery schools, such as those at the Yale Psycho-Clinic or at Iowa State College, "stood in sharp contrast to those of the psychoanalytic tradition or the Nursery School for the Bureau of Educational Experiments in New York City" (Weber, 1969).

Then, as now, there is little agreement as to what the early childhood curriculum should contain. At one end of the continuum are those who see the natural play of the child as the foundation for the curriculum in early childhood. As Nativists, these educators subscribe to the philosophy that reason is the prime source of knowledge. Knowledge begins with experience, but it doesn't originate with experience (Kant, 1781/1887). A framework of thought relationships over and above raw sense data is necessary for learning to occur. The mind is central and active in processing and making sense of sensory input and in constructing cognitive structures.

Because learning is internal, curriculum based on Nativist theories is child centered. Children initiate and are in control. The teacher responds to the cues given by the children. Children are trusted to initiate their own activities, do their own learning and evaluating. Within a safe and stimulating environment, children are the chief initiators of their own learning.

Doris Pronin Fromberg, in the chapter "Play Issues in Early Childhood Education," traces early childhood educators' intrigue with using the play of children as the curriculum. The values of play for children's learning, their total growth and development, are delineated in this chapter. Fromberg also illustrates the sharp distinction between work and play found in many early childhood classrooms.

At the other end of the continuum are those who endorse the empiricist theories. These educators view knowledge as the result of simple sensory experiences that, through association, become ideas. All knowledge, even the most complex of ideas, can be reduced to simple sensory input and the associative links between them.

The learner is believed relatively passive in the empiricist theories, the waiting receiver of sensory input from the environment. Curriculum based on these ideas is controlled by the teacher or someone else. Prespecified goals and objectives, and detailed instructions on how children will achieve these, characterize the curriculum. "This means that educational planning is essentially a 'top down' experience. Broadly defined adult roles and values form the basis of a formal K–12 span of educational requirements. Early childhood curricula, as preschool-kindergarten, are conceived to facilitate successful adaptation to existing primary programs and so on" (Evans, 1982, p. 110).

Russell Gersten and Nancy George describe this approach in the chapter "Teaching Reading and Mathematics to At-Risk Students in Kindergarten: What We Have Learned from Field Research." Gersten and George make the case that direct instruction is not punitive nor are children totally passive. Simply because teachers direct the activity does not mean children are unhappy, dissatisfied, or subjected to harsh punishment. Rather, Gersten and George claim, children are active and happy, and they achieve. Further, the authors document the long-lasting benefits of instruction.

Neither totally child centered nor teacher directed is another approach to the curriculum. Based on the idea of an active learner, one who constructs knowledge, the cognitive psychologists approach the curriculum as a process of interacting. Both the teacher and child initiate the curriculum. Control is shared. At times, teachers direct the activities; at other times, children do. It's like a ballet between a sensitive adult and a child: both are in control, both initiate, both respond, and both take cues from each other.

In this open framework, teachers do set objectives, but how these will be achieved is determined by the children. As in a child-centered approach, play is seen as the vehicle for learning. But this play is used more actively by the teacher to stimulate children's thinking and is exploited for learning opportunities, and the theories of Piaget and Dewey are used to support the approach, not those of the psychoanalytic theorists.

Margaret Lay-Dopyera and John E. Dopyera call this child-centered curriculum: Type B. They point out the differences between a totally child-centered curriculum based solely on children's play and the more clearly defined child-centered curriculum: Type B. In a Type B curriculum, children have sufficient control over the curriculum and so do their teachers.

Just as Gersten, George, and Fromberg cite research to support their views, so do the authors of the chapter "The Child-centered Curriculum." Margaret Lay-Dopyera and John E. Dopyera discuss research findings in order to build a case for the validity of the child-centered curriculum: Type B.

Today, any discussion of issues in early childhood curriculum would not be complete without consideration of the role of technology. The technology of the computer is a part of early childhood education, either as a mode of instruction or as a tool for learning in and of itself. Melissa Kaden, in the chapter "Issues on Computers and Early Childhood Education," discusses the role of the computer in today's early childhood curriculum. She takes the approach that any technology for young children ought to be examined with the same criteria used to critique any other curricula experience. Kaden uses the National Association for the Education of Young Children's *Developmentally Appropriate Practice in Early Childhood Programs Serving Children From Birth Through Age 8* (Bredekamp, 1987) as the base for evaluating the use of computers in programs for young children. She reviews the research on the effectiveness of the computer in early childhood, claiming that whether teachers want to or not, they will have to incorporate the computer into the curriculum. The question is not if they should use the computer, but only how it will be used.

MAKING DECISIONS

In a democratic society, diversity is valued whether in people, theories, or attitudes. Diverse opinions as to what the best curriculum is, are to be expected and respected.

Nevertheless, despite the valuing of diversity, unity is present in a democratic society. The goal of educating children to become fully functioning members of a democratic society unites us. Thus, decisions about the early childhood curriculum can be made in the context of the nature of a democratic society. Dewey wrote: "Since education is a social process, and there are many kinds of societies, a criterion for education criticism and construction implies a particular social ideal" (Dewey, 1944, p. 99).

Within the particular ideal of democracy then, decisions about the nature of the early childhood curriculum are made. A curriculum that gives children a "personal interest in social relationships and control" is necessary. Whether the approach to the curriculum in early childhood should be play, direct instruction, child-centered Type B, or transmitted through the computer may not be the issue. The issue is, rather, given any particular curriculum, will children learn to make choices and experience the consequences of these choices and will they learn to participate in the social life of the group, value equality, and develop "the habits of mind which secure social changes without introducing disorder?" (Dewey, 1944, p. 99)

WHAT SHOULD THE CURRICULUM CONTAIN?

As you read the following chapters, ask yourself

- On what dimensions could different curricula be compared?
- What are the benefits of direct instruction, a child-centered curriculum of free play, or a planned program of play?
- Is there only one best curriculum for all children in early childhood?
- What qualifications would teachers need to implement each of the approaches?

REFERENCES

Blow, S. (1894). *Symbolic education.* New York: D. Appleton.

Bredekamp, S. (1987). *Developmentally appropriate practice in early childhood programs serving children from birth through age 8: Expanded edition.* Washington, DC: National Association for the Education of Young Children.

Dewey, J. (1944). *Democracy and education.* New York: The Free Press.

Evans, E. D. (1982). Curriculum models and early childhood education. In B. Spodek (Ed.), *Handbook of research in early childhood education* (pp. 107–135). New York: The Free Press.

Hill, P. S. (1902). The value of constructive work in the kindergarten. *Proceedings of the Ninth Convention of the International Kindergarten Union* (pp. 51–55). New York.

Kant, I. (1887). *Critique of pure reason* (J. M. D. Meiklejohn, Trans.). London: George Belt. (Original work published 1781).

Weber, E. (1969). *The kindergarten.* New York: Teachers College Press.

Williams, L. (1987). The early childhood curriculum. In C. Seefeldt (Ed.), *The early childhood curriculum: A review of the current research.* New York: Teachers College Press.

9

The Child-centered Curriculum

MARGARET LAY-DOPYERA
Syracuse University
JOHN E. DOPYERA
Cumberland Hill Associates–Syracuse

Various terms have been used to describe programs that allow children to follow many of their own inclinations for large portions of the program day in choosing and carrying out activities. One such term is *child-centered*. The following quote illustrates the diversity of names used for child-centered curriculum approaches during the seventies:

> Let's look at some of the potential synonyms ... [open education], British Infant School, individualized instruction, informal education, Bank Street Model, child development model, EDC model, responsive day care, responsive environment, continuous progress, family plan, integrated day, schools without walls, free school, Summerhill school, architecturally open schools, British primary school, open plan school, Leicestershire plan, integrated curriculum, non-graded schools, ungraded system, progressive education, affective education, Parkway program, life-adjustment education, open learning environments, vertical groping, humanistic education, North Dakota plan, infant school, Nuffield math, activity centers, informal teaching, learning centers, flexible model, street academies, responsive instruction, unobtrusive teaching, flexible curriculum, interrelated studies, Piaget-based curriculum, experimental approach and unscheduled or unstructured day (Dopyera, 1972, p. 47).

A great many additional program names could now be added to such a list (e.g., whole language classrooms). The collection of names represents a commonality of child-centeredness, but also a wide array of different program dimensions that we will not attempt to sort out in this chapter. For purposes of clarification, however, we do wish to distinguish between two general types of child-centered curricula represented on the preceding list, which for the purposes of this chapter we will designate as child-centered curriculum: Type A and child-centered curriculum: Type B.

In Type A, the curriculum is derived almost totally by the children according to their individual and/or group interests and inclinations. Except for very young children (nursery and kindergarten), little prestructuring of options or advance preparation of the environment is considered appropriate in Type-A programs. Children are expected to decide what they want to have in their program environment, the kind of schedule they wish to follow, and the agreements they wish to make for their mutual benefit. Adults who staff such programs attempt to give the responsibility for learning, or not learning, to children. They may quite literally refuse to do more than respond to children's requests for help, fearing that if they impose their values or learning goals, children will develop in less creative and wholesome ways. In the days of so-called "progressive" education, this model was parodied in memorable fashion by a cartoon showing a small child appearing at the classroom door and saying to the adult (teacher), "Do I have to do what I want to do again today?" The consistent practitioners of a Type-A program would have to respond to such a child in the affirmative. They would do this with the expectation that the child will eventually learn to choose well and become an eager seeker of the world's knowledge. Outside of *Summerhill* (Neill, 1961) and some free schools, few such programs have been available as exemplars. Nevertheless, this is the image held by many persons, especially the relatively uninformed critic, of what a child-centered curriculum would be like.

Type-B programs may be very like Type-A programs in many respects, but there are also some very significant differences. Although children direct much of their own activity in Type-B programs, this is not due to an abdication of authority by their teachers (as in Type A), but instead because the teachers believe that learning is facilitated by children's active involvement in making choices, following through on projects, and seeking solutions to problems they set for themselves. Type-B teachers do not hesitate to direct children's activities in some situations. They are, however, convinced that it is more productive to follow children's leads and inclinations in many situations. They see learning as an active, constructive, and goal-oriented (toward the learner's goals) process. There is a great deal of advance preparation and "provisioning" in Type-B programs by the teacher, based, first, on knowledge of the kinds of activities that are likely to be involving to the age range to be enrolled and, second, after the program start-up, on knowledge of the actual interests and levels of interaction observed among enrollees. A time schedule is set by the teacher, and very specific expectations are derived from the teacher's own experience and from research on the kind of environment that is supportive of development and learning. There *are* significant numbers of Type-B programs. It is Type-B programs that are extensively described in this chapter under the name *child-centered curricula*.

CHARACTERISTICS OF A CHILD-CENTERED CURRICULUM: TYPE B

The following is a list of characteristics we associate with the child-centered curriculum: Type B:

1. Teachers reliably follow a time structure that has at least half of the total program day and at least one time segment of 1½ hour duration during which children structure their own involvement(s), choosing from among many genuinely different activity options.
2. Teachers structure the environment into activity centers, each of which provides multiple options for children's involvement, and few of which are designed to be used in uniform or "correct" ways.
3. Workable procedures for accessing, using, and replacing materials, for interacting with peers, for requesting and using help, etc., are emphasized by the teacher until thoroughly understood and adopted by the children.
4. Some program time and some classroom space are routinely dedicated to sharing and evaluation.
5. The teacher uses a broad and varied repertoire for interacting with children to further their involvement and learning in relation to their self-selected activities.
6. Teachers, other program staff members, and parents cooperate in creating a record or profile for each individual child, based on behavioral observations rather than tests, using a set of developmental categories, such as repertoire for language usage, social interactions, classification, and comparisons, using mathematical labels and concepts, causal relations, literacy, etc.
7. The classroom enrollment includes a broad mix of peers that may include differing ages; differing racial, ethnic, and linguistic backgrounds; differing socioeconomic backgrounds; differing ability levels.[1]

CONTRASTS WITH CONVENTIONAL ACADEMIC CURRICULA

Both Type-A and Type-B child-centered curricula contrast sharply with conventional academic curricula. Conventional academic curricula are sometimes referred to as highly structured, academically oriented, teacher-dominated, teacher-controlled direct instruction. In these programs, the curriculum is imposed by the teacher on

---

[1]There is accumulating evidence (Roopnarine, 1987; Slavin, 1987) to support heterogeneous versus homogeneous grouping in programs for young children. A mix of peers becomes even more critical in a program in which peer modeling and extensive collaboration between peers are expected and encouraged.

the children. It is usually imposed on the teacher as well from one or more of the following sources: curriculum guides (developed and distributed at federal, state, local district, program, or building levels), policy mandates (directives from funding agencies, state or local educational agencies, boards of directors, local administrators, or team leaders), published materials (textbooks, workbooks, or packaged teaching materials), texts (norm-based or criterion-based), pronouncements of educational "experts" (consultants, in-service trainers, university professors, researchers or "specialists"). Nearly all primary classrooms follow a conventional academic curriculum. Increasingly, curricula in preschools and kindergartens are also adopting curricula of this type. A great deal of concern has recently been expressed about the potential detrimental effects of these programs (Egertson, 1987; Elkind, 1987, 1988; Hatch & Freeman, 1988).

A personal note may be helpful here in emphasizing the contrast between child-centered and conventional academic approaches. Long ago, when I[2] was a primary-grade teacher, one of the positions I held was at the campus school of Antioch College in Yellow Springs, Ohio. The program I offered would be classified, according to the above criteria, as a Type-B program. In my classes, I had children of mixed ages labeled not as kindergartners, first graders, or second graders but as the "younger" group. Typically, there were twenty-five or so five, six, and seven year olds. Our classroom was clearly unusual, then as well as now, since much of the curriculum was child centered rather than subject centered. That was 25 or so years ago.

During one of those years in which I was the teacher of the younger group, Nate, age six, one of the children in my class, moved to another school in a different part of the country for a portion of the school year. As I remember it, the following story came back to me via Nate's mother. Nate's complaint about his new classroom, however, went as follows. "At the Antioch School," he said, "we kids got to do everything that was interesting, and Miss Lay helped us if we needed help. At this school, the teacher does everything that is interesting, and we have to just do what she tells us to do."

To Nate, the experience of his new school was something he had to tolerate only until he got back home again. For vast numbers of other children, there was not (and still is not) an alternative image, and so, being pliable and eager to please the adults who are so important to their well-being, they adapt, with only a few complaints, to a classroom that is teacher dominated and subject centered. Many things don't make sense to them. But they become accustomed to the classroom and learn to play the role of student. Schooling appears to be the initiation one must go through in the process of growing up. Everyone does it. Why not? The intent of this chapter is, first, to say why not, and, second, to discuss how curriculum for the young is different when the program follows a Type-B mode of being child centered.

---

[2]In this chapter, the referent *we* refers to both authors; the referent *I* refers to the first author.

THE RATIONALE FOR THE CHILD-CENTERED CURRICULUM

The central reason why the individual child needs to have significant control of a personal curriculum is that what is happening must make sense from the child's point of view if learning is to occur. Whether teachers recognize it or not, what the child gains from the lessons and activities provided in the classroom requires that the child understand what is going on, using what has been experienced in the past as the sieve through which the current happenings are screened. Only to the extent that children can make sense out of "lessons" and "assignments" do those efforts have any constructive effect. Many of the lessons that constitute the conventional academic program do not have the intended effect on children's learning, even when the lesson objectives may appear to have been accomplished. Children often lack awareness of what it is that teachers intend them to be learning from lessons.[3] By contrast, in the child-centered curriculum, it is the teachers' responsibility to correctly discern the meanings and intent of the children they teach, rather than the children's responsibility to discern the meanings and intent of the teachers. This constitutes a critical point of difference between child-centered and conventional academic programs.

IS THERE A CORE CURRICULUM?

Suppose, for the moment, that all of us become convinced of the case that we're making in this chapter that the work of the teacher is to create a setting that can foster children's constructive involvement and then facilitate the efforts of individual children to "drive" their own curricula within that environment. Suppose we do away with all of those district and state curriculum guides that have been written across the years that so often seem to get in the way of teachers seeing what children are really learning and/or already know. Suppose we do away with the workbooks, textbooks, and dittos that so often lead children into thinking that doing pages is what adults

---

[3]Increasingly, researchers are focusing on how learners react to the lessons they experience. Michel (1988) reports that first graders, for example, often describe what reading is by naming the tasks or procedures that happen in the lessons they experience. Thus, reading was described as "sitting and doing work" (p. 30) or "when the teacher says circle the word or you have to put a check on it" (p. 29). Anderson (1981) examined children's reported thoughts about their classwork and found that their primary goal was task completion, not gaining an understanding of the material being taught. Leinhardt and Putnam (1987) have described a model of the skills a student needs to have to make sense of lessons. They point out that a child in a classroom setting must spend a considerable amount of energy and effort trying to determine what the point of a lesson is and what demands are going to be made. Children try to make sense of what they encounter in school but often come to quite erroneous impressions of the meanings of their teachers' attempts to provide didactic instruction. Steinberg and Cazden (1979) videotaped children in various classroom situations and remarked, "There were marked differences between the picture of the child that emerged from the official, teacher-led part of the classroom day, and the picture that emerged from the activities that the children carried on by themselves" (p. 263).

think learning is all about. Suppose we do away with tests, both norm based and criterion referenced, both of which lead teachers and parents to think that there is a very close relationship between whatever is put on those tests and children's learning. Suppose we did away with these items—curriculum guides, workbooks, textbooks, ditto sheets, and tests. What if teachers then were successful in providing a stimulating set of possibilities for children's involvements and helped them learn in relation to their own efforts? Would children learn? The answer, resoundingly, is YES! Would different children learn quite different things, with little overlap between any one child's curriculum and the others'? No. Although clearly there would be some unique areas for each child, there would be a great deal of overlap. Children living in our society all want to learn to write, count, read, calculate, and communicate.[4] The general areas of learning are the same as when adults structure the curriculum. The difference is that a child trying to figure out about print or counting or a foreign language or a science concept as part of a personal agenda does it far more sensibly than adults.

THE ROLE OF TEACHERS IN THE CHILD-CENTERED CURRICULUM

Teachers are tremendously important in a child-centered curriculum. They interact with children in vital ways to assist and to enhance their learning. Teachers provide the arrangements and communicate to children what can be selected, how and where they can work, and how to acquaint others with what they have done. Teachers comment or question in ways that assist children with the development of clearer understandings. They do this without taking the initiative or motivation away from the children. They are important as authorities who set the tone that school is the place for learning. They communicate to children that school is not for being passive or frivolous; it is a place for being active listeners. Teachers set this tone. Their role is different in a child-centered program than in a subject-centered program but not less important. A later section will specify in more detail the kinds of interactions that teachers have with children and parents in a child-centered curriculum. Let's first talk about how the teacher sets the stage.

Setting the Stage

Time Arrangements

The child-centered curriculum has two essential time requirements. First, there must be long time periods for activity so that children can really get into a single project

---

[4]The only exceptions may be "disadvantaged" children who lack in their environment what the rest of us take for granted (books, letters, elaborated conversations, newspapers); children who have had highly traumatic life encounters; and children who have had premature instruction in academic areas, leading to failure and distaste.

or have the chance to do several different things of their own choosing. Children need to know that they will not just get started with something and then be told to stop. Second, there must be time for verbally sharing with others, including both the adults and other children, what has been accomplished during the activity periods.

There are a number of different models for how to structure time that fit the child-centered curricula. My Antioch School program had the following schedule:

News Time—sharing out-of-school life in various ways

QWT (Quiet Work Time)—choices of quiet activities, such as drawing, painting, using small manipulative toys, sewing, using the listening center, doing puzzles, or using the scrap box

Sharing—showing and/or talking about the products and experiences of QWT

Recess—outdoor play with multiple options

Book Time—looking at books and other print/picture materials, reading to self or another, writing, or making books

Math Time or Writing Time—individual and small-group work, with intermittent large-group discussion and sharing

Lunch

Story Time—teacher-read or told stories and/or individual reading or looking at books

NWT (Noisy Work Time)—QWT choices, as indicated above, plus noisier alternatives using blocks, water, dramatic play, carpentry, clay, musical instruments, or dancing

Sharing—showing and/or talking about the products and experiences of NWT

Unit Activities—group and individual activities related to interest themes, e.g., museums, spring, Glen Helen, restaurants

The above is only an example of the kind of program schedule within which a child-centered curriculum emerges. It is characteristic of programs that have a child-centered emphasis to arrange time under labels and definitions that are related to the kinds of activities the children are expected to engage in at each point in time, rather than the specific subject that they are supposedly learning about (e.g., science or reading). Choices between activities for any particular time period, e.g., Book Time, remain fairly constant across time. This is in contrast to subject-centered time arrangements in which the kinds of activities children engage in on any particular day depends upon the teacher's lesson plan. In contrast, planning and decision making are important functions for children in child-centered programs as well as for teachers.

Space and Equipment

Establishing the physical environment necessary to the child-centered curriculum requires a broad variety of activity involvements, ample supply of expendable raw materials, and organization for ease of access and maintenance by children. The material arrangements need to be discernible to children and the storage scheme obvious. This point is made by a great number of program developers who provide for child initiation. For example, in speaking of the Cognitively Oriented Curriculum, Hohmann, Banet, and Weikart (1979) point out, "Classroom space works best for children who make their own choices when it is divided into distinct work areas" (p. 30). The Cognitively Oriented Curriculum for preschool, which is child centered according to our classification schema, specifies the inclusion of a block area, a house area, an art area, a construction area, a music and movement area, a sand and water area, an animal and plant area, and an outdoor play area.

Teachers who use a child-centered curriculum do not attempt to constantly create new teacher-made and commercial games and devices to place in centers so that there is always something new and different. Children learn how to use the basic set of equipment provided in each center and can then operate autonomously and creatively.

In my classroom for primary-age children at the Antioch School, I had a block area (open carpeted space with bins for block storage), a drama area (stage, curtain, dress-ups), various art areas (clay, painting, scrap box), table manipulatives and board games, book area (shelves, display space, rug, cushions), writing area (blank books, paper, pencils, felt pens, etc.), a miniature house (transformable into various unit/theme representations), etc.

Zimiles (1987) described the materials found in the child-centered Bank Street Approach as follows:

> The materials used in a BSA [Bank Street Approach] classroom for young children provide for a functional reading environment: charts that summarize experience, guide management and record attendance; labels; written messages; bulletin boards with schedules; news of class activities and interests; committee listings; student contributions. Also present are cooking materials, building blocks and table clocks, and materials to be used in dramatic play, such as puppets and miniature household furniture.
>
> In order to underline the organizational structure of the classroom and to focus on learning, the classroom activities are arranged in centers. Reading materials to be used in a reading center will include student-made books, trade books, basal readers and reading kits, reference books, books related to special activities of the class, current magazines, and newsletters. A listening center has a tape recorder, record player, and earphones. The writing center has paper of various sizes, shapes and colors, different kinds of writing tools, manipulative alphabet letters, a typewriter, word banks, spelling books, picture collections, filmstrips, books without words and other story starters, children's journals, diaries, and writing books. The math center included childmade collections of found materials for counting, commercially-produced counting materials, some structured math materials such as Cuisenaire rods, Dienes blocks, attribute materials, measuring equipment such as rulers, measuring cups, scales, timers, geometric shapes that are two and three dimensional, number lines and 100 squares, math games and puzzles, task cards, and workbooks.

A science center will have plants, terrarium, animals, aquarium, materials that can be used for investigation such as food coloring, soap flakes, oil, and equipment for observing and recording, e.g., magnets, magnifying glasses, batteries, prisms. The art center will have paints, clay, collage materials, drawing materials, and hand puppets. The materials typically found in a BSA classroom convey the program's heavy reliance on handmade materials and its overriding commitment to provide a rich, cognitively stimulating environment (p. 171).

While there may be some differences between the three programs just cited (Antioch School, Cognitively Oriented, Bank Street), there are many similarities, as attested to by the given descriptions.

Establishing Classroom Procedures

Scheduling, space arrangements, and environmental maintenance all contribute to program involvement and need to be carefully planned. Both research (Emmer, Evertson, & Anderson, 1980) and common sense tell us that a key factor in successful classroom management is detailed advance planning of how the classroom environment is going to be used throughout the program day. This advance planning allows the teacher to teach children about the procedures that will work smoothly and, thus, facilitates their independence. This is true for all programs. It is, however, even more crucial for the program using a child-centered curriculum since it is only as children are constructively engaged in satisfying activities that the teacher can enter into other kinds of activities with the children, individually and in groups (for example, dialogue and observation). If the teacher must continue to interact with children over procedural issues, there is little possibility of making significant contributions to their learning.

Let's consider some examples of procedures that facilitate rather than discourage children's involvement and activity. What, for example, were children expected to do when a Noisy Work Time was over in my Antioch School classroom? First came a warning signal, which indicated that there were about 5 minutes left of the work period. Children were expected to think about how to complete their work and to decide whether they had something to share. Next, there was an announcement: "Noisy Work Time is over. Please move over to the rug for sharing time or begin to work very quietly where you are so that you can hear what is happening." There was a place for papers and objects to be shared to be temporarily placed nearby. The children knew that I would follow a systematic routine for asking, e.g., "Who has created a play for us to see today?" "Do you have any announcements about the performers, the scene, or anything else about your play?" and to the audience, after the performance, "Do you have any questions or comments about what you just saw?" Finally, after the sharing about block structures, water-play inventions, math manipulative designs, artwork, drama and music productions, illustrated and authored books, etc., came the announcement, "Now, it is time to clean up. Please start with the cleanup of the areas you used and when you finish, move to the other areas to help out. Sandy is going to play *Stars and Stripes Forever* during cleanup today. We'll have a snack in the book corner as soon as cleanup is done." As children snack, they are asked, "What did we do especially well during Noisy Work Time, Sharing, or Cleanup today?" and then, "Were there any problems?" "How could we do that better next time?"

TEACHERS' INTERACTIVE BEHAVIOR IN THE CHILD-CENTERED CURRICULUM

The child-centered curriculum develops through the interaction of the teacher and child(ren) in a well-prepared environment. Teachers use their attention, insights, and cognition to help children continue to accomplish their own goals and to extend their own understandings of the world around them. Teachers develop their abilities to engage children in dialogue, either individually or in small groups. The purpose is to extend children's thinking and to develop their communication skills.

What teachers actually do as they engage in dialogues with young children has been discussed in a number of publications (Cazden, 1981; Coppler, Sigel, & Saunders, 1984; Lay-Dopyera & Dopyera, 1987; Mehan, 1979; Tizard & Hughes, 1984; Tough, 1985). There is much yet to be learned about the most productive practices for helping children learn without didactic instruction. A number of desirable practices, however, are frequently cited.

One guideline has to do with the position of the teacher in relation to the child or children. Teachers situate themselves so that they are on the children's level. This sometimes requires kneeling or sitting on the floor or on a small chair. They then can maintain easy eye contact with the children as they listen to them talk about what they are doing and what they are thinking about. Sometimes the conversations include several children; more often the teacher talks with one individual at a time. When small groups are formed, the focus is almost always on cross-group sharing and mutual effort, rather than the flow of information and/or questioning coming unidirectionally from the teacher to the children.

In dialogue, the teacher makes use of rephrasing frequently to check on the accuracy of what is heard and to model other ways of speaking. The teacher sometimes also describes to the child what the child doing.

Open-ended questions are often posed to the child. Questions that require only a yes or no answer or a "right" answer are avoided. If the teacher knows the answer to a question before asking it, the question is avoided. The idea is to engage the children in dialogue, not interrogate them as to what they know or don't know. Kamii (1985), for example, points out that the most general principle for the teacher to keep in mind is to reduce adult power as much as possible and to exchange points of view with children. She appears to agree with the point made earlier in this chapter that while the teacher is responsible for the classroom, most teachers use more power than is necessary. It is also important, according to Kamii, to encourage the exchange and coordination of points of view among peers.

Forman (1987) emphasizes that the goal of the educator should not be to teach facts but, instead, to teach children to think about how they know a fact to be true. He says that when children are asked to talk about the thinking behind their conclusions, wrong answers are more helpful than correct answers in fostering reflection. Forman further points out that meaningful learning results only when the learner can ask questions. The following statements elaborate his perspectives:

> A child seeking to answer his or her own question is more likely to understand the significance of the ultimate answer. A child who is asked to seek the answer to the teacher's question may ultimately be successful, but may still not relate the answer to previously held concepts. On the other hand, the question itself already indicates a link to a wider domain of understanding. For instance, a question like "Where does the shadow go when I turn off the flashlight?" indicates that the child has constructed a contrast between real objects (they don't leave when the lights go off) and shadows. If the teacher had asked this question, the child would be less likely to treat it as a misapplication of real object concepts. Their answers would dangle in a world without many interrelations (Forman, pp. 72–73).

Sigel and Saunders (1979) report on the effectiveness of particular kinds of questioning. They, like others, recommend the use of open-ended questions. Further, they urge questioning that encourages children to "distance" themselves from the here and now in time and space (Cataldo, 1978; Sigel & Saunders, 1979):

> Whereas a closed question usually has a clear reference as well as a clear message, an open question forces the respondent to decide what is appropriate and how much to say. For example, "What can you tell me about your trip to the orchard?" is an open-ended question allowing for many options: the child can begin at any point in the history of the trip, relate any number of possible events, feelings, or what not. This is in contrast to closed questions, e.g., "Did you go to the orchard? . . . How did you get there?"

Through discussion of topics related to the immediate activity of the child or prior and/or anticipated future experiences, the teacher engages the child's thought processes and uses whatever the child verbally or nonverbally produces as the cues for the kind of interaction to pursue.

In the child-centered curriculum, dialogue is the primary teaching responsibility of the teacher. As the above paragraphs suggest, the teacher needs to carefully develop and use abilities to engage the children in talk and action that contributes to understanding. This kind of dialogue is applied to children's interest in making sense of the print in books, to their interests in physical and mathematical phenomena, and to their social interactions. With prekindergartners, the teacher moves about the classroom making contact with individual children as deemed appropriate at the particular point in time. In kindergarten and the primary grades, the teacher sometimes uses children's work periods for prescheduled "conferences." For example, in my Antioch School classroom, I daily posted on the chalkboard the names of children with whom I wanted to talk during the Quiet Work Time and Noisy Work Time. I also always left time and room for sign-ups of others who wished to arrange a conference. Such conferences were usually not individual lessons. They were, instead, dialogue about the ongoing efforts of children that ordinarily but not always involved endeavors that could be called "academic" (e.g., reading a book, solving problems, writing a letter, discovering math patterns).

OUTCOMES OF THE CHILD-CENTERED CURRICULUM

A tremendous expenditure of resources (time, money, and attention) has been devoted to comparing curriculum approaches in the past decades. Some of these comparisons included child-centered approaches (of various types) with academically oriented programs. The extent to which these programs actually involved classrooms that meet the criteria discussed in this chapter for child-centered curriculum: Type B is generally unknown.

A number of studies have demonstrated that academically focused programs are more successful in producing achievement test outcomes in impoverished children, at least in the short term, than programs that are more child centered. Among these studies are Becker and Gersten (1982); Miller and Bizzell (1970); Smith (1975); Stallings (1975); and Stebbins, St. Pierre, Proper, Anderson, and Cerva (1977). Such studies have been frequently cited in national media, in government publications (i.e., "Programs That Work," etc.), and in commercial advertising. The impression gained by a casual exposure to the popular reporting of such studies is often that academically oriented programs are far superior. There is, for example, a general belief among the public and among professionals as well that open education, the child-centered curriculum approach practiced during the seventies, had been proved to be unsuccessful. This belief was fueled by a study of British school practices (Bennett, 1976) that presented negative findings and served to discourage what American educators, emulating the British, had found promising. Walberg (1986), however, points out that three extensive syntheses of open education found that "students in open classes do slightly or no worse in standardized achievement" (p. 217). He further laments,

> Unfortunately, the negative conclusion of Bennett's (1976) single study—introduced by a prominent psychologist, published by Harvard University Press, publicized by the New York Times and by experts that take that newspaper as their source—probably sounded the death knell of open education, even though the conclusion of the study was later retracted (Aitken, Bennett, & Hesketh, 1981) because of obvious statistical flaws in the original analysis (Aitken, Anderson, & Hinde, 1981) (Walberg, 1986, p. 226).

The other significant influence in the decline of open education in America's elementary schools came from the widely publicized success of direct instruction in follow-through comparisons. The greatest achievement differences were obtained by curricula fashioned after the Academic Preschool of Bereiter and Engelmann (1966) in its Direct Instruction version. The Direct Instruction program was based upon the premise that positive reinforcement is essential to modifying student behavior and maximizing children's academic success. To implement the belief that children can be trained to succeed, a carefully sequenced curriculum and a rigidly controlled instructional process are required. A review by Stallings and Stipek (1986) of the planned comparison of the Direct Instruction and other models, including more child-centered alternatives, in Project Follow Through, stated, "Results over time have indicated that children who continued in this structured academic program eventually won the academic marble game" (p. 738).

There has been a recent note of warning, however, about the possible consequences of such programs from the comparative study of three preschool curricula reported upon by Schweinhart, Weikart, and Larner, (1986). They reported that impoverished children randomly assigned to preschool programs within either one or another of two child-centered approaches (cognitively oriented or traditional nursery school) fared better at age fifteen than children randomly assigned to a program with an academic focus (Distar/Direct Instruction) in regard to delinquency, relationships with their families, participation in sports, school job appointments, and reaching out to others for help with personal problems. These findings must be viewed with considerable tentativeness, however, since they come from only one study with a small sample.

Where variables other than achievement test scores are considered, the child-centered approaches often outdo the academic programs. According to Walberg (1986), Giaconia and Hedges (1982), in an analysis of open-education studies, concluded that open classes on the average enhance several nonstandard outcomes (attitude, creativity, self-concept) without detracting from academic achievement. Only those considered most extreme (perhaps what we would call Type-A programs) had lower academic achievement. Syntheses of open-education studies find more positive results in open education on attitudes toward school, creativity, independence, curiosity, and cooperation (Horwitz, 1979); independence and attitudes toward teachers (Peterson, 1979); and cooperativeness, creativity, and independence (Hedges, Giaconia, & Gage, 1981). From classroom observation data obtained in the widely varying models of Project Follow Through, Stallings (1975) reported the following to be associated with the more child-centered models: better attendance, higher rates of child independence, higher rates of child questioning, smiling, and laughing.

Studies of both short-term and long-term differences between aspects of early childhood curricula are clearly needed. We need to continue to fine-tune the rather gross indicators of program parameters and program effects that are now available to us. In regard to the issue of child-centered curricula, the following propositions are among those that need to be further tested:

- Enriched multifaceted program environments elicit more diverse involvement and greater educationally relevant involvement by children than impoverished, unidimensional program environments.
- Children in programs with predictable time sequences develop greater autonomy and self-regulated behavior than children in programs where time sequences are more whimsically determined.
- Children who encounter more diverse program experiences develop more diverse skills (e.g., social problem-solving skills) than children whose experiences are limited to focused, directed uniform instruction.
- Children who have many opportunities to become engaged in self-selected activities, with the expectation that they will then reflect on and discuss their involvements, develop more effective verbal, social, and problem-solving skills than those children who do not have these opportunities.
- Children who encounter greater variability in class composition (i.e., age, ability, racial, ethnic) in child-centered programs develop (a) greater appreciation of others and (b) more generalizable problem-solving skills than children who have little opportunity to freely interact with children different from themselves.
- Teachers with a broad repertoire of provisioning and dialogue skills are more effective in facilitating the health, well-being, and development of children, both short and long term, than those with a more limited repertoire.
- Children who have frequent one-on-one encounters with adults who engage in dialogue with them regarding their activities develop greater confidence, skill, and understanding than children who are predominantly taught in groups.

SUMMARY

The characteristics of programs that have a child-centered curriculum have been described in this chapter as typically including a broad mix of peers, a reliable time structure with ample provision of activity options for student initiatives, workable procedures, sharing and evaluation, and behavioral records to which all responsible adults contribute. Another common characteristic of the program with a child-centered curriculum is that time periods are arranged under labels and definitions related to the kinds of activities the children engage in at each point of time, rather than according to subject designations. The final and most important feature of the program with a child-centered curriculum is the teacher, whose predominant activity is engaging in dialogue with children and asking open-ended questions that encourage reflection and the exchange and coordination of points of view among peers. From these features, it seems reasonable to hypothesize greater long-term gains in learning and development for these programs than from those with the conventional academic emphasis.

REFERENCES

Aitken, M., Anderson, D., & Hinde, J. (1981). Modeling of data on teaching styles [With discussion]. *Journal of the Royal Statistical Society (Series A)*, *144*, 419–461.

Aitken, M., Bennett, S. N., & Hesketh, J. (1981). Teaching styles and pupil progress: A re-analysis. *British Journal of Educational Psychology*, *51*, 312–319.

Anderson, L. (1981). Short-term student responses to classroom instruction. *Elementary School Journal*, *82*, 97–108.

Becker, W. C., & Gersten, R. (1982). A follow up of Follow Through: The later effects of the direct instruction model on children in fifth and sixth grades. *American Educational Research Journal*, *19*, 75–92.

Bennett, S. N. (1976). *Teaching styles and pupil progress*. Shepton Mallet, Somerset, England: Open Books.

Bereiter, C., & Engelmann, S. (1966). *Teaching disadvantaged children in the preschool*. Englewood Cliffs, NJ: Prentice-Hall.

Cataldo, C. Z. (1978). A follow-up study of early intervention (Doctoral dissertation, State University of New York at Buffalo, 1977). *Dissertation Abstracts International*, *39*, 657-A. (University Microfilms No. 7813990)

Cazden, C. B. (1981). *Language in early childhood education*. Washington, DC: National Association for the Education of Young Children.

Copple, C., Sigel, I. E., & Saunders, R. (1984). *Educating the young thinker: Classroom strategies for cognitive growth*. Hillsdale, NJ: Lawrence Erlbaum.

Dopyera, J. (1972). What's open about open programs? In D. D. Hearn, J. Burdin, & L. Katz (Eds.), *Current research and perspectives in open education* (pp. 45–61). Washington, DC: American Association of Elementary-Kindergarten-Nursery Educators.

Egertson, H. A. (1987, May 20). Recapturing kindergarten for 5-year-olds. *Education Week*, pp. 7–9.

Elkind, D. (1987). *Miseducation: Preschoolers at risk*. New York: Alfred A. Knopf.

Elkind, D (1988, September 11). Overwhelmed at an early age. *Boston Globe Magazine*, pp. 18, 40–46, 54–58.

Emmer, E., Evertson, C., & Anderson, L. (1980). Effective classroom management at the beginning of the school year. *Elementary School Journal*, *80*, 219–231.

Forman, G. (1987). The school for constructive play. In J. L. Roopnarine & J. E. Johnson (Eds.), *Approaches to early childhood education* (pp. 72–82). Columbus, OH: Merrill.

Giaconia, R. M., & Hedges, L. V. (1982). *Identifying features of open education*. Stanford, CA: Stanford University.

Hatch, J. A. & Freeman, E. B. (1988). Kindergarten philosophies and practices: Perspectives of teachers, principals, and supervisors. *Early Childhood Research Quarterly*, *3*, 151–166.

Hedges, L. V., Giaconia, R. M., & Gage, N. L. (1981). *Meta-analysis of the effects of open and traditional instruction*. Stanford, CA: Stanford University, Program on Teaching Effectiveness.

Hohmann, M., Banet, B., & Weikart, D. P. (1979). *Young children in action*. Ypsilanti, MI: High/Scope Press.

Horwitz, R. A. (1979). Psychological effects of the open classroom. *Review of Educational Research*, *49*, 71–86.

Kamii, C. (1985). *Young children reinvent arithmetic: Implications of Piaget's theory*. New York: Teachers College, Columbia University.

Lay-Dopyera, M., & Dopyera, J. (1987). *Becoming a teacher of young children* (3rd ed.). New York: Random House.

Leinhardt, G., & Putnam, R. T. (1987). The skill of learning from classroom lessons. *American Educational Research Journal, 24*, 557–587.

Mehan, H. (1979). "What time is it, Denise?" Asking known information questions in classroom discourse. *Theory into Practice, 18*, 285–294.

Michel, P. A. (1988). *Children's perceptions of reading*. Unpublished doctoral dissertation, Syracuse University, Syracuse, NY.

Miller, L., & Bizzell, B. G. (1970). *Experimental variation of Head Start curricula: A comparison of current approaches* (Progress Report No. 5, Grant No. CG 8199, OEO). Louisville, KY: University of Louisville.

Neill, A. S. (1961). *Summerhill: A radical approach to child rearing*. New York: Hart.

Peterson, P. L. (1979). Direct instruction reconsidered. In P. L. Peterson & H. J. Walberg (Eds.), *Research on teaching* (pp. 112–131). Berkeley, CA: McCutchan.

Roopnarine, J. L. (1987). The social individual model: Mixed-age socialization. In Roopnarine, J. L., & Johnson, J. E. (Eds.), *Approaches to early childhood education* (pp. 143–162). Columbus, OH: Merrill.

Schweinhart, L. J., Weikart, D. P., & Larner, M. B. (1986). Consequences of three preschool curriculum models through age 15. *Early Childhood Research Quarterly, 1*, 15–45.

Sigel, I. E., & Saunders, R. (1979). An inquiry into inquiry: Question-asking as an instructional model. In L. Katz (Ed.), *Current topics in early childhood education* (Vol. 2, pp. 169–193). Norwood, NJ: Ablex.

Slavin, R. E. (1987). Ability grouping and student achievement in elementary schools: A best-evidence synthesis. *Review of Educational Research, 57*, 293–336.

Smith, M. S. (1975). Evaluation findings in Head Start planned variation. In A. M. Rivlin & T. M. Timpane (Eds.), *Planned variation in education* (pp. 48–63). Washington, DC: Brookings Institute.

Stallings, J. (1975). *Relationships between classroom instructional practices and child development*. Menlo Park, CA: Stanford Research Institute. (ERIC Document Reproduction Service No. ED 106 297)

Stallings, J., & Stipek, D. (1986). Research on early childhood and elementary school teaching programs. In M. C. Wittrock (Ed.), *Handbook of research on teaching* (3rd ed., pp. 727–753). New York: Macmillan.

Stebbins, L. B., St. Pierre, R. G., Proper, E. C. Anderson, R. B., & Cerva, T. R. (1977). *Education as experimentation: A planned variation model. Vol. IV-A: An evaluation of Follow Through*. Cambridge, MA: Abt.

Steinberg, Z. D., & Cazden, C. (1979). Children as teachers of peers and ourselves. *Theory into Practice, 18*, 258–266.

Tizard, B., & Hughes, M. (1984). *Young children learning*. Cambridge, MA: Harvard University Press.

Tough, J. (1985). *Talking and learning*. London: Ward Lock Educational.

Walberg, H. J. (1986). *Handbook of research on teaching* (3rd ed., pp. 214–229). New York: Macmillan.

Zimiles, H. (1987). The Bank Street Approach. In J. L. Roopnarine & J. E. Johnson (Eds.), *Approaches to early childhood education* (pp. 163–178). Columbus, OH: Merrill.

10

Play Issues in Early Childhood Education

DORIS PRONIN FROMBERG
Hofstra University–Hempstead, N.Y.

Imagine being offered a gift of the automobile of your dreams. Imagine the color and shape as it rolls off the assembly line with a full tank of gas, registered in your name. Only one thing is missing—the oil to lubricate it.

Imagine the human body as you studied it in school. You studied the various systems, such as the skeletal, nervous, reproductive, digestive, respiratory, endocrine, and circulatory. Most of these systems can be visualized structurally with ease. It is more difficult, however, to pinpoint the lymphatic system in a structural way. Like the oil for your automobile, it pervades the system, and makes possible the integration and functioning of the human machinery.

Play functions in human life, in ways similar to oil or lymph fluids, as an ultimate integrator of human experience. When children play, they integrate social, emotional, physical, cognitive, and imaginative experience. Play integrates the aesthetic and the logical, the real and the imagined. Play is episodic, rather than focused on some future goal. For example, fantasy play need not follow a beginning, middle, and end structure.[1] Play can be an end in itself. At the same time, it is a condition of learning, along with other conditions of learning. Other conditions of learning in early childhood include physical experience, induction, cognitive dissonance, social interaction, and competence (Fromberg, 1987a).

For young children, play is voluntary, meaningful, active, symbolic, rule bound, and usually pleasurable, even when dealing with serious matters. Play has been

---

[1] Indeed, different cultures offer alternative ways in which to structure stories (Sutton Smith, 1989).

223

studied with increasing interest in recent years, and various reviews of the literature exist (Bergen, 1988; Fein & Rivkin, 1986; Fromberg, 1987b; Monighan-Nourot, Scales, Van Hoorn, with Almy, 1987; Smith, 1986). This chapter, rather than a review of the research literature, will highlight selected issues concerning play as it relates to the work of early childhood teachers. These issues will be considered in the context of various theories of learning and acting. An opening issue resides in the contrasts between these theoretical positions.

TRYING TO UNDERSTAND PLAY

Two major approaches to an understanding of play are the individual and the social views. The psychological orientation, represented by the Piagetian (1962, 1965)/ Freudian (1916/1960, 1925/1958, 1928/1959) study of individual development, can be contrasted with the cultural, anthropological orientation, represented by the Vygotskian (1976, 1978, 1986)/Batesonian (1971, 1976, 1979)/Geertzian (1976) studies of contextual influences in play.

While differing about the emphases in interpreting play, both the psychological and cultural perspectives accept that play is significant in children's development. Both positions recognize that the child's self-directed, intrinsically motivated play activity is pivotal in the construction of understandings.

These intersecting contentions are constant with a relatively recent focus on the nature of the individual's subjective experiencing of play. The subjective feeling of "flow," an "optimal experience" (Csikszentmihalyi, 1976, 1979, 1988a, 1988b, 1988c) in which one is unaware of time passing, is satisfying and focused enough in the present to transcend the moment.

Orientation to the Past

Boldly stated, the psychological orientation holds that when children play, they practice what they already know, "assimilative" behavior as termed by Jean Piaget (1962). Play, in this sense, is an expressive form of cognitive development. This view is based primarily on research into children's interactions with the physical world and the manipulation/influence of other people. Views based on Freud's work present play as a personal catharsis for emotions, an opportunity for wish fulfillment and mastery.

The stages that each of these major theorists has presented have recently been called into question as male-oriented perspectives. Carol Gilligan (1982), for example, contends that an assessment of play that is based upon rules and the nature of morality stages in particular is hierarchical. When she accounts for the different socialization afforded to females, she points out that different is not more or less advanced but relative to socialization. That is, girls have been found to focus on relationships and connectedness rather than competition and separateness (Gilligan, 1982; Whiting & Edwards, 1988).

Orientation to the Future

The cultural, anthropological orientation contends that play functions in advance of development, "accommodative" behavior. For example, the Zone of Proximal Development, put forward by Lev Vygotsky (1986), suggests that play serves as a bridge between objects and thoughts. Children use objects and situations symbolically as a "pivot." For example, a stick substitutes for a horse (Vygotsky, 1976).

Vygotsky focuses attention on the rule-bound nature of play and contends that children accept rules when they enter into playing. Anthropologist Gregory Bateson (1979), similarly, talks about children moving into and out of the play frame. Their need to continually clarify what is inside of the play frame and what is outside of the play frame extends their social awareness. It reflects their capacity to communicate about their communication (metacommunication) in advance of their years (1971, 1976, 1979). For example, children step outside the play to suggest, "You be the big brother," and then step inside the play and behave in relation to the big brother. In effect, children move from the imaginative capacity, considering "What if," to behaving in play "As if." They demonstrate their capacity to classify what is and what is not play. In these ways, the children subordinate themselves voluntarily and meaningfully to the "rules" of the pretend play. The more they play, the more they learn about the rules by interacting with others who provide feedback.

In these ways, play leads development. You can see this taking place as the surface behavior of children's play becomes a vista through which to view their deeper understandings.

Another aspect of the cultural, anthropological view is reflected in the agreement of what is playful in the context of each culture and each situation (Schwartzman, 1978). Clifford Geertz (1976) highlights the nature of play in the context of each culture, where who may and who may not engage in activity, or the nature of the activity, is defined as play or ritual, frivolity or technical behavior. When children are needed to participate in a subsistence economy, for example, the time and opportunities for play often occur in the work setting (Whiting & Edwards, 1988). Some people may or may not engage acceptably in play (Morgan, 1982). Thus, play is a relative phenomenon. It is also a political phenomenon (Wertsch & Lee, 1984), and the personal content (text) of play occurs within a particular cultural context.

THE RELATION OF PLAY AND WORK

If you think of the classroom as a culture of its own, created anew by each unique group of children with their teacher each year, it becomes apparent that play is a political and relative phenomenon. In some classrooms, play is integrated in natural ways. It is a condition of learning much of the time. There are extended blocks of time set aside during which subgroups of children can convene in various areas. There are provisions in one area for sociodramatic play with varied, suggestive, and changing thematic props. There is another area in which construction materials are available. In still other areas, art materials or varied manipulative materials or language-related materials are used, and so forth. These provisions of space, time, and material resources are conducive to children's use in alternative ways.

In other classrooms, there are sharp distinctions drawn between work and play. Anthropologist Frederick Erickson (Erickson & Mohatt, 1982) contends that teachers who create sharp divisions between work and play use work as the area of their power. This suggests that play, the area in which children are permitted power, is less significant. Anne Haas Dyson (1987) makes the point that children's "off task" behavior, their playful conversational exchanges, their imaginative and fanciful play, is the source of significant learning. It is the source of useful feedback from their peers that provides them with reflections that heighten their self-awareness, in advance of what might be expected. Thus, children learn from interacting with other children. Put another way, children teach each other to perceive alternatives to their own perceptions. In this way, the power to teach is shared.

When classrooms are organized for "work first, play later," scholarship is not served as well as when such distinctions are absent. According to Greta Fein's (1985b) study, young children define work in terms of "obligation and duty" and play as "voluntary." Play is not, in this sense, an enrichment of work, nor should it be a release from work that is perceived as drudgery. Play is valuable in itself. Children may work at play, but play may or may not be serious. When you see play as a condition of learning, you see it in the context of events that change with the child's experience.

John Dewey (1933) suggests a continuum between fooling, play, work, and drudgery. When work becomes satisfying in itself and functional autonomy occurs (Allport, 1958), work may become play, in which the end is not in the future but in the present. "From the perspective of subjective experience, work and play are not necessarily opposite . . . [and] the quality of the experience might be a more valid guide than the nature of the activity" (Csikszentmihalyi, 1988c, pp. 8–9). Dewey proposes that play and work that is playful are relevant school activities.

HOW PLAY INFLUENCES OTHER DEVELOPMENTS: IMAGINATION, SOCIAL COMPETENCE, LANGUAGE, AND COGNITION

There is a considerable body of research pointing to the influence of play in stimulating creative and imaginative thinking and developing social competence, language skills, and cognition.[2] With such a rich lode of products to mine, teachers may be seduced into unduly intruding and eroding play, activity that is centered in

---

[2]There are a few studies that do not find support for these views. Genishi and Galvan (1985) found support for social, but not creative, correlations with play. Simon and Smith (1985a, 1985b, 1986) criticize the rigor of research techniques used in studies of the correlation between play and problem solving.

children's present-time, nonliteral, voluntary, and often seriously enjoyable concerns. It is important, therefore, that teachers remain vigilant and provide for play.

On the one hand, the human need to play deserves our respect. On the other hand, the school's purpose of expanding and extending what children bring to school is served by such opportunities. In order to support teachers in their provision of play, and provide information that may be shared with other adults, selected research findings are presented. The focus will be on representational and interactive play.

Play and Imagination

Imagination is central to play and to the content of education. When children move between "what if" plans and "as if" execution of those plans, they are employing significant imaginative skills. It is imagination, after all, that makes progress possible in all disciplines of knowledge. As Vygotsky (1986, p. 349) contends, "Alongside the images that are constructed in the immediate cognition of reality, man constructs images that are not found in completed form in reality. . . . Imagination is a necessary, integral aspect of realistic thinking."

This raises the issue of the hierarchy in Western cultures of disciplines, such as the sciences, mathematics, and language, that are valued more than the arts and social studies. In the present educational climate, separate specified academic skills that may be evaluated on standardized tests, such as mathematics, reading, and a body of factual information, are valued. The arts, imagination, and play are devalued. Kieran Egan (1988), however, proposes a nonhierarchical relationship between orality and literacy. He recognizes and outlines unique strengths in the structures of orality, which often are sacrificed with the advent of literacy. Pretend play, usually an oral interaction, demonstrates significant dynamics, which are detailed in a later section.

Sublime First, Mundane Second, If at All

Some research on children's capacity to be imaginative found that children who were exposed to realistic (mundane) toys before choosing activities were less imaginative than children who were exposed to less-realistic toys (McGhee, Etheridge, & Berg, 1984). This type of finding suggests that the rise in use of workbooks, and the decline of art and sociodramatic play, in early-childhood education may reduce children's opportunities to develop imaginative (sublime) capacities. The basic dynamic of the workbook is to move on. Typically, the teacher explains once and expects children to retain the information and then prove it by working alone, silently, page by page. When children begin to achieve new learnings, however, a contrast with formerly mastered concepts, they delight in repeating the situation. In this way, they confirm the validity of their perception as well as the predictability or orderliness of the phenomenon. The opportunity to engage in self-directed play, sometimes repetitive-with-variations-on-a-theme play, supports children's sense of competence, self-esteem, and sense of power.

Educators, in the first place, need to question the presence of linear, test-oriented workbooks in early-education settings. The rote learnings that are expected represent an impoverished alternative to the rich experiences of direct participation with materials and play with others. To "challenge children's elaborative capacities," Jerome Bruner (1980, 1986) found that groups of three or more young children did better than a child alone, but that pairs of children did best, in stimulating one another's imagination. This is consistent with Dyson's findings, cited previously, as well as the work of others who find that children are a source of learning from one another (Johnson, Johnson, Holubec, & Roy, 1984). Piaget (1965) also saw cognitive development, decentration, and reversible thinking growing out of individuals' interactions with their peers.

Through modeling, asking divergent questions, and providing contrasts, unstructured materials, and appreciation for alternatives, teachers can stimulate imagination. According to researchers, sociodramatic play activities that children build spontaneously also offer these strategies. Researchers have found that children who played with unstructured materials (Dansky & Silverman, 1976; Freyberg, 1973; Pulaski, 1973), who were encouraged to engage in divergent play (Pepler & Ross, 1982), and who were asked divergent questions (Feitelson & Ross, 1973) showed more imaginative and varied play, produced more originality and associative fluency, and employed more alternatives.

Those children whose parents model or encourage fantasy play are likely to engage in imaginative storytelling, use more analogies, and show more perseverance and the capacity to wait quietly (Connolly & Doyle, 1984; Moran, Sawyers, Fu, & Milgram, 1984; Singer, 1973; Singer & Singer, 1979). These various capacities are more and less acceptable in the cultures of different classrooms. Teachers usually appreciate children's abilities to wait quietly (even if children engage in the fantasy that helps make it possible). Imaginative storytelling and the use of analogies are often valued. Associative fluency, exploring alternative solutions, and sometimes original outcomes have been welcomed with less enthusiasm by some teachers (Torrance, 1962). Those teachers labeled children who engaged in such creative behavior as difficult.

When we consider a world in which global technology, economy, and communication undergo rapid change, however, the most productive individuals will be those who are capable of collaborative work, connection making, and setting and solving problems in unique ways. Children acquire aspects of these important personal and social attributes through experiences and learnings generated in spontaneous social and pretend play.

Play and Social Competence

Researchers have described the constructs that help to illuminate the relation of play and social competence. Their views on decentration, decontextualization, and integration are integrated in this section (Bretherton, 1984; Fein, 1975, 1985a; Fenson & Schell, 1986; Monighan-Nourot et al., 1987; Rubin & Howe, 1986).

Social pretend play reveals progress in *decentration*. As children interact with others, contrast between one child's perspective and those of other children occur. It is as if children become a responsive audience to one another, an audience whose voice is heard and serves to alter the course of play and perceptions. Children learn to anticipate others' reactions and respect their respective positions sufficiently to adapt their behavior.

Social pretend play reveals progress in *decontextualization*. As children engage in pretend play, they increasingly become less dependent on prototypical objects. This is evidenced by their symbolic substitutions. They transform a block into a nursing bottle, a plate into an airplane steering wheel, and a friend into a mythic character. They move from pretending to feed oneself (self-reference), to pretending to feed a doll as if it were real (other-reference), to assuming both roles (agent-reference).

Social pretend play reveals progress in *integration*. As children interact with one another, they increase the array of symbolic actions from a single transformation to multischeme combinations. They may begin by pretending to feed a doll and then add comforting, bathing, putting to sleep, and covering. As their play integrates more schemas or action sequences, they increase their use of speech.

Caution is needed in assessing the developmental significance of children's play performances. Their competence, according to Roberta Corrigan (1987), may be masked by the situational context and vary accordingly: "Children are not at a particular level or stage across-the-board" (p. 104). Inge Bretherton concurs (1984).

The issue of privacy contrasted with participation has arisen. Children are able to express their need for privacy more clearly as they mature. A typical progression of play, however, excerpted from the early work of Mary Parten (1971), suggests that social play is more advanced than parallel play, when children play alongside one another, or solitary play. More recently, some researchers contend that solitary play may serve to assist imagination and need not always be judged as less-mature behavior (Olszewski, 1987; Rubin & Howe, 1986; Singer, 1973). An alternative view suggests that there may be a "relative predominance" (Monighan-Nourot et al., 1987, p. 78) rather than an absolute progression: Indeed, "a 5-year-old might typically remark, 'I'm doing this now. I'll come to your restaurant later.' In contrast, a 3-year-old might either physically fight intrusion on his solitary activity by grabbing objects and shouting 'No! Mine!' or retreat from play" (p. 68).

Teachers need to be concerned that a balance is present between opportunities for privacy and participation. For those children whose style of play appears to be more solitary, it makes sense to help them feel welcome and to offer opportunities to share materials with more forthcoming peers. Grossly unbalanced solitary activity, however, may hinder development. For example, research indicates that the "frequent display of nonsocial classroom pretense in kindergarten is predictive of social skills deficits when children are in grade two" (Rubin, 1988, p. 70).

Play and Language

While social play provides us with access to children's language development, it also has been considered an important *stimulant* to language development. A body of research, for example, has found that story comprehension improved after children were tutored in thematic fantasy play and were provided with opportunities for role playing (Marbach & Yawkey, 1980; Pellegrini, 1984, 1985; Pellegrini & Galda, 1982; Williamson & Silvern, 1984).

Sarah Smilansky's (1968) study of children from different socioeconomic groups suggests that language development can be stimulated by sociodramatic play and teacher involvement. She also found that cognitive development was influenced by opportunities for sociodramatic play. Vygotsky (1986) contended that imagination, emotions, language, and social interaction are "interfunctional" (p. 348). The relation of play and language, therefore, is viewed as dynamic, not serial (Roth & Clark, 1987). There is an interaction between play and language in that, "as children become able to use more complex language in their play, their episodes become longer, more complex, and less dependent on the use of concrete objects. Language helps them to extend the realms of their imaginations" (Monighan-Nourot et al., 1987, p. 64).

Teachers stimulate children's language development by providing time, space, and appreciation for social interaction in classrooms, whether in a sociodramatic area, or throughout other areas in which social interaction is recognized as educative (Dyson, 1987; see also Cazden, 1988). Researchers have found that children's language development was stimulated when varied themes were introduced into the repetitive housekeeping area, such as hospital, grocery, and circus (Dodge & Frost, 1986; Levy, Schaefer, & Phelps, 1986). A reflective teacher reported that children understand her better, and she them, when inquiries are in the form of role playing and sociodrama (Paley, 1986). This is consistent with identification of the contrasts in cognitive dissonance, a condition of learning cited previously.

Pretend play has been viewed as an opportunity to rehearse language for native speakers (Bruner, 1980) as well as for second-language learners (Heath with Chin, 1985). Also, as children rehearse roles and strategies that can influence social competence, they add to their experience in communicating with different audiences. In this way, play contributes to children's rehearsal of their later need for considering different perspectives and voices, part of what writers do. Bretherton recommends that, "if we must look at the future implications of pretend play in childhood, it may be more profitable to think of it as the hallmark of an emerging artistic and literary ability" (1988, p. 211).

Play and Cognition

Play tutoring has been employed successfully to improve the cognitive and academic skills of children from lower-class families (Levenstein, 1976, 1985; Smilansky, 1968) and others (Ghiaci & Richardson, 1980; Sylva, Bruner, & Genova, 1976). The transferability and long-term results of conservation of quantity training (Golomb, Gowing, & Friedman, 1982), however, are difficult to measure because children change so quickly and school practices intervene that shape behavior. In any case, in the natural course of events, children will achieve conservation, by their own construction, from direct experiences. Results of the body of studies that attempt to prove exclusively cognitive increments from play are confounded by issues such as language intervention that becomes intertwined, especially in a culture that emphasizes literacy.

While this chapter focuses on children's representational and interactive play, a word needs to be said about the significance of games for cognitive development. Games are a form of play that bridges external rules with children's creation of rules. Young children become increasingly able to employ the rules of games with increasing consistency as they develop.

Most games in United States culture are competitive and leave more losers than winners. It is possible to create lotto boards in which all children finish together, although the elements are mixed differently on each card. It is possible to move a single playing piece toward a common goal across a board game that is directed by a spinner, cards, dice, or a grab bag. It is possible to move a single playing piece toward a common goal across a board game that is directed by a spinner, cards, dice, or a grab bag. It is possible to focus on each person's completion rather than only the first person to finish. Perhaps it is time to consider that it is also possible, as in the Tengu culture of New Guinea, reported by Bruner (1986), that games come to an end when each player has an equivalent position.

Thus, the cooperation:competition issue is a consideration in the use of games. The playful medium of games welcomes children's voluntary participation in potential learning or practice activities. Constance Kamii and Georgia DeClark (1984) and Constance Kamii and Rheta DeVries (1980), among others (Downie, Slesnick, & Stenmark, 1981), suggest many playful games in which children can construct understandings.

It does appear that there is a recursive relationship between play and cognitive development. Advances in play are reflected in readiness for extending learnings. As children learn more, they can integrate new themes and extended language use in their play.

EQUITY IN PLAY

Inasmuch as there is a recursive relationship between play and cognition, language, social competence, and imagination, it is particularly relevant to assure that children have equitable opportunities. There are individual differences between children based upon gender, cultural background, individual variations, and special learning needs.

Play and Gender

Gender differences in play have been documented. They are related to cultural conditions and adult intervention. Girls, for example, appear to remain closer to their teacher (who is often found at sedentary activities) (Serbin, 1978) and closer to home (Whiting & Edwards, 1988), and appear to be more dependent (Saracho, 1987). They receive more attention for compliant, positive behavior while boys receive more attention for more assertive, negative, and independent behavior (Fagot, 1988). Boys engage in more adventurous and more rough-and-tumble play (Blurton Jones, 1976; Pellegrini, 1987; Whiting & Edwards, 1988). Boys engage in more group play that requires strategy and teamwork, and constructive play with objects such as blocks (Maccoby & Jacklin, 1974; Paley, 1984; Serbin, 1978).

Group play and constructive play assist in the development of visual spatial skills that are important for mathematical development, providing an advantage to those children who engage in such play. Inasmuch as girls appear to play more at housekeeping, there appears to be a need for stimulating alternatives. When teachers place themselves in the block-building area, girls have been found to engage in construction (Serbin, 1978). When access to blocks was assured, sometimes through planning or doubling the supply and space, no gender difference in amount of use was found (Rogers, 1985).[3] Thus, minimal teacher intervention can influence children's opportunities for experiences.

Play and Cultural Background

Cultural influences are significant in how children play, what they do, when they do it, with whom, where it is done, and how adults intervene. Shirley Brice Heath (1983) studied middle-class and working-class, urban and rural, black and white children in North Carolina for 10 years. She found that the middle-class, urban black and white children arrived at school with similar backgrounds. Different from the middle-class children, the working-class black and white children arrived with backgrounds that were different from one another.

The play of this particular Piedmont population of working-class black children included uniquely creative narratives and powerful uses of metaphors and humor. They were exposed to interage and intergenerational activities and fluid alternatives in the uses of time and space. These strengths were not generally appreciated by their teachers until the intermediate grades, by which time many children had become alienated and discouraged. The play of the other working-class and middle-class children was more separated from the larger community and family activities. Self-closing toys were heavily employed. The other working-class children were taught to

---

[3]Rogers also found that children selected same-sex dyads. This is consistent with cross-cultural findings that children increasingly begin to select same-gender chums beginning with four year olds (Whiting & Edwards, 1988).

seek the "right" way to do things, an outlook that was valued in school through the primary grades. These restricted outlooks were not as useful in the connection making needed in the intermediate grades.

Another cultural variation is overly scheduled after-school time. When children are scheduled for lessons and competitive sports events after school, there is less time for the pretend play that fuels narratives, language development, social competence, and a sense of personal competence.

In subsistence economies, anthropologists have found that children who are assigned work create islands of opportunities to play (Whiting & Edwards, 1988), just as children in United States schools engage in "off task" fantasy play that tends to enrich the quality of schoolwork (Dyson, 1987). Those teachers who appreciate the strengths that children bring to school, who welcome alternative solutions to problems, who ask questions for which more than one response is expected—in short, who adapt to children—provision classrooms for play.

Play and Individual Variations

Individual children manifest unique play profiles. "Patterners" appear to focus on the mechanical aspects of objects while "dramatists" seem to prefer social and interpersonal situations (Gardner, 1982). High-fantasy and low-fantasy children have been identified (Connolly & Doyle, 1984; Feitelson & Ross, 1973; Freyberg, 1973; Pulaski, 1973; Singer, 1973). "Master players" have been distinguished by creativity, risk taking, and personalized relationships (Fein, 1985a).

Younger nursery-school children manifest distinctive play behaviors. They are more likely to engage in physically oriented play, such as grasping, banging, and mouthing, and less likely to struggle over large objects than small ones (Bergen, Smith, & O'Neill, 1988). They need more space and less furniture than kindergarten or primary children. They may need varying degrees of opportunities to explore and play with objects in general as well as art materials:

> Art materials at the toddler age are primarily used as sensory play materials. Toddlers do not care about making a product. Space for messy art activity such as sand and water play should be provided, preferably in a separate room or area out of sight of the other activity areas. Prone to herding, toddlers are likely to leave the paint table and run to the climber with paint-covered hands if they see the excitement increasing on the climber and slide (Bergen et al., 1988, p. 203).

While developmental differences and individual dispositions are observable in children's play, cultural influences also are reflected in the thematic content with which children concern themselves. Thematic content, such as war play, superheroes, or Barbie dolls, reflects larger societal issues, gender influences, and the influence of communications media. There is concern that heavy television viewing limits children's opportunities and accomplishments in sociodramatic play, thereby reducing "the general ability to organize and comprehend new material" (Singer, 1988, p. 78).

Many women teachers are uncomfortable with superhero and rough-and-tumble play. Children have always played out good and evil, aggression and accommodation, monsters and saviors. The use of signals and symbols, and practice in negotiation, are significant aspects of rough-and-tumble play (Pellegrini, 1987). While one way of coping with superhero and violent play is to harness it at a separate role-playing time planned with the teacher (Paley, 1984) there have been alternatives offered. Cautioning against intrusiveness in favor of facilitation, Nancy Carlsson-Paige and Diane E. Levin (1987) recommend helping children see alternatives to stereotypes and repetitiveness by such strategies as adding props, differentiating reality from fantasy, and raising questions that generate fresh problems and benevolent alternatives. In these various situations, the purpose would be to see that children feel a sense of competence and personal power.

Teachers face a complex task in attempting to understand the cultural contexts and unique personal expectancies of children. Social play may reveal some cultural sources. These observations suggest that there is a need to legitimize a variety of ways in which children may function in schools.

Play and Special Learning Needs

Children who have special learning needs, need opportunities to play. This needs to be stated because children with special learning needs, as well as children who come from diverse economic and cultural backgrounds, are often faced with rote learning tasks and weighty external controls.

In working with special needs, teachers accept the possibility that children will move at a slower pace in entering a play setting. Children with special needs may need more time to explore ("What does this do?" [Hutt, 1976, p. 211]) before they would be expected to play ("What can I do with this?" [p. 211]). (See Hutt, 1976, 1979, on exploration.) Through exploration, children learn the perceptual properties, and through play, they learn the functional properties, of objects (Collard, 1976). The teacher's playful outlook and encouraging interactions are significant in helping children feel competent.

Materials and toys may need to be adapted to the children's special needs. Children's play is sustained when they are able to influence what happens. Adapted mechanisms have been recommended, such as varied switches, and the activation of materials by blowing, sucking, breaking a light beam, and pressing sensitive pressure pads (McConkey, 1986).

Children need to be able to have as much independent access to their surroundings as possible. Enough space should be provided between sturdy furniture so children can move safely if they are impulsive or uncoordinated or use appliances for mobility. Ramps or elevators might be needed. Contrasts between varied environments, and textures and bright color contrasts within them, are also recommended (Phyfe-Perkins & Shoemaker, 1986; Ramsey & Reid, 1988).

The same considerations apply for all children—opportunities to play, the provision of space and other material resources, a receptive environment, the legitimization of choices and social interactions, and the chance to feel independent and competent. While suggestions for teacher intervention are interspersed in preceding sections, the discussion that follows highlights related issues.

IMPLICATIONS FOR TEACHERS

There has been debate about the degree and type of teacher intervention in children's play. Practitioners have taken positions from laissez-faire only to controlling and scheduling a few minutes of games each day. Sometimes, the arts have been categorized as play and offered as a minimal presence in school.

Rational arguments, developmental evidence, children's behaviors, and research notwithstanding, decisions about play in schools also are made on the basis of valuing. It is important to consider that play is worthwhile and developmentally appropriate. When children engage in play, they can be independent, thereby empowering the teacher to work with small groups and individuals. It makes possible the sharing of power between teachers and children. It is the lymphatic system for integrating the logical and the emotional. The imagery and metacommunication stimulated by, and employed in, play interact in the service of problem solving. Play nourishes opportunities and accomplishments in connection making, problem solving, imagining, and creating across disciplines.

If play can improve children's learning and imagination, then it would follow that teachers need to create different environments for children than if learning and imagination were uninfluenced by play. In the interest of pursuing this issue, it is useful to consider the transformational dynamics of how the play process may be functioning to affect development. Then, there is a discussion of the types and degrees of interventions, and the place of play in early childhood education.

Play and Transformational Dynamics

An understanding of the dynamics of play can help us plan how to juxtapose activities in space and time. It helps to think of the fluidity of pretend play within the context of a kind of underlying syntactic structure. "Script model" theory suggests that young children represent their experiences through "event schemata," a series of shared play elements that keep changing in the interactive context (Bretherton, 1984; Kreye, 1984).

The latent structure of such a script theory may lie in the infinite personal varieties of each child's experiences. This interaction, between shared and personal play events, may be similar to the relationship between the universal and personal symbols of dreams, as expounded by Carl Jung (1970). This view would be compatible with the notion that there are "affective representational templates" that reflect the nondiscursive, fluid emotional experiences of early childhood (Fein, 1985b).

> In a way, script theory posits a kind of syntactic structure for sociodramatic play which contains a finite set of figurative structures that can generate an infinite set of combinations, a kind of grammar for play. While children understand the signals of play such as voice change, posture, gestures, or facial expression, they seem to follow certain organizational rules that are developmentally more or less complex. Their implicit understanding of the "script" is explicitly represented in their play (Fromberg, 1987b, p. 42).

The isomorphic aspects of these considerations are paralleled in other disciplines that have been concerned with transformational knowledge, such as the sciences, mathematics, linguistics, communications, anthropology, and psychology. The use of isomorphic imagery as a natural consideration in creating developmentally appropriate, as well as substantive, early-childhood interdisciplinary curriculum is relevant and has been discussed elsewhere (Fromberg, 1987a).

From a different perspective, a holistic, biocultural outlook suggests that human beings

> learn through all sensory modalities simultaneously . . . [and] the senses also . . . sample internal states related to effort, tension, and emotions. The information is stored in the brain in the form of a multisensory holograph, which is first indexed by and most accessible through affective components, although other cognitive indexes are constructed. In humans, the polyphasic [multisensory] learning ability contributes to the integrating function of play; it provides the necessary physical vehicle for holistic learning (Dobbert, 1985, p. 161).

To consider transformational dynamics in the context of play, therefore, is to imagine the development of thematic content that is constructed in fresh ways by the ongoing perceptions, feelings, social expectancies, and competencies of the participant children. These processes cut across separate fields of knowledge and support interdisciplinary understandings.

Play and Intervention

The teacher's role in the context of such evolving texts is to combine the functions of an occasional coauthor, a supportive connoisseur, and a nurturant editor. The teacher as a coauthor provides alternative resources and themes; as a supportive connoisseur, focuses on, appreciates, and encourages the positive; as a nurturant editor, assists in extending the best and phasing out the least valuable. In order to perform these functions with sensitivity, teachers consider children's development and the context in which play is taking place. This concern for both development and context is symmetrical with the more and less individual or cultural interpretations of play with which this chapter began.

Questions to ask about children's *development* would include the following:

- How are children using the play frame? How can a facilitative question stimulate perspective taking? (For example: What can you do so that you/they can tell the truth? How can you solve that so that everybody is happy?)
- How are children able to work out their differences?
- How are children varying the duration of their activities? How are they extending the duration of their play?
- How are symbolic representations becoming more sophisticated? How may children be repeating the same themes in the same ways over an inordinately long period of time? (Repetition in context, such as operating a vehicle, undressing a doll, selling shoes, or having a birthday party, is to be expected from time to time.) What are the imaginative extensions of themes?
- In what ways are language skills expanding? To what extent are you engaging in "verbal harmony" (appreciatively describing what children are doing at times that may extend play)?

Questions to ask about the play *context* would include the following:

- What is the mix of children involved? How are materials sufficient to stimulate cooperation? Which indoor and outdoor activities stimulate social interaction? How are children moving between areas? (There should be no assigned seats. Materials are available in the areas of use, and children store personal belongings in designated areas.)
- What background and personal experiences are evident in the play? How are egalitarian values manifested in themes and access to resources?
- How does the play relate to preceding experiences?
- When are long blocks of time available?
- What space is allocated for privacy and participation at different degrees of more or less activity? What are the opportunities for outdoor play?

Teachers can intervene in *indirect ways* through such means as

- provision of space (creating an area or revising traffic patterns by moving furniture)
- addition of materials that stimulate thematic variety
- addition or removal of props
- planning activities that add to the children's knowledge of themes through trips, films, literature, or resource visitors.

Another indirect intervention is through parent conferences or group meetings. Between after-school gymnastics, puppetry, library story times, music instruction, Sunday school, television, and so forth, perhaps there is a need for parents to schedule more time in which children might choose to look at clouds; observe ants, construction crews, and older children at play; spend time with a friend; and choose or not choose to play.

Teachers can intervene in more *direct ways* through such means as

- being present at a play site
- entering the play frame by taking a role, using a play voice or gesture, asking a question, or varying a routine
- raising a question about the play frame or about clarifying content
- modeling, by imitating children's play with extended or altered content.

It is important to deal with what children bring to the play situation without a hierarchical judgment. Whatever the teachers does or does not do has consequences. Therefore, it is important to attempt to be conscious of what is not being done as well as what is being done. Teachers have been able to raise their awareness by tape-recording their interactions with children from time to time. The teacher's most useful direct intervention is maintaining a playful attitude, and accepting and encouraging children's independent problem setting, problem solving, and connection making.

SUMMARY

Early childhood education has been characterized by integrated teaching and learning. This means that separate subjects typically are not as central as in later years. For example, a science activity is sensorial and involves measurement (mathematics) and language experience, as well as drawing or three-dimensional representation of concrete experiences that children and their teacher have shared. This is consistent with young children's development in which early undifferentiated experiences become increasingly differentiated. Schools, however, traditionally have separated subjects for instruction. Whereas formal education is organized hierarchically and in parallel ways, there are always needs for connection making and perspective taking. Even at the frontiers of adult knowledge, scientists are trying to make connections (Gleick, 1987).

Play is a distinctive, significant condition of learning in early childhood education. Play helps to define the integration of knowledge because it blends language, thought, affect, and imagination. Play leads development and stimulates children to extend their self-directed, rule-governed behavior.

To play or not to play is not the question. The question is how to provision for it. In the exemplary and sometimes utopian worlds of developmentally appropriate environments, teachers and children just get on with it.

REFERENCES

Allport, G. W. (1958). The functional autonomy of motives. In C. L. Stacey & M. F. DeMartino (Eds.), *Understanding human motives* (pp. 68–81). Cleveland: Howard Allen.

Bateson, G. (1971). The message "this is play." In R. E. Herron & B. Sutton Smith (Eds.), *Child's play* (pp. 261–266). New York: Wiley.

Bateson, G. (1976). A theory of play and fantasy. In J. S. Bruner, A. Jolly, & K. Sylva (Eds.), *Play—its role in development and evolution* (pp. 39–51). New York: Basic Books.

Bateson, G. (1979). *Mind and nature*. New York: E. P. Dutton.

Bergen, D. (Ed.). (1988). *Play: A medium for learning and development*. Portsmouth, NH: Heinemann.

Bergen, D., Smith, K., & O'Neill, S. (1988). Designing play environments for infants and toddlers. In D. Bergen (Ed.), *Play: A medium for learning and development* (pp. 187–207). Portsmouth, NH: Heinemann.

Blurton Jones, N. (1976). Rough-and-tumble play among nursery school children. In J. S. Bruner, A. Jolly, & K. Sylva (Eds.), *Play—its role in development and evolution* (pp. 352–363). New York: Basic Books.

Bretherton, I. (1984). *Symbolic play: The development of social understanding*. New York: Academic Press.

Bretherton, I. (1988). Reality and fantasy in make-believe play. In D. Bergen (Ed.), *Play: A medium for learning and development* (pp. 209–211). Portsmouth, NH: Heinemann.

Bruner, J. S. (1980). *Under five in Britain*. Ypsilanti, MI: High/Scope.

Bruner, J. S. (1986). Play, thought and language. *Prospects, 16*, 77–83.

Carlsson-Paige, N., & Levin, D. E. (1987). *The war play dilemma*. New York: Teachers College Press.

Cazden, C. (1988). *Classroom discourse*. Cambridge, MA: Harvard University Press.

Collard, R. R. (1976). Exploration and play. In B. Sutton Smith (Ed.), *Play and learning*. (pp. 45–68). New York: Gardner Press.

Connolly, J. A., & Doyle, A. (1984). Relation of social fantasy play to social competence in preschoolers. *Developmental Psychology, 20*, 797–806.

Corrigan, R. (1987). A developmental sequence of actor-object pretend play in young children. *Merrill-Palmer Quarterly, 33*, 87–106.

Csikszentmihalyi, M. (1976). The Americanization of rock-climbing. In J. S. Bruner, A. Jolly, & K. Sylva (Eds.), *Play—its role in development and evolution* (pp. 484–488). New York: Basic Books.

Csikszentmihalyi, M. (1979). The concept of flow. In B. Sutton Smith (Ed.), *Play and learning* (pp. 257–274). New York: Gardner Press.

Csikszentmihalyi, M. (1988a). The flow of experience and its significance for human psychology. In M. Csikszentmihalyi & I. S. Csikszentmihalyi (Eds.), *Optimal experience: Psychological studies in flow consciousness* (pp. 15–35). New York: Cambridge University Press.

Csikszentmihalyi, M. (1988b). The future of flow. In M. Csikszentmihalyi & I. S. Csikszentmihalyi (Eds.), *Optimal experience: Psychological studies in flow consciousness* (pp. 364–383). New York: Cambridge University Press.

Csikszentmihalyi, M. (1988c). Introduction. In M. Csikszentmihalyi & I. S. Csikszentmihalyi (Eds.), *Optimal experience: Psychological studies in flow consciousness* (pp. 3–14). New York: Cambridge University Press.

Dansky, J. L., & Silverman, I. W. (1976). Effects of play on associative fluency in pre-school children. In J. S. Bruner, A. Jolly, & K. Sylva (Eds.), *Play—its role in development and evolution* (pp. 650–654). New York: Basic Books.

Dewey, J. (1933). *How we think*. Boston: Heath.

Dobbert, M. L. (1985). Play is not monkey business: A holistic biocultural perspective on the role of play in learning. *Educational Horizons, 63*, 158–163.

Dodge, M. K., & Frost, J. L. (1986). Children's dramatic play: Influence of thematic and nonthematic settings. *Childhood Education, 62*, 166–170.

Downie, D., Slesnick, T., & Stenmark, J. K. (1981). *Math for girls and other problem solvers*. Berkeley, CA: Lawrence Hall of Science, University of California.

Dyson, A. H. (1987). The value of "time off task": Young children's spontaneous talk and deliberate text. *Harvard Educational Review, 57*, 396–420.

Egan, K. (1988). The origins of imagination and the curriculum. In K. Egan & D. Nadaner (Eds.), *Imagination and education* (pp. 91–127). New York: Teachers College Press.

Erickson, F., & Mohatt, G. (1982). Cultural organization of participation structures in two classrooms of Indian students. in G. Spindler (Ed.), *Doing the ethnography of schooling* (pp. 132–174). New York: Holt, Rinehart & Winston.

Fagot, B. I. (1988). Toddlers' play and sex stereotyping. In D. Bergen (Ed.), *Play: A medium for learning and development* (pp. 133–135). Portsmourth, NH: Heinemann.

Fein, G. G. (1975). A transformational analysis of pretending. *Developmental Psychology, 11*, 291–296.

Fein, G. G. (1985a). The affective psychology of play. In C. C. Brown & A. W. Gottfried (Eds.), *Play interactions* (pp. 19–28). Skillman, NJ: Johnson & Johnson.

Fein, G. G. (1985b). Learning in play: Surfaces of thinking and feeling. In J. L. Frost & S. Sunderlin (Eds.), *When children play: Proceedings of the International Conference on Play and Play Environments* (pp. 45–53). Wheaton, MD: Association for Childhood Education International.

Fein, G. G., & Rivkin, M. (Eds.). (1986). *The young child at play*. Washington, DC: National Association for the Education of Young Children.

Feitelson, D., & Ross, G. S. (1973). The neglected factor—play. *Human Development, 16*, 202–223.

Fenson, L., & Schell, R. E. (1986). The origins of exploratory play. In P. K. Smith (Ed.), *Children's play: Research developments and practical applications* (pp. 17–38). London: Gordon & Breach.

Freud, S. (1958). *On creativity and the unconscious* (I. F. Grant Doff, Trans.). New York: Harper & Row. (Original work published 1925)

Freud, S. (1959). *Beyond the pleasure principle* (J. Strachey, Trans.). New York: Bantam. (Original work published 1928)

Freud, S. (1960). *Jokes and their relation to the unconscious* (J. Strachey, Trans.). New York: W. W. Norton. (Original work published 1916)

Freyberg, J. T. (1973). Increasing the imaginative play of urban disadvantaged children through systematic training. In J. L. Singer (Ed.), *The child's world of make-believe: Experimental studies of imaginative play* (pp. 129–154). New York: Academic Press.

Fromberg, D. P. (1987a). *The full-day kindergarten*. New York: Teachers College Press.

Fromberg, D. P. (1987b). Play. In C. Seefeldt (Ed.), *The early childhood curriculum: A review of current research* (pp. 35–74). New York: Teachers College Press.

Gardner, H. (1982). *Art, mind, and brain: A cognitive approach to creativity*. New York: Basic Books.

Geertz, C. (1976). Deep play: A description of the Balinese cockfight. In J. S. Bruner, A. Jolly, & K. Sylva (Eds.), *Play—its role in development and evolution* (pp. 656–674). New York: Basic Books.

Genishi, C., & Galvan, J. (1985). Getting started: Mexican-American preschoolers initiating dramatic play. In J. L. Frost & S. Sunderlin (Eds.), *When children play: Proceedings of the International Conference on Play and Play Environments* (pp. 23–30). Wheaton, MD: Association for Childhood Education International.

Ghiaci, G., & Richardson, J. T. E. (1980). The effects of dramatic play upon cognitive structure and development. *Journal of Genetic Psychology, 136*, 77–83.

Gilligan, C. (1982). *In a different voice: Psychological theory and women's development.* Cambridge, MA: Harvard University Press.

Gleick, J. (1987). *Chaos: Making a new science.* New York: Viking.

Golomb, C., Gowing, E. D. G., & Friedman, L. (1982). Play and cognition: Studies of pretense play and conservation of quantity. *Journal of Experimental Child Psychology, 33*, 257–279.

Heath, S. B. (1983). *Ways with words: Language, life, and work in communities and classrooms.* New York: Cambridge University Press.

Heath, S. B., with Chin, H-K. (1985). Narrative play in second language learning. In L. Galda & A. D. Pellegrini (Eds.), *Play, language, and stories: The development of children's literate behavior* (pp. 147–166). Norwood, NJ: Ablex.

Hutt, D. (1976). Exploration and play in children. In J. S. Bruner, A. Jolly, & K. Sylva (Eds.), *Play—its role in development and evolution* (pp. 202–215). New York: Basic Books.

Hutt, C. (1979). Exploration and play (#2). In B. Sutton Smith (Ed.), *Play and learning* (pp. 175–194). New York: Gardner Press.

Johnson, D. W., Johnson, R. T., Holubec, E. J., & Roy, P. (1984). *Circles of learning: Cooperation in the classroom.* Alexandria, VA: Association for Supervision & Curriculum Development.

Jung, C. G. (1970). *Analytical psychology.* New York: Vintage. (Original work published 1968)

Kamii, C. K., & DeClark, G. (1984). *Young children reinvent arithmetic.* New York: Teachers College Press.

Kamii, C., & DeVries, R. (1980). *Group games in early childhood.* Washington, DC: National Association for the Education of Young Children.

Kreye, M. (1984). Conceptual organization in the play of preschool children: Effects of meaning, context, and mother-child interaction. In I. Bretherton (Ed.), *Symbolic play: The development of social understanding* (pp. 299–336). New York: Academic Press.

Levenstein, P. (1976). Cognitive development through verbalized play: The mother-child home programme. In J. S. Bruner, A. Jolly, & K. Sylva (Eds.), *Play—its role in development and evolution* (pp. 286–297). New York: Basic Books.

Levenstein, P. (1985). Mothers' interactive play behavior in play sessions and children's educational achievements. In C. C. Brown & A. W. Gottfried (Eds). *Play interactions* (pp. 160–167). Skillman, NJ: Johnson & Johnson.

Levy, A. K., Schaefer, L., & Phelps, P. C. (1986). Increased preschool effectiveness: Enhancing the language abilities of 3- and 4-year-old children through planned sociodramatic play. *Early Childhood Research Quarterly, 1*, 133–140.

Maccoby, E. E., & Jacklin, C. T. (1974). *The psychology of sex differences.* Stanford, CA: Stanford University Press.

Marbach, E. S., & Yawkey, T. D. (1980). The effect of imaginative play actions on language development in five-year-old children. *Psychology in the Schools, 17*, 257–263.

McConkey, R. (1986). Changing beliefs about play and handicapped children. In P. K. Smith (Ed.), *Children's play: Research developments and practical applications* (pp. 93–108). London: Gordon & Breach.

McGhee, P. E., Etheridge, L., & Berg, N. A. (1984). Effect of level of toy structure on preschool children's pretend play. *Journal of Genetic Psychology, 144*, 209–217.

Monighan-Nourot, P., Scales, B., Van Hoorn, J., with Almy, M. (1987). *Looking at children's play: A bridge between theory and practice.* New York: Teachers College Press.

Moran, J. D., III, Sayers, J. K., Fu, V. R., & Milgram, R. M. (1984). Predicting imaginative play in preschool children. *Gifted Child Quarterly, 28*, 92–94.

Morgan, R. (1982). *The anatomy of freedom: Physics and global politics*. Garden City, NY: Anchor.

Olszewski, P. (1987). Individual differences in preschool children's production of verbal fantasy play. *Merrill-Palmer Quarterly, 33*, 69–86.

Paley, V. G. (1984). *Boys and girls: Superheroes in the doll corner*. Chicago: University of Chicago Press.

Paley, V. G. (1986). On listening to what the children say. *Harvard Educational Review, 56*, 122–131.

Parten, M. (1971). Social play among preschool children. In R. E. Herron & B. Sutton Smith (Eds.), *Child's play* (pp. 83–95). New York: Wiley.

Pellegrini, A. D. (1984). Identifying causal elements in the thematic-fantasy play paradigm. *American Educational Research Journal, 21*, 691–701.

Pellegrini, A. D. (1985). The relations between symbolic play and literate behavior: A review and critique of the empirical literature. *Review of Educational Research, 55*, 107–121.

Pellegrini, A. D. (1987). Rough-and-tumble play: Developmental and educational significance. *Educational Psychologist, 22*, 23–43.

Pellegrini, A. D., & Galda, L. (1982). The effects of thematic-fantasy play training on the development of children's story comprehension. *American Educational Research Journal, 19*, 443–452.

Pepler, D. J., & Ross, H. S. (1982). The effects of play on convergent and divergent problem-solving. *Child Development, 52*, 1202–1210.

Phyfe-Perkins, E., & Shoemaker, J. (1986). Indoor play environments: Research and design implications. In G. G. Fein & M. Rivkin (Eds.), *The young child at play* (pp. 177–193). Washington, DC: National Association for the Education of Young Children.

Piaget, J. (1962). *Play, dreams, and imitation in childhood* (C. Gattegno & M. F. Hodgson, Trans.) New York: W. W. Norton.

Piaget, J. (1965). *The moral judgment of the child* (M. Gabain, Trans.). New York: The Free Press.

Pulaski, M. A. (1973). Toys and imaginative play. In J. L. Singer (Ed.), *The child's world of make-believe: Experimental studies of imaginative play* (pp. 73–103). New York: Academic Press.

Ramsey, P., & Reid, R. (1988). Designing play environments for preschool and kindergarten children. In D. Bergen (Ed.), *Play: A medium for learning and development* (pp. 213–239). Portsmouth, NH: Heinemann.

Rogers, D. L. (1985). Relationships between block play and the social development of children. *Early Child Development Care, 20*, 245–261.

Roth, F. P., & Clark, D. M. (1987). Symbolic play and social participation abilities of language-impaired and normally developing children. *Journal of Speech and Hearing Disorders, 52*, 17–29.

Rubin, K. H. (1988). Some "good news" and some "not-so-good news" about dramatic play. In D. Bergen (Ed.), *Play: A medium for learning and development* (pp. 67–71). Portsmouth, NH: Heinemann.

Rubin, K. H., & Howe, N. (1986). Social play and perspective taking. In G. G. Fein & M. Rivkin (Eds.), *The young child at play* (pp. 113–125). Washington, DC: National Association for the Education of Young Children.

Saracho, O. N. (1987). Cognitive style characteristics as related to young children's play behaviors. *Early Child Development and Care, 29*, 163–179.

Schwartzman, H. B. (1978). *Transformations: The anthropology of children's play*. New York: Plenum.

Serbin, L. A. (1978). Teachers, peers, and play preferences: An environmental approach to sex typing in the preschool. In B. Sprung (Ed.), *Perspectives on non-sexist early childhood education* (pp. 133–150). New York: Teachers College Press.

Simon, T., & Smith, P. K. (1985a). Play and problem solving: A paradigm questioned. *Merrill-Palmer Quarterly, 31*, 265–277.

Simon, T., & Smith, P. K. (1985b). A role for play in children's problem-solving: Time to think again. In J. L. Frost & S. Sunderlin (Eds.), *When children play: Proceedings of the International Conference on Play and Play Environments* (pp. 55–59). Wheaton, MD: Association for Childhood Education International.

Simon, T., & Smith, P. K. (1986). Problems with a play paradigm: A reply to Dansky. *Merrill-Palmer Quarterly, 32*, 205–209.

Singer, J. L. (1973). *The child's world of make-believe: Experimental studies of imaginative play*. New York: Academic Press.

Singer, J. L. (1988). Imaginative play and human development: Schemas, scripts, and possibilities. In D. Bergen (Ed.), *Play: A medium for learning and development* (pp. 75–79). Portsmouth, NH: Heinemann.

Singer, J., & Singer, D. (1979). The values of imagination. In B. Sutton Smith (Ed.), *Play and learning* (pp. 195–218). New York: Gardner.

Smilansky, S. (1968). *The effects of sociodramatic play on disadvantaged preschool children*. New York: Wiley.

Smith, P. K. (Ed.). (1986). *Children's play: Research developments and practical applications*. London: Gordon & Breach.

Sutton Smith, B. (1989). Radicalizing childhood. In L. R. Williams & D. P. Fromberg (Eds.), *Defining the field of early childhood education: Proceedings of invitational conference* (pp. 77–151). Charlottesville, VA: W. Alton Jones Foundation.

Sylva, K., Bruner, J. S., & Genova, P. (1976). The role of play in the problem-solving of children 3–5 years old. In J. S. Bruner, A. Jolly, & K. Sylva (Eds.), *Play—its role in development and evolution* (pp. 244–257). New York: Basic Books.

Torrance, E. P. (1962). *Guiding creative talent*. Englewood Cliffs, NJ: Prentice-Hall.

Vygotsky, L. S. (1976). Play and its role in the mental development of the child. In J. S. Bruner, A. Jolly, & K. Sylva (Eds.), *Play—its role in development and evolution* (pp. 537–554). New York: Basic Books.

Vygotsky, L. S. (1978). *Mind in society*. Cambridge, MA: Harvard University Press.

Vygotsky, L. S. (1986). In R. W. Reiber & A. S. Carton (Eds.), *The collected works of L. S. Vygotsky: Vol. 1. Problems of general psychology* (N. Minick, Trans.). New York: Plenum.

Wertsch, J. V., & Lee, B. (1984). The multiple levels of analysis in a theory of action. *Human Development, 27*, 193–196.

Whiting, B. B., & Edwards, C. P. (1988). *Children of different worlds: The formation of social behavior*. Cambridge, MA: Harvard University Press.

Williamson, P. A., & Silvern, S. B. (1984). Creative dramatic play and language comprehension. In T. D. Yawkey & A. D. Pellegrini (Eds.), *Child's play: Developmental and applied* (pp. 347–358). Hillsdale, NJ: Erlbaum.

11

Teaching Reading and Mathematics to At-Risk Students in Kindergarten: What We Have Learned from Field Research[1]

RUSSELL GERSTEN
University of Oregon–Eugene
NANCY GEORGE
University of Oregon–Eugene

In 1987, the Association for Supervision and Curriculum Development (ASCD) convened a task force of prominent early childhood educators to address issues in the public school education of four and five year olds. As can easily be imagined, one of the most controversial issues discussed was whether or not reading and other academic subjects should be directly taught to kindergarten students, especially those low-income, at-risk students who enter school with limited experience with books and academic concepts.

A debate raged, with some arguing that forcing academic content on these unsuspecting, "unready" students could create a lifelong aversion to learning. They argued for a "developmental," low-key curriculum that puts few demands on these students. A recent survey conducted of elementary principals (Educational Research Service, 1986) found that only 22% saw academics as the primary focus of kindergarten. Half the principals felt reading should be taught only to students who demonstrate they are ready and able.

Others, including the senior author of this chapter, argued that it is imperative to teach reading and mathematics to these students at an early age so that they can

[1]Portions of this chapter are adapted from an article entitled "Effectiveness of a Direct-Instruction Academic Kindergarten for Low Income Students," published in *Elementary School Journal*, November 1988. This research was supported by Grant Number G007507234 from the United States Department of Education. The authors wish to acknowledge their debt to Wesley Becker for his work on the initial evaluation research, his conception of the program, his dedication to the population, and the catchy title of his 1977 *Harvard Educational Review* piece. The authors also wish to thank Geneva Blake for her perceptive feedback on earlier versions of this chapter.

compete with their middle-class peers in the elementary grades. They cited research and experiences demonstrating that reading could be taught to low-income, at-risk five year olds with no apparent negative side effects.

After listening to both sides of the debate and reviewing the research, the task force finally reached a compromise, concluding, "Although most five-year-olds *can* learn to read, the question that requires conscious decision making at the local level is whether they *should* learn to read" (ASCD Task Force, 1988, p. 108).

This chapter has several major objectives. The first is to describe in some detail the research that documents that even extremely disadvantaged five year olds can be taught to read in kindergarten, and that—contrary to popular belief—there is no evidence of negative side effects. In fact, there is some preliminary evidence suggesting enduring positive effects on the students' later lives.

The second objective is to describe what an effective academic component of a kindergarten is like, to give those in early childhood education a guideline or standard by which they can assess whether the academic component of a kindergarten is productive, is sensitive to the needs of the students. The final objective is to argue that a kindergarten program can and should contain an academic component coupled with a range of other developmentally appropriate activities and projects.

A review of the early childhood education literature reveals that those who object to teaching academic content in kindergarten (Katz, 1988; Weikart, 1988) often create an either/or dichotomy by assuming that academic kindergarten programs automatically ignore children's social and emotional needs and that time allocated to reading and language precludes time for social interaction and play. We believe such a dichotomy need not exist. The functions of gaining knowledge and socialization are not mutually exclusive.

MISCONCEPTIONS ABOUT ACADEMIC KINDERGARTEN

Some educators propose that the primary focus of kindergarten programs for all students—including those who enter with weak language skills and low academic readiness—should be on building a strong knowledge base in oral language, reading, mathematics, and listening comprehension. A major goal of a kindergarten program should be to prepare these students to enter first grade with a knowledge base in reading, mathematics, and language concepts as children not at risk.

There are several misconceptions about academically oriented programs that need to be dispelled. The first is that students in academic kindergartens are primarily passive. Nothing could be further from the truth. Though five year olds are not asked to articulate the objectives of each day's lesson, and the teacher, not the child, determines the sequence of instruction, students are extremely active in academic early childhood programs. The majority of instruction is conducted in small groups; students constantly respond to teachers' questions and each others' comments. The structure of academically focused programs insures that students will receive clear and immediate feedback from the teacher, and be provided with additional practice, if necessary.

A second misconception is that students spend all their time filling out worksheets, and no time interacting with other students and teachers. Again, this is not true. The majority of instruction is done in small groups, involving constant interaction. Only a small amount of follow-up worksheet activities are included.

Two other misconceptions prevail. The first, articulated by psychologists such as David Elkind (1988), is that academic programs can destroy a child's pleasure in reading. Only inept academic programs do so. Intelligent academic programs include a blend of a oral reading (including listening to stories read by teachers) and systematic practice in sounding out words. The final misconception is that academically focused programs preclude time for play, socialization, and art. Again, this need not be the case.

This chapter describes a kindergarten program that successfully promotes acquisition of knowledge in reading, language, and mathematics while also enabling students to develop socially. We present findings from research that document both the immediate and long-term benefits of an academic kindergarten approach.

To the best of our knowledge, no research formally and rigorously compares and evaluates specific approaches toward teaching low-income kindergartners. Our goal is to describe and document an approach that has been effective in accelerating the academic progress of disadvantaged students and to explain components of the program that led to its success. We conclude with a discussion of what we see as critical issues in developing and implementing effective academic kindergarten programs especially geared for at-risk students.

CONCEPTIONS OF AN ACADEMIC PROGRAM

A recent essay by Eugene Campbell (1988), superintendent of Newark's schools, eloquently addresses the need for academic kindergarten programs for disadvantaged students:

> Middle class parents are able to enhance their children's development because of their own educational background and their economic ability to provide not only the necessities of life, but also such amenities as cultural outings, educational toys, and travel experiences. Regardless of the age of school entry, their children thus have a competitive edge. They are "readier" for school because they have been "pushed" at home; their parents expect academic rigor at school.
>
> Those of us who cling to the hope that education can promote equity support public preschool education policies that give similar advantages to children who do not have alternative resources.
>
> If such a policy means that administrators and teachers, rather than parents, must do the "pushing," then so they should. If it means that the content of today's prekindergarten or kindergarten curriculum must be more rigorous than yesterday's, for all children, then so it should (p. 30).

The academic kindergarten program to be described in this chapter was implemented in twelve low-income communities between 1968 and 1985 as part of Project Follow Through, a large-scale program for economically disadvantaged students. In the views of the developers of the program, a major function of kindergarten for disadvantaged students is to deal effectively with the dramatic, often difficult transition between preschool and first grade.

Carnine, Carnine, Karp, and Weisberg (1988) describe the transition this way:

> The preschool for four-year olds is clearly child centered. The children are normally given wide latitude in choosing what to do, and experience almost complete acceptance of their responses. A picture of scribbles is acknowledged for the pretty colors, a jangle of toy cymbals for the making of music. The goals are primarily participation and expression. . . . The child is a success. An important transition from home to school has begun.
>
> In contrast, first grade is content centered. Reading, language arts, and mathematics . . . dictate the schedule. Choices are curtailed. Mere participation and expression are no longer sufficient to gain praise. A narrow range of responses is acceptable. Reading the sentence "I saw a cat" as "Once upon a time" won't do; nor will calling a six "nine". . . . Many of these children feel their success and confidence slowly erode" (p. 74).

Perhaps the central image that guided the conceptualization of the academic kindergartens in Project Follow Through was the image of students learning new concepts each day, but in such a way that they experienced *unremitting success*. Instructional sequences were designed to match the attention span of a typical five year old. Symbols and other concepts were introduced at a much slower rate and in a much more interactive fashion than the readiness series that accompany conventional basal reading series (Sprick, 1986). Much of the academic content of the program was taught through games.

COMPONENTS OF THE ACADEMIC KINDERGARTEN IN PROJECT FOLLOW THROUGH

A good deal of the kindergarten day (approximately 90 minutes to 2 hours) was devoted to building academic skills. For the reading, math, and language sessions, students worked in groups of six to ten with a teacher or an instructional aide. Each of these sessions lasted 20–30 minutes. Typically, each session consisted of six or seven brief 3-minute teaching sequences that covered a wide range of activities. These sequences accommodated the relatively short attention span of most of the students and enabled them to participate in a variety of different activities in the course of one lesson. Because teachers also moved quickly from one activity to the next, student interest and motivation typically remained high during the 20-minute lesson (Gersten, Carnine, & Williams, 1982). Supplementary gamelike activities were integrated with the content of the small group sessions, and served a very important purpose: additional practice and mastery of key concepts that students were acquiring. Because games and instruction were interwoven and so closely aligned, students had the opportunity not only to practice key concepts but to enjoy doing so.

Students spent about 30 minutes a day in academically related independent activities. They practiced writing letters and numbers, they colored in pictures related to the stories they had read, and, as the year progressed, they wrote words and sentences and answered simple comprehension questions about the stories they read.

As they learned how to read, the children devoted time to independent silent reading. A unique feature of the reading program was the use of short paperback storybooks that students could read independently after only a few months of school. These books contained simple, often humorous stories written with words the children could read. Students took these books home with them and could read them to parents, brothers, and sisters. Thus, from the very beginning, children learned that the purpose of learning to read was to read and enjoy stories.

The enjoyment and understanding of stories were a big part of the kindergarten program. Teachers read out loud to students daily. In addition, a home reading program provided parents with a variety of books to read to their children; teachers actively encouraged them to do so.

The oral language program was designed to build students' understanding of concepts and to help them describe the world around them. Students learned about colors, shapes, and time. They practiced describing objects and describing relationships. The listening comprehension component of this program is seen as the basis for subsequent work in reading comprehension.

The reading curriculum utilized a synthetic phonics approach, breaking all skills into small steps with repeated practice. The sequence of introducing new letter-sound correspondences was carefully controlled according to research-based principles of curriculum design. For example, sounds or symbols that students were likely to confuse, such as *b* and *d*, or *i* and *e*, were separated by several weeks (Carnine, 1981). The rate at which new sounds were introduced was much slower than the readiness level of the major basal series. Students were allowed as much time as necessary to learn each new sound before the next was introduced. Students were systematically taught how to blend sounds before they were asked to sound out simple words. Within several weeks, students began reading simple stories and answering questions about these stories.

Most of our discussion has focused on the relatively unique nature of the academic portion of the kindergarten program. The remainder of the full-day program consisted of more-traditional kindergarten activities—play with dolls, puppets, blocks, and board games; art projects; music; and projects related to holidays and social studies. This part of the day afforded students with an array of informal social interactions with the teacher and each other.

RELEVANT RESEARCH

A major independent evaluation of the Direct Instruction Follow Through Project was conducted for the United States Office of Education by Abt Associates and the Stanford Research Institute (SRI). These results have been extensively reported (Becker, Engelmann, Carnine, & Rhine, 1981; Stebbins, St. Pierre, Proper, Anderson, & Cerva, 1977), and are briefly summarized here.

Academic Benefits: The East St. Louis Evaluation

The evaluation intensively examined the academic progress of two cohorts of low-income minority children. Although both cohorts of Follow Through students began school in the fall of 1970, one cohort began kindergarten and the other first grade, with no previous kindergarten experience. For each cohort, the Abt evaluation included a demographically similar comparison group that received the district's traditional curriculum. One comparison group began kindergarten in 1970; the other began first grade in 1970 (with no kindergarten experience). Essentially, the evaluation allowed for two important comparisons: (a) whether 4 years of a Direct Instruction academic K–3 program led to more achievement than 4 years of the district's traditional K–3 program, and (b) whether the year of academic kindergarten enhanced achievement.

Demographics and Entry-Level Skills

The demographics (gender, family income, mother's education, ethnicity) for the Direct Instruction and comparison groups were quite similar in both cohorts of East St. Louis students. All the Direct Instruction and comparison students who received only a first- through third-grade program (i.e., no kindergarten experience) were black. Eighty-nine percent of the Direct Instruction students in the K–3 program were black, and 76% of the comparison students were black. Approximately 65% of the families in both samples had female heads of households. Over 70% of the students' families were receiving welfare (AFDC).

Pretest data on the Wide Range Achievement Test (Jastak & Jastak, 1965) showed that the comparison students began with slightly higher academic skills than the Direct Instruction groups, although the difference was minor. To control for this initial small difference in entry skills, the researchers utilized analysis of covariance.

Academic Achievement at End of Third Grade

In the spring of third grade, both cohorts were administered all subtests of the Metropolitan Achievement Test (Durost, Bixler, Wrightstone, Prescott, & Balow, 1970). The test is a fairly comprehensive measure of most facets of academic achievement.

See the upper portion of Table 11.1 for the results of the evaluation for students who received Direct Instruction in first through third grade only (the No-Kindergarten Direct Instruction group). See the lower portion of Table 11–1 for analogous data for the sample of students receiving the academic Direct Instruction program beginning in kindergarten. As the top part of Table 11–1 illustrates, the first- through third-grade Direct Instruction program was more effective than the district's program in the areas of mathematics and language. Students in the Direct Instruction program were at or above grade level in math concepts and math problem solving, while the

TABLE 11–1

End of third grade achievement: mean raw scores (and percentile equivalents) on the Metropolitan Achievement Test for students in East St. Louis Direct Instruction and comparison programs

First- Through Third-Grade (No Kindergarten) Programs (1970–1973)							
	Direct Instruction (N = 96)			Comparison Group (N = 45)			
	%ile	M	SD	%ile	M	SD	p
Total Reading	28th	37.3	13.8	28th	37.0	15.4	NS
Word Knowledge	30th	20.9	8.7	30th	21.1	9.6	NS
Reading (Comp.)	28th	16.6	5.8	26th	15.9	6.9	NS
Language	56th	28.1	9.8	20th	14.6	5.7	.01
Spelling	38th	18.0	12.0	40th	19.4	11.2	NS
Total Math	36th	54.5	20.2	16th	40.2	12.6	.01
Math Computation	74th	22.7	7.4	17th	14.8	4.5	.01
Math Concepts	62nd	19.9	7.1	22nd	14.4	5.7	.01
Prob. Solving	42nd	15.8	7.3	18th	11.0	4.6	.01

Kindergarten Through Third-Grade Programs (1970–1974)							
	Direct Instruction (N = 56)			Comparison Group (N = 45)			
	%ile	M	SD	%ile	M	SD	p
Total Reading	43rd	49.2	17.1	37th	44.6	16.5	.01
Word Knowledge	41st	27.7	9.9	37th	25.3	9.6	.01
Reading (Comp.)	47th	21.5	7.8	39th	19.3	7.6	.01
Language	68th	32.1	9.8	52nd	19.1	7.3	.01
Spelling	44th	23.2	11.3	44th	21.4	11.4	.01
Total Math	56th	68.2	18.7	26th	46.9	21.4	.01
Math Computation	77th	28.8	6.5	36th	19.4	7.2	.01
Math Concepts	49th	21.8	6.9	23rd	14.8	8.4	.01
Prob. Solving	47th	17.7	7.0	25th	12.8	9.2	.01

Source: Adapted from *Education as Experimentation* (Vol. IV, p. C–344) by L. Stebbins, R. G. St. Pierre, E. C. Proper, R. B. Anderson, and T. R. Cerva, 1977, Cambridge, MA: Abt Associates.

local comparison students were at the twenty-second and eighteenth percentiles. Although the 3-year students often performed better than their peers in the district in reading comprehension and vocabulary (word knowledge), they were well below grade level, and no significant effect was found.

A different picture emerges in the data presented in the lower part of Table 11–1, the achievement of students who had the additional year of academic kindergarten. Here the Direct Instruction sample consistently outperformed the comparison sample, in reading as well as mathematics and language. All these differences are statistically significant (except spelling).

What is particularly impressive is that the low-income students who experienced the year of academic kindergarten were at or near the national median (grade level) in all academic measures (see Table 11–1 and Figure 11–1). In contrast,

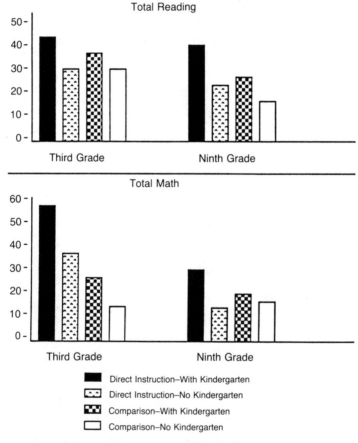

FIGURE 11–1
Achievement levels of students in total reading and total mathematics in percentiles

students who had a Direct Instruction program in first through third grade, but no academic kindergarten, were at only the thirty-sixth percentile in math and the twenty-eighth percentile in reading. These data clearly indicate the benefits of an additional year of well-designed academic kindergarten.

Self-Concept

As a supplement to the evaluation, the effects of the Follow Through program on self-concept were also assessed. Obviously, self-concept is a good deal more difficult to measure than achievement. The Coopersmith (1967) Self-Concept Inventory was administered individually to each student at the end of the third grade. Results on the Coopersmith indicated statistically and educationally significant positive effects of both groups of students who received Direct Instruction. As with achievement, the magnitude of the treatment effect was stronger for students who had the extra year of academic kindergarten, .46 standard deviation units rather than .30 standard deviation units.

Long-Term Academic Benefits

Many argue that, although academic programs for young disadvantaged students may present some immediate benefits, the long-term effects may be detrimental (Katz, 1988; Schweinhart, Weikart, & Larner, 1986). They argue that when students leave the world of carefully sequenced lessons and consistent teacher guidance and feedback and deal with the harsh realities of the intermediate grades and middle school, they will not be able to learn independently. Furthermore, some feel that the pressure put upon the students at an early age will have detrimental effects on their social lives.

The only way to study this issue is through longitudinal research that examines long-term effects of the program. The longitudinal study of the high school careers of the former East St. Louis Direct Instruction students allowed such an examination.

Follow Through students who received either the 3-year Direct Instruction program (that began in first grade) or the 4-year program (that included an academic kindergarten) were tested in reading, math, and language on the California Achievement Test at the end of ninth grade in the spring of 1979 and 1980. Again, their performance was contrasted with that of demographically similar students who received the district's typical curriculum in the early grades. Comparison schools were matched on the basis of percentage of students from homes receiving AFDC (welfare), ethnicity, and student mobility. (See Gersten, Carnine, Keating, and Tomsic, 1984, and Gersten and Keating, 1987, for technical details.)

In these analyses, mean standard scores (rather than raw scores) were used, a more accurate procedure than that employed by Abt Associates. See Table 11–2 for percentiles, grade equivalent scores, and significance values.

As Table 11–2 illustrates, in general, Direct Instruction Follow Through students outperformed comparison students on all achievement measures 6 years after the

TABLE 11–2

East St. Louis grade 9 CAT (California Achievement Test) scores for Direct
Instruction and comparison students

	No Kindergarten				
	Direct Instruction (N = 59)			Comparison (N = 139)	
	G.E.	%ile	G.E.	%ile	t
Reading	7.4	23	6.9	18	2.01*
Language	8.9	42	8.1	33	1.72*
Math	7.4	19	7.2	18	.76

	Kindergarten				
	Direct Instruction (N = 54)			Comparison (N = 121)	
	G.E.	%ile	G.E.	%ile	t
Reading	8.8	40	7.6	26	2.99**
Language	10.2	59	8.6	39	3.12**
Math	8.3	30	7.5	20	2.75**

* $P < .05$

**$P < .01$

Source: Adapted from *Education as Experimentation* (Vol. IV, p. C–344) by
L. Stebbins, R. G. St. Pierre, E. C. Proper, R. B. Anderson, and T. R. Cerva, 1977,
Cambridge, MA: Abt Associates.

program ended. (The only nonsignificant effect is math for the first grade cohort.)
Although both cohorts of Direct Instruction students performed significantly
better than the comparison groups in reading, students who received the year of
academic kindergarten demonstrated stronger effects. These students' achievement was at the fortieth percentile on the California Achievement Test, within ten
percentile points of their middle-income peers. The students without kindergarten, though reading at a higher level than the comparison group, scored at only
the twenty-third percentile.

The same pattern persists in language. Again, although the Direct Instruction
students in the first- through third-grade program performed significantly better than
the comparison sample (forty-second versus thirty-third percentiles), they are considerably below the level of the students who received kindergarten. Effects are less
dramatic in math. The cohort of students who experienced academic kindergarten
performed significantly higher than the comparison group, while no effect was found

for the 3-year students. The overall mathematics performance is substantially lower than that in reading or language.

It is clear that in each area of achievement, stronger effects were found for the students who experienced academic kindergarten than for those who only began an academic program in grade one.

FACTORS CONTRIBUTING TO PROGRAM SUCCESS

Some reasonable hypotheses can be developed concerning what led to the success of the program described. In the following section, we articulate what seem the most plausible reasons for its success and discuss implications for those considering implementing academic kindergarten programs.

The curriculum used in the academic kindergarten was in no way a "watered-down" first-grade reading program but rather a program uniquely developed for kindergarten. The sounding out and blending strategies practiced in kindergarten were the basis for more sophisticated word attack strategies taught in first grade. The practice in aural comprehension of a wide range of language concepts served as a basis for the reading comprehension material in the first- and second-grade curricula. Similarly, major emphasis was given to teaching preskills necessary for first- and second-grade arithmetic systematically. Students learned what the equals and addition signs meant on both the concrete and conceptual levels. Mastery of these concepts in kindergarten served as a basis for students' understanding of the various algorithms and strategies presented in first and second grade.

A Gradual But Systematic Transition

The program envisioned kindergarten as a *gradual but systematic* transition between the child-centered, accepting atmosphere of most preschools and day-care centers and the structured environment of most first grades. Beginning in the first weeks of school, teachers began, in a step-by-step fashion, to (a) build the skills and knowledge necessary for success in first grade, and (b) help the students gradually increase their attention span and their ability to focus on academic material presented in small-group instruction.

Each academic or cognitive objective was taught in brief 2- to 5-minute segments, aimed to match the five year olds' attention span. As the year progressed, the length of these segments increased. However, the program always mixed the more serious aspects of learning with games. A major goal was to ensure that students' first exposure to academic learning was fun.

Unique Features of the Curriculum

There were several important underlying features of the curriculum that should be made explicit so that they can serve as criteria for evaluating or adapting curricula that might be used in kindergartens for at-risk students. The rate of presentation of new content was slower than is typically found in basal readiness series (Kameenui, 1987; Sprick, 1986). Many basal readiness series introduce sound-letter correspondences at three to five times the rate of the curriculum used in this kindergarten program. This can lead to frustration, as was evident in observations of children in low-achieving schools (Gersten, Davis, & Green, 1986).

A second unique feature of the curriculum that led to the success of the kindergarten program was the provision of an adequate number of examples of each concept and a large amount of practice and review of each new concept. A recent review of traditional basal language programs revealed that they typically provide only a few examples of each concept and review new material only three or four times during the year (Kameenui, 1987). Early childhood educators such as Katz (1988) urge teachers to use only small numbers of naturally occurring examples of a concept. In contrast, the curriculum used in this program provided up to twenty examples of each new concept and briefly reviewed all new material on a daily basis for weeks, until students had mastered it. If students did not display mastery, additional brief review segments were added to lessons.

Perhaps the most important component of this curriculum was that it was designed so that students succeeded. The carefully sequenced instruction and the amount of practice, interaction, and praise all created numerous successful academic experiences for these kindergartners. Interviews with the parents of students in one of the academic kindergarten programs revealed that none of the parents reported that their children experienced undue stress (Gersten, True, & Moore, 1987).

Highly Interactive Teaching Strategies

A final factor that appears to account for the success of the program was that the academic lessons were highly interactive. Worksheets comprised a small portion of each child's day. Most of the time was spent in small- or large-group instruction. Reticent students who lacked the self-confidence to volunteer answers were always given an opportunity to respond by the use of choral as well as individual turns. Typically, students were asked to respond between nine and twelve times per minute (Gersten, 1984). Rather than listen to a teacher rhyme words for a few minutes for a few days, all students in these kindergartens practiced rhyming until they had mastered the skill and could apply it to beginning reading words. The instruction involved active responding by the students. The average observed success level of the students during the small-group sessions was between 80% and 90% (Gersten et al., 1982).

Teachers utilized most of the principles that researchers have found to be effective with low-income students in the elementary grades (Brophy & Good, 1986). However, these principles were adapted to meet the needs of five year olds. As the

Brophy and Good research findings suggest, the lessons had clear academic objectives, reviewed relevant preskills, and had students practice until mastery. Explanations were clear and consistent. Students were asked many questions with right/wrong answers and were provided with immediate, clear feedback about the accuracy of their answers.

DEVELOPMENT OF NEW TEACHING STRATEGIES: TEACHER TRAINING AND EVOLUTION OF ATTITUDES

Implementation of such a program can be difficult; intensive staff development activities are required. In Follow Through, this involved practice and role-play sessions as well as classroom observations and feedback sessions by mentor teachers or consultants.

Initially, some kindergarten teachers resisted this approach, feeling that too much pressure was being put on the students. This initial reaction has occurred often. However, in a case study of the evolution of teachers' attitudes and perceptions, the researchers found that the attitudes of most of the "resistant" kindergarten teachers shifted as the year progressed and they saw this new approach to teaching kindergartners succeed with their five and one-half year olds (Gersten, Carnine, Zoref, & Cronin, 1986).

SUMMARY

The results of these studies indicate that reading *can* be taught to virtually all kindergarten students, regardless of their scores on readiness tests or limitations of their home backgrounds. Teaching reading in a developmentally appropriate fashion to these students is a challenge—but it can lead to enduring benefits to the students involved.

The dramatic success of the academic kindergarten program in the East St. Louis and the New York Projects (Meyer, 1984; Meyer, Gersten, & Gutkin, 1983) gives an inkling of what can be accomplished with an academic curriculum that is based on research-based principles of effective teaching, yet is sensitive to the needs of five year olds.

The programs implemented in both these communities attempted to integrate academic activities with more informal child-centered activities. There is an increasing need to create this sort of integrated experience. Often, it seems as if the world of early childhood education is divided into two irreconcilable camps— those with a developmental approach and those with a more "academic" approach. These results provide a glimmering of what can be done when an attempt at integration of the two approaches is made. They strongly suggest that almost all low-income kindergarten students can be taught to read in a developmentally appropriate fashion.

REFERENCES

ASCD Task Force. (1988). Analysis of issues concerning public school involvement in early childhood education. In C. Warger (Ed.), *A resource guide to public school early childhood programs* (pp. 99–118). Alexandria, VA: ASCD.

Becker, W. C., Engelmann, S., Carnine, D., & Rhine, R. (1981). Direct Instruction models. In R. Rhine (Ed.), *Encouraging change in American schools: A decade of experimentation* (pp. 95–154). New York: Academic Press.

Brophy, J., & Good, T. (1986). Teacher effects and student achievement. In M. Wittrock (Ed.), *Third handbook of research on teaching* (pp. 328–375). New York: MacMillan.

Campbell, E. C. (1988). Early-childhood programs and the pursuit of "equity." *Education Week, 7*(17), 30.

Carnine, D. W. (1981). Reducing training problems associated with visually and auditory similar correspondence. *Journal of Learning Disabilities, 14*, 276–279.

Carnine, D., Carnine, L., Karp, J., & Weisberg, P. (1988). Kindergarten for economically disadvantaged students; The direct instruction component. In C. Warger (Ed.), *A resource guide to public school early childhood programs* (pp. 73–99). Alexandria, VA: ASCD.

Coopersmith, S. (1967). *The antecedents of self-esteem*. San Francisco: W. H. Freeman.

Durost, W. N., Bixler, H. H., Wrightstone, J. W., Prescott, G. A., & Balow, I. H. (1970). *Metropolitan achievement test*. New York: Harcourt Brace Jovanovich.

Educational Research Service. (1986). A kindergarten survey. *Principal, 66*(5), 22–23.

Elkind, D. (1988). The resistance to developmentally appropriate educational practice with young children: The real issue. In C. Warger (Ed.), *A resource guide to public school early childhood programs* (pp. 53–62). Alexandria, VA: ASCD.

Gersten, R. (1984). Follow Through revisited: Reflections on the site variability issue. *Educational Evaluation and Policy Analysis, 6*(2), 109–121.

Gersten, R., Carnine, D., Keating, T., & Tomsic, M. (1984, April). *The long-term effects of Direct Instruction: Longitudinal analysis of 1500 low-income students*. Paper presented at the annual meeting of the American Educational Research Association, New Orleans.

Gersten, R., Carnine, D., & Williams, P. (1982). Measuring implementation of a structured educational model in an urban setting: An observational approach. *Educational Evaluation and Policy Analysis, 4*, 67–79.

Gersten, R., Carnine, D., Zoref, L., & Cronin, D. (1986). A multifaceted study of change in seven inner-city schools. *Elementary School Journal, 86*, 257–276.

Gersten, R., Davis, G., & Green, W. (1986, April). *The fragile role of the instructional supervisor in school improvement*. Paper presented at the annual meeting of the American Educational Research Association, San Francisco.

Gersten, R., & Keating, T. (1987). Improving high school performance of "at risk" students: A study of long-term benefits of Direct Instruction. *Educational Leadership, 44*(6), 28–31.

Gersten, R., True, M., & Moore, L. (1987). *Hispanic parents' perceptions of sheltered English programs in the primary grades*. Eugene, OR: University of Oregon.

Jastak, J., & Jastak, S. (1965). *Wide range achievement test*. Wilmington, DE: Jastak Associates.

Kameenui, E. (1987). *A design of instruction analysis of concept teaching in five basal language programs: Violations from the bottom up*. Manuscript submitted for publication.

Katz, L. (1988). Engaging the minds of young children: Curriculum implications of recent research. In C. Warger (Ed.), *Public school early childhood programs* (pp. 32–53). Alexandria, VA: ASCD.

Meyer, L. (1984). Long-term academic effects of the direct instruction Project Follow Through. *Elementary School Journal, 44*, 380–394.

Meyer, L., Gersten, R., & Gutkin, J. (1983). Direct Instruction: A Project Follow Through success story in an inner-city school. *Elementary School Journal, 84*, 241–252.

Schweinhart, L. J., Weikart, D. P., & Larner, M. B. (1986). Consequences of three preschool curriculum models through age 15. *Early Childhood Research Quarterly, 1*, 15–45.

Sprick, M. (1986). *Adapting basal reading programs for low performers: A Direct Instruction approach*. Eugene, OR: Teaching Strategies.

Stebbins, L., St. Pierre, R. G., Proper, E. C., Anderson, R. B., & Cerva, T. R. (1977). *Education as experimentation, Vol. IV*. Cambridge, MA: Abt Associates.

Weikart, D. (1988). Quality in early childhood education. In C. Warger (Ed.), *Public school early childhood programs* (pp. 63–73). Alexandria, VA: ASCD.

12

Issues on Computers and Early Childhood Education

Early Childhood Coordinator and Computer Coordinator
Erring Elementary School–Millers Falls, MA

Imagine! It's 9:30 A.M., activity time in preschool. Children are dispersed into small groups throughout the room, actively playing and conversing in the dramatic play corner, the block area, the housekeeping area, and the puzzle and manipulatives corner; easel-painting in the art area; playing on the computer. Hold it! Playing? Or thinking? Or both? Watch more closely. Two four-year-old children are working to complete an electronic maze. Under ordinary circumstances, an individual would accomplish this easily. But in this scenario, where children work in pairs, the teacher has established some important rules. First, no one is allowed to remove another child's hands from the keyboard. Second, each child is in charge of moving the cursor in only one direction. One child is in charge of "up and down"; the other controls "sideways." And third, the children must plan their route together before they begin. These simple rules force the pair to plan and execute a collaborative solution, communicate verbally, cooperate and coordinate their efforts, and complete the task (move an electronic cursor through a maze from Point A to Point B).

The children look at the maze before them on the monitor. They begin to discuss and describe their common task. Together, with their pointer fingers, they trace their projected route on the monitor. They reach agreement about the plan and begin. Back and forth, commands are heard. "Go up, up, up more." "Turn, now. Go over." "No! Not that way. The other way. Toward Snoopy." "Okay. Just when it gets to the opening, press the down button." "Go there!" "Where?" "Down." The words *there* and *turn* and *over* aren't sufficient; the children must clarify meaning and describe directionality. This necessity to communicate precision and meaning is quite difficult. Here, children are practicing precise communication skills, in a situation that has been carefully constructed for this purpose.

Some educators and parents are skeptical about the value of the above interaction. The children playing at the computer were NOT playing with blocks or doing a puzzle. Is this an activity teachers of young children should be offering? Computers, like pencils or chalkboards, are not good or evil. It is what we choose to do with them that determines their educational and social significance. Although research often plays a significant role in the decision-making process, educators who choose to introduce technology into their classrooms should pay attention to what is most important—the children. Just as knowledge of child development helps to mold the teacher's goals for young children, so too, these goals can serve to guide the teacher in making choices about technology in the classroom. The introduction of technology into education ought to be viewed as a teacher's ideal opportunity for self-reflection. Teachers can examine their use of technology for the all-important match between child development theory, goals for children, and classroom practice.

Using the example at the beginning of this chapter, the reader can make an educated guess about the goals for these children:

Use and practice language skills throughout the day.

Share and cooperate with others while engaging in classroom activities.

Gain experience in solving problems cooperatively—social and cognitive conflicts.

Grow toward becoming self-sufficient learners.

Gain opportunities to make choices and decisions.

Plan and implement their choices.

Reflect on and revise their plans, choices, and implementations.

Each of the above goals is reflected in the experience the two children had when they worked on an electronic maze together. The rules established by the teacher ensure that the above goals are practiced. The children's exchange was natural, playful, collegial, and always on task. The children were focused and engaged in active learning, which is often an important and primary goal of early childhood educators.

How goals are specifically carried out varies with each teacher and each child. Teaching practices differ from classroom to classroom, influenced by many variables. However, if teachers are always careful to know what it is they want children to gain from school experiences, and if they are diligent in offering children the opportunities to help achieve those objectives, then the computer will become another tool, like blocks, puzzles, crayons, and paint. The selection of computer activities that we present in our classrooms is the critical factor. Our knowledge of child development, coupled with the individual needs of children, should be reflected in our classroom materials and tools.

Passions have arisen around certain issues involving the use of computers with very young children. The social development of children has been by far the most discussed and controversial of those critical concerns. Other issues that have sparked research and generated lively discussion among educators are the effects of gender on children's use of computers and the influence of using computers on the development of children's self-esteem and confidence, as well as on their creativity. Also, educators have been intrigued by the potential for computers to enhance or augment children's problem-solving skills, reflectivity, and understanding of abstract concepts of the physical world. The intent of this chapter is to establish a solid link between children's development, appropriate teaching practices, and the use of computers in early childhood classrooms.

Recently, the National Association for the Education of Young Children (Bredekamp, 1987) published an important set of appropriate practices for early childhood programs. These suggestions have already been enthusiastically accepted by educators, many of whom are responding by examining and refining their programs. This outline is the first comprehensive program analysis of early childhood practices published in a widely read professional journal. Not only does this article describe what we ought to be doing in early childhood programs to accomplish our goals for children, it also specifically highlights what practices we should avoid.

It is under this light that technology for young children ought to be examined. The NAEYC goals and program components can help to form our decisions about computer activities in classrooms. Teacher-facilitated computer management and their software selections must stand up to this test of appropriate developmental practice.

The NAEYC curriculum goals for four- to five-year-old children include a call for experiences that stimulate every aspect of children's development—social, emotional, cognitive, and physical. Computers certainly have the flexibility to offer activities that enhance every area of development; however, sometimes the computer environment needs to be constructed by the teacher to focus on specific goals. The scenario described in the beginning of this chapter is a good example. The program used by the children, Peanuts Maze Marathon (1984), can be used in a straightforward fashion—one child sitting at the computer completing the maze. When used in this way, the developmental focus might be considered within the cognitive domain, specifically, visual tracking, an important precursor to the ability to follow the printed lines for reading (Anselmo & Zinck, 1987). But when two children must complete this maze together, following the rules established by the teacher, the focus shifts. Now this becomes an important social and language activity. Children must work cooperatively toward a common goal. Not only do they tend to talk to each other, an important goal for young children, but they also must refine their language to communicate very specific directions.

Many of the decisions educators make when developing programs for children are supported by current educational research. There is now a growing and informative body of research on young children and computers, which educators can use to assist them when integrating technology into their programs. The current body of research includes information about six aspects of children's development, each of which will be discussed in this chapter: social development, gender, emotional development, cognitive development, thinking skills, and physical development. Computers can be particularly useful tools for enhancing social, language, and cognitive skills. For this reason, the bulk of the technology research falls into these categories. The following discussion summarizes some of the current research about computer use and preschoolers. When the NAEYC goals for early childhood programs are matched with the current research on technology and young children, it becomes clear that computers can hold a unique place in a developmentally appropriate classroom.

SOCIAL DEVELOPMENT

Children between the ages of three and five spend much of their time practicing new social and language skills. The NAEYC identifies important social objectives for this population in its statement on appropriate practices: "Children are provided many opportunities to develop social skills such as cooperating, helping, negotiating, and talking with the person involved to solve interpersonal problems. Teachers facilitate the development of these positive social skills at all times" (Bredekamp, 1987, p. 55).

Most of the opportunities provided for young children in preschools keep the objective of positive social skills in the forefront. Computers have been shown to be helpful in facilitating such skills as cooperation, sharing, conversation, helping, and mutual planning.

Early in the new field of early education and computers, researchers began to investigate the computer and its effects on the social development of young children. Critics of computers in early childhood education were convinced that computers would isolate children in the crucial years when they were just developing new social skills. Many studies reveal that, in fact, computers encourage more cooperation and collaboration in young children (Bracey, 1982; Vaidya & McKeeby, 1985). And some research has shown that students are often less competitive and more cooperative in attempting to solve common computer problems (Watt, 1982; Zonderman, 1982). More peer tutoring and conversation has also been observed (Hawkins, 1982; Spencer & Baskin, 1981). And so, researchers at this early stage have demonstrated evidence that, rather than causing the isolation of children, computers can enhance their social development in areas of cooperation, peer assistance, and sharing of possible solutions to common problems.

Later research continued the attempt to answer criticism in the social domain with a major focus on the early childhood classroom. The Children and Technology (CAT) Project (1983) at the University of North Carolina at Greensboro, under the direction of Daniel Shade, published several research reports on the effects of a computer on preschool children's social behavior. Results indicate that as much social behavior occurred around the computer as in other typical play areas (Watson,

Nida, & Shade, 1983). The computer does not lead to social isolation or have deleterious consequences on the social development of young children (Nida, Shade, Lipinski, & Watson, 1983). Researchers found that rarely were the children alone at the computer; they were usually in dyads or triads. In a similar study (Watson, Nida, & Shade, 1983), the investigators examined the effects of the microcomputer on young children's free play choices. After the novelty of the computer wore off, its presence did not dominate children's classroom activity preferences. This same year, the CAT Project observed children's interactions with age-appropriate software and reported some interesting conclusions about their social development, as well as their technical ability. Using the Stickybear (1983) software, the children soon realized that they would all get turns at the computer, competition decreased, and their helping behaviors increased. Initially, the children spent their time jockeying for turns at the keyboard. Over time, though, the focus became centered on the use of the software and proper use of the computer. Children began to form natural dyads, and there was less aggression toward the machines and their classmates. The teacher's presence at the machine also served to decrease any aggression toward the machine and increased the children's interest in the computer. Indeed, the teacher's apparent availability for assistance increased the children's independence. The CAT Project found that more children using the machine tended to increase the amount of aggression observed, so dyads and triads seemed an ideal strategy for reducing competition. Most of the children liked working with the teacher at the computer, and most also liked programs that gave them control over their interactions. Class "experts" emerged from this preschool group. Children who watched the monitor made an easier connection between the keyboard and the resulting action on the monitor. These children, as a result, stayed at the computer longer, and soon were considered the "experts" to ask for advice by classmates. Other researchers, too, reported that most children spend time at the computer with a peer, and look to class "experts" for computer assistance more than assistance with other classroom tasks (Muller & Perlmutter, 1983; Nieboer, 1983; Sheingold, Jewson, Gearhart, & Berger, 1983; Taylor, 1983).

Still another report by the CAT group (*Children and Technology [CAT] Project*, 1983) describes a two-study investigation of the effect of the microcomputer on preschoolers' social behavior. Conclusions were that the only difference in children's social interaction patterns was in their antisocial behaviors. The research group found that the critical factors affecting antisocial behavior were the ratio of children to computers and the amount of structure provided by the classroom teacher. A ratio of 10–1 and appropriate teacher-initiated structure, rather than 20–1, reduced aggression significantly. Clearly, this research has strong implications for the use of the computer in a preschool setting. The role of the teacher is still central to the effectiveness of computer use in the classroom.

Educators, it seems, have looked thoroughly at the effects that computers might have on young children's social development. One reason for this focus might be that this area of development is so crucial for preschoolers and educators would not want to facilitate any obstacles to this already difficult arena for children. Also, when computers were first introduced onto the early childhood scene, there was vociferous criticism of the new technology, and fears were expressed that preschoolers would become social isolates from using computers. And so, this hot issue became one of the first to be investigated. Now that the fires have cooled, and information has filtered from the research lab to the classroom, it is clear that computers will not make children social isolates, nor do they seem to have any deleterious effects on children's social development. In fact, evidence exists that computing may serve to promote the NAEYC goals of independence as well as cooperation in children.

GENDER

Another concern expressed by many educators is that boys would be more interested in the computer and, therefore, use it more than girls, broadening a gender gap that already concerns early childhood teachers. Lipinski, Nida, Shade, and Watson (1983) discussed the issue of gender in one of their reports. In one study, they found no significant sex differences in children's free-play choices. But in another study, discussed in the same report, they observed that boys did spend more time at the computer than girls. And so, the debate and research continue on this issue. But both studies found that with the children with high and medium competency, both sexes spent equal time at the computer. Beeson (Beeson & Williams, 1983) looked at this issue as well. She found a significant difference between five-year-old male and female use of the computer. Males chose the computer much more frequently than females. But with older children (six year olds), neither gender nor age influenced their computer usage. Research on this issue is still being conducted in order to clarify the effects of gender and age on children's use of computers. It is clearly an element of computer use that needs to be closely monitored and managed by the classroom teacher.

EMOTIONAL DEVELOPMENT

The development of self-esteem and confidence are two important goals of a typical early childhood program. The NAEYC identifies two additional goals for young children that may be augmented by technology: "Children's natural curiosity and desire to make sense of their world are used to motivate them to become involved in learning activities" (Bredekamp, 1987, p. 56). Computers and other electronic technologies are still a novelty to young children. They therefore are a natural attraction—materials children will want to manipulate and discover. It is also important that the experiences offered to children with this technology are stimulating and interesting. Without continuing challenge and interest, once the novelty wears off, children's sustained interest will wane. In every area of the curriculum, teachers are always alert to children's interests, and establish environments that engage and challenge the students. So, too, with computers, teachers must select experiences that are exciting and interesting.

Children's preferences in computer software has, therefore, been a topic of interest to educators. Research in this area is informative for teachers making software selections. Recent research has examined children's software preferences. In a study by Sherman, Divine, and Johnson (1985), four-year-old children indicated an overwhelming preference for problem-solving software over drill and practice software. Children tend to avoid activities, like drill and practice software, that are relatively passive and offer little freedom of choice. Drill and practice software offers few opportunities for invention (Sheingold, 1986). Instead, computers could be machines that children could use for making, doing, and creating, using dynamic, user-controlled software environments. Sheingold outlines the potential of computers for children in her discussion of the computer's unique properties. These properties are what ought to be emphasized when planning computer activities for young children.

Computers are programmable and show movement. Children are introduced to the concepts of choice and control, cause and effect. When young children interact with a preschool keyboard, Muppet Learning Keys (1984), they quickly discover the effects of their keyboard actions. This oversized keyboard offers an alphabetically ordered set of letters, a color palette, number keys in numeric sequence, and several function keys. Using the accompanying software, the children are encouraged to explore the keyboard and discover on their own the results produced by different keystrokes. Every key press produces a graphic response on the monitor, but does not cause any program errors or crashes, which could inhibit exploration. Thus, the children exhibit the excitement of producing a graphic display, moving scenes, or a musical composition from experimenting with the unique properties of the microcomputer, this specially adapted keyboard, and selected software. Pairs of children can be heard laughing and chattering about the often silly images on the screen: a singing sock, dancing hamburgers, a dressed-up alligator, or fire-breathing dragons, all with accompanying songs or noises. Children instruct each other to "make the alligator blue, now green, now red." Or order, "Let's get the arrows and make them move. Stop them; press the 'go' button"; "Let's say good-bye to Kermit." There is also incidental learning occurring when the children make the pictures black. Nothing shows on the screen. And when they press the number "0," again no pictures light up the monitor. Figuring out why, cooperatively, is often difficult but fun and satisfying. This opportunity to make their own discoveries, and to be in control of their interaction with the computer, can only serve to enhance the children's motivation, interest, willingness to take risks, and self-confidence.

These machines can also offer the opportunity for children to bypass previously necessary prerequisites for musical composition or story writing. No longer is it essential for children to be able to form letters, or understand the musical notation system. Children can now compose music or stories, using the computer's abilities to form letters and notate. In this way, technology, supplementing more traditional educational media, can serve a developmentally appropriate curriculum by addressing children's aesthetic development in a unique form. The NAEYC goal that "children have daily opportunities for aesthetic expression and appreciation through art and music" (Bredekamp, 1987, p. 56) can be assisted by technology. "Children experiment and enjoy various forms of music. A variety of art media are available for creative expression, such as easel and finger painting and clay" (Bredekamp, 1987, p. 56), computer graphics, word processing, and music activities. It is clear that technology has a unique role to play in facilitating the achievement of these objectives in an early childhood setting.

COGNITIVE DEVELOPMENT

Cognitive development is another area of crucial significance in the development of a young child. Many of the goals identified by the NAEYC in this area can be tapped by a teacher's creative use of technology. Here, the computer best displays its unique properties that can be harnessed to offer novel intellectual experiences for young children.

The NAEYC emphasizes that it is important that "children develop understanding of concepts about themselves, others, and the world around them through observation, . . . and seeking solutions to concrete problems" (Bredekamp, 1987, p. 56). Suggestions for curriculum include observing changes in the environment. Most preschools offer many opportunities for children to learn about their worlds. They explore the properties of natural materials, such as clay, sand, and water. They explore their neighborhoods and communities, walking in the woods to discover the properties of nature. They observe classroom animals, monitor plant growth, and nurture classroom life. Computers offer a unique opportunity (difficult or impossible to derive from other media) to manipulate the variables in the physical world and to discover the effects of each. Many of these opportunities would be otherwise out of reach.

Computer simulations can be significant opportunities offered within a classroom, which can create novel experiences for young children. This software can simulate experiences in the real world and allow users to manipulate variables to gain understandings of the physical world or previously inaccessible events. Thus, with currently available software, older elementary students can play with elements of physics, such as gravity, momentum, elasticity, force, and speed. Or they can plunge into the worlds of economics or politics by operating a railroad company or pretending to be an immigrant to this country and enjoying or suffering the consequences of economic, political, or social decisions affecting them. Simulations also explore factors affecting plant life, animal life, erosion, or the internal workings of a computer.

> The microcomputer environment can simulate experiences from other environments as well as create unique experiences. These environments may facilitate the acquisition of knowledge at ages earlier than educators and psychologists thought

> possible. One result of such early knowledge acquisition may be that children will
> reach adulthood with not only more knowledge but a greater variety of knowledge.
> . . . Such experience-rich adults should be better productive thinkers than the adults
> in today's world (Hofmann, 1986, p. 100).

What an interesting and stimulating way to gain understandings about our world.

Developmentally appropriate simulations could be designed that would offer even very young children opportunities to explore aspects of their worlds. For example, computers and appropriate software can provoke children's reflective thinking in a previously unexplored way. Children intuitively know how to build a block tower. Suppose a computer program allowed children to move block images on the screen to "reconstruct" this same tower. Here, the child would need to teach the computer how to do what the child intuitively did in the three-dimensional medium. The translation from muscles to symbols is important thinking.

Software developers ought to take note of these unique properties of computers, and work to develop software that allows children to easily incorporate computers into their play. LEGO/Logo (1987) is an important step in this direction. Here, LEGO blocks are combined with gears, motors, sensors, and the Logo programming language. Students construct vehicles, conveyor belts, or other moving objects and write Logo programs to control their movements. This learning material combines the symbolic world of computer programming with the three-dimensional world of LEGO to create a stimulating, exciting learning environment.

What might children be learning from such a stimulating microenvironment? Would we be reaching our educational aims if our students engaged in such computer activities? The "project management skills" refined by use of LEGO/Logo, as well as the conceptual understandings gained, may also be acquired by younger children interacting with simple robots. Dynamic turtles programmed in Logo, or robot construction sets, previously manufactured by Milton Bradley, also allow children to interact with principles of motion, leverage, torque, mass, and gravity. In the process, their cooperative efforts provoke explicit language and new vocabularies (Forman & Kaden, 1987).

Reports on investigations into children's experiences with Logo indicate continued controversy about its promise and use. Clements (1986) assessed the effects of Logo and computer-aided instruction (CAI) on specific cognitive skills, metacognitive skills, and achievement of six- and eight-year-old children. His posttests revealed that children who were in the Logo group scored significantly higher on measures of classification and seriation, creativity, metacognition, and on skill in describing directions. Reports by Carmichael and others (Carmichael, Burnett, Higginson, Moore, & Pollard, 1985) indicate important positive effects on children's creativity, confidence, and self-esteem. Carmichael found that creative uses of computers fostered the development of independence and original thinking. These are surely some of the goals of many early childhood educators and are identified as developmentally appropriate objectives by the National Association for the Education of Young Children. Carmichael also concluded that a computer environment that encourages exploration leads to extensive social interaction among students. Students are more willing to express, refine, and revise their ideas.

But Jan Hawkins (1987) disagrees. She reported a case study of two teachers who introduced Logo into their third-fourth-grade and fifth-sixth-grade classrooms. These teachers were involved in an intensive 2-month pilot and then an experimental year with Logo and drew some important conclusions, even though the children were older than those in the early childhood stage of development. The teachers reported that there was constant tension between the discovery approach to learning Logo and their belief that some formal structure was necessary to achieve effective learning. They were never able to overcome the wide range of individual differences in skill and interest. This was partially due to the nature of its place in the curriculum. Work in Logo was treated differently than other areas of the curriculum—there were no specific expectations, no evaluations, no apparent accountability. As a result, some students seemed to treat their work less seriously; they seemed to put less effort into it and questioned its legitimacy as part of their curriculum. And so in practice, it is very difficult to effectively integrate Logo and other computer activities into an ongoing curriculum.

Curriculum integration is a crucial concern for teachers of young children. But before they attempt to integrate Logo into an already-full program, it is important to know if there is any significant benefit from its addition. Many of the goals described by the NAEYC as important to the development of young children were also described as the goals being accomplished in a Logo project engaged in by two six-year-old children. Kull (1986) described, in a case study, what these children were learning while they explored Logo. They were

- Gaining control over the computer
- Acquiring or reinforcing a concept of number
- Beginning to recognize cause and effect—direct correspondence between what they typed and what appeared on the monitor
- Becoming aware of required precision in communicating with the Turtle
- Developing a style of communicating with each other
- Continuously using and practicing language skills
- Cooperating in the task of solving problems
- Sharing results with adults and other children
- Learning about learning.

Here, Logo was making a significant contribution to the development of these young children, providing the teacher with a tool to assist in the implementation of sound curriculum.

Research with preschoolers using Logo has begun to take on increasing importance in the literature. The Logo research previously reported, particularly in *BYTE* magazine (*BYTE*, 1982) described older students. Now that even four- and five-year-olds are learning Logo, serious research in this new arena has begun. The Center for Children and Technology (CCT) at the Bank Street College of Education in New York emerged as a leader in this area of computer research. Researchers there published numerous reports on their work with upper elementary children and Logo. Much of their research refutes claims made by Seymour Papert and the developers of Logo. Papert has repeatedly said that young children can acquire knowledge through self-discovery by experimenting "though a process that takes place without deliberate or organized teaching" (1980, p. 8). He thus developed Logo to provide such a discovery playground for children. Reports on the research by CCT with eleven- and twelve-year-old children indicate that most avoid all but the simplest programs and do not gain a deep understanding of the important concept of recursion (Kurland & Pea, 1984). Clearly, CCT researchers indicated that even with fourth through sixth graders, the promise of Logo was not being totally fulfilled.

What, then, were preschoolers and kindergartners learning from computers and Logo? Brady and Hill (1984) did an extensive review of the literature on young children and microcomputers. They raised the question of whether early childhood is the appropriate time to learn Logo. And Barnes and Hill (1983) strongly believe that children ought to reach the stage of concrete operations before they begin working with computers. Yet many researchers have begun to investigate preschoolers using computers and disagree with Barnes and Hill's argument. Brummel and Jaworski (1984) studied a group of twenty-eight first graders after working with them for 10 weeks on computer skills and then Logo. The children developed the required keyboarding skills to interact with the machine, and all exhibited some degree of logical thinking demonstrated by the use of Logo for the development of a final graphic display. They all exhibited enthusiasm when they were in control of their own learning on the computer and proudly finished their final products. Research has shown that there is no question that preschool through third-grade children can interact successfully with a computer and learn to program in Logo. The continuing questions remain: Should they be learning Logo? Is it an efficient and beneficial use of student and teacher time? What are they really learning? The debate continues.

THINKING SKILLS

More recently, research with young children and technology has focused on thinking skills and computers. Forman (1984) suggests that interactive video may enhance children's reflectivity by allowing the child to gain new perspectives previously impossible with three-dimensional toys. Interactive video offers control as a new element to computer play. Children can manipulate variables and experiment with the effects of their changes. Forman and Kaden (1987) suggest also that video replay can be a powerful tool for provoking reflective thought in children. Using Smurf Paint and Play (1985), children can create and enact scripts for Smurf characters and animate them in a playful, immediate mode. A record-and-replay option is available that allows children to have the computer record their Smurf play and then play it back to them. The viewers tend to reflect back on what they did with their Smurfs.

When the replay is paused, children may be asked, "What did you do next?" This kind of reconstructive thinking can lead to premeditated play. In other words, children may animate the Smurfs and edit their scripts with an awareness of future replay. Perhaps increased exposure to these new forms of play and reflection will have long-term effects on problem solving by today's children and will invite them to think about their own thinking.

Additional research on problem solving by young children with computers has been reported by Clements and Gullo (1984). Their research observed first graders programming in Logo. They found that the children showed improved results on two specific thinking tests after learning Logo, but not on an overall thinking test. Logo tended to increase their creativity and ability to reflect on their own thinking, but there was no revolutionary change in their overall cognitive development. Such data will certainly help educators develop reasonable expectations for using computers in our classrooms. Researchers still are exploring implications of computing with young children and are providing fuel for continued lively discussion.

PHYSICAL DEVELOPMENT

The role that computers play on children's physical development is minor. The predominant question is whether very young children have the dexterity and coordination to successfully use a computer and peripherals. Observations have revealed that even three year olds, with instruction, can use a traditional keyboard, handle disks carefully, insert disks into the disk drive and close the disk drive door, and turn on the computer and necessary peripherals. Young children have also demonstrated the ability to use the joystick, a touch pad, and other input devices (Borgh & Dickson, 1986). According to Borgh and Dickson, adults have seen these young children use many construction toys that require even more dexterity, and should not be surprised that they can handle electronic equipment successfully. So, by simply observing young children, it is clear that there is no longer any question about their physical ability to use a traditional configuration of computer hardware.

SUMMARY

There is now so much research indicating the benefits of technology in the early childhood classroom that the time has come for teachers to decide how, not if, they want to incorporate it into their curricula. But again, the educators disagree on the most beneficial and effective ways to use computers.

Brummel and Jaworski (1984) recommend using Logo with first graders based on their research. Roy Pea (1984) from the Center for Children and Technology at Bank Street suggests that educators ought to give children more purposeful uses for computers applicable to society's broader uses. This might imply that tools such as word processing and simulations of real world events might be more appropriate.

Silvern (1983) writes that computers should be used as tools for thinking, not as drill and practice machines. And still other researchers report that computers are appropriate as graphics tools for young children. It will be the teachers' responsibility to determine the most effective uses for technology for their particular students.

We now recognize that computers are being used successfully by even the youngest students. Computers will not make children social isolates, nor do they seem to have deleterious effects on their social development. In fact, evidence exists that computing may serve to promote independence as well as cooperation in children. There is contradictory evidence concerning the effects gender may have on children's abilities with, and interest in, computing. It appears that for the youngest children, gender does not have an overpowering influence on children's interest in the computer. But this question will continue to be addressed. Many researchers recommend the use of Logo with young children and claim it helps to improve problem-solving ability. There is some evidence to support this claim, but this debate, too, is far from over. And it is clear that children's physical development will not interfere with their ability to use a microcomputer. Indeed, they have the dexterity and coordination to operate most of the available hardware. Now research on computers and early childhood education is beginning to examine some crucial issues by investigating the computer's effect on such areas as problem solving, reflective thinking, and the cognitive development of young children.

Increasingly, classroom teachers will be able to refer to a growing body of knowledge about computers—and to the NAEYC's appropriate practices, now widely accepted—to guide them in their decision making about integrating technology into their already rich and diverse curricula.

REFERENCES

Anselmo, S., & Zinck, P. A. (1987). Computers for young children? Perhaps. *Young Children, 11*(42), 22–27.

Barnes, B. J., & Hill, S. (1983). Should young children work with microcomputers: Logo before Lego? *The Computing Teacher, 10*(9), 11–14.

Beeson, B.S., & Williams, A. (1983). *The effects of gender and age on preschool children's choice of the computer as a child-selected activity*. Muncie, IN: Ball State University.

Borgh, K., & Dickson, W. P. (1986). Two preschoolers sharing one computer. In P. Campbell & G. Fein (Eds.), *Young children and microcomputers* (pp. 38–44). Englewood Cliffs, NJ: Prentice-Hall.

Bracey, G. (1982, November/December). What research shows. *Electronic Learning*, pp. 51–53.

Brady, E. H., & Hill, S. (1984). Young children and microcomputers: Research issues and directions. *Young Children, 39*(3), 49–61.

Bredekamp, S. (1987). *Developmentally appropriate practice in early childhood programs serving children from birth through age 8*. Washington, DC: National Association for the Education of Young Children.

Brummel, B. & Jaworski, A. P. (1984). *Introducing computer education into an early elementary curriculum*. Rochester, MI: Oakland University. (ERIC Document Reproduction Service No. ED 250059)

BYTE. (1982). 7(8).

Carmichael, H. W., Burnett, J. D., Higginson, W. C., Moore, B. G., & Pollard, P. J. (1985). *Computers, children, and the classrooms: A multisite evaluation of the creative use of microcomputers by elementary school children* (Final report). Urbana, IL: Educational Resources Information Center. (ERIC Document Reproduction Service No. ED 268 994)

Children and Technology (CAT) Project. (1983). Greensboro, NC: Department of Child Development/Family Relations, University of North Carolina.

Clements, D. H. (1986). Effects of Logo and CAI environments on cognition and creativity. *Journal of Educational Psychology, 78*, 309–318.

Clements, D. H., & Gullo, D. (1984). Effects of programming. *Journal of Educational Psychology, 76*, 1051–1058.

Forman, G. (1984). *Computer graphics as a medium for enhancing reflective thinking in young children*. Paper presented at the Annual Conference on Thinking, Harvard University, Cambridge, MA.

Forman, G., & Kaden, M. (1987). Research on science education for young children. In C. Seefeldt (Ed.), *The early childhood curriculum: A review of current research* (pp. 141–164). New York: Teachers College Press.

Hawkins, J. (1982). *The flexible use of computers in classrooms* (Technical Report No. 6). New York: Bank Street College of Education, Center for Children and Technology.

Hawkins, J. (1987). The interpretation of Logo in practice. In R. Pea & K. Sheingold (Eds.), *Mirrors of minds* (pp. 3–34). Norwood, NJ: Ablex.

Hofmann, R. (1986). Microcomputers, productive thinking, and children. In P. Campbell & G. Fein (Eds.), *Young children and microcomputers* (pp. 87–101). Englewood Cliffs, NJ: Prentice- Hall.

Kull, J. (1986). Learning and Logo. In P. Campbell & G. Fein (Eds.), *Young children and microcomputers* (pp. 104–128). Englewood Cliffs, NJ: Prentice-Hall.

Kurland, D., & Pea, R. (1984). *Children's mental models of recursive Logo programs* (Technical Report No. 10). New York: Bank Street College of Education, Center for Children and Technology.

LEGO/Logo. (1987). Enfield, CT: Lego Systems.

Lipinski, J., Nida, R., Shade, D., & Watson, J. (1983). *Competence, gender, and preschooler's free-play choices when a microcomputer is added to the classroom*. Greensboro, NC: University of North Carolina at Greensboro, Department of Child Development-Family Relations.

Muller, A., & Perlmutter, M. (1983). *Preschool children's problem-solving interactions at computers and jig-saw puzzles*. Unpublished manuscript, University of Minnesota, Minneapolis.

Muppet Learning Keys. (1984). Pleasantville, NY: Sunburst Communications.

Nida, R., Shade, D., Lipinski, J., & Watson, J. (1983). *Introducing the microcomputer to a preschool classroom: The effects on children's social interactions*. Greensboro, NC: University of North Carolina at Greensboro, Department of Child Development-Family Relations.

Nieboer, R. (1983). *A study of the effect of computers on the preschool environment*. Unpublished master's thesis, Oakland University, Rochester, MI.

Papert, S. (1980) Mindstorms: *Children, computers, and powerful ideas*. New York: Basic Books.

Pea, R. (1984). *Symbol systems and thinking skills: Logo in context*. New York: Bank Street College of Education, Center for Children and Technology.

Pea, R., & Kurland, D. M. (1983). *On the cognitive prerequisites of learning computer programming* (Technical Report No. 18). New York: Bank Street College of Education, Center for Children and Technology.

Peanuts Maze Marathon. (1984). New York: Random House.

Sheingold, K. (1986) The microcomputer as a symbolic medium. In P. Campbell & G. Fein (Eds.), *Young children and microcomputers* (pp. 26–34). Englewood Cliffs, NJ: Prentice-Hall.

Sheingold, K., Jewson, B. J., Gearhart, L., & Berger, R. (1983). *Microcomputers in schools: Impact on the social life of elementary classrooms*. New York: Bank Street College of Education, Center for Children and Technology.

Sherman, J., Divine, K., & Johnson, B. (1985, May). An analysis of computer software preferences of preschool children. *Educational Technology*, pp. 39–41.

Silvern, S. (1983). Opening the door to the microworld. *Childhood Education, 59*, 219–221.

Smurf Paint and Play. (1985). Avon, CT: Coleco Industries.

Spencer, M., & Baskin, L. (1981, November/December). Classroom computers do make a difference. *Classroom Computer News*, pp. 12–15.

Stickybear. (1983). Middletown, CT: Optimum Resource, Inc.

Taylor, H. (1983). *Microcomputers in the early childhood classroom*. Lynwood, WA: Edmonds Community College. (ERIC Document Reproduction Service No. ED 234845)

Vaidya, S., & McKeeby, J. (1985). Developing a Logo environment in the preschool. *Computers in the Schools, 2*, 81–89.

Watson, J., Nida, R., & Shade, D. (1983). *Young children should work with computers: Logo with Lego!* Greensboro, NC: University of North Carolina at Greensboro, Department of Child Development: Family Relations.

Watt, D. (1982). LOGO in the schools. *Byte, 7*(8), 116–134.

Zonderman, J. (1982, September/October). Toying with education. *Classroom Computer News*, pp. 26–28.

PART FIVE

How Will Early Childhood Education Be Evaluated?

How should early childhood education be evaluated? Some may even ask *why* children and their care and education should be evaluated. Evaluation of the growth, development, and learning of young children is problematic in and of itself. And given all the methodological problems involved in evaluating the effectiveness or benefits of programs for young children, the worth of evaluations—the time and money involved for the amount of information gained—can be challenged.

Other questions about the nature of evaluation in early childhood education continue in the field today. Should the evaluation focus on children? On outcomes such as their academic achievement, gains in intelligence, or obtainment of specific goals and objectives? Or is it the teachers and administrators of programs who should be evaluated? Should evaluations revolve around the questions of cost benefits, or are there other variables equally as important in the assessment and evaluation of early childhood education?

Evaluation, defined as "systematic formal appraisal of the quality of educational phenomena" (Popham, 1988, p. 7), has been a continuing issue in the field of early childhood education. The variety of types of evaluation—informal, summative, and formative—confound the issues, as do the numerous variables that could be the focus of evaluation—the program, children, teachers.

Nevertheless, despite the issues and problems, evaluation is an essential part of early childhood care and education. There is the necessity of maintaining standards and ensuring the quality of young children's early educational experiences. Through the process of evaluation, information about the strengths and weaknesses of programs can be used to enhance program quality. Sue Bredekamp, in the chapter

"Achieving Model Early Childhood Programs Through Accreditation," describes the use of evaluations in enhancing the quality of early childhood education. She suggests that the nature of the National Academy of Early Childhood Programs accreditation process can positively affect program quality.

Accountability is also required. Some proof that a program is effectively carrying out the mission set for it is necessary in today's world. Evaluation as a means of accounting is written into nearly every new law relating to children's services or programs. The Child Abuse and Neglect Law, 94 457, and others not only require evaluation of programs and services, but mandate annual review and analysis of research and program activities in the field.

John E. Dopyera and Margaret Lay-Dopyera, in the chapter "Evaluation and Science in Early Education: Some Critical Issues," discuss the history of evaluation as a means of accounting for program effectiveness and program quality. They describe why programs receiving any type of external funding must demonstrate that they are meeting the funding guidelines and specifications.

From the practical view of society, scientific evaluation of early childhood programs of care and education is necessary for the advancement of the human welfare. Simply because children and their families are involved in care and education, evaluation is essential. To ask seriously, utilizing all of the methods of the scientist, how a specific program affects the individual and group, is proper.

PROGRAM EVALUATIONS

Nevertheless, early childhood educators are cautious about the use of evaluation in early childhood care and education. Past misuses and misinterpretations of program evaluations contribute to educators' concerns.

In the past, programs have been given an indelible stamp of approval or disapproval based on outcomes of faulty evaluations. Once labeled on the basis of limited data, or narrow concepts of program quality, programs were judged effective or ineffective. "Many policy makers viewed evaluation as a definitive procedure for determining whether a particular program was worth its salt, or, in the case of several competing programs, which program was saltiest. High-level policy makers, in particular, began to believe that formal evaluations could provide the information needed in order to determine whether a particular program should be scrapped or saved" (Popham, 1988, p. 5).

An example is the Westinghouse/Ohio evaluation report of the effectiveness of Head Start programs, which concluded that Head Start had only a few weak and fleeting effects (Cicirelli, 1969). The Nixon administration, intent on dismantling the previous Johnson administration' war on poverty, embraced these conclusions. Concern that the Westinghouse report would be used to eliminate the popular Head Start program was prevalent. Discussion about the validity of the measures used in the report, the sampling procedures, and basic research design followed.

On the other hand, belief that judgment about the "saltiness" of a program could lead to decisions about the continuation of the program did not materialize in the case of Head Start. Popham (1988) believes this is not an isolated instance of the results of a program evaluation being ignored. He believes it is actually rare for the results of evaluations to yield "results so unequivocal that decision makers" are able to act in accord with the summative evaluations' results. "The majority of summatively oriented educational evaluations, at least those conducted during the past two decades, have proved to be far less influential than their architects had hoped . . . rarely has an ongoing program truly been expunged on the basis of a summative evaluation's findings" (Popham, 1988, p. 15).

Standards for Evaluation

To ensure that a given program evaluation will be fairly and adequately carried out and will serve to improve the quality of the educational program, a set of *Standards for Evaluation of Educational Programs, Projects, and Materials* (Joint Committee on Standards for Educational Evaluation, 1981) were developed. These thirty separate standards were organized under four different concepts and offer the early childhood community a list of "first-rate things to think about" when carrying out educational evaluations (Popham, 1988). The standards are organized around four concepts:

- **Utility:** The utility standards are intended to ensure that an evaluation will serve the practical information needs of a given audience.
- **Feasibility:** The feasibility standards are intended to ensure that an evaluation will be realistic, prudent, diplomatic, and frugal.
- **Propriety Standards:** The propriety standards are intended to ensure that an evaluation will be conducted legally, ethically, and with due regard for the welfare of those involved in the evaluation, as well as those affected by its results.
- **Accuracy Standards:** The accuracy standards are intended to ensure that an evaluation will reveal and convey technically adequate information about the features of the object being studied that determine its worth and merit.

ASSESSING CHILDREN

Assessing the growth, development, and learning of young children is as essential as program evaluations. In fact, the assessment of children is often seen as the major component of program evaluation. Testing, either for individual children or for groups of children, is believed the "handmaiden of evaluation" (Bradley & Caldwell, 1974). If gain scores on tests of achievement or intelligence can be found, then the success of the program is believed documented.

Irrespective of program evaluation, however, is the fact that educators do want information on the status of the children with whom they work. The information gleaned from assessment permits educators to predict children's growth and development, and can lead to the improvement of the teaching/learning process.

The difficulties of testing young children are fully known. Young children's uneven growth and development is well documented. Children who may walk or talk fluently one day may not demonstrate these skills again for any number of days or weeks. Or a child who speaks in two-word sentences one day may suddenly speak in full paragraphs the next.

Children also have a limited understanding of the testing situation. Frequently they are unable to accurately interpret the requests of the examiner or understand the task they are asked to do. Humorous anecdotes of children's responses during a testing situation are familiar to all. One five year old came home from kindergarten and informed her mother that she was the smartest child in the entire class. When her mother asked her why she had reached this conclusion, the girl replied, "Well, the teacher gave us a test today that would tell how smart we were, and I marked all the answers in the book before she even handed it out to the other kids."

Then, too, children have a limited repertoire of behaviors that can be tested. The behaviors typical of young children are typically not those traditional to the testing situation. Typical behaviors also vary dramatically over the period of early childhood. Behaviors at birth differ greatly from those at age one, as do children's behaviors at age one from any other age. These diverse behaviors serve to confound the issue of testing during the period of early childhood education.

Nevertheless, despite the problems of testing young children, we are witnessing the most blatant misuse of testing young children today. In many school systems, children are being required to pass a readiness test in order to be admitted to kindergarten. On the basis of a single test score, on tests that are of dubious value, children are being denied access to education.

On the basis of a single test score, young children are being tracked into "differential programs." Here is another situation in which research or evaluation results are unrelated to practice. The damaging effects of tracking have been known since the 1930s. Findings from current research strongly indicate the negative effects of this practice. And yet today's young children are being placed in transitional, developmental, or other forms of differential programming on the basis of a single test score.

Carol Seefeldt, in the chapter "Assessing Young Children," reviews the problems involved in testing and suggests alternative methods of judging children's progress and gaining information that would be useful in the improvement of children's early educational experiences.

Standards for Testing

In selecting tests to assess young children, educators should consider the characteristics of tests. In addition to the standards of reliability and validity and the type of information provided by the test, the American Psychological Association (1985) provides several other useful criteria for judging the practical worth of tests. These include

- **Relevance:** Test data are collected to meet certain purposes, and if they do not relate to those purposes, they are useless. The criterion of relevance asks whether or not the purposes are, in fact, served.
- **Importance:** A great deal of information can be collected that is nominally relevant to some purpose; but, obviously, not all information is equally important.
- **Scope:** Information may be relevant and important but lack sufficient scope to be useful.
- **Credibility:** Credibility relates to the quantity of trust or belief one can have in the data. Not all users of test information are in a position to determine its validity, reliability, or objectivity. They need to be able to trust the information provided by the test.
- **Timeliness:** The best test information is useless if it comes too late or too soon.
- **Efficiency:** After test data have been examined for adequacy in meeting the practical criteria, there are probably still alternatives that differ in terms of such requirements as time, cost, and personnel. The criterion of efficiency can be employed as a means of guiding the educator to the appropriate alternative.

MAKING DECISIONS

Evaluation and testing are facts. Both are complex activities requiring constant examination, change, and refinement. Testing and evaluation are neither good nor bad. The use to which evaluation and testing results are put, however, can foster and enhance children's development and education, or they can be used to hinder and negate children's progress.

Early childhood educators can assume responsibility for understanding the issues involved in program evaluation and testing and for ensuring that evaluations and tests are used in constructive ways. Should our knowledge of evaluation and testing be used to foster the goals of a democratic society or to deny individuals their right to their own freedom of choice, action, and equality of educational opportunity?

HOW WILL EDUCATION BE EVALUATED?

As you read the following chapters, ask yourself

- How can tests and evaluations be used to improve the status of young children and their care and education?
- What is the relative importance of both formative and summative evaluations in early childhood education?

- What goals will be evaluated? In evaluating programs of technical education, or adult education, the goals may be specific and easily assessed. In early childhood education, however, program goals vary widely, are often global, and do not lend themselves to specific assessment.
- How can measurement and assessment of young children be improved?

REFERENCES

American Psychological Association. (1985). *Standards for educational and psychological testing*. Washington, DC: Author.

Bradley, R. H., & Caldwell, B. M. (1974). *Issues and procedures in testing young children*. Princeton, NJ: Educational Testing Service.

Cicirelli, V. (1969). *The impact of Head Start: An evaluation of Head Start on children's cognitive and affective development. A report submitted to the Office of Economic Opportunity*. Washington, DC: National Bureau of Standards, Institute for Applied Technology.

Joint Committee on Standards for Educational Evaluation. (1981). *Standards for evaluation of educational programs, projects, and materials*. New York: McGraw-Hill.

Popham, W. J. (1988). *Educational evaluation* (2nd ed.). Englewood Cliffs, NJ: Prentice-Hall.

13

Evaluation and Science in Early Education: Some Critical Issues

JOHN E. DOPYERA
Cumberland Hill Associates–Syracuse

MARGARET LAY-DOPYERA
Syracuse University

Across the past decades there has been a great deal of evaluation activity directed toward early education. Although the results of these efforts have been suggestive for funding and program direction, a great deal of confusion and controversy continue regarding the care and education of young children. Recently, major associations representing professionals with concerns for children (Association for Childhood Education International, 1987; Bredekamp, 1987; Early Childhood and Literacy Development Committee of the International Reading Association, 1985; National Association of Early Childhood Specialists in State Departments of Education, 1987; Southern Association on Children Under Six, 1984) have attempted clarification by publishing position statements on appropriate practice. The majority of educational programs across the nation, however, especially in public schools and in for-profit day-care and learning centers, continue to operate with little regard for what is recommended by the professional associations. In this chapter, we will explore how this state of affairs may have come about. We will first discuss the roots and history of educational evaluation. We will then describe four types of evaluation, the first of which is intuitive evaluation, a common form of human cognitive activity. The other types of evaluation are of the formal variety that comprise the work of professional evaluators. They include objectives-based, standards-based, and evaluation research. We will discuss some major problems and issues with evaluation efforts as they are currently conducted and suggest some future directions for early education evaluation that we believe have an enhanced probability of resolving some of these problems.

HISTORICAL PERSPECTIVES

Prior to World War I, most scientific study was conducted by individuals, working independently in settings that they themselves had created. The nature and direction of the work and the time schedule for its completion was up to the individual. As the scientific enterprise developed, in the form of both research and development activities, public funding became more prevalent. With public funding, accountability was an issue of concern. Government funding required the specification of the product that would result from the work. Accountability was linked to the extent to which the funded effort was successful in meeting the "specs" (specifications) set out by the funding agency. A particular kind of expertise was required to determine the extent to which the final product met the project specifications. Thus, the profession of evaluation as distinct from research was born.

As more and more educational and social programs of the Great Society (such as E.S.E.A. Title I, Head Start, and Follow Through) came into existence, each with congressional mandates for evaluation, the number of persons involved in evaluation activities increased rapidly. To support the work of this professional group, societies and associations were formed, and specialized publications were created. Professional organizations developed "SIGs" (Special Interest Groups) and special divisions for an emphasis on evaluation. Academic institutions hired researchers to train advanced-degree candidates as specialists in evaluation.

As the evaluation profession grew, there was a consolidation of concepts, strategies, and membership requirements. Those within the profession were set apart from other professionals based on their presumed knowledge of the techniques for doing evaluation. Within the profession, standard practice, which could be applied to any educational evaluation endeavor, embraced an emphasis on the product-oriented concepts of "behavioral" objectives, criterion-referenced testing, the distinction between formative and summative evaluation, and scores of other related concepts.[1] Increasingly, the conduct of evaluation was seen as the province of the specialist and beyond the capability of the practitioner. Practitioners have become convinced of this as well. The work of evaluators has increasingly been seen as keeping practitioners accountable to funding or sponsoring agencies, according to criteria that have been established prior to the start of programs. Although the initial impetus to this direction came from governmental funding and concerns for accountability, the generalized expectation for evaluation now holds for the evaluation of all educational and many other social and technological programs, whatever the source of sponsorship. The way in which the evaluation field has developed has had

---

[1] For further explication, consult standard references such as the following:

Cook, T. D., & Campbell, D. T. (1979). *Quasi-experimentation: Design and analysis issues for field settings*. Boston: Houghton-Mifflin.

Cronbach, L. J. (1982). *Designing evaluations of educational and social programs*. San Francisco: Jossey-Bass.

implications for the extent to which evaluation studies have contributed to knowledge and practice in many fields, including but not limited to early education.

TYPES OF EVALUATION

An examination of the evaluation activities that are relevant to early education leads to various discriminations and categories. For the purposes of this chapter, a discrimination between intuitive evaluation, a universal human propensity, and formal evaluation, the province of the professional evaluator, appears useful. Within formal evaluation, there are relevant subclassifications.[2] A further delineation of these different types of evaluation is included in the upcoming subsections.

Intuitive Evaluation

Intuitive evaluation concerns how we each in our own way survive and function each moment of our existence. Intuitive evaluation is so commonplace in our lives that we seldom recognize that it is occurring. When a discrepancy occurs between our expectations and what occurs, we act to remedy the discrepancy.

On reflection, each of us can identify within a short period of time instances of our own intuitive evaluation systems in operation. For example, in our kitchens, as we prepare a meal, cutting a piece of beef for stew, we evaluate whether a piece we have just cut is too large or just right. If too large, we cut it smaller. When we taste the stew for flavor, we evaluate whether it is not salty enough or is okay. If not salty enough, we add more salt. Our lives are filled with evaluation activities, moment by moment, to assure that our internal standards are met.

As in more formal evaluation, criteria and standards are involved in intuitive evaluation. Data is the signal of a discrepancy, just as data is involved in determining results of formal evaluations.

Intuitive evaluations appear to be critical to the way professional teachers conduct their work. Several years ago, we became interested in how adults working with young children got the children to conform to their expectations, i.e., use time productively, follow classroom procedures, become social beings, etc. We (Dopyera, 1969, 1974) systematically observed eighty children in their respective classrooms (eight children in each of ten Head Start classes) in small time segments. Children were observed individually, and three kinds of information were recorded: first, what the child was doing, including who the child was with and what was initiated by the

---

[2]The scope of this chapter does not allow for a critical review of the major decision points in conducting formal evaluations. The interested reader may wish to consult references such as the following:

Dopyera, J. E., & Pitone, L. (1983). Decision points in planning the evaluation of training. *Training and Development Journal, 37,* 66–71.

Nevo, D. (1983). The conceptualization of educational evaluation: Analytical review of the literature. *Review of Educational Research, 53*(1), 117–128.

child; second, what was being said or done by peers or adults to the child; third, the context within which these activities were occurring. We were especially interested in noting child behaviors that were "discrepant" for the teacher and what the teacher did or said when such behaviors occurred. It became very clear that each teacher carried within her head a set of notions, a map if you will, of what constituted appropriate child behavior.

Teacher maps, of course, were not all the same. Although there was a broad range of agreement, there were distinct differences. When Jimmy would climb to the top of the jungle gym and yell, "Look at me," some teachers would smile and wave back. Others would look anguished and/or run over to tell Jimmy to "get down before you hurt yourself." For given teachers, maps had time-specific, space-specific, and/or child-specific aspects. Some child behaviors were okay at some times but not at others, e.g., using blocks was fine during free play but not during circle time; running was okay out-of-doors but not inside; wearing a dress was okay for Sally but not for Johnnie.

If teachers we were observing became aware that the intuitive evaluations they were making of the events around them were different from those of other professionals, they probably assumed that the other persons were remiss in their judgments. By definition, intuitive evaluations are largely unexamined. Internal maps become the focus of conscious consideration when there is a significant clash between our own assumptions and those of others whom we respect, or between our own assumptions regarding the outcomes of our decisions and what actually ensues. At the point of such a discrepancy, the mental map that is the basis of intuitive decision making is sometimes redrawn.

The practitioner's reliance on intuitive evaluation for guiding professional decisions and actions, if it is recognized worthy of comment at all by those who write about professional evaluation, is typically seen as unimportant or as an unfortunate aspect of professional functioning. For example, Goodwin and Driscoll (1980) quote LaCrosse (1970) regarding the intuitive orientation of teachers of young children as being in sharp contrast with the inquiring, rational outlook of the psychologist-researcher. According to Goodwin and Driscoll, "the implication is that early childhood educators, with their uncomplicated view of causality and their allegiance to intuition, feel no need for the products of a solid evaluation effort" (p. 30). After reviewing such "solid evaluation efforts" in the upcoming paragraphs, we shall return to the topic of intuitive evaluation and its potential contribution to a science of early education.

Formal Evaluation

We shall describe three types of formal evaluation. Two of these are concerned with accountability, as previously mentioned. They are objectives-based evaluation and standards-based evaluation. Objectives-based evaluation focuses on what learners achieve; the other, standards-based evaluation, focuses on the characteristics and requirements for programs. The third is evaluation research, which goes beyond accountability in seeking data helpful in understanding causal relationships between program parameters and outcomes for participants.

Objectives-based Evaluation

Objectives-based evaluation informs decision making by providing information on the extent to which predetermined objectives of an event or a program are achieved. This is the activity that is most often referred to when educational professionals, or the lay public, talk about evaluation. Most persons with the professional designation of "evaluator" define their work in these terms. The basic question asked is, "Is the event or program achieving its goals?" The first thing the evaluator must do to conduct this kind of evaluation is to learn what the program objectives are so that information can be obtained to answer the question of whether the program is successful in meeting these objectives.

Program-specific or curriculum-specific criteria are also often used in objectives-based evaluations for determining the worth of a program. For example, in one school district (Cipfl, 1984), evaluation of the instructional program included components consisting of (a) a skills continuum, reflecting decisions of district faculty about what skills should be taught at what level; (b) exit tests, measuring how much students have learned from classes; and (c) objective evaluation, depending on analysis of the exit tests to determine the effectiveness of the program for individual students, classes, schools, or the entire district. These approaches are commonly used in both local and national evaluation efforts. Johnson (1987) represents this view when he says, "Evaluation is the process of selecting, gathering, and interpreting information in order to form a judgment about the worthwhileness of a program or the value of an approach to solving a specific problem or accomplishing a prescribed set of objectives" (p. 15). He, like others who follow the objectives-based evaluation paradigm, also emphasizes the importance of discrimination between formative and summative evaluation. *Formative evaluation* refers to the use of data to assess the effectiveness of various facets of the program while it is being tried out initially and while changes are still being contemplated. *Summative evaluation* refers to the use of data to judge the overall effectiveness of a program after it has been fully developed. Johnson claims, "The importance of thorough evaluation of early educational programs, both summative and formative, has received widespread recognition by professionals and researchers within the field of early childhood education. . . . Summative evaluation could not be a substitute for formative evaluation and vice versa, regardless of the study design" (p. 17).

Standards-based Evaluation

Standards-based evaluation differs from objectives-based evaluation in that it is not looking at the evidence of outcomes of particular conditions or elements in a program, event, or other phenomena under scrutiny. Instead, the focus is on whether that program or event meets certain criteria believed to be desirable. Everyday examples of standards-based evaluations are real estate appraisals and automobile inspections.

Judgments and decisions based on standards-based evaluation are frequently used in early education evaluation. The most prominent example is the National Association for the Education of Young Children's accreditation effort through the National Academy of Early Childhood Programs (Bredekamp & Apple, 1986; Bredekamp & Berby, 1987). Within the accreditation process, program descriptions receive ratings for each of ten components (interactions among staff and children, curriculum, staff-parent interactions, staff qualifications and development, administration, staffing, physical environment, health and safety, nutrition and food service, and evaluation) that are believed significant to children's development, welfare, or learning. There are specific criteria for each component. Raters are early childhood professionals with diverse experiences in early childhood programs who have "a high level of knowledge in early childhood/child development, a diverse range of first-hand experiences, and a national perspective on the field" (Bredekamp & Apple, 1986, p. 34). During 1987, nearly 2,000 programs across the country were involved in self-study preparatory to seeking accreditation, and almost 400 had been accredited (Hymes, 1988).

Other comparable standards-based evaluation practices in the field of early childhood education include the credentialing processes involved with Child Development Associates (CDA National Credentialing Program, 1984), and the Guidelines for Teacher Education (National Association for the Education of Young Children, 1982), which are used by the National Council for the Accreditation of Teacher Education (NCATE) to determine accreditation for colleges that prepare teachers of young children.

Evaluation Research

Evaluation research contrasts with the two types of accountability evaluation described above. Evaluation research may go well beyond the concern of whether a particular set of objectives are achieved or whether a particular set of criteria are met (in the provision of a program or an event or a performance of a teacher). There is, instead, an emphasis on how various aspects of that which is being evaluated (event, program, teacher performance, environment, etc.) are related to variations in outcomes for participants. The purpose of evaluation research is to construct a better understanding of the forces that interplay within a given situation. The more complex questions of cause/effect relationships motivated the Head Start and Follow Through Planned Variation projects in which governmental funding supported the mounting of quite different program approaches to determine whether some were more effective than others.

One of the examples of this kind of evaluation in early childhood education is the High/Scope (Schweinhart, Weikart, & Larner, 1986) longitudinal comparison of three different preschool curriculum models on a range of measures assessing such variables as achievement, delinquency, family relations, and activity involvement. Schweinhart et al. reported their findings as follows:

> The three preschool curriculum groups [the High/Scope model, the Distar model, and a model in the nursery school tradition] differed little in their patterns of IQ and school achievement over time. According to self-reports at age 15, the group that had attended the Distar preschool program engaged in twice as many delinquent acts as did the other two curriculum groups, including five times as many acts of property violence. The Distar group also reported relatively poor relations with their families, less participation in sports, fewer school job appointments and less reaching out to others for help with personal problems. These findings, based on one study with a small sample, are by no means definitive; but they do suggest possible consequences of preschool curriculum models that ought to be considered (p. 15).

The authors of this report urge the initiation of longitudinal studies on the long-term intellectual and social effects of teacher- and child-initiated curriculum approaches in early childhood education. They suggest, "Like the field of medicine, we must conduct rigorous, long-term evaluations under careful conditions to uncover unintended consequences or undesirable side effects of programs that we create based on any theory" (p. 44). This search for understanding about any effects, not just those that are seen as the objectives of the program, marks one important difference between objectives-based evaluation and evaluation research. The pursuit of evidence rather than the acceptance of assumptions about what is good marks the difference between evaluation research and standards-based evaluation. The evaluation research methodologies include both qualitative and quantitative methods (experimental, quasi-experimental, correlational, path analysis, etc.). Well-known evaluation research studies on early education include Berrulta-Clement, Schweinhart, Barnett, Epstein, and Weikart, 1984; Lazar, Darlington, Murray, Royce, and Snipper, 1982; Miller and Dyer, 1975; and Stallings, 1975a, 1975b. In evaluation research, as in both types of accountability research, the investigatory activity has been the domain of the evaluation professional.

PROBLEMS AND ISSUES

Of the four types of evaluation presented herein, only the three formal types are typically seen to be of any consequence by those in the evaluation profession. Intuitive evaluation is seen as the unscientific approach of the "untrained" and unsophisticated. Many evaluators acknowledge, on the other hand, that there are grave problems with formal evaluation approaches. The following are simply a sampling of the comments of professional evaluators with long-term affiliations with evaluation and evaluation research in education. They exemplify the controversy and criticism of formal evaluation studies.

In the words of Sanders (1981), "We now have had more than two decades of experience in this [evaluation] enterprise. Billions of dollars have been spent by government and private agencies in deliberate efforts to use science and technology to improve educational practices and operations. The effort has endured long enough so that it is possible to discern some of its effects, and unfortunately, they are more than disappointing" (p. 8). He concludes that the expected educational improvements have not ensued and that unexpected consequences have resulted in undesirable changes.

According to Zimiles (1977), "The more our current efforts to evaluate educational programs strive for relevance, the more invalid they become" (p. 63). He suggests that the "evaluation of impact has had the effect of circumscribing the scope of a classroom. It fosters an approach to teaching in which the teacher works backward from the evaluation procedure, her concept of her goals and her methods become increasingly bound to the content of the evaluation instruments" (p. 70).

House and Hutchins (1979), in writing about the model comparisons of the Follow Through evaluation, declared, "In a society as pluralistic as the United States, people often disagree on outcome measures to assess programs. And the cause and effect relationships in the social sciences are exceedingly complex. Perhaps the final judgment is that the Follow Through evaluation was inappropriate for the context in which it was employed" (p. 10). We (Lay-Dopyera & Dopyera, 1982; Neisworth, Dopyera, & Lay, 1976) also address the problems of model comparisons, pointing out the wide variation from class to class and within a single classroom and variation from teacher to teacher. Even when sponsors of specific program models guide the implementations, as occurred in the Follow Through study, there are substantial differences across classrooms within models (Stallings, 1975b). As Fein and Clarke-Stewart (1973), Zimiles (1977), and Shelly and Charlesworth (1980) suggest, evaluation efforts must go beyond model comparisons to provide information on how specific encounters differentially affect children to provide a basis for program improvement.

The evaluation activity, as it has been formally conceptualized and practiced, appears not to be adequate to guide the development of the field of early education in ways that are necessary. And yet the need is great. Even the most optimistic Pollyannas among us cannot ignore the evidence that our society, and, hence, our educational system, has critical problems. We daily read in our newspapers about some of these problems—the shocking illiteracy rates, the cultural ignorance of our teenagers, the failure of children beyond the primary grades to achieve adequately, the increasing dropout rates, drug use, delinquency. We are besieged with national reports expressing alarm at the weaknesses of our educational system. From *A Nation at Risk: The Imperative for Educational Reform* (National Commission on Excellence in Education, 1983) to *A Nation Prepared: Teachers for the 21st Century* (Carnegie Forum on Education and the Economy, 1986) and *Time for Results: The Governors' Report on Education* (National Governors' Association, 1986), we are told that our educational system must be reformed.

Given the critical nature of societal problems, there is good reason for early educators to seek to insure that programs enhance rather than detract from children's health, well-being, learning, and development. It seems essential that we make every effort to develop our abilities and our "dispositions" (to use Lillian Katz's term) to become accountable for our early education practices, that is, accountable in the sense of continuing to learn about the milieu that we provide for children and how they and we use that milieu to seek better understandings. When we consider how evaluation efforts have contributed to that learning to date, we are disappointed in what we find. Instead of substantial contributions, we see the following: (a) a confusing glut of information, (b) fractionalized roles, and (c) hyperrationalized decision making.

A Confusing Glut of Information

Paradoxically, early childhood practitioners lack information on how programs affect children while they are, at the same time, inundated with possibilities for seeking information. There is at the present time an abundance of journals, newsletters, microfiche documents, books, textbooks, conferences, workshops, resource centers, etc. Few practitioners have the time and patience to sift through this profusion of possibilities in preparation for making decisions about how to provide programs for children. When one attempts to do so, there is the problem of determining what information is of most worth, since significant portions of it are confusing and/or contradictory. This state of affairs appears to come about because evaluation efforts have primarily been directed toward trying to determine which of contrasting programs work best, on the average, for specific objectives (objectives-based evaluation), rather than attempting to learn what is happening to learners with various characteristics within various program configurations. This latter has not been accomplished for a number of reasons. The major reason is that the product model of evaluation has predominated and the study of more refined causal relationships has only been undertaken on a more fragmented, piecemeal basis. A simple but comprehensive means for describing program configurations or child outcomes that are understandable and usable for both teachers and other classroom observers has not as yet been developed.

Fractionalized Roles

In the conduct of early childhood programs, there is a clear demarcation between practitioners and evaluators. This separation is inherent in the formative versus summative view of objectives-based evaluation. The problem with this view, as we see it, is that the reactions of children and the impressions and judgments of teachers, program administrators, or program developers are in prime focus only in formative stages. The learning derived from formative stages seldom is known about by those outside an immediate setting or project. It is the summative results that are disseminated in print, at conferences, etc. Summative evaluation is seen as the work of a special group of persons who test, observe, collect and analyze, and interpret data. Not only are roles separate; in the general hierarchy of roles, it is clear which group has higher status. The unfortunate outcomes from this artificial separation of roles are twofold. First, there is often resistance on the part of practitioners to agree to participate in evaluation studies. Even when there is consent, the tasks set by evaluators are often carried out in ways that distort the findings. Second, there is usually minimal communication between teachers, parents, or others involved with the programs on a day-to-day basis, and the summative evaluation personnel are not, therefore, informed by the practitioners about the nuances of the milieu that is being evaluated. Each group has a different agenda and follows a different set of priorities. The fractionalization of roles serves to lessen the effectiveness of evaluation efforts.

Hyperrationalized Decision Making

It has frequently been pointed out that educational decision making is seldom based on sufficient evidence to fully justify one alternative over another. And yet nearly all educational practices are presented as though the scientific method was carefully applied in support of each decision. Educators, especially at the level of policy formation, tend to pride themselves on being scientific. The problem seems to be that there is, as yet, insufficient knowledge on which to base sound decisions. Sanders (1981) cites Wise (1978) and Goodlad (1978) and discusses this problem as follows:

> In the absence of knowledge about how educating processes work . . . policy makers focus on the specification of educational ends (in measurable form) and means (in technological form) and seek to improve schooling through centralized and bureaucratized decision making. [Difficulties] arise, however, because every policy incorporates both an aim to be achieved and a theory— often an implicit theory— that provides the basis for believing that the action taken will produce the desired result. If powerful policy makers believe in certain ideas about education and if they seek to implement those ideas through a policy or succession of policies, eventually the schools change to reflect those ideas in operational form. If the theories are incomplete or mistaken, the result may be "hyper-rationalization, . . . an effort to rationalize beyond the bounds of knowledge" (Sanders, 1981, p. 8).

When evidence is cited to support a decision, it is typically evidence that has been selected to bolster policymakers' preconceived notions (intuitive evaluations) of the way things ought to be. The issue for early childhood education professionals, at this point, is to sort out which of the barrage of "scientific" findings presented in support of policy decisions are really based on firm evidence and which are some combination of intuitive evaluation and biased selection of corroborating studies. Fully qualified academics find this sorting process difficult, given the current milieu; most practitioners find it an impossibility.

SCIENCE AS A MODEL FOR INQUIRY

In this chapter, we have reflected on the genesis of the evaluation profession. We have also examined the function intuitive evaluation plays in the ongoing decision making of practitioners (as well as the rest of us). We have suggested that if early education is to make significant societal contributions, evaluation processes must involve and influence practitioners' intuitive functioning. We have also reviewed the nature of evaluation studies conducted of early education and found them wanting. As a result of these reflections, we propose a shift of emphasis for early education evaluators (and, concomitantly, for practitioners) in several conceptual and attitudinal arenas. Those who serve in leadership positions in the evaluation of early education will, we believe, do well to move toward an emphasis on (a) inquiring openly and skeptically rather than drawing premature conclusions about the outcomes of program encounters for children, (b) describing practices and effects rather than seeking prescriptions for practice and outcome measures, and (c) learning about practitioners' implicit hypotheses rather than holding them accountable to predetermined objectives and methods.

There is a critical need for the development of an early education science that is rooted in the work of practitioners. What is necessary are collaborative efforts to move toward a scientific approach to finding out what works with individual children and under what circumstances. Science requires, minimally, commonly shared terminology as well as propositions (beliefs) that are testable, that continue to be tested in experience, and that may be revised and/or reframed entirely, based on that experience.

We envision individual practitioners "observing" the program settings they implement and examining with empirical documentation the consequences of those settings for the well-being, learning, and development of individual children. We envision practitioners (teachers, administrators, and support personnel) engaging much more in the reflective process suggested by Schon (1983). (See also Dopyera and Lay [1975] for a practical process for assisting some aspects of teacher reflection.) On the basis of these experiences, we envision the further collaboration of practitioners with professional evaluators to generate questions and hypotheses that are drawn from the insights of both groups, and then to align evidence from their respective experiences to "test" the propositions articulated.

A different starting point might be for early education practitioners and professional evaluators to work together in stating in propositional forms (hypotheses) and testable forms the major themes contained in the position statements (Bredekamp, 1987) published by NAEYC. This activity could certainly include the reflection by mature teaching professionals, based on their prior experiences, as to whether they have explicit evidence that is supportive and/or evidence that is contrary to these propositions. It is our guess that these activities would produce a number of benefits, including the building of mutual respect. Such collaborative, coordinated activity would go a long way toward addressing and rectifying many of the problems associated with the glut of information, the fragmentation, and the hyperrationalization cited earlier as prevalent today. If practitioners are to be included in the processes of establishing a knowledge base, they will require experiences such as these to increase awareness that early education can be studied, that they can participate fully in that study, and that when that study occurs, benefits accrue to all.

The work of these groups would be greatly facilitated when the following are developed:

1. A common vocabulary for describing behaviors, settings, behavior changes (teachers', children's)
2. Mechanisms/procedures for recording observations of conditions, settings, encounters, and behaviors in comparable form
3. A compilation from existent literature of hypotheses and propositions for which some evidence exists but that need further testing and replication
4. A clearinghouse, free from distracting agenda, to coordinate, receive, and compile data for use in testing propositions and to disseminate results to practitioners as well as to researchers.

If these were available, we believe that several shifts in practice would follow. There would be more coordinated programmatic studies and fewer piecemeal efforts. There would be more continuous data collection and less reliance on using one-shot library reviews as the justification for practice or as the basis for the design of isolated studies. There would be less speculation about best practices and more active data collection to learn about how individual children relate to, and benefit from, their educational environments.

Several desired goals would begin to be met in early education, early education evaluation, and early education science:

- Early education practitioners would become more reflective, more focused, and more professional in their endeavors with "educating" young children.
- A body of data would be developed that would clarify the hypotheses inherent in many of the statements of standards recently adopted by professional organizations.
- The values associated with early education professions would be discussed and become clarified.
- A more productive collaboration between professionals in different disciplines (early education/educational research and evaluation, professional associations, social psychologists) would come about that would further enhance early education science.

SUMMARY

What is being proposed herein is a radical shift in the conceptualization of early education evaluation away from the narrow conceptions of objectives-based evaluation or the reliance on the standards-based evaluations as it is usually undertaken by external evaluators. We propose an enlistment of practitioners to go beyond their intuitive evaluation to cooperate with each other and with professional evaluators to conduct evaluation science projects designed to be relevant to the issues of daily program decision making. We recognize the value of the many thousands of formal evaluation studies of various types that have been done in the past by competent and committed professionals. We also recognize, however, that most decisions regarding early education planning in our increasingly complex and pluralistic society are rooted in authority that is conceptually based in past rather than current knowledge. There is no ongoing comprehensive accumulation of new data to correct the suppositions of the past about how children in the here and now learn and develop. Also, there is no "vehicle" or constituency currently organized for focusing on and developing the critical mass of needed data. Therefore, we somewhat audaciously have suggested a different evaluation path, knowing full well that what we have described suggests a direction, but not does not supply a blueprint, for what should be done. In this respect, we rely on the adage of the wise native American who has been quoted as saying, "Go as far as you can see and when you get there you will see further."

A major advantage of this direction, beyond those listed above, is that what *is* learned will have a greater likelihood of improving the well-being and development of children. Any effort that improves teachers', parents', and caregivers' understanding of how children relate to, and benefit from, experience will further contribute to resolving major social problems for which we believe we all share responsibility.

REFERENCES

Association for Childhood Education International. (1987). *The child-centered-kindergarten*. Wheaton, MD: Author.

Berrulta-Clement, J. R., Schweinhart, L. J., Barnett, W. S., Epstein, A. S., & Weikart, D. P. (1984). Changed lives: The effects of the Perry Preschool Program on youths through age 19. *Monographs of the High/Scope Educational Research Foundation, 8.*

Bredekamp, S. (Ed.). (1987). *Developmentally appropriate practice in early childhood programs serving children from birth through age 8.* Washington, DC: National Association for the Education of Young Children.

Bredekamp, S., & Apple, P. L. (1986). How early childhood programs get accredited: An analysis of accreditation decisions. *Young Children, 42*(1), 34–37.

Bredekamp, S., & Berby, J. (1987). Maintaining quality: Accredited programs one year later. *Young Children, 43*(1), 13–15.

Carnegie Forum on Education and the Economy. (1986). *A nation prepared: Teachers for the 21st century.* Washington, DC: Author.

CDA National Credentialing Program. (1984). *CDA competency standards and assessment system.* Washington, DC: Author.

Cipfl, J. J. (1984). *How to evaluate your school instructional program.* Urbana, IL: Educational Resources Information Center. (ERIC Document Reproduction Service No. ED 247647)

Dopyera, J. (1969). *Assessing the micro-environments of individual preschool children* (Contract No. OEO4120). Washington, DC: Office of Economic Opportunity Research Division.

Dopyera, J. (1974). Behavior-sanction-interaction observation schedule. In G. Boyer, A. Simon, & G. Karafin (Eds.), *Measures of maturation: An anthology of early childhood observation instruments* (Vol. 2, pp. 911–924).

Dopyera, J. E., & Lay, M. Z. (1975). Assessment of openness in program structures. In B. Spodek & H. J. Walberg (Eds.), *Studies in open education* (pp. 127–142). New York: Agathon.

Early Childhood and Literacy Development Committee of the International Reading Association. (1985). *Literacy development and pre-first grade reading instruction and recommendations for improvement.* Newark, DE: International Reading Association.

Fein, G. G., & Clark-Stewart, A. (1973). *Day care in context.* New York: John Wiley & Sons.

Goodlad, J. (1978, February). *Accountability: An alternative approach.* Third Annual DeGarmo Lecture, Society of Professors of Education, Pacific Oaks, CA.

Goodwin, W. L., & Driscoll, L. A. (1980). *Handbook for measurement and evaluation in early childhood education.* San Francisco: Jossey-Bass.

House, E. R., & Hutchins, E. J. (1979). Issues raised by the Follow Through evaluation. In L. G. Katz (Ed.), *Current topics in early childhood education* (Vol. 2, pp. 1–11). Norwood, NJ: Ablex.

Hymes, J. L. (1988). *Early childhood education: The year in review. A look at 1987.* Carmel, CA: Hacienda Press.

Johnson, J. E. (1987). Evaluation in early childhood education. In J. L. Roopnarine & J. E. Johnson (Eds.), *Approaches to early childhood education* (pp. 15–33). Columbus, OH: Merrill.

LaCrosse, E. R., Jr. (1970). Psychologist and teacher: Cooperation or conflict? *Young Children, 25,* 223–229.

Lay-Dopyera, M., & Dopyera, J. E. (1982). Evaluation as an administrative function. *Topics in Early Childhood Special Education, 2*(1), 84–93.

Lazar, I., Darlington, R. B., Murray, H., Royce, J., & Snipper, A. (1982). Lasting effects of early education. *Monographs of the Society for Research in Child Development, 47*(2–3, Serial No. 195).

Miller, L., & Dyer, J. L. (1975). Four preschool programs: Their dimensions and effects. *Monographs of the Society for Research in Child Development, 40*(5–6, Serial No. 162).

National Association of Early Childhood Specialists in State Departments of Education. (1987). *Unacceptable trends in kindergarten entry and placement.* Lincoln, NE: Author.

National Association for the Education of Young Children. (1982). *Early childhood teacher education guidelines.* Washington, DC: Author.

National Commission on Excellence in Education. (1983). *A nation at risk: The imperative for educational reform.* Washington, DC: U.S. Government Printing Office.

National Governors' Association. (1986). *Time for results: The governors' report on education.* Washington, DC: Author.

Neisworth, J., Dopyera, J. E., & Lay, M. Z. (1976). Comparing preschool programs. In K. F. Riegel & J. A. Meacham (Eds.), *The developing individual in a changing world: Vol. 2. Social and environmental issues* (pp. 39–77). The Hague: Mouton.

Sanders, D. P. (1981). Educational inquiry and developmental research. *Educational Researcher, 10*(3), 8–13.

Schon, D. A. (1983). *The reflective practitioner: How professionals think in action*. New York: Basic Books.

Schweinhart, L. J., Weikart, D. P., & Larner, M. B. (1986). Consequences of three preschool curriculum models through age 15. *Early Childhood Research Quarterly, 1*(1), 15–45.

Shelly, M., & Charlesworth, R. (1980). Expanded role in evaluation. In S. Kilmer (Ed.), *Advances in early education and day care: A research annual* (Vol. 1). Greenwich, CT: JAI Press.

Southern Association on Children Under Six. (1984). *Position statement on developmentally appropriate experiences for kindergarten*. Little Rock, AR: Author.

Stallings, J. (1975a). Implementation and child effects of teaching practices in Follow Through classrooms. *Monographs of the Society for Research in Child Development, 40*(7–8, Serial No. 163).

Stallings, J. (1975b). *Relationships between classroom instructional practices and child development*. Menlo Park, CA: Stanford Research Institute. (ERIC Document Reproduction Service No. Ed 106 297)

Wise, A. (1978). The hyper-rationalization of American education. *Educational Leadership, 35*, 354–361.

Zimiles, H. A. (1977). A radical and regressive solution to the problem of evaluation. In L. Katz (Ed.), *Current topics in early childhood education* (Vol. 1). Norwood, NJ: Ablex.

14

Achieving Model Early Childhood Programs Through Accreditation

SUE BREDEKAMP
Director of Professional Development,
National Association for the Education of Young Children–Washington, DC

The development of model early childhood programs and delivery systems undoubtedly will be affected in the future by the recent launching of a professionally sponsored, national voluntary accreditation system—the National Academy of Early Childhood Programs, a division of the National Association for the Education of Young Children (NAEYC). NAEYC is the nation's largest professional organization of early childhood educators. The purpose of the accreditation system is to improve the quality of group programs available for young children and their families and also to provide recognition for those programs that substantially comply with national standards for high quality. In this chapter, the accreditation system is described, then its theoretical base is presented, followed by a summary of relevant research and implications. The chapter concludes with recommendations for using Academy accreditation as a major delivery system for providing model programs for four year olds in public schools in North Carolina and throughout the country.

DESCRIPTION OF THE ACCREDITATION SYSTEM

The accreditation system is designed for any full-day or part-day group program serving children from birth through age five and/or school-age children in before- and after-school child care. Therefore, it applies to both publicly and privately sponsored programs for four year olds. The accreditation is based on NAEYC's Criteria for High Quality Early Childhood Programs (NAEYC, 1984a). The criteria were developed by NAEYC over a period of 3 years from a review of existing standards, from a review of the research literature on the effects on children of

301

various aspects of a group program, and from input of teachers, administrators, and other experts in early childhood education (Bredekamp, 1985). NAEYC's criteria address the areas of interactions among staff and children, curriculum, staff-parent interactions, staff qualifications and development, administration, staffing, physical environment, health and safety, nutrition and food service, and evaluation.

The accreditation process involves three steps: a self-study by the directors, teachers, and parents; an on-site validation visit by specially trained validators; and the accreditation decision by a commission of nationally recognized early childhood professionals. The system is structured in that the Academy provides the instruments to study the program (the Early Childhood Classroom Observation, Staff Question-naire, and Parent Questionnaire) and provides guidance on how to do the self-study (NAEYC, 1985b). The validation procedure is also structured. Validators use the same observation instrument program that personnel used to rate the quality of the individual classrooms, and validators must follow carefully prescribed procedures to ensure reliability of the system (Bredekamp, 1985; NAEYC, 1985b).

Program personnel decide to initiate the self-study process, and then they determine when they are ready for the validation visit. There are no time limits between self-study and validation. An individual program may take 2 months or 2 years to complete the self-study, or program personnel may determine that the self-study alone was sufficient to meet their needs for program evaluation and improvement. There is no obligation to submit to a site visit.

NAEYC's accreditation is similar to other accreditation systems, such as that of the National Council for the Accreditation of Teacher Education (NCATE) (1985). However, it differs slightly from other systems in that it uses a structured rating scale for reporting and validating results, called the Program Description (NAEYC, 1985a). The use of the Program Description was instituted to facilitate the reporting task for directors. Rather than describe the program's compliance with each criterion, the director rates compliance with each criterion using a three-point rating scale (with *3* meaning the criterion is fully met, *2* meaning the criterion is partially met, and *1* meaning the criterion is not met). When criteria are rated partially met or not met, the director explains what is not met or how the criterion is met through alternate means. Other accreditation systems are more open-ended and require that ad-ministrators and staff members prepare voluminous descriptions of their programs. The more structured approach to reporting used by the Academy is not only ad-vantageous to directors, but it has advantages for researchers, since it produces both quantitative and qualitative data for analysis.

THEORETICAL BASE

Accreditation is a somewhat new concept for the field of early childhood education. The regulation of early childhood programs has been almost exclusively a governmental function implemented through state and local licensing. The similarities and differences between licensing and accreditation have been well articulated (Morgan, 1982). A brief comparison of the two approaches to ensuring quality of delivery systems reveals the theoretical foundation of NAEYC's accreditation. Both systems have as an underlying goal the improvement of quality, but the strategies for achieving that goal are very different.

Licensing is mandatory; accreditation is voluntary. Programs must be licensed in order to operate legally. Participation in accreditation is voluntary, self-initiated, and self-paced.

Licensing standards are minimum requirements; accreditation standards define high quality. Licensing is designed to provide a baseline of protection for children in group care (Morgan, 1982). Accreditation, on the other hand, defines a ceiling of quality.

Licensing requires 100% compliance; accreditation is based on substantial compliance. Because licensing standards are often established as minimum standards, the assumption is that they must all be met at an equal level of compliance. Because accreditation standards define higher quality, compliance is determined on the basis of professional judgment, and 100% compliance is not required.

Licensing is governmentally regulated; accreditation is professionally sponsored. As government regulations, licensing standards are designed to protect the public. Accreditation systems are sponsored by professions to define and monitor the quality of services that are offered on behalf of the profession (Ade, 1982).

Licensing is operated at the state and local level, accreditation is national. The myriad of existing state and local licensing standards are enormously diverse (Johnson & Associates, 1982). NAEYC's criteria fill the void left by the absence of Federal Interagency Day Care Requirements, by providing a national standard for quality in early childhood programs. The assumption is that although local standards exist, the needs of children are the same regardless of geographic location, and in a highly mobile society such as ours, a national standard is important.

Licensing punishes noncompliance; accreditation recognizes and awards achievement. When operators fail to comply with licensing standards, they are in effect operating illegally and are subject to a number of sanctions, including revocation of their license. As a result, licensing standards and licensors often pose a threat to operators, who approach them defensively. Accreditation, on the other hand, promises reward and recognition to those who substantially comply. Achieving accreditation is the incentive for program personnel to become involved in a process of self-study/validation that will most likely result in program improvement.

The theoretical base for the accreditation system derives from the field of organizational development and change. One of the most important concepts in organizational theory is that for change to be real and lasting, it must be initiated from within the organization (Arends & Arends, 1977). Hence, the voluntary nature of the accreditation. Similarly, one of the most effective strategies for program improvement and change is a collaborative problem-solving approach (Berman & McLaughlin,

1975). This collaborative model is at the foundation of the Academy's system—involving administrators, teachers, and parents in a systematic study of the program's strengths and weaknesses.

The theoretical base for the accreditation system is obviously eclectic. At its core is the assumption that for substantive programmatic change to occur and last, it must be intrinsically motivated. Participants must voluntarily choose to participate; they must be internally motivated toward improving. At the same time, extrinsic incentive is offered—the potential for achieving accreditation, the reward for substantially complying with high standards.

RELATED RESEARCH

Having only been in operation since 1985, the Academy's system has not as yet been thoroughly evaluated. However, the research that has been done indicates that the system is a reliable and valid mechanism for identifying good-quality early childhood programs.

The most systematic study to date was the field test of the process (Bredekamp, 1985; NAEYC, 1984b). A thorough discussion of the results is beyond the scope of this chapter. However, a brief summary reveals important information about the system. The field test was conducted in thirty-one early childhood programs in four states: California, Florida, Minnesota, and Texas. During the field test, program personnel conducted limited self-studies and submitted to validation visits. Of the thirty-one programs, twenty-three had two independent validation visits by different validators on different days. The purpose of this study was to evaluate the reliability of the system over time and among different observers. Results revealed a high level of agreement between validation visits for each program ranging from 67% agreement to 94.9%. Percentages of agreement between validation visits for each criterion were also high, ranging from 48% to 100% agreement. Of 157 criteria, only 22 or 14% achieved percentages of agreement below 70% (Bredekamp, 1985).

Achieving reliable validation results is difficult considering the amount of change that takes place in early childhood programs over time, such as staff turnover, changing enrollments, and developmental differences in individual children. In light of the realities of the field, the results of this study were encouraging but will need to be replicated now that the system is fully operating.

An equally important research question concerns the validity of the accreditation system. Is it measuring that elusive element called program quality? Validity is a multidimensional concept. To date, two types of validity have been relatively well established for the accreditation system—content validity and construct validity. Future studies will need to address other forms of validity, such as discriminant validity. The content validity of the accreditation system is derived from its development—the research and expert opinion on which the system is based (Bredekamp, 1985). A measure of the construct validity was achieved by conducting a study of the internal consistency of the Early Childhood Classroom Observation, using data from the field test (Bredekamp, 1986). Results of factor analysis and item analysis of the Early Childhood Classroom Observation consistently demonstrated that the items on the instrument that correlated most highly with the total score and with each other related to curriculum and positive interactions among staff and children. Similarly, a study of the first ninety-five accreditation decisions (Bredekamp & Apple, 1986) reveals that commissioners place the greatest weight on the program's compliance with the criteria related to curriculum and interactions among staff and children, and that programs are most frequently deferred for noncompliance in those critical areas.

One of the most pressing research questions regarding the accreditation system is how well it achieves its goal of bringing about lasting change and improvement in programs. To date, only qualitative evidence exists. Directors whose programs participated in the field test reported that they had made measurable program improvements as a result of the process (NAEYC, 1984b). In fact, the level of agreement between validation visits during the field test was lowered due to the fact that directors continued to make changes in their programs between visits. In a nonrandom survey of directors of validated programs, similar reports of widespread program improvement were found (Carter, 1986). A systematic study using a pretest/posttest design is needed to fully answer the question regarding the impact of the system on program improvement. Such research will be difficult to conduct in the presence of many intervening variables, but is nevertheless needed to fully address the question of the system's validity.

APPLYING ACCREDITATION TO PUBLIC SCHOOLS

The application of the Academy's accreditation system to public schools raises several questions. Does this system apply to prekindergarten programs in public schools? What benefits accrue from public school involvement? And finally, what problems, if any, must be addressed?

Most certainly, the criteria apply to public school programs, particularly those that serve four year olds. The common denominator of programs that are involved in the accreditation system is that they enroll four year olds. All of the programs in the field test included this age group, and of 122 programs accredited during the first year of operation, 120 serve four year olds. In fact, the first 122 accredited programs include one public school kindergarten in New Mexico and one public school prekindergarten in Maryland.

There are several benefits of public school involvement in the accreditation process, primarily for the public schools but also for the early childhood profession. The most obvious benefit is that public school programs would be subject to nationally recognized standards of quality and monitoring. In most states, schools are not subject to the licensing standards of the state and must conform only to standards of the school system. Most states have had little previous experience serving children younger than age five. The developmental needs of this age group and the ways young children learn are quite different from those of older children. As a result, many standards for programs that serve older children do not apply or are inappropriate. Currently, a major concern of early childhood professionals is that programs are placing undue emphasis on instruction in narrowly defined academic skills. In effect, schools are applying teaching methods designed for older children to groups of younger children (Elkind, 1986; NAEYC, 1986). Because schools are traditionally involved in the business of education, there is a tendency to separate "teaching" or instructional time from other activity, primarily playful interaction, through which young children acquire knowledge. The tendency to see "education" as a separate function from "development" is one that has potentially negative long-term implications for our nation's young children. Research is beginning to show that rigidly implemented instructional programs do not help and may actually harm long-term socioemotional development (Schweinhart, Weikart, & Larner, 1986).

Using NAEYC's accreditation standards will help to educate both public school administrators and consumers about what is developmentally appropriate for young children and how they learn. Some of the items in the accreditation system that are frequently not met or that cause accreditation to be deferred are items specifically designed to address the issue of the degree to which the program is developmentally appropriate. For example, routine tasks are to be individualized as much as possible and used as learning experiences. Children are to be given choices throughout the day and given the opportunity to choose not to participate in a given activity at times. One of the most seemingly innocuous criteria requires that there be a balance of teacher-initiated and child-initiated activity and a similar balance between large- and small-group and individual activity. Programs that are rigidly academic find it difficult to fully meet these criteria, and these are criteria that weigh heavily in the commission's decision. In fact, the issue of the developmental appropriateness of program practice has become so critical that NAEYC recently adopted two position statements to help define and describe developmentally appropriate practice (NAEYC, 1986).

Therefore, using NAEYC's accreditation system as a delivery system for monitoring the quality of public school prekindergartens will help to ensure that such programs meet the nationally recognized standards of the early childhood profession. Holding the programs to these criteria will also raise public awareness about what is appropriate for young children. Many parents assume that young children learn the same way adults do and expect that schools should introduce paper-and-pencil tasks regardless of the age group served. Once the public is educated regarding appropriate instructional methods for four year olds, demands for inappropriate demonstrations that children are "really learning," through ditto sheets and direct reading instruction, should diminish.

A further benefit to public schools relates to the demands on the system for accountability. Public schools must account to legislators, administrators, and decision makers at various levels, as well as to taxpayers and consumers. Accreditation is a concept that is well understood by the general public. Most Americans would hesitate to enroll their child in an unaccredited college or university or to be treated in an unaccredited hospital. Achieving accreditation is one vehicle for demonstrating that a publicly funded educational program is accountable and provides a high-quality service.

Even if public school programs do not wish to seek accreditation by the Academy, the self-study materials are valuable tools for program evaluation. The instruments can easily be used by programs for staff performance evaluation or to obtain parent input. The self-study model is a useful tool for program evaluation and improvement regardless of whether the results are used only internally or for accreditation decisions.

What are the problems that might arise in adopting accreditation for the public schools? The primary concern is that if the public schools choose to participate in voluntary accreditation, it will most likely occur as a bureaucratic decision by administrators or supervisors for principals and teachers. As such, the system will lose the tremendous value of intrinsic motivation on which it is based. For program change to be real and lasting, it is best initiated from within. If classroom teachers see accreditation as a vehicle to help them achieve their goals for children and use it to communicate with principals and higher administrative officials, the potential for achieving goals is greater than if the initiative comes from above in the administrative hierarchy.

One of the serendipitous effects of involving public school programs in this process is that the system is designed to actively involve the program administrator in evaluation of classroom practice. During the self-study, the director and teachers observe and rate the quality of the classroom independently and then must compare their ratings and come to consensus. Since the "director" in a public school is usually the principal, the system has great potential for educating administrators, few of whom would have any early childhood training, about good-quality programs for young children.

Early childhood educators have expressed grave concerns about public school involvement in programs for four year olds (National Black Child Development Institute, 1986; Zigler, 1986). This concern is founded in the notion that public schools have not always been successful at serving the diverse population of elementary-age children and the unproven assumption that elementary methods of instruction will be imposed on young children. The opposite effect could potentially occur, in that introduction of younger children and greater numbers of trained early childhood educators into the public schools could influence the teaching in the kindergarten and primary grades—the trickle-up theory, so to speak. Unfortunately, recent trends in kindergarten curriculum do not support such an eventuality. However, if prekindergarten programs in public schools were subject to national standards of accreditation by the early childhood profession, influence would certainly be increased. The criteria are equally applicable to public school kindergartens, and the need to set standards for those programs may be even more critical at this point in time.

SUMMARY

This brief description of NAEYC's accreditation system can only begin to describe its potential for improving the quality of group programs for young children. In many ways, the public schools are a natural vehicle for serving young children. However, caution must be used in establishing programs. If the quantity of programs for four year olds increases without attention to the quality of service, more harm may be done. A tested vehicle already exists for ensuring model programs and delivery systems—the accreditation system of the National Academy of Early Childhood Programs. It is now up to the schools to initiate a collaborative relationship with the early childhood profession toward the goal of providing high-quality programs for all four year olds and their families.

REFERENCES

Ade, W. (1982). Professionalization and its implications for the field of early childhood education. *Young Children, 37*(3), 25–32.

Arends, R. I., & Arends, J. H. (1977). *Systems change strategies in educational settings*. New York: Human Sciences Press.

Berman, P., & McLaughlin, M. W. (1975). *Federal programs supporting educational change: Vol. 4. Findings in review*. Santa Monica, CA: Rand.

Bredekamp, S. (1986). The reliability and validity of the early childhood classroom observation scale for accrediting early childhood programs. *Early Childhood Quarterly Review, 1*, 103–118.

Bredekamp, S., & Apple, P. L. (1986). How early childhood programs get accredited: An analysis of accreditation decisions. *Young Children, 42*(1), 34–39.

Bredekamp, V. S. (1985). *The reliability of the instruments and procedures of a national accreditation system for early childhood programs*. Unpublished doctoral dissertation, University of Maryland, College Park.

Carter, M. (1986). NAEYC's center accreditation project: What's it like in real life? *Child Care Information Exchange, 49*, 38–41.

Elkind, D. (1986). Formal education and early childhood education: An essential difference. *Phi Delta Kappan, 4*, 631–636.

Johnson, L., & Associates. (1982). *Comparative licensing study: Profiles of state day care licensing requirements*. Washington, DC: U.S. Department of Health and Human Services.

Morgan, G. (1982). Regulating early childhood programs in the eighties. In B. Spodek (Ed.), *Handbook of research in early childhood education* (pp. 375–398). New York: Free Press.

National Association for the Education of Young Children. (1984a). *Accreditation criteria and procedures of the National Academy of Early Childhood Programs*. Washington, DC: Author.

National Association for the Education of Young Children. (1984b). NAEYC field tests accreditation system. *Young Children, 40*(2), 40–46.

National Association for the Education of Young Children. (1985a). *Early childhood program description*. Washington, DC: Author.

National Association for the Education of Young Children. (1985b). *Guide to accreditation by the National Academy of Early Childhood Programs*. Washington, DC: Author.

National Association for the Education of Young Children. (1986). NAEYC position statement on developmentally appropriate practice in early childhood programs serving children from birth to age 8. *Young Children, 41*(1), 3–19.

National Black Child Development Institute. (1986). *Child care in the public schools: Incubator for inequality*. Washington, DC: Author.

National Council for the Accreditation of Teacher Education. (1985). *Standards for the accreditation of teacher education*. Washington, DC: Author.

Schweinhart, L., Weikart, D., & Larner, M. (1986). Consequences of three curriculum models through age 15. *Early Childhood Research Quarterly, 1*, 15–46.

Zigler, Edward. (1986). Do four-year-olds belong in kindergarten? *Working Parents, 8*, 8–10.

15

Assessing Young Children

CAROL SEEFELDT
University of Maryland

Study your children for assuredly you do not know them," wrote Jacques Rousseau in 1762 (Rousseau, 1947). And we have heeded Rousseau's advice. Motivated by the goal of uncovering the mystery of children's thinking, and truly understanding their growth, development, and learning, we have studied children.

Curiosity about the child's mind, "the width and depth of the chasm which yawned between the infantile and adult mind" (Hall, 1907, p. 15), led G. S. Hall to study children and their childhood. He argued that any real advance in educational theory or practice would stem only from an ever clearer, more precise understanding of childhood itself. He believed that childhood, with "its different stages of development," would become the norm for all the method and manner of teaching. Through the use of questionnaires, anecdotal records, and observations, Hall (1907) believed he had uncovered *The Contents of Children's Minds*.

Intrigue with children and their thinking led Piaget to his life's work. In his autobiographical sketch, Piaget emphasized the importance of the time he spent in 1919 at the school for boys in rue Grange-aux-Belles (Murchinson, 1952). It was here that, in carrying out Theodore Simon's suggestions, he standardized the French version of tests of reasoning by Cyril Burt. This task started Piaget on his lifelong study of the development of children's thinking.

Piaget interviewed children at length. "The children did not complain. They found this 'M'sieu' amusing. With him, one was not bored at all. Instead of simply noting the responses given by the children to the test items, the young Swiss biologist was interested in the how and the why of the answers. What had been at the outset nothing but a boring and annoying test situation became a real dialogue with

311

suggestions, and counter suggestions, an argument developed, a deepening of the child's thought, a new method of interrogating children was born" (Gruber & Voneche, 1977, p. 53). Piaget's intrigue with the study of children changed the way the world thinks about them and their childhood.

At around the same time, for quite a different reason, and for a very different purpose, Thorndike was also studying children's minds. To Thorndike, it wasn't the content of children's minds that was of interest, but rather the way the total organism responds to its environment. The role of the educator, Thorndike believed, was to build sequences of ideas that would form a right set of mental habits. The laws of learning—those of readiness, exercise, and effect—could be applied to structure the mind of the child. For young children, the law of effect was of special interest. The proper instincts of young children, such as their natural curiosity, could be strengthened through the provision of satisfying effects. To eliminate or weaken the undesirable instincts of young children, one would make certain that these would be followed by dissatisfying effects.

Thorndike taught in a school of education. In the business of training teachers, he was constantly faced with the challenge of using psychology to solve real problems of education (Hilgard & Bower, 1981). Being an empiricist, he championed the ideas of educational measurement and the statement of clear educational goals. Thorndike believed that educational methods should be regulated "according to specific practices" (Hilgard & Bower, 1981, p. 47). Specificity of desired outcomes, control of the educational process, through the law of effect, and then frequent testing to measure the effect were advocated.

IDIOGRAPHIC AND NOMOTHETIC ASSESSMENT

Driven by the same desire to study children, to understand them, and to improve and shape their early care and education, today's early childhood educators study children by measuring and assessing their growth, development, and learning. As in the past, very different philosophies and theories direct this assessment.

Idiographic Assessment

One group of educators endorse the philosophy of the rationalists. These view children as goal-seeking, thinking individuals, who construct their own knowledge. Learning is thus internal and individual. Each infant and child is an absolutely unique phenomenon. While all infants and children are alike in many respects, no one is like another.

To make sense of the individual, idiographic methods of assessment are believed most suitable. With intensity, each individual is studied. Each child is believed a complex organism, stemming from both biological and cultural factors, and each functions within a social setting. Thus, not only is the individual studied, but the setting, situation, and interactions between the child and others are studied as well.

Idiographic methods of assessment focus on the individual. Normative information, such as standardized test scores, is considered useful only as it promotes greater insight and understanding of the individual or the situation. To the rationalist, a test score alone is rather meaningless, even when converted to a percentile rank or standardized score. Normative data, indicating the degree to which a child departs from the average, does not add much information about a specific child. It doesn't tell how the child handles frustrations, solves problems, relates with others, or does anything else. Any given test, standardized score, or percentile rank cannot be understood without understanding the test, the test items, and the norms to which the score or percentile rank refers. "If a score is used to distort what a child is or what a child can do, then it is the result of blind and unwarranted faith in the probity and usefulness of test scores" (Burns, 1979, p. 27).

Through idiographic assessment, insight and understanding of children grow. As insight and understanding grow, so does artistry (Almy, 1975). Through this insight, the optimum educational environment is planned and arranged.

Various Methods

Idiographic techniques of assessment vary, but the goal of understanding the growth, learning, and development of children in order to foster their health, education, and welfare and enable each to develop their full potential does not. Idiographic methods include observations, case studies, interviews, and other methods that focus on the individual.

Observations.   Observing is probably the oldest, most frequently used, and most rewarding method of assessing children, their growth, development, and learning. Simply observing children as they play, interact with others and their environment, leads to greater knowledge and understanding of them. Teachers, especially, find they can identify an individual child's unique strengths and weaknesses through observation. The National Association for the Education of Young Children calls for an increase in the use of systematic observation of student performance (Bredekamp & Shepard, 1989). By focusing observations on an individual child, insights into that child's pattern of response, perceptions of self and others, and thoughts and feelings develop. A general understanding of not only the child being observed, but of all children is the result.

Observing, a rewarding tool of assessment, also fits the nature of young children. As Snow and Ferguson (1977) pointed out, the methods of assessment must adapt to the phenomenon being studied, rather than to try to force the phenomenon to adapt to the assessment. Young children, who have a limited repertoire of behaviors that can be assessed, may best be studied through observation. In fact, to assess young children, who are unable to express themselves fully with words, with any method other than direct observation may not be possible. Further, young children reveal themselves through their behaviors. Unlike older children and adults, the young are incapable of hiding their feelings, ideas, or emotions with socially approved behaviors, so observing them often yields accurate information.

Observing is far from a singular assessment technique. There are numerous observational techniques and methods possible. Fassnacht (1982) lists nineteen terms to describe different types of observations and any number of systems for recording and storing observations, as well as analyzing the data.

The purpose of the observation directs the choice of methods and types of observation used. "The differing purposes lead to differences in strategies for observation, levels of systematization, and levels of formality. These factors lead to differences in design and implementation" (Evertson & Green, 1986, p. 163). Teachers may use informal and naturalistic methods of observations to better understand children. They will resist establishing preset categories (Genishi, 1983), coding systems, or prior decisions about recording behaviors and elect to record behaviors as they occur with a running narrative. Barker and Wright's classic, *One Boy's Day* (1951), is an example of a natural, unstructured, observation.

At times, naturalistic observations are used in combination with a structured environment. Duckworth's (1978) African Primary Science Project is an example. She observed what children did when they were brought into a room filled with the typical materials of a "hands-on" science program.

Researchers, studying children's learning under differing conditions, select more structured systems of observation. Event sampling, time sampling, and the use of rating scales or specimen description are more structured quantitative methods of observations. These usually follow a predetermined coding system or categorization of behaviors. Event sampling observes naturally occurring behaviors as they occur. Phinney, Feshbach and Farver (1986) used event sampling to observe children's response to peer crying. Each time a child cried, narrative descriptions of the episodes were coded as to the cause of crying, teacher and peer response, and context.

Highly sophisticated observations are possible with current technology. Through the use of technology, observations can gain precision. With the use of video, audiotapes, and computer technology, a permanent record of behaviors can be made. The permanence of the observation makes possible multiple analyses and approaches to data analysis. With the use of technology, units and categories of behaviors can be predetermined and measured, and the tapes can be replayed.

Despite its usefulness in understanding children, observing is not without limitation. Observer bias, sampling problems, and the continual issues of reliability and validity plague data obtained through observation. Observer bias affects both the behaviors selected for observations and the interpretation given the behaviors. The use of technology and closed and other structured systems of observation limit observer bias. Yet the judgment of the observers, their initial impressions, and their failure to acknowledge their own biases can become sources of error in observational data (Evertson & Green, 1986).

The issues of what is sampled, when, and where; when sampling decisions are made; and timing in sampling are related to the issues of the stability and validity of observations. The way one samples within any given observational study is related to the questions asked and the framework guiding the observations. The question is, "Does the sample provide a high degree of confidence that reality has been represented validly?" (Evertson & Green, 1986, p. 182)

As a field, early childhood education is a long way from being able to use observations of children as a means of accountability. The development of systematic yet open frameworks for observing individual children's growth, development, and learning has yet to be perfected.

Additionally, we are far from defining what children do learn, how they learn it, and what they are to learn in a preschool setting. A taxonomy of simple descriptions of children's development of increasingly complex thinking, problem solving, social skills, and attitudes may be necessary to develop in order to focus observations and describe children's learning and growth.

Case studies.   Decades old, the case study is defined as the intensive analysis of a single object of social inquiry (Stake, 1978). The investigator becomes immersed in the dynamics of a single subject and tries to uncover insights that might be missed with more superficial methods. Through systematic investigation, the individual is studied. This investigation can include the use of observations, standardized tests, interviews, and other evidence collected in order to know the individual. Informal, naturalistic methods of observing can also be used as the source of data in a case study, with Virginia Axline's classic, *Dibs: In Search of Self* (1964), being a prime example.

In a case study, every source of data is used to gain a better understanding of the individual child. Personal documents, interviews, objective test data, and projective responses are included in order to assess a child or evaluate learning, growth, and development. Prescott, in 1957, listed seven sources for obtaining anecdotal information:

1. Observing the child in action in the classroom, on the playground, and elsewhere in and around the school
2. Studying the child's accumulating records
3. Making visits to the child's home
4. Observing the child's life space and recording descriptions of it and the things going on in it
5. Conferring with colleagues who have taught the child in the past
6. Collecting and examining samples of the child's work
7. Conversing with the child individually and informally.

No hypotheses direct the collection of evidence. Rather than being guided by preconceived questions or hypotheses, teachers or researchers conducting case studies collect whatever information is available. Standardized test scores can be included in this information, but these are not likely to be unique to the subject, and therefore not of high interest. Once researchers or teachers believe they know a child through the accumulation of evidence, "the daring exercise in constructing a theory to fit the individual" (Cronbach, 1988, p. 132) takes place. Only after the collected evidence has been reviewed and analyzed are hypotheses advanced.

Case studies have also been used nomothetically, as a method for uncovering laws that govern human behavior. In the search for laws of human behavior, Darwin (1877) completed a case study of his son, William. Although Darwin's conclusions that the infant's behavior was a living record of our species' evolutionary history were discredited around the turn of the century, his belief that the study of children was a valid part of understanding humans continued to influence the field of psychology.

Piaget's observations of his own three children could be considered another type of case study. Following his three children as they grew, observing their actions and reactions to the environment at different ages, Piaget collected new information each year on children's intellectual growth and advanced new hypotheses. In *The Psychology of Intelligence* (1950), Piaget reported the results of his study of the development of intelligence.

The case study approach can be a valuable method of assessing children. Keeping anecdotal records over a school year, collecting paintings, scribbles, and other work, and analyzing the child's interactions with others offer rich insights into a single child's development and learning. The approach itself matches the nature of young children. Because there are no preconceived hypotheses, the investigator can be flexible and is able to "adopt the methods to the task of discovery rather than to impose methods that may prevent the latter" (Biddle & Anderson, 1986, p. 238).

Case studies are luxurious. They are rich, elegant, enjoyable, and sumptuous accounts of one child's life. But as something luxurious, they are costly, expensive, and grand. It's a rare person who has all the theoretical sophistication, the prior knowledge and understanding of children's growth and development, the insight, and the artistic talent required to complete a useful case study.

Even if one had the luxury and ability to immerse oneself in the case study of each child over a year, or throughout the primary school years, the case study alone is not complete for the assessment of young children. Biddle and Anderson (1986) believe the case study could be useful in the generation of hypotheses or theories about an individual child, yet it has limitations. The case study is a poor one "for testing theory, since the data obtained by the researcher were not gathered systematically and do not represent any population of events to which the researcher may wish to generalize" (p. 238).

Then, too, Popham (1988) describes the case study as more of a historical work than a respectable research method. With no reliability of sampling behaviors, products, or interviews, nor any validity, the meaning of the observations, of the entire case study, is highly questionable.

Interviews. Face to face, one on one, the clinical interview is widely used and popular with adults. Applicants for professional schools, colleges, and universities are routinely interviewed, as are candidates for business positions. The interview, however, can be highly useful as a tool for the assessment of young children.

Piaget perfected the technique with children and demonstrated the power of an interview to uncover children's thought processes. Entering into a dialogue with children, the amusing Monsieu Piaget found the interview a simple, direct, and fruitful method of assessment, one that was "a long step from the hodgepodge of traditional testing" (Gruber & Voneche, 1977, p. 53).

The interview has a number of virtues that make it ideal for use with young children. It is a flexible technique. The interviewer can go over some questions, probe others more intently, and direct and adapt the interview to obtain as much information as possible. Response rate is high. When the interviewer sees a child is confused about a question, or resistant, the question can be rephrased or reworded to elicit a response. The interview can motivate children to answer or to give more complete answers.

Areas of children's growth and learning that could not be examined by any other means can be explored through an interview. Piaget's ingenious methods, his astute questioning and structured tasks, provide powerful models for the use of interviews with children. Given the richness of the interview, and its potential for assessing young children, it is puzzling as to why the technique has not yet been perfected for wide use in the field of early childhood education and care.

Cazden (1983) noted that interviewing students is much less common than interviewing teachers. The most extensive interview of pupils, according to Cazden, is Morine-Dershimer and Tenenberg's (1981) study of classroom discourse. In this study, upper-grade pupils were shown videotapes of a lesson in which they had participated and were individually asked to report on what other students said.

Interviews can take any number of forms. They can range from unstructured to highly structured, and the questions asked can be open or closed. As with observing, the purpose of the interview determines the selection of method. A structured interview, with closed questions, will yield responses that are readily scored and interpreted. The results of unstructured interviews, with open-ended questions, though more flexible and offering greater potential for rich, individual response, are more difficult to analyze and interpret.

Darrow (1964), in *Research: Children's Concepts*, describes open-end interview techniques. She suggests that listening to what children say, watching what they do, and being willing to poke and pry behind their words and deeds are necessary (p. 1). Trying to get children to tell all they know about something, without any guiding cues and without questions with implied answers, she suggests asking children open-ended questions: What can you tell us about . . .? What can you draw or write about . . .? What can you do to show us about . . .?

As Piaget, Darrow was interested in the analysis of children's errors revealed during the interview. She believed a deeper understanding of children's thinking would result from the analysis of children's errors for consistency of response, patterns, and logic. Probing children's responses by asking additional questions, such as "How did they get their answer?" "Why did they say what they did?" and "What might happen if they did that?" resulted in still more knowledge of children's ideas.

Open-ended questions have been used to explore older children's knowledge. Rogers and Stevenson (1988) used free association to examine students' understanding of a unit on Robert Frost. The first question was "What can you tell me about the Frost unit?" If the student was hesitant, additional questions, such as "What went well for you?" and "What did you enjoy the most?" were posed. These questions, along with asking for concrete examples of specific learnings and opinions, yielded information sufficient to evaluate the unit.

Jantz and Seefeldt (1976) found this technique useful in their studies of children's attitudes toward the elderly. Asking children to tell all they know about old people, Jantz and Seefeldt found that children's responses, for the most part, were easily categorized into three types. It was found that the results of this one question provided the same type and amount of information about children's attitudes and concepts of age and the elderly as did the use of a Semantic Differential and a standardized picture sort task.

Anderson and Smith (1986) used a combination of interviews and drawings to successfully evaluate children's science concepts. They asked children to draw pictures of how the sun helps people see a tree, and to use directional arrows and words as needed to help them complete their drawings. Others have asked children to draw pictures following some experience, as a means of evaluating that experience. In order to evaluate the effects of children's visits to old people in nursing homes, children have been asked to draw pictures of old people before and after these visits (Seefeldt, 1987). In designing a fire safety unit, children were also asked to draw pictures of what they would do in specific fire situations (Seefeldt, 1988).

Performance tasks offer an alternative interview model. These have been used for many years with adults. The skills of adolescents are assessed with performance tasks in high school, and to assess the effectiveness of job training, adults are asked to perform tasks. Asking students to perform a specific task could be used diagnostically so evaluating children could facilitate their learning; or summatively so instruction could move them from one educational level to another; or formatively so program quality or development could be improved.

Performance tasks can take place in the actual or real-world setting. If one is interested in examining children's communication skills, then assessment logically takes place in a situation in which they have an opportunity to demonstrate their skills. If one is interested in assessing children's competence with mathematical skills, then asking children to play a math game and interviewing them about their actions makes sense.

Unstructured, unstandardized, and highly dependent upon the skills of the interviewer, the interview shares the same strengths and weaknesses of observations and case studies. Reliability and validity, and the subjectivity of the interview technique itself, limit the usefulness of the technique for assessing children.

Nomothetic Assessment

Another group of educators is guided by the theories of the empiricists. As Thorndike, this group views children as passive and learning as something that occurs through contiguous association of events and ideas. The acquisition of habits, through reinforcement or trial and error, rather than insightful problem solving, accounts for learning and development. Specificity is necessary in order to come to know the child. Without specificity, Thorndike (1913) maintained, one would not be able to do anything.

To the empiricists, idiographic methods are imprecise, personal, and too general to be of any use. Nomothetic methods—the search for general laws that govern human growth, learning, and behavior—are believed better suited to the study of young children. The discovery of "general laws governing the relationships between particular conditions of stimulation and associated behavioral responses" (Stern, 1963, p. 409) would lead to understanding children's learning, growth, and development. With knowledge of general laws, children's care and education could be controlled and improvements made.

As with idiographic assessment, the purpose of nomothetic methods is to know the individual. But to know the individual means to be able to use knowledge of general laws to describe the individual accurately and fully. More importantly, to be able to describe the individual completely is to be able to predict and control how the individual will behave in any given situation. These general laws are understood to be normative in character, derived from the study of representative samples or cases, and applicable to the individual insofar as the individual represents an instance of the general case (Stern, 1963).

The mathematical elegance of the normal curve, in which relationships are predictable and exact, provides a frame of reference for the desired specificity. The symmetry and exactness of the normal curve allow for the quantification of principles and laws and the use of numbers to express psychological qualities. With the normal curve, one can identify how an individual deviates from the standard. Without normative standards derived from the statistical analysis of group data, it would be impossible to make meaningful evaluations about an individual case.

If you want to know more about how an individual child thinks, feels, acts, and reacts in different situations, and under differing educational experiences, then idiographic methods of study are of value. Observation, case studies, and interview techniques will produce knowledge "for its own sake" (Popham, 1988, p. 77). While many find knowledge of individuals useful, others find they can ill afford the luxury of engaging in "inquiry merely for the sake of better understanding the relationships among educationally relevant variables" (Popham, 1988, p. 77).

Various Methods

Nomothetic methods require the norms of standardized testing. Intelligence testing, standardized achievement tests, and the procedures of diagnosis and screening are examples of nomothetic techniques.

Intelligence tests. For the psychologists who first administered intelligence tests in the early 1900s, intelligence was a concrete, invariant entity that could be measured with accuracy, just as you could measure anything, say a bar of steel (Yerkes & Foster, 1923). Boring's statement (1923) that intelligence was what the intelligence tests measure, rather than being facetious, reflected how psychologists in the early 1900s defined intelligence.

As the time, psychologists embraced the idea of assessing intelligence. G. S. Hall, anxious to move psychology from philosophy into a scientifically experimental direction, was impressed with the idea of scientifically measuring intelligence through testing. He confidently maintained that the Binet-Simon intelligence test, brought to the United States from Europe in 1908 by Goddard, was amazingly accurate and would be very easily applied in all settings.

Hall's confidence in the Binet-Simon to accurately assess intelligence stemmed from a number of scientific studies. One was the study of children at the Vineland, New Jersey, Training School for Feeble-Minded Boys and Girls in 1911, in which the test did classify the Vineland pupils in a way consistent with the staff's experience of them. In another study of 2,000 children, Goddard noted that he could accurately classify "idiots" from "imbeciles" or "morons" (Kevles, 1984b). And in 1917, Goddard reported the results of the Binet-Simon administered to a small group of immigrants at Ellis Island. He found that two out of five of those who had arrived in steerage were in fact, "feeble-minded." Goddard declared that Alpine and Mediterranean "races" were "indeed intellectually inferior to the representatives of the Nordic race" (Kevles, 1984b, p. 79).

For others, the idea that there was a general ability called intelligence, and that it could be measured accurately with intelligence tests, was absurd. Lippmann in 1922 wrote in *The New Republic* that intelligence tests had "no more scientific foundation than a hundred other fads, vitamins and glands and amateur psychoanalysis and correspondence courses in will power, and it will pass with them into that limbo where phrenology and palmistry and characterology and the other Babu sciences are to be found" (Kevles, 1984a, p. 105). Lippmann insisted that "intelligence is not an abstraction like length and weight; it is an exceedingly complicated notion which nobody has yet succeeded in defining" (p. 105). Carl Campbell Brigham at Princeton in 1923 wrote that to say the Binet-Simon measures something called general intelligence was to indulge in "psychophrenology" (Kevles, 1984a, p. 105).

Nevertheless, the Binet test, and the measurement of intelligence, did not prove to be a fad. Today, the argument is not whether or not intelligence exists and can be measured, but rather whether intelligence is a global, general capacity for acquiring knowledge, reasoning, and problem solving, or if it is composed of many separate mental abilities that operate more or less independently. The "lumpers," beginning with Spearman (1927), believe that even though some people may be more facile with mathematics, for instance, it doesn't really matter, because all tests require a common factor of general intelligence. Binet and Simon, as well, believed intelligence was a general faculty. "To judge well, to comprehend well, and reason well, these are the essential activities of intelligence" (Binet & Simon, 1905, p. 191).

On the other hand, "splitters" see intelligence as being composed of many separate mental abilities that operate more or less independently. Thurston (1938) identified seven factors he believed made up intelligence, and Guilford and Hoepfner's taxonomy (1971) listed 120 separate mental abilities.

Sternberg (1986) presents a triarchic theory of intelligence, relating intelligence to the internal world of the individual, specifying the mental mechanisms that (1) lead to more intelligent or less intelligent behavior; (2) indicate at what point in a person's experience with handling tasks or situations intelligence is most critically involved; and (3) relate intelligence to the external world of the individual—environmental adaptation, environmental selection, and environmental shaping.

In many ways, disagreements over the nature of intelligence, or even if it exists and can be measured, have little to do with the field of early childhood. To attempt to measure the intelligence of an infant or a young child, whether intelligence is viewed as a general ability or specific abilities, seems ludicrous. Infants, who organize their world without a store of memories, with no fund of information with which to think, who construct knowledge through the organization and elaboration of simple reflexes, are poor subjects for intelligence testing regardless of theoretical approach.

Yet the search for infant intelligence, and how to measure it, is as old as the debate on whether intelligence exists and can be measured. In the 1920s, Arnold Gesell pioneered the work in measuring the mental abilities of infants. He and his coworkers at Yale listed 915 items that were used to appraise the mental, motor, and social development of infants between the ages of 3 and 30 months.

Nancy Bayley (1969) and her colleagues at the Berkeley Growth Study developed the Bayley Scales of Infant Development over 30 years ago. These, believed the most carefully researched measures of infant intelligence, are divided into three sections: (1) the Mental Scale; (2) the Motor Scale; and (3) the Infant Behavior Profile. The Mental Scale assesses perception, memory, learning, and problem solving; vocalization and response to verbal instructions; and early signs of ability to generalize and classify.

Even though the Bayley Scales and other tests of infant intelligence, such as the Cattel and the Brazelton Neonatal Behavioral Assessment Scale, are widely used and have been shown to be correlated with later intellectual functioning (Broman, Nichols, & Kennedy, 1975), the attempt to measure infant intelligence continues to seem strangely inappropriate. Some suggest that it is inappropriate to try to assess the intelligence of infants with the same approach used to assess the intelligence of ten, twenty, or thirty year olds (Siegler & Richards, 1982). What it means to be intelligent at 3 months isn't the same as what it means at 30 years.

Others point to the lack of a pool of common experiences on which to base test items as a complicating factor in the measurement of infant intelligence (Anastasi, 1976), while the lack of reliability of infant intelligence tests is criticized by still others (Thorndike & Hagen, 1977).

The measurement of intelligence in children 2 years old and older isn't any less problematic. Although those children have a greater repertoire of behaviors that can be assessed, and any number of intelligent tests are available, issues remain.

The most widely used measure for children ages two through eight, the Stanford-Binet, fourth edition, is itself controversial. The Stanford-Binet, which is individually administered and asks preschool children to identify parts of the body on a paper doll, build a tower with blocks, recognize objects in terms of their functions, string beads, and copy simple geometric designs, is interesting to children.

Examiners, too, find administration of the Binet interesting. As Piaget, they find administering the tasks to young children revealing. Children's wrong answers, the way they try to solve problems, and their spontaneous comments all add to a clearer understanding of children's thought processes.

Coming to know more about a child through administration of the Binet is not the issue. The issues stem from the use to which the scores are put, and from the abstract, verbal nature of the test. As in the early 1900s, the scores on a Binet are believed to be an accurate index of intelligence and are interpreted as a fixed, precise, and enduring entity. Perhaps the terms *moron* and *imbecile* are no longer used, yet children are still labeled on the basis of their scores on the Binet as either bright or stupid, gifted or slow.

The verbal nature of the test, although somewhat reduced in the fourth edition, continues to penalize children whose background is not middle class. Children from lower-income homes, minorities, and those without fluency with English as their first language are often those who find themselves either excluded from educational programs or placed in "special" differentiated programs on the basis of their scores on the Binet.

Stern, in the 1930s, recognized that the Binet was being used to discriminate between groups of children (1938). He cautioned that to "base any pedagogical estimate upon the IQ alone for practical purposes (e.g., for assignment to opportunity classes), is indefensible" (pp. 310–311).

The National Association for the Education of Young Children (NAEYC) (1988) states that language and cultural variations of children are ignored too frequently in intelligence testing. With young children, language and culture are essential aspects of their learning and development. Any test in English given to a nonnative English speaker, or children who speak a dialect of English, is first and foremost a language test, regardless of its intent.

Other measures of preschool intelligence are available. The Wechsler Preschool and Primary Scale of Intelligence, for children ages 4 to 6½ is based on the concept that intelligence consists of separate skills and abilities. Tests based on Piagetian theories and tasks have been developed (Goldschmid & Bentler, 1968; Laurendeau & Pinard, 1970). Nevertheless, as these and other measures of intelligence gain their validity in correlation with the Binet, the question of what intelligence is, and how it is measured, becomes mute. To paraphrase Boring, intelligence is what the Binet intelligence test measures.

Achievement tests. Intelligence tests purport to assess a child's ability; achievement tests assess what a child has been taught or has learned. "Achievement suggests a deed in the real world, a contribution one makes to society, such as designing a bridge, composing a symphony, or formulating a theory of learning. So called achievement tests actually assess what a person has learned in a given area of instruction. The individual's test performance is a sample of what he or she is able to do at the time" (Anastasi, 1980, p. 3).

Standardized achievement tests do have a place in preschools and the early grades. Fundamental to any educational program is the need to account for education and to assess each child's progress and achievement. Standardized tests enable schools to do this. They are designed to assess the progress a child has made, to determine the degree to which a child has acquired information or skills taught, as a child's readiness for new learning.

Unlike idiographic techniques, standardized tests of achievement are believed to have precision. With an achievement test, the standing of an individual child may be determined by reference to the norms of the tests. Scores can be converted to percentiles, or standard scores of a child on tests, and compared to establish a relative level of achievement, or the converted scores may be compared with similar scores from aptitude tests to see whether achievement is consistent with what would be expected.

Comparison is possible with standardized achievement tests. The achievement of an individual or group can be compared with others, or achievement in different skills or subject areas can be compared. The progress of individual children or children in different programs or schools, using the common base of an achievement test, can be compared. Children's progress, over time, can also be compared.

There is a plethora of standardized achievement tests designed for the preschool/primary child. Astonishing in their abundance, achievement tests are available in every variety, for every category, and for any purpose. "There are formal tests, informal tests, verbal tests, personality tests, perceptual motor tests—the categories of tests, and the numbers of tests within each category, are mind boggling" (Burns, 1979, p. 12). Popular preschool measures include the Metropolitan Readiness Test, the Cooperative Preschool Inventory, Tests of Basic Experiences, the Cognitive Skills Assessment Battery, and others describing a child's current level of skill achievement or preacademic preparedness.

Even though abundant and unique, all standardized achievement tests share common characteristics. They all have standardized materials, such as forms, instructions, and scoring procedures. They usually have a manual that contains the statistical data to support the test. And usually they are commercial, designed to be marketed and sold and to be profitable.

Most importantly, however, standardized achievement tests are normed. These norms are critical, for individual children's scores on the tests will be interpreted in comparison with them. If the child taking the achievement test is not like those of the norming sample, then the test score will make little sense.

Examples of inadequate and inappropriate norming populations abound. The Gesell Preschool Test was normed 20 years ago on a sample of fifty boys and fifty girls per age level who were white and came from Connecticut (Bredekamp & Shepard,

1989). Thus the only children for whom this test might provide useful information are white children from Connecticut. The test further reports no standard deviation of scores. Without that, it is not possible to tell anything about a child's performance.

National norms also presume that "all children, in all schools, in all parts of the country are presented with the same knowledge, information, and skills which are measured by one of these 'national' achievement tests" (Burns, 1979, p. 61). Thus normed achievement tests rarely reflect what has been taught and learned in any individual class, or by any specific group of children. Normed achievement tests, then, are not flexible tools. They cannot be adapted to special current needs, local emphasis, or a particular course of study.

Rather than the assessment measure being selected to assess what a group of children have been taught, instruction often becomes based on what the standardized test measures. Thus the standardized test determines the curriculum. When this happens, the curriculum is defined as the specific academic skills assessed by the standardized test. Thorndike's theories of the law of exercise and effect are employed to shape children's achievement, and the once cognitively rich early childhood curriculum disappears.

Reliability and validity are other issues to be considered. Messick (1989, p. 5) states that the issue of validity is at the core of issues surrounding tests: "To what degree—if at all—on the basis of evidence and rationale, should the test scores be interpreted and used in the manner proposed?" He asks the following:

- What balance of evidence supports the interpretation or meaning of the scores?
- What evidence undergirds not only score meaning, but also the relevance of the scores to the particular purpose and the utility of the scores in the applied setting?
- What rationale makes credible the value implications of the score interpretation and any associational worth of the test in terms of its intended and unintended consequences?

The best protection against invalid achievement tests and inappropriate score interpretations of tests is to limit and guard against the adverse consequences of tests. Cronbach (1988, p. 3) claims that "the bottom line is that validators have an obligation to review whether a practice has appropriate consequences for individuals and institutions, and especially to guard against adverse consequences. You may prefer to exclude reflection on consequences from meanings of the word validation, but you cannot deny the obligation." Practitioners also have an obligation to recognize that a child's score on any standardized measure of achievement is just that—only a score. It alone cannot be the basis of decisions about a child's educational placement, retention, or promotion. "Use valid standardized tests as one of many sources of information" (Bredekamp & Shepard, 1989, p. 22).

Diagnosis and screening. Just as schools have the right and responsibility to assess young children's achievement, so they are responsible for identifying potential learning problems and providing remediation for young children at risk (Meisels, 1987). Diagnosis and screening consist of a brief assessment procedure designed to identify children who may need further evaluation and educational intervention (Meisels, 1978).

Standardized tests of achievement may be used in the diagnosis and screening of children, but they are used for a different purpose than assessing a child's achievement in any given subject or area. The purpose of standardized tests of achievement for screening is to survey a child's abilities in all areas of functioning.

Meisels (1986) lists four criteria for the selection of a developmental screening instrument:

1. It must be a brief procedure designed to identify children who may have a learning problem or handicapping conditions that could affect their overall potential for success in school.
2. It must primarily sample the domain of developmental tasks rather than the domain of specific accomplishments that indicate academic readiness.
3. It must focus on performance in a wide range of areas of development, including speech, language cognition, perception, affect, growth, and fine motor skills.
4. It must have classificational data available concerning the reliability and validity of the instrument.

The purpose of screening is to enable children to achieve their full potential. The intent is to intervene to assist a child to achieve and function at optimal development level. Early intervention may include developmental services; speech, occupational, and physical therapy; social work; and psychological and nursing services. A range of services may be provided in the child's home, in a setting such as a nursery or family day-care home, or in a specialized developmental and therapeutic program, based on an assessment of a child's individual needs and the needs of the family.

Screening should also be used to assess children's ability to acquire skills, rather than the skills they already have acquired. These tests should be used only as a first step in identifying children who may be in need of further diagnosis of a specific development or educational problem. The results of screening tests should NOT be used to place children in special education programs or remove them from the regular classroom. Placement decisions should be made ONLY on the basis of a complete diagnosis assessment of an individual child (NAEYC, 1988).

ASSESSING—FOR WHAT PURPOSE?

Purpose is all. Unfailing purposefulness directs humans. With a clear purpose in mind, careful observations of conditions and the means available for reaching our end, the proper order or sequence in the use of means, and making choices between alternatives are possible (Dewey, 1944).

The study of children is directed by the purpose of the study. Idiographic and nomothetic methods of studying children share the same purpose of increasing knowledge of children, just as they share weaknesses and strengths. If an understanding of each individual child is the purpose, then idiographic methods of assessment are selected. When the purpose is to know how the individual child compares with a norm group, then nomothetic methods of assessment are selected. Through the understanding of children arising from assessment, wise decisions that contribute to the improvement of children's care and education can be made.

Another Purpose

Regardless, assessment currently has little to do with the purpose of studying children. Our society has placed great expectations in the early years. For the child of poverty or the child of wealth, the early years are filled with hope for the years to come. Whether for the child of poverty or the child of wealth, the expectation that enduring academic achievements, intelligence, and social and emotional health have their foundation in the early years of life directs the purpose of assessment.

Great expectations in the power of the early years of life to affect the future influence decisions. Programs for early care and education are funded for the child of poverty, or at risk, because of these expectations—not because care and education are a right of all children, but because the programs are believed to result in "payoffs" in the future for society. And children not at risk are now enrolled in every type of class—violin, dance, gymnastics—all in an attempt to make certain their early years will be a solid-enough foundation for hoped-for future success.

Great expectations are accompanied by the desire for accountability. As a society, we need evidence that our hope is not misplaced, that our expectations in the early years are being fulfilled. When hope is so great, the need to account for the time, money, or energy invested in fulfilling hope is present. To study children, regardless of the philosophy of assessment selected, simply for the sake of understanding children, seems an ill-affordable luxury when the need to account is paramount.

The need to account is especially great when tax dollars fund early childhood programs. Legislators want to make certain their investment in children will be returned with long-lasting achievement gains. "The school will conduct annual evaluations to determine the extent to which it attained the measurable goals. Evaluation is based on the collection, compilation and analysis of empirical data" (Maryland State Department of Education, 1988, p. 49). "After all," one legislator declared, "we are investing six million dollars in these programs. You will have to account for that money and measure what children are learning."

As a result, assessment is now being used to make "high-stakes" decisions. Assessment of children is for the purpose of deciding the worth of a program, the teacher, and even the child. When assessment is linked to "high-stakes" purposes, only techniques that permit comparison are selected. Once comparison begins, competition follows. Young children's test scores are published and compared, school by school, grade by grade, and even class by class so all may judge the worth of groups of young children and the education they receive. Bredekamp and Shepard (1989) state that "anyone who doubts that high stakes are involved in the testing of young children need only turn to commercial publishers who now produce curriculum kits on test-taking skills for pre-K, K, and 1st graders, or sponsor 'CAT Academies' in Georgia to prepare kindergartners to take the required California Achievement Test, or publish books like *The Baby Boards, A Parents' Guide to Preschool and Primary School Entrance Tests*" (pp. 14–15).

Future Purposes

Educational evaluators are aware of the changing purposes of assessment and caution against its misuse. Popham (1988) believes educational evaluators are responsible for the use and misuse of assessment. He suggests the evaluator must use caution both in the assessment of young children and in the reporting of results to educators. He writes, "Educational evaluators must realize that by presenting a few means, standard deviations, or percentages they can dramatically influence the nature of educational decisions that will affect many human beings. This is a heavy responsibility" (p. 81). Being sensitive to the tendency of educators to ascribe almost magical significance to measurement results should cause evaluators not only to advise caution to the users of measurement data, but to exercise such caution themselves.

Evaluators believe educators can determine the purpose of assessment and thus the choice of assessment methods. This may be the case. When the Binet was first introduced in the United States, teachers said they had little power over the test, and decisions involving placement, promotion, and retention of children were made based on scores on the Binet. In Britain, however, teachers quickly rejected the Binet, resisting making decisions on the basis of a single test score. British teachers believed their own authority and professionalism was being threatened by the test, and the Binet never achieved the same status in England as in the United States (Kevles, 1984b).

SUMMARY

Today, early childhood educators in the United States are determining the purposes of assessment. Through the National Association for the Education of Young Children, educators have taken a position on assessment. This position states

1. All standardized tests used in early childhood programs must be reliable and valid according to the technical standards of test development.
2. Decisions that have a major impact on children, such as enrollment, retention, or assignment to remedial or special classes, should be based on

multiple scores of information and should never be based on a single test score.

3. It is the professional responsibility of administrators and teachers to critically evaluate, carefully select, and use standardized tests only for the purpose for which they are intended and for which data exists demonstrating the tests' validity.

4. It is the professional responsibility of administrators and teachers to be knowledgeable about testing and to interpret test results accurately and cautiously to parents, school personnel, and the media.

5. Selection of standardized tests to assess achievement and/or evaluate how well a program is meeting its goals should be based on how well a given test matches the locally determined theory, philosophy, and objectives of the specific program.

6. Testing of young children must be conducted by individuals who are knowledgeable about, and sensitive to, the developmental needs of young children and who are qualified to administer tests.

7. Testing of young children must recognize, and be sensitive to, individual diversity.

Today, early childhood educators, with the clear goal of improving the quality of life for young children, heed the advice of Rousseau to study their children. With this purpose, early childhood educators act with purpose, observing conditions and the means available to reach their goal and making wise choices between alternatives (Dewey, 1944).

REFERENCES

Almy, M. (1975). *The early childhood educator at work*. New York: Teachers College Press.
Anastasi, A. (1976). *Psychological testing* (4th ed.). New York: Macmillan.
Anastasi, A. (1980). *Psychological testing* (5th ed.). New York: Macmillan.
Anderson, C. W., & Smith, E. L. (1986). *Children's conceptions of light and color: Understanding the role of unseen rays* (Research Series No. 166). East Lansing, MI: Institute for Research on Teaching.
Axline, V. M. (1964). *Dibs: In search of self*. New York: Houghton Mifflin.
Barker, R., & Wright, H. (1951). *One boy's day*. New York: Harper & Row.
Bayley, N. (1969). *Bayley scales of infant development*. Cleveland: Psychological Corporation.
Biddle, B. J., & Anderson, D. S. (1986). Theory, methods, knowledge, and research on teaching. In M. C. Wittrock (Ed.), *Handbook of research on teaching* (3rd ed., pp. 230–255). New York: Macmillan.
Binet, A., & Simon, T. (1905). New methods for the diagnosis of the intellectual level of subnormals. *Annals of Psychology, 11*, 191.
Boring, E. G. (1923, June). Intelligence as the tests test it. *New Republic*, pp. 35–37.
Bredekamp, S., & Shepard, L. (1989). How best to protect children from inappropriate school expectations, practices, and policies. *Young Children, 44*(3), 14–23.

Broman, S. H., Nichols, P. L., & Kennedy, W. A. (1975). *Preschool IQ: Prenatal and early developmental correlates*. Hillsdale, NJ: Erlbaum.

Burns, E. (1979). *The development, use, and abuse of educational tests*. Springfield, IL: Charles C. Thomas.

Cazden, C. (1983). Contexts for literacy: In the mind and in the class room. *Journal of Reading Behavior, 14*, 413–427.

Cronbach, L. J. (1977). *Educational psychology* (3rd ed.). New York: Harcourt Brace Jovanovich.

Cronbach, L. J. (1988). Construct validation after thirty years. In R. L. Linn (Ed.), *Intelligence: Measurement theory and public policy* (Proceedings of a symposium in honor of Lloyd G. Humphreys. Manuscript copy). Urbana: University of Illinois Press.

Darrow, H. F. (1964). *Research: Children's concepts*. Washington, DC: Association for Childhood Education International.

Darwin, C. (1877). A biographical sketch of an infant. *Mind: Quarterly Review of Psychology and Philosophy, 2*, 285–294.

Dewey, J. (1944). *Democracy and education*. New York: The Free Press.

Duckworth, E. (1978). *The African primary science program: An evaluation*. Grand Forks, ND: North Dakota Study Group on Evaluation.

Evertson, C. M., & Green, J. L. (1986). Observation as inquiry and method. In M. C. Wittrock (Ed.), *Handbook of research on teaching* (3rd ed., pp. 162–214). New York: Macmillan.

Fassnacht, G. (1982). *Theory and practice of observing behavior*. London: Academic Press.

Genishi, C. (1983). Observational research methods for childhood education. In B. Spodek (Ed.), *Handbook of research in early childhood education* (pp. 563–592). New York: The Free Press.

Goldschmid, M. L., & Bentler, P. M. (1968). *Manual: Concept assessment kit-conservation*. San Diego: Educational and Industrial Testing Service.

Gruber, H. E., & Voneche, J. J. (1977). *The essential Piaget*. London: Routledge & Kegan Paul.

Guilford, J. P., & Hoepfner, R. (1971). *The analysis of intelligence*. New York: McGraw-Hill.

Hall, G. S. (1907). *The contents of children's minds*. Boston: Ginn.

Hilgard, G. H., & Bower, E. R. (1981). *Theories of learning* (5th ed.). Englewood Cliffs, NJ: Prentice-Hall.

Jantz, R. K., & Seefeldt, C. (1976). *The CATE: Children's attitudes toward the elderly. Test manual*. Urbana, IL: Educational Resources Information Center. (ERIC Document Reproduction Service No. ED 141 860)

Kevles, D. J. (1984a, October 5). Annuals of eugenics. Part II. *New Yorker*, p. 52 + .

Kevles, D. J. (1984b, October 24). Annuals of eugenics. Part III. *New Yorker*, p. 92 + .

Laurendeau, M., & Pinard, A. (1970). *The development of the concept of space in the child*. New York: International Universities Press.

Maryland State Department of Education. (1988). *Standards for prekindergarten programs*. Baltimore: Maryland State Department of Education.

Meisels, S. J. (1978). *Developmental screening in early childhood: A guide*. Washington, DC: National Association for the Education of Young Children.

Meisels, S. J. (1986). Testing four- and five-year-olds: Response to Salzer and to Shepard and Smith. *Educational Leadership, 44*(3), 90–92.

Meisels, S. J. (1987). Uses and abuses of developmental screening and school readiness testing. *Young Children, 42*(3), 4–7.

Messick, S. (1989). Meaning and values in test validation: The science and ethics of assessment. *Educational Researcher, 18*(1), 5–12.

Morine-Dershimer, G., & Tenenberg, M. (1981). *Participant perspectives of classroom discourse* (Executive Summary, NIE No. G-78-0161). Washington, DC: National Institute of Education.

Murchinson, C. (1952). *Autobiography: A history of psychology in autobiography.* Worcester, MA: Clark University Press.

National Association for the Education of Young Children. (1988). *Testing of young children: Concerns and cautions.* Washington, DC: Author.

Phinney, J. S., Feshbach, N. D., & Farver, J. (1986). Preschool children's response to peer crying. *Early Childhood Research Quarterly, 1*, 207–221.

Piaget, J. (1950). *The psychology of intelligence.* London: Routledge & Kegan Paul.

Popham, W. J. (1988). *Educational evaluation* (2nd ed.). Englewood Cliffs, NJ: Prentice-Hall.

Prescott, D. (1957). *The child in the educative process.* New York: McGraw-Hill.

Rogers, V. R., & Stevenson, C. (1988). How do we know what kids are learning in school? *Educational Leadership, 45*(5), 68–75.

Rousseau, J. J. (1947). L'Emile ou l'education. In O. E. Tellows & N. R. Tarrey (Eds.), *The age of enlightenment* (pp. 416–513). New York: F. S. Crofts.

Seefeldt, C. (1987). The effects of preschoolers' visits to infirm elders in a nursing home. *The Gerontologist, 27*, 228–232.

Seefeldt, C. (1988). *Evaluation of a fire safety curriculum.* Unpublished manuscript, University of Maryland, College Park.

Siegler, R. S., & Richards, D. D. (1982). The development of intelligence. In R. J. Sternberg (Ed.), *Handbook of human intelligence* (pp. 897–971). Cambridge, England: Cambridge University Press.

Snow, C., & Ferguson, C. (1977). *Talking to children.* Cambridge, England: Cambridge University Press.

Spearman, C. (1927). *The abilities of man.* New York: Macmillan.

Stake, R. E. (1978). The case study method in social inquiry. *Educational Researcher, 7*(2), 5–8.

Stern, G. G. (1963). Measuring noncognitive variables in research on teaching. In N. L. Gage (Ed.), *Handbook of research on teaching.* Chicago: Rand McNally.

Stern, W. (1938). *General psychology* (H. D. Spoerl, Trans.). New York: Macmillan.

Sternberg, R. J. (1986). *Intelligence applied.* San Diego: Harcourt Brace Jovanovich.

Thorndike, R. L. (1913). Educational psychology: The psychology of learning. *Vol. II. Teachers College Record, 41*, 699–725.

Thorndike, R. L., & Hagen, E. P. (1977). *Measurement and evaluation in psychology and education* (4th ed.). New York: Wiley.

Thurston, L. L. (1938). *Primary mental abilities* (Psychometric monographs, No. 1). Chicago: University of Chicago Press.

Yerkes, R. M., & Foster, J. G. (1923). *1923 revision: A point scale for measuring mental ability.* Baltimore: Warwick & York.

Index